EASTERN SYSTEMS FOR WESTERN ASTROLOGERS

AN ANTHOLOGY

EASTERN SYSTEMS FOR WESTERN ASTROLOGERS

AN ANTHOLOGY

Introduction by
Thomas Moore
THE ASTROLOGICAL VISION

Ray Grasse
ASTROLOGY & THE CHAKRAS

Robin Armstrong
THE DEGREES OF THE
ZODIAC & THE I-CHING

Bill Watson
CHINESE FIVE-ELEMENT
(TZU P'ING) ASTROLOGY

Michael Erlewine
TIBETAN ASTROLOGY

Hart deFouw
THE HUMANISM OF VEDIC ASTROLOGY

Dennis Flaherty
THE EASTERN MOON
THROUGH WESTERN EYES

James Braha
PREDICTION EAST

Richard Houck
LIFE & DEATH—EAST & WEST

SAMUEL WEISER, INC.

York Beach, Maine

First published in 1997 by
Samuel Weiser, Inc.
P.O. Box 612
York Beach, ME 03910-0612

Library of Congress Cataloging-in-Publication Data
Eastern systems for Western astrologers / Robin Armstrong ... [et al.] ;
    introduction by Thomas Moore.
        p.   cm.
    Includes index.
    ISBN 1-57863-006-1 (pbk. : alk. paper)
    1. Astrology.   2. East and West.   I. Armstrong, Robin.
BF1708.1.E27   1997
133.5´925—dc21   97-1457
                                                                          CIP
EB

Typeset in 11 point Bembo

Printed in the United States of America

04   03   02   01   00   99   98   97
10   9   8   7   6   5   4   3   2   1

TABLE OF CONTENTS

PUBLISHER'S PREFACE

T HERE IS A RAPIDLY GROWING interest in Eastern Systems of astrology in the English speaking world. Many astrologers who are presently using the "Western" systems are hungry for practical information about other systems, especially since Project Hindsight* began to issue modern translations of classical literature. What could be more "classical" than exploring ancient astrological themes from China, India, and Tibet?

This book contains a general overview of what's going on in a very broad field. Because most astrologers are familiar with the word chakras, the anthology opens with an article by Ray Grasse, who discusses the symbolism contained in the chakras to obtain new insights into the Western chart. Robin Armstrong follows with an exploration of the horoscope using the I Ching and horary concepts. He has been working with his own system of I Ching relationships and how they can be applied to astrology; this article is the result of many years of study.

Bill Watson explores Chinese Five-Element (Tzu P'ing) astrology, a completely different system than the one Western astrologers use. He explains how Chinese astrologers use this symbolism, from both a cultural and an astrological point of view, and then shows us how we can work with this system. Michael Erlewine has written an exciting introductory chapter on Tibetan Astrology, translating new material, and providing a different set of insights. Both authors stress that we cannot combine Western charts and Eastern symbols, which means that we can-

*Project Hindsight, translating famous classic texts for astrologers. To support the organization, or to purchase copies of the many classics that have been translated into English, please write P.O. Box 002, Berkeley Springs, WV 25422.

not take an Eastern technique and apply it to a Western chart. We can, however, work with both the Western and the Eastern chart, drawing conclusions from both systems.

It is clear that we can't combine the systems of East and West. Westerners also mistakenly feel that Eastern systems are not humanistic. Hart deFouw addresses this common belief and talks to the more psychologically-based astrologer, explaining the humanism of Vedic Astrology. Dennis Flaherty follows with an extremely comprehensive article on the differences between the Eastern and Western view of the Moon and Moon cycles that all astrologers will benefit from reading.

James Braha is the author of several well-known books on the subject of Vedic Astrology, and provides practical advice and instruction for working with Jyotish, or Vedic Astrology.

We close the book with Richard Houck's view of death, and with his explanation of the Nadi Grantha reading and free-will. The word "death" makes Westerners uncomfortable. It is the end of a cycle, and people who have walked away from strict religious observances no longer have the traditions to make them comfortable with the process. Some astrologers secretly see death all around them (listen to them talk about Solar Returns) but feel that its unethical to talk about it. Richard Houck shares a look at his own chart, and provides an interesting read for anyone who wants to delve into the subject.

These authors bring passion and enthusiasm for the subjects presented here. We hope that their enthusiasm will excite readers to explore at least one of the these ancient traditions and concepts. The information about chakras and the I Ching can readily be applied to your own systems. Chinese Astrology is a study by itself, as is Tibetan Astrology and Vedic Astrology (or Jyotish). Since we are approaching the millennium, and because prediction is a "hot topic" now, these ancient Eastern systems can be invaluable to contemporary Western astrologers.

THOMAS MOORE

THE ASTROLOGICAL VISION

NOT SO MANY GENERATIONS ago, both intellectuals and ordinary folk assumed an astrological worldview, and as a result they
felt more connected to nature and to the timings and rhythms in their
own lives. Even today some form of astrological sensibility can be found
all around the world, and yet our own technologically advanced and ra-
tionalistically explained culture is generally not able to appreciate it.

To some extent astrologers, themselves, are to blame for astrology's
bleak presence in modern life, for they often feed the notion that astrology is a new age practice, or that it belongs in an essentially esoteric
approach to life. The ordinary person looks at astrology as quaint, superstitious, and irrelevant in any serious effort to understand ourselves and
our world. To give astrology wider acceptance, it may be useful to imagine it in ways not so split off from mainstream thinking.

To some extent, astrologers have tried to claim relevance by placing
their work on a solid scientific basis, or at least they have tried to make
it look like science. In this century, many fields of knowledge, the social
sciences for example, have tried that approach, but ultimately the attempt
to secure acceptance by clinging to the coattails of science doesn't work,
because science tries to shake off hangers-on it doesn't approve of, and,
besides, the beauty of astrology lies in its alternative values and vision.

We might restore astrology to at least some of its former glory by
developing a new appreciation for its fundamental ingredients and methods—poetic and symbolic thinking, divination, and attention to nature,
process, and movement. None of these ingredients needs to be imagined
only esoterically, for each can have a central role in ordinary living, and
each can co-exist fruitfully and smoothly with rationality and science.
Astrology is a fundamental way of looking at the world in which we

live. It provides a context for our lives, and only secondarily does it unfold into a divinitory means of knowledge.

Astrology is based on the idea that to look into ourselves and our experience we need an external source of imagery. The alchemist of old peered intensely into the materials that make up the stuff of the world, and found there images and a language that reveal elements and dynamics of human life that might otherwise remain hidden. Mythology portrays the most profound patterns and themes of human life, and it, too, often emerges out of a simple manifestation of nature—a mountain that evokes the notion of a residence of the gods and goddesses, or the rising and setting of the sun suggesting beginnings and endings, or the hero's journey. The poet draws upon every particle of nature and experience for its metaphoric value. In each case, the concrete world is the impetus for a life-shaping imagination.

Astrology focuses on the sky, finding there not only an image of the mystery and vastness of human life, but a fully articulated theater of cycles, colors, animal shapes, stories, heroes, geometries, and rhythms. Nothing in nature offers so much to the imagination as the night sky, and nothing evokes divinity and mystery so palpably.

Broadly speaking, an astrological sensitivity may consist of little more than an awareness that in autumn the days grow shorter, or that the moon is waxing or waning, or that the sunset is particularly captivating. Of course, astrology becomes infinitely more complex, but the essential perspective of astrology can sometimes get lost in the intricacies of the fully developed system, and often that system can be explored without reference to the simple natural developments in the sky that quite directly can set the most ordinary person to thinking poetically about fate and destiny.

In the spirit of the times, people today tend to understand developments in their lives with exclusive reference to experiences that may be current or past. We blame our childhood and our parents for current adult difficulties, or we look to external conditions for explanation. The resulting imagination of ordinary life is narrowly personalistic and blaming. An astrological view, in contrast, encourages us to look at our essential natures and at the rhythms of unfolding life. We don't blame anyone else for what has befallen us, and therefore we have the opportunity to enjoy the weight and pleasures of living our own lives responsibly. It's possible, of course, to use astrology as an excuse, to avoid responsibility by blaming the stars, but approached intelligently, astrology offers a way to acknowledge the stuff of which we are made and the cycles of its realization.

In a key statement, Herakleitos, the Greek philosopher of the sixth century B.C., said: "The soul has its own principle of unfolding." As we respond to and care for our soul, we might watch its unfolding, not looking to the literal events of life for the soul's reasons, but rather learning something about its own elements, rhythms, and timings. Astrology offers an excellent means for observing and naming the soul's own movements, and so in this sense, astrology is a mythology of the soul, an applied poetics, that allows us to behold our own natures, to see ourselves as nature just as the stars are nature.

The implications of this restoration of astrology include an intimacy with nature stemming from a deeply felt awareness that there is no essential gulf between the world out there and the felt world of our interior lives. We might revere nature more on account of this awareness, so that astrology could become the basis for a grounded ecological sensibility. We might also respect more the movements in our own hearts, responding to them with respect rather than judgment.

With this basis—a less personalistic view of our own subjective experiences and increased intimacy with nature—a divinatory approach to everyday decisions and understanding makes "natural" sense, and may not appear so esoteric. If the world holds the secrets to our own make-up and rhythms, admittedly in the sense of applied poetry, then it makes sense to look outside ourselves for clues about how to engage life. A purely rational approach would be inadequate, since rationality doesn't respect sufficiently the mysteries of the soul and of nature. Nor would a purely willful approach do, for then we are back in the realm of the personalistic.

The divinatory method of astrology is essential to its basic premises, and offers an alternative to the modern approach to decision-making. Ordinarily people make decisions by trying to understand the issues at hand, weighing the pros and cons, considering past experience, and hoping to have everything under control. A divinatory approach asks for intuition, faith, openness, and even a certain degree of ignorance or respect for mystery. Everyone knows that life is never fully predictable or under our control, yet our usual methods imply that we can be fully in charge. Divination leaves plenty of room for mystery and mistakes. I would go so far as to say that divination is the proper way in which the soul finds its way, while the more rational weighing of alternatives and options is the way of the mind.

A divinatory way of life in general looks for signs in all places. Signs waken the imagination and lead us into a profoundly intuitive approach to the design of life. Astrology is one area in which we can become sophisticated in our reading of a certain group of signs—the movements of the planets. Modernism trusts only the latest bit of knowledge and the latest technological invention, while astrology finds its confidence in a long line of authorities and in ancient traditions of interpretation and their own kinds of technology.

Whereas modern rational thinking always looks for *advances* in information and thought, divinatory forms of knowledge place more confidence in the breadth and depth of experience *behind* its method. Astrology has developed out of centuries of imagination and experimentation, and this wealth of subtle imaginal analysis is available to us in various astrological traditions around the world. From Africa to the Americas to Asia, various ways of reading the stars expand our very notion of what astrology is, and at the same time offer increasingly sophisticated directions for the Western practice.

The East is particularly important for its traditions of sacred poetry and divination. The East is sometimes called, often disparagingly, more mystical than the West, but contrasting the pragmatism of the West with the mysticism of the East creates a false dichotomy. Both East and West have extraordinary traditions in care of the soul. Both have astounding technologies, both have astounding mystics. We can turn to the East, not as though toward a world opposite ours, but rather to a culture that has explored our own concerns with imagery that could be fresh and enlightening.

We might also realize that East and West are such broad categories that they mean little in specific terms. The East embraces a host of traditions that are varied and often contradictory. From country to country, from region to region, from one time period to another, we find many different ways of imagining the same quests and concerns.

Still, we Westerners find the East a land of mystery. All peoples seem to share the profoundly mythic experience of imagining some other people as opposite themselves. It's an archetypal pattern. Renaissance Europe was mesmerized by ancient Egypt, the classical Greeks were charmed by the god Dionysus, who was a foreigner, and we can still fantasize little green people from outer space as bearers of an as yet unknown way of being in life.

So, by all means, let us turn eastward and deepen our own way of looking at the heavens. But at the same time, let us make a special effort to make astrology friendly to our own people, for those of us who value astrology are like foreigners to the majority of our own people. Let us not indulge in our esoteric aloofness, but rather let us find inviting language and an inclusive attitude as we nourish our own culture, so starved of soul and poetry, with gifts of an ancient and a worldwide astrological vision. In a time dominated by materialistic, mechanistic, and rationalistic thinking, we need the gifts of astrology: the mystery of the sky, the sure guidance of divination, ancient stories and personalities associated with the stars, a holy reverence of nature, and love of the human being whose fate is signaled in the outlay and the dance of the heavenly bodies.

RAY GRASSE

CHAPTER I

ASTROLOGY
AND THE CHAKRAS

Understand that thou thyself art another world in little, and hast within thee the Sun and the Moon, and also the stars.

—Origen

WHAT I WOULD LIKE TO EXPLORE in this chapter is the exciting possibility of bridging two of history's greatest psychological systems, that of astrology and the chakras. Conventionally, these two systems have been seen as having little or nothing to do with each other, the former primarily concerning the outer world, or macrocosm, the latter largely seen as concerning the inner world, or microcosm. In fact, as we shall soon see, these two systems are two sides of the same coin, each one complementing the other in ways that can enhance our understanding of both. Through understanding this connection we stand to acquire an entirely new way of perceiving our own horoscope, as framed in the context of one of the great spiritual psychological systems devised by the yogic sages of antiquity.

The basic system of correspondences our discussion will be based upon can be found in several sources. Although I have personally learned it from teachers in the Kriya Yoga lineage (Goswami Kriyananda of Chicago, and Shelly Trimmer, a direct disciple of Paramahansa Yogananda), one finds the same essential system described by such writers as David Frawley *(Astrology of the Seers)*, Jeff Green *(Uranus)*, Titus Burckhardt *(Alchemy)*, and Marc Edmund Jones (in his privately circulated "Sabian Assembly" lessons), derived in each case from largely independent sources. While the specific method of "chakric horoscopes" and their guidelines of interpretation used throughout this chapter are my own, they are, I believe, faithful to the basic principles I have learned from my teachers on this subject. With that said, let us begin by examining some of the basic elements of chakric philosophy.

WHAT ARE THE CHAKRAS?

In Sanskrit, the term *chakra* (sometimes spelled "cakra") literally means "wheel." In yogic philosophy, this term refers to the psycho-spiritual centers located along the length of the spine, each of which is associated with a different archetypal principle of consciousness. These are sometimes described as energy centers or "vortexes" which convert spiritual energy from subtler to grosser levels of experience. Although there are literally thousands of chakras situated throughout the subtle body, yogic philosophy normally stresses only seven or eight of these. Let us briefly review these primary points and their key associations. (See figure 1.)

  Chakra (1) is called, in Sanskrit, *Muladhara*. Its element is Earth. It psychologically concerns one's relationship with the material plane, and archetypally relates to the principle of limitation in both its constructive and destructive forms. In its more unbalanced expression, it therefore

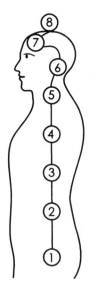

Figure 1. The chakras.

governs such states as greed and the drive for survival, while at its more subtle levels, it rules the wise relation to matter, one's body, and the physical universe generally.

Chakra (2) is called *Svadisthana*. Its element is Water, and it psychologically concerns the experience of emotions generally. At its lower levels of expression, it governs states such as escapism, excess, and dogmatism, and in its more subtle expression, the more constructive states of enthusiasm and spiritual devotion.

Chakra (3) is called *Manipura*. Its element is Fire, and it rules over emotions of a more dynamic and energetic type. In its less refined state, this relates to anger and combativeness, and more positively as strength and assertiveness. By way of analogy, if the emotionalism of the 2nd chakra were likened to that found at a religious revival meeting, the emotionalism of the 3rd chakra is more akin to the enthusiasm of an athelete in competition, or a soldier marching into battle.

Chakra (4) is called *Anahata*. Its element is Air. Its psychological focus is toward love, beauty, allurement of all types, and governs the capacity for harmony in all romantic and social interactions. In its unbalanced form, it produces a tendency toward hedonism, pleasure-seeking, and excessive "sweetness" of temperment; while in its balanced form it produces an exceptional sense of aesthetics or even unselfish love.

Chakra (5) is called *Visshudha*. Its element is Ether, and its psychological focus is pure mind, or intellectuality. Unbalanced, it produces uncontrolled thoughts or communications; in balanced form, it gives rise to creative or spiritual thinking and refined communication skills.

Chakra (6) is called *Chandra*. Though not mentioned in most published discussions of the chakras, Paramahansa Yogananda described this as the feminine polarity of the brow chakra, or "third eye" (to be considered next). It is not formally associated with any element, although for the sake of explanation one may refer to it as "Divine Water," in contrast to the "common water" of the 2nd chakra. Its psychological focus is awareness in its most reflective or introspective mode, and governs such qualities as nurturing compassion and psychic sensitivity, and, more destructively, such states as fearfulness, emotional dependency, and a preoccupation with the past.

Chakra (7) is called *Ajna*, and is located in the center of the forehead, also known as the "third eye." As with the Chandra chakra, it also is traditionally associated with no element, although it can for the sake of description be expressed as "Divine Fire." By way of analogy, if we associate the 3rd chakra with ordinary fire, the third eye can be compared to nuclear fire. It psychologically governs the principle of pure consciousness in its most active and expressive form, as well as the higher will. In its balanced state, it rules creativity, spiritual energy, and self-expression generally, while in unbalanced form it can manifest as egotism, willfulness, and "dry" awareness without compassion.

Chakra (8) is called *Sahasrara*, or the "crown chakra" or "thousand-petaled lotus," and exists at the top of the head above the other chakras. (Note: Since most accounts do not include the lunar chakra at the back of the head, this top chakric point is commonly numbered as the 7th stage of consciousness.) Whereas the previous Ajna chakra represents the quintessential expression of personal divinity (perceived in meditation in the form of a five-pointed star), the Sahasrara rules our point of contact with the transpersonal divine. However, since this point represents a transcendental point beyond the more personal chakras below (and, by inference, their astrological correlaries), and is largely dormant for most individuals, we will for purposes of clarity leave it out of our subsequent discussion.

THE PLANETS AND THE CHAKRAS

In turn, each of the personal chakric centers can be related to the seven visible planets of classical astrology. (As we will see shortly, the newly discovered outer planets play a role within this model as well, but in a more subtle and indirect manner.) Starting from the bottom up, figure 2 shows the relationship.

> The 1st (or lowest) chakra is associated with Saturn;
> The 2nd chakra with the planet Jupiter;
> The 3rd chakra with the planet Mars;
> The 4th chakra with the planet Venus;
> The 5th chakra with the planet Mercury;
> The 6th chakra with the Moon;
> And the 7th, or brow chakra, with the Sun.

Importantly, these last two centers, associated with the Sun and the Moon, are in some respects the most fundamental of all, serving as the seat and source of consciousness for the entire chakric system. In traditional mythic imagery, these represent the proverbial land of "milk

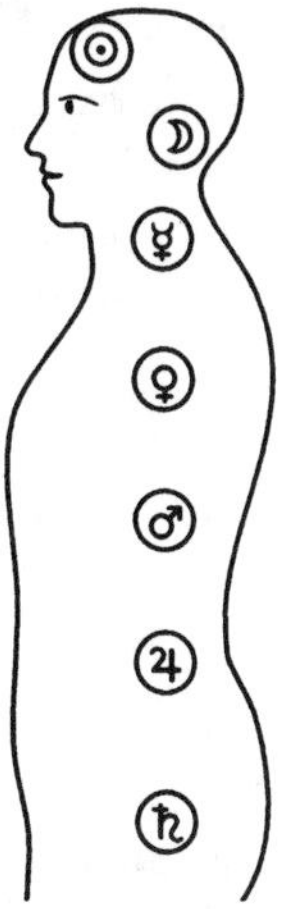

PLANET	METAL	ELEMENT	TRAIT
Sun	Gold	(. . . .)	Creativity, Will
Moon	Silver	(. . . .)	Receptivity
Mercury	Mercury	Ether	Rationality
Venus	Copper	Air	Love, Harmony
Mars	Iron	Fire	Drive
Jupiter	Tin	Water	Emotionality
Saturn	Lead	Earth	Practicality

Figure 2. The relationship between chakras, planets, elements, and traits.

(Moon) and honey (Sun)," the promised land we are aspiring toward in our pilgrimage to enlightenment. Noting the hermetic system of metallic correspondences shown in figure 2, we further glimpse an important insight into the traditional alchemical practice of transmuting lead into gold, which is here revealed to be a psycho-spiritual process involving the raising of energies from the lowest Saturn chakra to the highest Sun chakra, or third eye.

THE TWELVE SECONDARY CHAKRIC STATES

Chakric astrology takes this basic system an important step further. What we have been looking at thus far are the chakras only in their simplest possible description. In reality, most of the chakras possess at least *three different* aspects, or faces: feminine (introverted), masculine (extroverted), and spiritual (balanced). That is, each chakra can be expressed or diverted over to its right side, or over to its left side, or in a perfectly balanced fashion within the very center of the spine. In each of these three aspects, the psychological energy of any given chakra will manifest in uniquely different but interrelated ways.

For example, in its expression off to the right or masculine side, the 5th/Mercury chakra will tend to manifest in terms of interpersonal communications in the waking world, while off to the left side it will tend to involve more internalized thought processes, perhaps within one's nightly dreams. In its balanced modality within the center, however, Mercury rules the mind in its most mystical aspect, as that aspect of mentality which truly communes with the spirit. More traditional esoteric sources expressed this same idea in the following way: Saturn rules Aquarius by day and Capricorn by night; Jupiter rules Sagittarius by day and Pisces by night; Mars rules Aries by day and Scorpio by night; Venus rules Libra by day and Taurus by night; Mercury rules Gemini by day and Virgo by night; while the Sun and Moon hold rulership over one sign each, Leo and Cancer. Yet it is only in the very center of each chakric level that the energy of that chakra truly manifests in a spiritually balanced fashion.

What this shows us is that the seven classical planets relate to the twelve signs in a startlingly precise way. One simply spins the zodiac around until they fall into line with these chakric placements.

What to do with the three outer planets? We find that they fall into line with the lower three chakras, in accordance with the zodiacal signs they have become associated with by rulership: Pluto with the feminine side of the Mars chakra (Scorpio), Neptune with the feminine side of the Jupiter chakra (Pisces), and Uranus with the masculine side of the Saturn chakra (Aquarius). (See figure 3.)

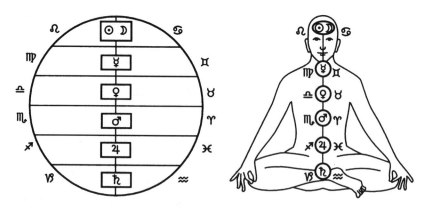

Figure 3. The zodiacal signs, their traditional planetary rulers, and the chakras in the body.

In yogic philosophy, each of these different zodiacal centers represents a kind of memory tract or "storage bin" for both karmas and life-impressions generally; whatever we feel, think, or experience is logged into the energy fields of the spinal column appropriate to it. In this way, habit patterns (or *samskaras*, in yogic terminology) are built up over time, etched into our subconscious psyche, and which continue to compel us toward particular behaviors from lifetime to lifetime. In fact, despite the seeming literalism of yogic philosophy and its discussion of karmic "seeds," I strongly suspect that karmas are not actually stored in specific points of space, but rather find a certain *resonance* with these chakric locations. In medicine, by way of analogy, a diseased liver would not be regarded by a holistic healer as a problem only of the liver, but as a systemic condition which simply has its greatest *focus* in that body organ—indeed, because of the symbolic correspondence between the liver and the planet Jupiter, we might even say that the liver problem extends all the way outward to encompass Jupiter itself! Similarly, it may be more accurate to say that karma represents a field-phenomenon which extends through both space and time, but which resonates to certain chakric points in especially concentrated ways.

THE THREE CHANNELS

There is one further element necessary for us to round out this basic introduction, that being the three channels or *nadis* that circulate around and through these different chakric centers. These may be thought of as the three courseways through which subtle energy (or *prana*) flows in and out of the body/mind system, and which in turn fuel the different chakric centers. In modern times, most of us are familiar with this system of currents through the symbolism of the caduceus employed by the modern medical profession (figure 4).

Figure 4.
The caduceus.

According to the teachings of Kriya Yoga, subtle energy is drawn in from the greater universe through the back of the head, or Moon chakra (also referred to as the "mouth of God"), then spirals down through the feminine side of the chakric tree with each inhalation, then spirals up through the masculine side of the chakras on each exhalation, where they are finally expressed outward back into the universe through the third eye. Specifically, the left hand channel or *nadi* is called *ida*, and relates more dominantly to the emotions and astral or dream awareness; the right hand channel is called *pingali*, and relates to the more rational world of waking awareness. Each of the secondary chakric "compartments" modifies the pranic energy in particular ways.

Between these two peripheral channels, however, lies the *nadi* known as *sushumna*, the channel of pure balanced awareness. It is this channel through which the spiritual energy known as *kundalini* flows upward toward the spiritual centers within and atop the head. Also known as the proverbial "crack between worlds," this point of our being relates to a state of awareness beyond the influence of karma, and which, therefore, plays a critical role in understanding the relationship of spirituality to the horoscope—a point we will return to later.

THE CHAKRIC SCIENCE OF PERSONALITY

Every personality is comprised of these basic archetypal elements, in widely varying combinations. Depending on an individual's karmic or samskaric patterns, energy (or *prana*) is siphoned off as it courses through these channels at each of the chakric levels, where it is then employed in either constructive or destructive ways. In this manner, complex patterns may be constellated among an individual's chakric centers. Although every person experiences all of the different centers to one degree or another, certain chakras will tend to be more dominant for some individuals than for others. Hence, a more artistic individual may have their 4th chakra more emphasized, whereas a more heavily intellectual type might have their 5th chakra more emphasized, and so forth.

One way that I find particularly helpful in illustrating this point is through the notion of *sub-personalities*, with each chakra having its own unique traits or personified qualities. Utilizing this system of correspondences, we may correlate the different chakras in the following way: the lowest, Saturn, chakra can be described in such terms as the "Inner Pragmatist," "Inner Disciplinarian," or the "Inner Architect." The 2nd, or

Jupiter, chakra may be variously described as the "Inner Optimist,""Inner Philanthropist," or (because of its occasionally evangelistic tendencies) the "Inner Preacher." The 3rd chakra is, plain and simple, the "Inner Warrior." The 4th, or Venus, chakra, is the "Inner Lover," or "Inner Artist." The 5th, or Mercury, chakra is the "Inner Communicator," or "Inner Intellectual." The 6th, or lunar, chakra is the "Inner Mother," or "Inner Queen." The 7th, or solar chakra is the "Inner Father," or "Inner King." Which chakra is emphasized in the horoscope will determine which of these inner sub-personalities are most dominant in any given individual. (Those familiar with the system of "archetypal psychology" developed by psychologist James Hillman may instead prefer to personify these centers in terms of their mythic correlaries. Hence, a strongly accented throat chakra would indicate a pronounced internal "Hermes," while a strong heart center would show a highly activated internal "Aphrodite," and a strong Sun center would indicate a pronounced internal "Apollo," etc.)

INTERPRETING THE HOROSCOPE AS A DIAGRAM OF ONE'S CHAKRAS

With these basic points as our foundation, we may now begin to explore some of the specific ways the horoscope can tell us about an individual's chakric energies. Having worked with this basic system for well over ten years now, I have come to believe that there are minimally three *primary* levels on which this can be approached. These are, in suggested order of importance:

1) The Planets. The specific character and condition of one's primary seven (intra-Saturnian) planets arguably represent the most significant indicator of those corresponding chakras within one. This would include examining any aspects formed to a planet, its power in terms of angular prominence (e.g., conjuncting the 1st or 10th house cusp), sign placement, and general condition in the horoscope. To use a very simple example, a person may have Mercury on the 1st house cusp conjuncting Jupiter, while exactly squaring Uranus. This would tend to indicate a very activated and open Mercury, or throat chakra (chakra locations are illustrated in figure 3, page 6), quite possibly a little too open, giving rise to unbridled thoughts and self-expression. Or, a prominently placed

Venus opposing Saturn exactly on an angle could indicate a blockage or limitation at an individual's heart center; though it is also possible that Saturn may be serving to bring the feelings of the heart into concrete manifestion, as we often see in the charts of many artists or musicians. It is for this reason critical that we never assign value judgments to any condition indicated in the chart, since even the most challenging configuration may have its constructive potentials.

Likewise, planetary significators are always modified by such factors as sign or house placement; having Venus in Capricorn in the 12th house would tend to indicate a more reserved and possibly late-blooming quality with regard to an individual's heart chakra, whereas a Venus in Aries on the 1st house cusp would modify the energies of the heart/Venus chakra in a considerably more expressive and uninhibited way.

2) The Signs. We have already seen how the twelve signs closely correspond with the different chakras in a binary fashion, as shown by spinning around the conventional zodiac until Cancer and Leo are located at the top of the wheel. The different planets as located within these different signs therefore provide important clues as to which chakric levels are more pronounced in a person's life. The simplest technique in this respect is noting which signs are most strongly accented, by planet or aspect. For example, any large constellation of planets in Libra or Taurus may indicate a heavy focus of attention, karmically, on the lessons of the heart level.

In a more complex fashion, the chart also reveals the complex relationship of energies *between* the different chakras. For instance, planets in the throat center signs (Gemini or Virgo) in aspect to planets in the 2nd chakric signs (Taurus or Libra) indicate an interaction of energies between intellect and religious devotionalism. Whether these connections would express themselves in a "hard" or "easy" way in turn depends not only on the aspects involved, but an individual's ability or resolve to channel the energies constructively.

Such intepretations as these can be refined considerably, since each planet contains subtle differences in the way it amplifies each chakric center. For example, Saturn in a chakra will produce a dramatically different effect than if Jupiter is found in that same chakric center. Whatever sign Saturn is located in shows where one will feel especially challenged to grow, or, in its most frustrating form, where one may even feel denied in some way (although in a more subtle sense, the placement of Saturn indicates the level at which one may also find one's greatest depth of wisdom as accumulated from past lives).

Whatever sign Jupiter is in, by contrast, shows the chakra where one experiences more obvious blessings and "good fortune," where there is a greater opening and flow of life-energies—possibly, however, to excess! By contrast, one would probably have to work for any results obtained in whatever chakric area Saturn was placed; however, for this very reason one might have that much more appreciation for the fruits of that area! Where Venus is placed shows the chakric level from which one draws the greatest pleasure, etc.

In purely quantitative terms, arguably the most powerful significators in this respect are the Sun, Moon, and Ascendant. Looking to these basic points of emphasis, one can learn much about an individual's chakric focus in this life. For instance, a Sun in Gemini will, by itself, indicate a great focus on the throat center of mentality and communication, whereas the Sun located in Capricorn would tend to show an intense directing of energies toward the earth plane and the attainment of success and/or recognition on this level.

As most astrologers know, each of these three astrological symbols has its own unique and subtly different shades of meaning. What these are exactly has been a source of lively debate among astrologers. My own experience with horoscopes over the years leads me to believe that the Moon indicates the chakric level one is *coming from*, both emotionally and karmically; the Ascendent shows where the everyday personality in this life is *presently at*, in the immediate here-and-now; while the Sun indicates the chakric direction one is *aspiring toward* and attempting to bring into creative manifestation in this life.

3) The Houses. In precisely the same way that we can spin around the signs to situate Leo and Cancer at the top, so we can also spin the houses of the horoscope until the 5th and 4th houses are perched atop the horoscope to correspond to the Sun and Moon chakras. By looking to the planets situated in the different houses, one can likewise determine primary points of focus, interests, key talents, or life-challenges. For example, a strong emphasis in the 3rd house may reflect a focus on the throat chakra, similar to that found in association with Gemini or Virgo, or through a strongly amplified Mercury. Or, a person with no planets in Capricorn or strong aspects to Saturn, but with many planets in the 10th house, may experience a strong drive toward success and recognition on the earth-plane, the domain of the Saturn chakra. Similarly, an individual with an unaspected Mars and no planets in either Aries or Scorpio, but with many in the 1st and 8th houses, can sometimes exhibit a surprisingly strong "Inner Warrior."

These then, are a few of the primary ways that we may begin to understand the chakric indicators in a common chart.[1] Seen in their entirety with an eye to any dominant trends, this host of factors can begin to reveal a picture of the energies constellated within an individual's subtle body. That is, if we could actually observe someone clairvoyantly, we would see the basic energies of his or her horoscope as translated into the energy patterns of the various chakras. I personally know of one incident, for example, where a highly intuitive yogi appears to have done just this, casually mentioning to a first-time student he never met before exactly what difficult transits the student had firing in his chart at that moment, based strictly on a psychic observation of the person's spinal energies—to the great surprise of that student, needless to say!

Yet in truth one hardly needs to be psychic, or an evolved yogi, to perceive such qualities in individuals; the person you meet who is just terribly "heavy," or gloomy, is clearly acting out of his or her Saturn, or root chakra, whereas a person who is "sweet" and light, to the point of excess, is most likely acting out an overly activated Venus chakra, etc. In

---

[1]There are, in my opinion, at least two further methods that can be utilized in extracting chakric information from a conventional horoscope. The first of these involves looking to the elemental preponderance of a chart, then applying this to the chakric level associated with that element. For example, if a person has most of his or her planets in earth signs, this would tend to indicate a heavy focus upon the lowest, Saturn chakra—regardless of whether or not Capricorn, Saturn, or the 10th house were strongly emphasized. Likewise, a heavy emphasis upon fire signs would suggest a strong 3rd, or Martian, chakra. The obvious drawback of this elemental technique is that it tells us little or nothing of the higher three (Mercury, Moon, and Sun) chakras, since astrology employs only four main elements.

The second method involves examining the relative balances of planets in positive or negative-polarity signs, and using this to determine which of the two subtle channels (*ida* or *pingala*) are more strongly emphasized within a person's chakric system and consciousness. For example, a preponderance of planets in feminine or negative signs would indicate an individual whose pranic energies are largely directed over to the left, or *idic* side of the subtle body (the channel governing both emotions and the dream state); whereas an individual with a preponderance of planets in masculine or positive signs would tend to have energies focused more within the *pingalic* side of the subtle vehicle (the channel governing rationality and the waking, outer world).

short, a little bit of character judgment and common perceptiveness can go a long way toward revealing much about the condition of another person's chakras.

In this same way, it can be instructive to contrast one's chart in terms of chakric emphases with one's own direct impressions of these various centers. Most of us are largely unaware of how the energies change and shift from moment to moment in our lives, let alone from year to year, or even decade to decade; yet these changes are occurring all the time and comprise the stuff of our emotions, body states, and thoughts at each moment. One of the ways I often begin lectures on this topic is to ask those in attendence to sit silently for a few moments and visualize a small sphere of light moving up and down their spines, and try to see if they feel any noticable blocks or concentrations of energy along the spine—then later compare these impressions against what they discover in their charts. One of the important values of this philosophical system is that it can help us, in a highly practical way, to become increasingly aware of the energies within our subtle bodies. As one becomes more sensitive in this way, one may also begin to notice increasingly more subtle patterns of relationship among the chakric centers, which often mirror those corresponding aspects between the planets in one's horoscope.

THE HOROSCOPE AND THE CHAKRAS: EIGHT CASE STUDIES

Let us now take a few examples and explore some possible ways this system can be used to tell us about an individual's chakras. For purposes of both clarity and consistency, I will focus here primarily (but not exclusively) on the second of our above-mentioned techniques, i.e., using the planets in the signs to assess the chakric emphasis within a chart. All of these horoscopes have been chosen on the basis of unusually dramatic planetary emphases and characteristics, from which the reader may then extrapolate more subtle patterns of meaning and interpretation. (Note: strictly for simplicity, I have not included such secondary factors as the nodes, asteroids, or Arabic parts. In all of the chakric horoscopes, where the zodiacal location of the Ascendant is known with any certainty, I have indicated it by "ASC." Finally, all charts here employ the tropical

zodiac; those sympathetic toward the sidereal, or constellation-based zodiac may wish to experiment with that system using these guidelines to
see how that approach works for them. My own experimentation with
both zodiacal systems over the years has led me to believe that whatever
other merits it may have to offer, the sideral approach is less effective in
delineating personality traits than the tropical, sign-based approach.)

Case Study No. 1: A Writer

For our first case, I will begin by showing this individual's conventional
Western chart (utilizing Placidus house cusps) followed by its conversion
to the chakric system. See figure 5, and figure 6 on page 15.

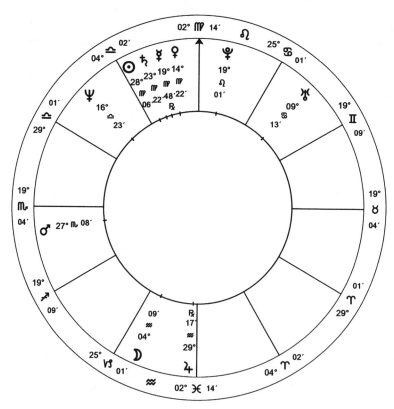

Figure 5. A writer. Birth data has been withheld for confidentiality.
Placidus houses. Chart computed using Solar Fire program.

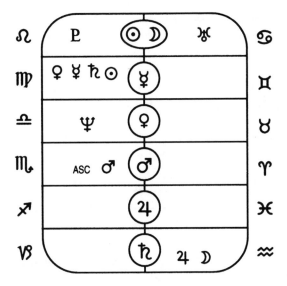

Figure 6. The writer's horoscope converted to show chakric emphasis.

Let us now take this chart (figure 6) and spin it around so as to position Leo and Cancer at the top, thus giving us the planets as they now appear located within the various chakric sub-compartments.

Here we see the chakric chart of a writer, specializing in works of a spiritual and yogic nature. He is highly prolific, hard working, and writes in a stylistically austere, yet clear and unusually insightful, manner. Most notable here is the group of planets located in the Virgo portion of the throat (Mercury) chakra. The fact that the stellium is placed in a Mercurial sign, and that Mercury is also included in this group, simply underscores the importance of this particular chakra in the horoscope. The additional fact that his conventional (non-chakric) horoscope shows these planets positioned in the angular 10th house further emphasizes this particular chakra in an even more dramatic way.

What this tells us, from a chakric standpoint, is that this individual possesses an extremely fertile and disciplined mind, suggesting a life directed in large part toward both knowledge and communication. Importantly, Saturn is in orb of a conjunction with Mercury, once again emphasizing the throat chakra in this person's life. As we already noted, one sometimes sees struggles or early frustrations in any area touched by

Saturn, although this connection also usually indicates a considerable depth of knowledge and discipline in those same areas.

Frequently, I have noticed that any major accentuation of the throat chakra can indicate the potential for healing abilities, or an involvement with health in some fashion. (Recall, for example, that the symbol of the winged caduceus is traditionally depicted as being held by Hermes, suggesting, I suspect, the important role of the mind in the healing process, and in the maintenence of psychic equilibrium throughout the chakric system generally.) Appropriately, this individual is highly knowledgable in Eastern forms of healing, particularly Indic and Chinese, having written both articles and books on this subject.

As might be expected with Saturn conjunct Mercury in Virgo, his overall approach is highly traditionalist in nature, championing the importance and value of time-proven ideas and techniques. What makes his case interesting, and somewhat paradoxical, is the added Aquarian element in his horosope; from the standpoint of mainstream academia, he is regarded as something of a maverick, precisely because of his extreme traditionalism, and his challenge to conventional modes of history with a more spiritualized and ancient model. Also noteworthy in this regard is his work in adapting ancient astrological wisdom for computer applications, as well as his involvement as a presenter and organizer of astrology conferences (Aquarius/11th house).

CASE No. 2: AN ARTIST

Here we see the chart pattern of an artist, as converted to the zodiacally-based chakric grid. (See figure 7 on page 17.) This artist is female, and spends the greater part of her time painting, writing, and giving workshops. Her artwork is spiritual in style and content, with a heavy emphasis on color and harmony of line and form. Note the astonishing emphasis on the heart level: first of all, not only is she a Sun in Taurus with Moon in Libra (both Venus-level signs), but all together there are seven planets in Venusian signs! That she chooses to express herself through artistic forms is therefore hardly surprising.

To reiterate an earlier point: it is important when working with any of these charts to avoid assigning any labels of "good" or "bad" when considering the different chakras. For example, some might be tempted to see the higher chakras as more intrinsically "good" or

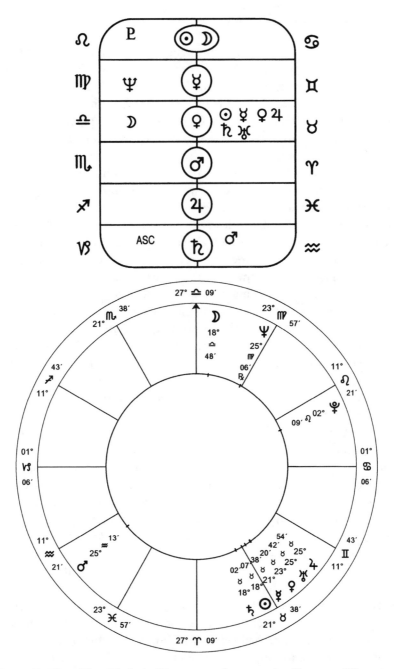

Figure 7. Top: The Chakric Horoscope for an artist. Bottom: Western-style Horoscope. Birth data has been withheld for confidentiality. Placidus houses. Chart computed using Solar Fire.

"spiritual," with the lower chakras being more intrinsically "negative" or "gross." In fact, there is no chakra that cannot be utilized in either a spiritual or destructive fashion, whether it be high or low upon the chakric tree. (Indeed, I find myself agreeing with one friend who remarked that the longer he is involved with spiritual practice, the more he realizes the importance of the lower three chakras in maintaining and fueling that practice!)

While this female artist has obviously used her Venusian energy in a more spiritually constructive fashion, we might do well to recall, by way of contrast, Adolph Hitler's horoscope, with its strong Taurus Sun and Libra Ascendant, likewise indicating a prominent 4th/Venus chakra. Indeed, Hitler nurtured a secret aspiration throughout his life to be an artist; yet this same energy, in considerably more imbalanced form, also produced in him a sensibility that often valued works of art over human lives, not to mention a preference for beautifully formed "Ayran" humans at that. Consequently, while it may be safe to presume that an individual with a powerfully activated heart area would be concerned or involved with matters of beauty or love, it is quite another thing determining what level they will choose to express that concern on.

As with conventionally drawn charts, one of the more telling features of chakric profiles is not only what they show but what they *don't* show; whenever one finds stelliums or important configurations channeling into certain areas, obviously certain other areas can come up short as a result. I have frequently found one of the most important challenges facing individuals with a highly prominent Venus chakra (whether indicated by planetary or zodiacal indicators), due to their acute sensitivity to harmony and beauty, can be learning to deal with the coarser energies and emotions of the lower chakras. This applies to Mars in particular, and its corresponding issues of assertiveness, anger, chaos, etc. In the artist's case, the fact that Mars is in challenging relationships with many of the planets in Taurus cuts both ways, helping to provide more energy or directness than might otherwise be expected for so Venusian a temperment, while also underscoring the potential difficulties in integrating that very same Inner Warrior energy. By this woman's own admission, her early life was indeed characterized by considerable challenges in dealing with anger and assertiveness, though in later years she has learned much more effectively how to deal with both of these areas.

Case Study No. 3: The Singer/Songwriter

Shown here (figure 8, page 20) is the chart of Bob Dylan, converted to the zodiacal-chakric grid. In this chart we see an example of what can arise with a strong emphasis on two different chakric levels at the same time. Whereas in Case Number 1 we saw a powerful emphasis primarily on the throat/Mercury chakra, and in Case Number 2 a strong dominance on the heart/Venus center, here we see both of these centers—the throat and heart—accentuated. Appropriately, Dylan became famous not only for his art (Venus) or his words (Mercury), but for his ability to combine these two elements in his craft, as a musician *and* lyricist.

Also worth noting here, incidentally, are the supporting aspects in the rest of Dylan's natal chart, such as Neptune and Mars square Mercury. One sometimes hears astrologers describe squares or oppositions as indicating a person's greatest faults or weaknesses, whereas trines show an individual's talents or virtues. Clearly, such a view is simplistic; so often, we find individuals who's greatest talents arise directly out of their most challenging aspects. One wonders whether a figure like Dylan, for instance, would have been as productive or creative in his career had these key aspects in his chart been trines instead of squares.

Yet another point to note here, in light of our chakric study, is Dylan's Mars in Pisces along with his Sagittarius Ascendant. This combination can often show a need to champion either spiritual or socially worthy causes, yet, as mentioned earlier, it can express itself sometimes in an evangelistic manner (hence, my partial designation of this chakric level as "the Inner Preacher"). With these chakric points emphasized in his chart, it is therefore not surprising that Dylan devoted several years of his career toward writing lyrics of an explicitly religious nature, in the wake of his born-again conversion to Christianity.

Case Study No. 4: The Religious Warrior

Depicted here is the chakric chart of Martin Luther (figure 9, page 21), the man who single-handedly broke ranks with the reigning Catholic authorities during the 16th century, thereby initiating the protestant reformation throughout Europe. Here again we see a good example of a chart in which not one, but two chakric levels are strongly emphasized.

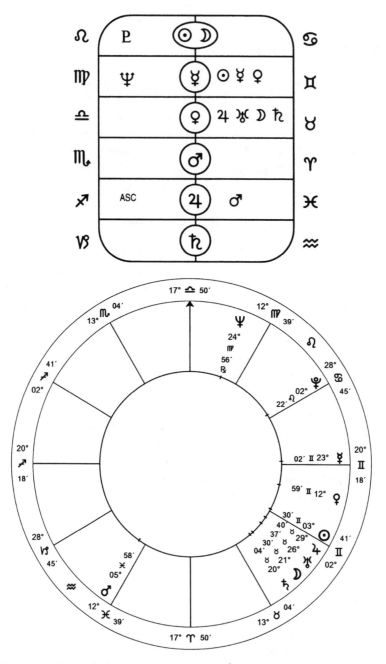

Figure 8. Top: Chakric Horoscope for Bob Dylan. Bottom: Western-style horoscope. Born: May 24, 1941, 9:05 P.M. CST, Duluth, MN. Placidus houses. Chart calculated by Solar Fire from data presented from *Contemporary Sidereal Horoscopes* and published in Lois Rodden's *Book of American Charts*.

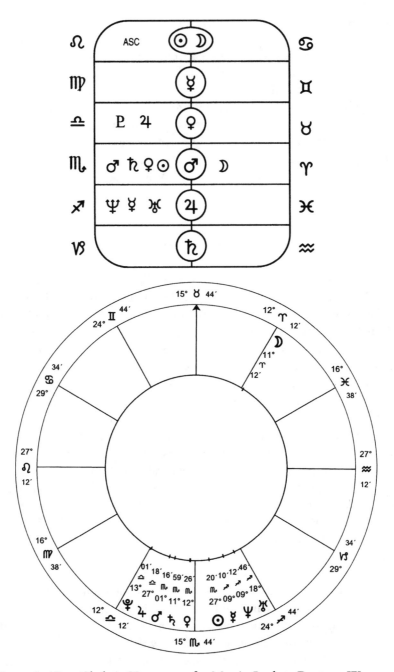

Figure 9. Top: Chakric Horoscope for Martin Luther. Bottom: Western-style Horoscope. Born: November 10, 1483 OS, 11:00 P.M. LMT, Eisleben, Germany. Placidus Houses. Chart calculated by Solar Fire based on information provided in Rodden's *Book of American Charts*. Data from mother's memory, confirmed from *Baker's Biographical Dictionary*.

In this case, these are the chakras specifically connected with what I have called the "Inner Warrior" and the "Inner Preacher," the 3rd and 2nd chakras. Certainly, Luther joined these two energies together, in his highly persistent and combative efforts to establish a more independent religious sensibility for his time. In the chakric horoscopes of almost all individuals I have studied over the years who played a pioneering or "revolutionary" role in initiating changes in their field, I have consistently found a dominant 3rd/Mars chakra to be a prominent feature.

CASE STUDY NO. 5: ACTOR/PLAYBOY/BUSINESSMAN

This is the chakric chart for actor Warren Beatty. (See figure 10.) As I noted before, one can often tell a great deal about an individual's chakric make-up simply from looking to the position of the Sun and the Moon. With Beatty's Sun in Aries and Moon in Scorpio, this chart shows a prominent emphasis on the "Inner Warrior." Indeed, Beatty has been known for his drive and aggressiveness both in and out of the movie industry. Early on, Beatty gave up a possible career in sports (playing quarterback in college football), to make his name and fortune as an actor and producer of numerous Academy Award-winning films. These capacities are effectively complemented by two planets in the heart-leveled Taurus (artistic and financial sensibility) as well as his root-chakra Jupiter in Capricorn (potential acumen and general success in earth-plane pursuits). Interestingly, his most personal and ambitious film was a lengthy and critically-acclaimed film about reporter-turned-revolutionary Jack Reed, called "Reds"—red being the color, of course, of both Mars and the Mars chakra! As an actor, he also won an early Academy Award playing a well-known gangster (or "*underworld* warrior") in the film "Bonnie and Clyde."

Not to be ignored here either is Beatty's concurrent reputation as a jet-setting playboy, having courted and seduced a seemingly endless string of actresses and glamorous women from around the world. While the sexual drive is commonly associated with the lowest two chakras, there is much to suggest that the 3rd/Martian chakra is central in this respect as well. In this vein, I have been repeatedly struck by how consistently a strong emphasis on this chakric level can indicate assertiveness as well as an extraordinary—and sometimes even uncontrollable—libido as well.

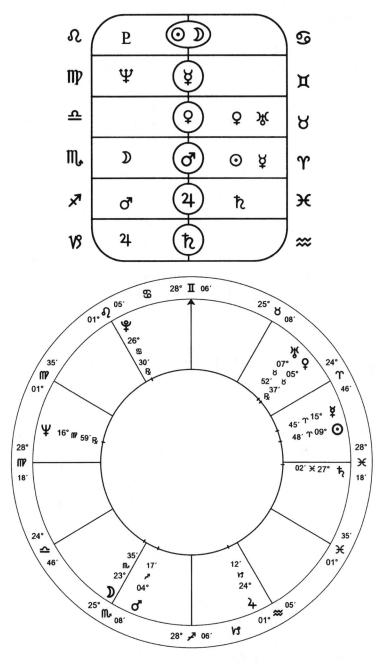

Figure 10. Top: Chakric Horoscope for Warren Beatty. Bottom: Western-style Horoscope. Born: March 30, 1937, 5:30 P.M. EST, Richmond, VA. Placidus Houses. Chart calculated using Solar Fire and "A" data from Rodden's *Book of American Charts.*

CASE STUDY No. 6:

THE BUSINESSMAN/ARCHITECT/ASTROLOGER

In this unusual confluence of energies in Capricorn, we see evidence of a temperment highly attuned toward the energies of the Saturn chakra, and the material plane generally. Now in his mid-30's, this man shows an innate talent for business and politics, as well as a great love for architecture (figure 11). In his own words, he has a great interest in "building" things generally, whether there be physical structures, businesses, ideas, or group activities—a fact which recalls our earlier designation of this chakra as the point of the "Inner Architect." With Mercury in Aquarius, he is also an avid astrologer, having studied this discipline since his mid-teens. Also worth noting is the fact that he was born into a highly prominent family, being the son of a famous psychologist. In other words, his life is inextricably bound up with earth-plane notoriety (or what in Capricornian terms might be called "life on the mountaintop").

One of the most curious facts about this individual is that, despite his clearly Capricornian/Saturnian skills and tendencies, his personality reveals a pronounced Jupiterian warmth and wateriness, rather than the more characteristic reserve one might expect from so Saturnine a chart. One possible answer to this is the placement of his Venus in Pisces, and the fact that, in his conventional chart, Jupiter is exactly on his Ascendant (within one degree of arc), while Neptune is positioned near the top of the chart. On the planetary level of importance, in other words, the two bodies associated with the Jupiter/water chakra are, by angular emphasis, the most highlighted symbols in his horoscope. This teaches us that we must consider all the information within a chakric horoscope in a holistic fashion, with a keen eye toward synthesizing the most prominent patterns on all these different levels.

CASE STUDY No. 7: THE VISIONARY ENGINEER

In figure 12 (page 26), we see an even more extraordinary convergence of energies, with no fewer than eight major indicators (including the Ascendant) located in Aquarius alone. By zodiacal emphasis, this likewise indicates a strong emphasis upon the lowest, or Saturn chakra—but with an intriguing twist. In contrast with Capricorn—an earth sign on

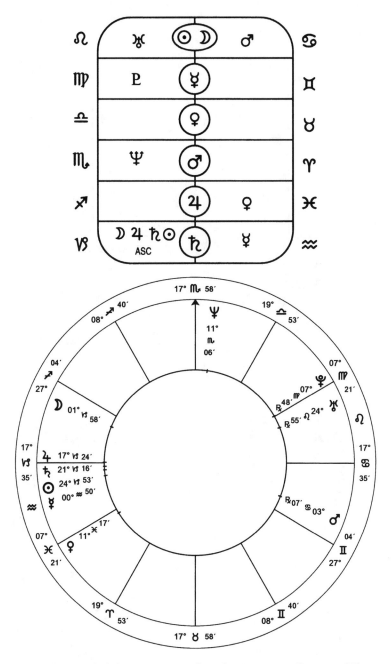

Figure 11. Top: Chakric Horoscope for a businessman. Bottom: Western-style Horoscope. Birth data has been withheld for confidentiality. Placidus houses. Chart calculated using Solar Fire. Source of data: birth certificate.

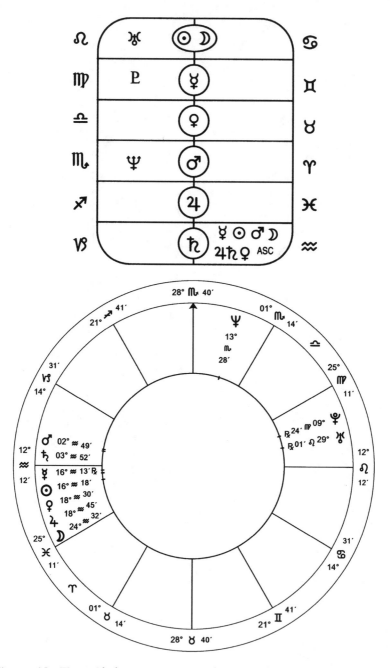

Figure 12. Top: Chakric Horoscope for visionary engineer. Bottom: Western-style Horoscope. Birth data withheld for confidentiality. Placidus houses. Chart calculated using Solar Fire. Source of data: birth certificate.

an earth chakra—Aquarius is an air sign transposed onto an earth chakra. As the element of mentality, *wherever we find air upon the chakric ladder is where we see the mind directed in its workings.* In Libra, for example, we see the air element transposed onto the heart chakra—hence, mentality in service of more aesthetic or interpersonal concerns. Librans are therefore often associated with the arts and diplomacy. In Gemini, we find air applied to the throat chakra—in short, the most purely platonic form of mentality in the zodiac, with relatively less concern for the practical applications of that knowledge. In Aquarius, however, we see the element of air applied to the earth chakra, thus the principle of mentality in service of more physical-plane material concerns. It is therefore fitting that we find this symbol so prominently emphasized in the charts of inventors, social reformers, scientists, or engineers. The person this chart belongs to is, in fact, an engineer, with far-ranging aspirations of changing the world through improved technology and living habitats.

On a broader level, it is worth considering how this elemental superimposition might help us grasp the deeper significance of the so-called "Aquarian Age" we find ourselves about to enter. By contrast, Pisces is a water sign transposed onto a water chakra, thus indicating an age of emotions, with a strong emphasis on religious devotion or dogmatism. The movement from Pisces to Aquarius therefore signals a movement from emotions (water) to intellect (air), yet within the context of a greater downswing to the Saturn, or earth chakra. Put these factors together (airy mentality applied to the realm of matter), and we may justifiably predict an age of spectacular technological and scientific achievements, and as well, potentially of considerably less emotional growth.

Also worth noting here is how this chakric connection can illumine the relationship of Uranus to the archetypal figure of Prometheus, as suggested by such astrologers as Richard Tarnas.[2] Recall that Prometheus was the Greek mythological figure who secretly brought fire down from Mt. Olympus to humankind, thereby giving mortals a newfound degree of power and independence. In association with Uranus (and to a lesser degree Aquarius), Prometheus represents that factor of consciousness which awakens us to the higher (intellectual?)

---

[2] Richard Tarnas, *Prometheus the Awakener: An Essay on the Archetypal Meaning of the Planet Uranus* (Dallas, TX: Spring, 1994).

potentials of our nature, and which can, in extreme cases, stimulate us toward titanic (or "Promethean") accomplishments as if in emulation of the gods themselves. Significantly, the period surrounding the discovery of Uranus in 1781 was one marked by the blossoming of democracy (personal participation in the political power structure) and capitalism (the entreprenuerial spirit), as well as the industrial revolution—all of which synchronistically converged within the birth of the American nation, as the collective embodiment of all these trends.

When we look at the position of Aquarius/Uranus upon the chakric tree, what we find is that it is directly opposite Leo, the symbolic point of God and the "third eye" (and, on the more mundane/political level, royalty). As one half of this vital dyad, in other words, it therefore represents that point where the light of divine spirit has descended completely into matter, where it has ventured furthest from its natural place, but where the possibility now exists for spirit to become manifest and practical. Here, emphasis thus shifts to the plane of material, political, and physical/bodily mastery, yet at the risk of forgetting the divine source.

With individuals who have either Uranus or Aquarius strongly emphasized in their horoscopes (especially in opposition to planets in Leo), we see the Promethean impulse operating on one of several possible levels. In politics or business, for instance, it may show itself as the desire to draw power down democratically from the "top" to the "bottom," as with democracy's founding fathers or even modern union organizers; in science, we find it in figures like Edison (an Aquarian), who brought down the electrical fires of heaven for everyday household use through such inventions as the lightbulb; in religion, it can express itself as the drive to "democratize" divinity through a message of personal God-realization, as we see in teachers like Omraam Aivanhov or Ramana Maharshi (with his appropriately titled technique of "Self-inquiry"); while in the creative field, it can indicate a desire to use one's creative powers as a conduit for helping or inspiring humankind, as in the case of Beethoven (who possessed a strong Uranus). Yet, on any of these levels, there is the ever-present danger of this energy shifting toward the more dictatorial or hubristic possibilities latent in this polarity, as exemplified by the literary figure of Dr. Frankenstein. In a slightly different vein, this same polarity may be expected to express itself as a shifting dance between the creative needs of the individual versus those of the greater collective (as provocatively illustrated in such films as "Brazil" and "Tucker").

CASE STUDY NO. 8: THE MYSTIC

Paramahansa Yogananda (figure 13, page 30) was the most famous proponent of Kriya Yoga in the West. Followed by his chakric horoscope I have employed in the previous cases.

There is much here of great interest when considered in light of Yogananda's life, such as the planets in Gemini (communication), or those in the warrior signs of Aries and Scorpio. Though not generally well known, Yogananda frequently claimed to be the reincarnation of William the Conqueror; and indeed, one might say his efforts to bring yoga to America was in its own way "establishing a beachhead" of sorts, though in a more spiritual than militaristic vein.

Particularly intriguing to my mind is the placement of his Sun down in the Capricorn side of the Saturn chakra. This may seem an odd placement for so mystical and spiritually-oriented a figure as Yogananda, yet its significance becomes clear once we realize the broader implications of his life's story. Rather than spending his life in a Himalayan cave, he instead chose (at the urgings of his teacher) to direct his spirituality into a more earthly expression, through a highly visible and successful mission of teaching in the secular world. Of relevance here, too, was the fact that this effort wound up requiring Yogananda's energies as a part-time administrator and manager for those selfsame organizations and projects he founded—a responsibility that frequently grew wearisome for him, as some former associates and disciples have noted. Furthermore, the more practical side of this chakra can be seen in Yogananda's efforts to present his teachings of Kriya Yoga to the West as a "*science* of spirituality"—a truly Capricornian approach indeed!

In figure 14 (page 31), I have taken the same basic horoscope and shifted it from the zodiacal-based system employed to the house-based method of chakric analysis we discussed earlier (figure 13). Here, instead of using the signs as our reference points, I have simply spun around the houses until Yogananda's 4th and 5th houses (relating to Cancer and Leo, respectively) were positioned at the top of the chart, and extrapolated the other chakric levels downward accordingly. I have also indicated the general placement of a major T-square in his chart, as converted to this house-chakra system, the meaning of which we will consider shortly.

This is a fascinating chart for several reasons, and provides us with a slightly different, but equally revealing, look into the character and

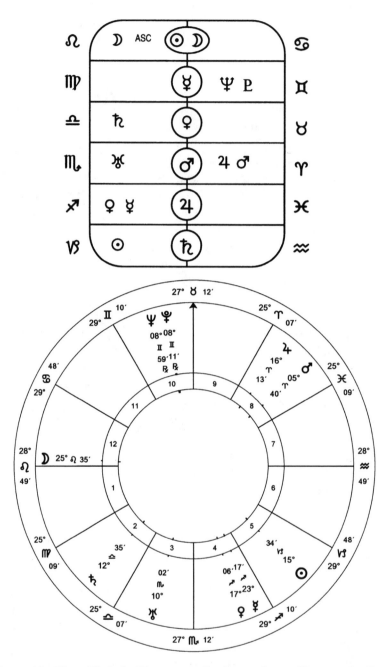

Figure 13. Top: Chakric Horoscope for Paramahansa Yogananda. Bottom: Western-style Horoscope. Born: January 5, 1883, 8:38 P.M. LMT, Gorakhpur, India. Placidus houses. Chart calculated according to data in Rodden's *Book of American Charts*. Chart source: according to the Sri, published in *Mercury Hour*, July 1976.

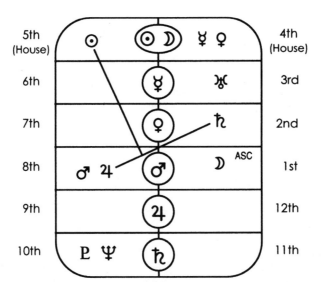

Figure 14. The house-based Chakric Horoscope for Yogananda.

destiny of Yogananda. As we have already discussed, the Sun, Leo, and
5th house all relate by chakric association to the spiritual center located
at the forehead, or third eye. In their more conventional form, these
three astrological factors tend to manifest themselves in such things as
pleasure, children, and child-raising, or creativity. Yet as some teachers
have pointed out, they can, in rare cases, indicate a focus on more spiritual concerns, even the quest for God-consciousness. On first hearing
this association many years ago, I asked my astrology teacher at the time,
Goswami Kriyananda, to explain it. His simple response was, "Because
God-consciousness is the greatest pleasure!"

There is, I believe, a more subtle reason implied in this statement.
As the seat and center of Self-awareness, the Solar/Ajna chakra represents the point of pure spontaneous, blissful consciousness—indeed,
what *is* enlightenment other than an absolute awareness of the present?
We experience this state in somewhat more mundane form during moments of play or creativity, but at its most subtle level, it represents nothing less than an awakening to the very foundation of our true nature, to
pure being in the present moment. The position or character of these
points within the birth chart (i.e., Sun, Leo, and the 5th house) can
therefore yield important clues as to an individual's access to this state of
pure spontaneous existence.

In the first, zodiacally-based chart erected for Yogananda (figure 13), we already saw a strong emphasis of the Ajna chakra indicated by the Leo Ascendant and Moon. Above and beyond this sign-emphasis, however, upon converting his chart to the house-based system shown in figure 14, we find this chakric point of the third eye further reinforced by a T-square to the 5th house, with Jupiter and Mars-Saturn focusing in on the Sun at the short leg of the aspect. In brief, using all three of the levels I suggested earlier—planetary (the Sun as the short leg of a T-square), sign (Moon and Ascendant in Leo), and house (the T-square focused into the 5th house), we see a chart overwhelmingly focused upon the Solar principle!

To be sure, a configuration like this could have just as well manifested in a far more prosaic fashion. It is not irrelevant, perhaps, that, of the highly diverse teachers of his lineage, Yogananda was one of the few to remain completely celibate: by contrast, his guru and guru's guru, Sri Yukteshwar and Lahiri Mahasaya, chose householdership and its responsibilities as an integral part of their path. One therefore has good reason to believe that had Yogananda not chosen this particular direction, his 5th-house T-square could have easily given rise to a far different destiny, possibly with regard to children or romantic entanglements of one sort or another. As a result of his decision, his T-square was transmuted into the more sublimated pursuit of God-consciousness with a degree of one-pointedness rare among contemporary teachers.

TIMING AND TRIGGERING FACTORS

In addition to what the natal chart can tell us about an individual's chakric constitution, astrology can reveal other insights about the chakras as well, in terms of the timing and unfoldment of an individual's subtle energies over the course of an entire lifetime. Utilizing such techniques as transits and progressions, we can begin to glimpse how the chakras are subject to various timing mechanisms in the way they manifest their energies. To use some obvious examples, for instance, transiting Jupiter crossing over a personal planet, like the Moon, would suggest a corresponding opening up of the Lunar chakra at the back of one's head; while Saturn conjuncting or squaring that same point might suggest a closing down or limiting of that chakric energy. Again, this does not mean that Jupiter is "good" while Saturn aspects are "bad"; indeed, Saturn periods are often the most constructive and discipline-producing times in a person's life. However, the psychological experience of that energy may be one of considerable frustration or heaviness, at least initially.

Of a quite different sort, Uranus aspects often indicate an activation or blowing-open of a chakric center sometimes even more extreme than Jupiter. Mars transits can show the chakric area where one's psyche tends to "heat up," which can thus be a point of considerable energy or even volatility. Neptune transits to a given chakric point can diffuse the energies of that center in a way which, if not creatively or spiritually channeled, may diffuse or "bleed" one's subtle energies in that area. And Pluto connections to any important points in the chakric chart can indicate areas where, not unlike Mars, intense energy will be drawn toward a radical restructuring and "death/rebirth" of that level of psychic concern.

I have likewise found that transiting returns of key planets to their own natal degree can be especially helpful checkpoints during which one can gain insight into the essential life-karmas of that given chakra. Every time Mercury returns to its natal position each year, for instance, one may notice certain recurring motifs or states relating to one's own unique lessons with matters of communication or thinking. In turn, each year these lessons may change in subtle ways, or accrue new and more subtle layers of meaning pertaining to the energies of that chakra. It is likewise useful during such times to observe one's dreams, or put aside time to meditate on those points of the chakric "ladder," to see what feelings or images arise in connection with those areas.

Another helpful technique involves looking to the degree number associated with that planet, and relating it to that corresponding year of one's life. If one's Venus, say, is 22 degrees and 30 minutes into Sagittarius, somewhere roughly midway between one's 22nd and 23rd birthdays one may see some key manifestation of that energy in one's life, as if one's Venus were somehow "coming-to-bloom" at that time. And as with transits or progressions, if one pays close attention to one's inner experience during such times, one may notice specific energies activating that relate to those symbolic areas. Applying this technique to the chakric system, these timing points can likewise shed light on one's life-karmas associated with those corresponding chakric points. These points can, in turn, echo at later stages in one's life at *30-year* (corresponding to 30-degrees) increments. Hence, if a person has a planet in the birth chart at 2 degrees and 30 minutes of a given sign, one might see echos of that energy during the middle of the 32nd, 62nd, and 92nd years as well.

On a more collective level, it is likewise instructive to study the transiting planets through the various signs for what they reveal about the *collective* consciousness upon these different chakric levels. This applies to any major configuration of energies throughout the zodiac, including eclipses, outer-planetary aspects, or major groupings (stelliums) of planets in any given sign. I recall during the Winter of 1993/1994, for example, when one such constellation of planets took place in Capricorn, as I anxiously perused news reports of the time for insights as to where we, as a culture, were at in relation to the energies of this lowest chakra. As it turned out, the biggest news story of the period was an ice-skating scandal involving Tonya Harding and Nancy Kerrigan, replete with Saturnian ice symbols, clubbed knees, even Nancy's big shiny teeth—all in the name of dog-eat-dog competitiveness and greed. Not a particularly flattering indicator of our collective bill of health at this chakric level, but a comically graphic one!

SPIRITUALITY AND THE HOROSCOPE

Finally, we might ask whether there is some reliable way of determining a person's degree or level of spirituality from the chart, chakrically or otherwise. For example, we saw with Yogananda's chart how a heavy emphasis on the Sun, Leo, and the 5th house helped contribute to a one-pointed orientation toward God-realization—although this, by itself, doesn't necessarily guarantee a spiritual or enlightened orientation. Additionally, in terms of house emphasis, astrologers have traditionally spoken of the 8th house (occult interests and abilities), 9th house (philosophical matters and the broadening of spiritual horizons), and 12th house (mystical pursuits and liberation) as indicators of an involvement with spiritual matters. And in terms of planetary symbols, the outer planets are commonly associated with spiritual growth and transformation, with Neptune, in particular, showing an individual's degree of spiritual sensitivity or capacity for transcendence.

For example, some teachers in the Kriya Yoga lineage have stressed one natal configuration as especially suggestive of a mystically-inclined temperment. This is, simply, *Neptune in hard aspect to one luminary while in easy aspect to the other luminary.* For instance, one might have Neptune square the Moon but trine the Sun, or conversely, Neptune trine the Moon but square or opposing the Sun. (According to this system, Neptune conjunctions and oppositions would be classified as "hard" or challenging aspects.) One suspects that the importance placed here on the Sun and Moon is due to their vital role in the chakric system as the primary poles of consciousness, with the single hard aspect to Neptune assuring a degree of intensity and a focused application frequently absent with easy aspects alone.

Yet there is a very different viewpoint suggested by certain astrologers and yogis: the idea that spirituality *cannot* be truly deduced from the horoscope. Why? Because the horoscope reveals one's karmic patterns "on the wheel," i.e., within the two channels of energy running to the right and left-hand sides of the spine (*ida* and *pingala*); but tells us nothing of one's degree of self-control or focused awareness within the central, *sushumnic,* channel.

An individual, for example, may have karmic tendencies to become a great military leader and in this role the leader could direct great armies and send thousands of soldiers into battle. Yet this person might choose, through a combination of self-awareness and self-discipline, *not* to respond to these compelling forces from the sides of the spine (in this case, specifically at the level of the Martian chakra) and, instead, simply witnesses these tendencies from the vantage point of the central spiritual channel. The karmic urges may still present themselves, but the individual has chosen not to be *controlled* by them. Legend tells us that early on the Buddha was himself faced with just such a challenge, between the prospect of becoming a great ruler or a world teacher. Through wisdom and self-discipline, he chose the more balanced of these two paths. In short, the chart reveals what the urges and propensities from the past may be, but does not reveal how successfully one will respond to, or balance out, those energies.

On this level, the chart could be thought of as offering a detailed blueprint of one's potential addictions, or "archetypal enslavements"— that is, the compelling karmic patterns during a given life. This is not to suggest these energies are "bad"; it's simply a matter (as Shelly Trimmer has expressed it) of *who's controlling who.* Are you in control of your chakras, or are your chakras in control of you? Likewise, are you in control of your planets, or are your planets in control of you? For one individual, the Mars chakra may be an uncontrollable source of pain or explosive anger, while for a yogi, that same exact "warrior" energy may prove useful in dealing with challenging life-situations or fueling spiritual practice.

In this sense, spiritual growth can be seen as a process of breaking free of increasingly more subtle addictions, ranging from such obvious habits like food or sex to more fleeting and intangible patterns of thought or mood. More surely than any other symbolic system I know of, the horoscope shows what an individual's potential archetypal addictions may be, whether gross or subtle in nature. Through an understanding of these patterns, one may begin to understand how best to transmute or counteract their influence in one's life. With this in mind, let us briefly look back at each of the chakric levels in terms of the potential allurements and habitual patterns they present, with an eye toward those levels which are most emphasized in one's own chart by planetary or zodiacal emphasis, or aspect (such as major conjunctions or T-squares). In a sense, every person has his or her "drug of choice," whether this takes the form of books, sex, power, or money, with no single addiction being better or worse than another. As some spiritual teachers have expressed it, gold handcuffs are ultimately no less confining than iron ones. The critical first step toward gaining control of those patterns is through becoming more conscious of what archetypes are specifically strongest in one's life.

• The 1st, or root, chakra (Saturn), involves a primary orientation toward the earth plane. A strong focus here can suggest a potential addiction to worldly prestige, success, or power (though in Aquarius this can take on a more social or organizational guise). On an emotional level, this can indicate a habitual tendency toward coldness or reserve.

• The 2nd chakra (Jupiter) concerns the allure of, or enslavement to, emotion in its most general sense, whether this take a more exhuberant and optimistic form (Sagitarius-9th house) or a more ethereal, escapist, or self-effacing form (Pisces-12th house). More subtly, at this level; there can be a habitual tendency to find solace or put faith in belief systems or ideologies of one sort or another.

• The 3rd, or Martian, chakra primarily concerns the expression of energy and power; a strong emphasis here shows the potential addiction to combativeness, anger, sex, or "being in control."

• A heavy emphasis on the 4th, or Venus, chakra shows the possibility of entrapment by beauty, and the allurements of comfort or even love (or, in the case of Libra, self-love).

• A dominance of energies at the level of the 5th, or Mercury, chakra shows the potential enslavement to ideas and thoughts, and the tendency to shield oneself from life by erecting mental walls around one.

• The 6th, or Lunar, chakra shows a possibly addictive need to nurture or to be nurtured, or the entrapping lure of memories (reflectivity) and excessive dwelling upon the past.

• The 7th, or Solar, chakra shows a potential addictiveness to ego, pride, and the need for attention and recognition in situations.

Once one has determined which levels are most emphasized in one's own chakric horoscope, one might then reflect how those express themselves in one's everyday experience. One might try devising ways of testing, transmuting, or overcoming those addictive patterns. For instance, in conversation with a fellow Gemini (someone with a strong emphasis on the throat chakra, in other words), I once jokingly remarked that if I were his guru, I'd probably tell him to try spending a month in a library without picking up a single book or magazine there! In other words, was he able to consciously control his hunger for information and data, as reflected in his relationship with those external symbols of mind, books, *or did those symbols have control over him?* Likewise, for an individual with the Moon, Cancer, or the 4th house accentuated by contact with key planets or a T-square, that potential enslavement may take the form of food, family, or nourishment issues, while for the Capricorn individual it may take the form of social status or the need for achievement.

By learning how to become more self-sufficient within oneself, one begins drawing in life-energy from the peripheral chakric channels toward the central sushumnic channel of the subtle body, in this way becoming free from the compelling influences of both the outer environment and the "inner horoscope." Through the cultivation of the higher (or "magical") will, the mystic in this way learns to direct the activity of the different chakras consciously and by choice rather than by compulsion.

At the more advanced levels of practice, this may also entail directing the energies not only in, but *up* the chakric ladder, toward the spiritual centers in (and above) the head region, then back down through the chakric levels again. In systems like Kriya Yoga, for example, this may be facilitated by meditation techniques involving the visualization of a current of light in the center channel of one's body, which is then directed up and down (or, in a circular fashion, around) the spinal column. This serves the purpose of not only enhancing mastery of the chakric energies generally, but of heightening one's awareness of (and access to) the higher states of spiritual consciousness.

As a result of such methods as these, the yogi ultimately develops a facility for manipulating states of consciousness not unlike a concert pianist who has mastered the keys of his piano. And so, in the end, it is through transcending the chart that we learn how to actualize its potentials to the greatest possible degree.

ABOUT THE AUTHOR

Ray Grasse has been a professional astrologer for over twenty years. He obtained a degree in filmmaking and painting from the Art Institute of Chicago, and studied yogic esoteric philosophy with two teachers in the Kriya Yoga tradition for sixteen years. He has written for such publications as *NCGR Journal, Welcome to Planet Earth, The Quest,* and *Magical Blend,* and was a contributor to the anthology *Karma: Rhythmic Return to Harmony (Quest).* He is also author of the book *The Waking Dream (Quest 1996),* a study of synchronicity and symbolism. He has been assistant editor for *The Quest* magazine for six years.

Readers who want to get in touch with Ray Grasse can write the following address:

Ray Grasse
c/o The Quest
1926 N. Main St.
P.O. Box 270
Wheaton, IL 60189

ROBIN ARMSTRONG

CHAPTER 2

THE DEGREES OF THE ZODIAC AND THE I CHING

BEFORE WE BEGIN TO WORK with the I Ching we need to have a brief overview of its history. The origins of the I Ching reach back beyond the beginnings of any recorded history. They are ascribed to a period of Highest Antiquity. This was the time of the Emperor Fu Hsi, 3322 B.C., more than five thousand years ago. Apparently Fu Hsi used the I Ching to direct the government and run the nation. By this time the I Ching would have been developed to an advanced state of social application and literacy, which means that its origins must be traced to a much earlier period.

The I Ching was an oral teaching, like many of the early beliefs. It was passed on from teacher to student; it emphasized the understanding of thoughts, rather than words. The implications of change were a primary concern. It was not until the time of King Wen, who brought about the downfall of the Yin Dynasty, that words were written and added to the I Ching. Before the beginning of the Kau Dynasty in 1122 B.C., King Wen was imprisoned for about a year. It was in prison in 1143 B.C., that words were added to the I Ching. Shortly thereafter Wen was freed and subsequently took over the country. The words just added to the I Ching consisted of meanings for the basic trigram to trigram relationships with each hexagram. King Wen also took the editorial liberty of rearranging the sequence of the trigrams. In so doing he altered our primary relationship to nature (old religions) and redirected it into a numerological and divinatory relationship (newer and more abstract theology). This process is generally accepted by historians without further thought. It is possible that the original clarity and vision of the I Ching and its changes were abstracted and obscured (a process we have experienced greatly over the last thousand years in the West). In any case, words were added, and accepted without question for thousands of years.

King Wen's son, Tan, the Duke of Kau, added words to the meaning of each line. He died in 1105 B.C., at which time the traditional text of the I Ching, as it stands today, was complete. Since then, many scholars have appended translations and commentaries to the I Ching. It was at the beginning of the Kau Dynasty that words and a new logic were added to the I Ching, replacing the old. The new logic was based on numerological associations, magical squares, and seemingly Quaballistic techniques. It ushered in an era of contemplative abstraction and meditation, replacing the older religions and our relationship to nature and to planets as Gods! As happened in early Christianity, the older teachings were incorporated into the new, and they were redirected.

The original I Ching was, and is, considered to be a Book of Changes. It represented the nature and implications of change and relationships. It was based on a concept of duality and its subsequent implications: such as light and dark, or firm and yielding. It included relationships to nature, to the heavens, to the gods, and to the earth. The I Ching was, in my opinion, the original astrological system, and a very advanced one at that. I believe that when words were added, the astrological clarity of the changes was obscured. It was the way of the new order; the times were changing. I am uncertain however, if the new order was an improvement. This seems to mark a period in history when people began to worship an abstract or inner God, separate from nature.

From this era, Confucianism developed. It was a time of great social and cultural refinement. The Confucian era was also an extremely puritanical and fundamentalistic period, where life, sex, and nature were to be controlled, so that people could be free! Such abstract moralism was too severe for the average person. It was difficult to live up to all the new idealized rules. Much of the addendums to the I Ching were written by Confucius or his students.

Taoism developed as a reaction to the puritanical repressive Confucian order. It brought in a more natural, spontaneous, sensual, and artistic balance as the way of the world. It was less rigid, and encouraged the development of a middle way between the senses and the silence.

Confucianism and Taoism both were based upon the ideas presented in the I Ching, and the development of both philosophies contributed to the evolvolution of the book. The concepts of Yin and Yang also came into existence during this period (about 500 to 300 B.C.).

In 213 B.C., the Emperor of China decided that all books must be burned. The only books to escape were books on medicine, husbandry, and divination. Some books escaped to Japan and surrounding countries, but much was lost. However, the divinational aspect of the I Ching survived. I believe that the remaining astrological literacy permeating the I Ching was rewritten, and from this time on, was hidden within the implications of the apparently divinatory wisdom. Astrology has been obscured in many places around the world over the centuries. China was one of these places. A highly advanced form of astrology remained buried or hidden within the I Ching and its words. It was brilliantly buried in the ideas behind the words: easy to see if one could only understand the great secret—the I Ching was, and is, an astrological text, and it was through astrology that the great wisdom and insights originated.

INTRODUCTION TO THE SYSTEM

In using the I Ching for divination, one asks a question and throws coins, or counts sticks, to obtain a figure from which meaning is derived. Take out the divination, add astrological computation, and we discover the essence of Horary Astrology! It is my premise that the I Ching, with its 64 hexagrams and subdivisions, was an original zodiac, a zodiac of 64 divisions.

I have spent over thirty years studying the I Ching and its relationship to astrology. Through this method I have developed many insights and correspondences. Each I Ching figure (hexagram) consists of six lines, either broken or solid, arranged on top of each other as in a totem pole. There are only 64 possible combinations of two distinct lines in a six level totem. These 64 hexagrams measure the circle and stand for the circle (or cycle) of all relationships. The position of each hexagram in the circle is unique, and critical for understanding the changes. One of the puzzles I struggled with, in the early years of my research, was that there are 384 lines in an I Ching circle and 360 degrees in the Western zodiacal circle. Both systems measure the same heavenly circles. In short, there are 24 appropriately placed lines that could be considered neutral. This would allow for a direct correspondence of each line of an

I Ching hexagram to a degree of the zodiac. Following upon this correspondence, I have extended the association to subsystems of the zodiac. I have worked vigorously over the last twenty years to confirm this correspondence through its application to individual horoscopes. The following material shows how the I Ching can assist and enhance astrological insights through natal chart evaluation. There are many other astrological techniques that can be further enlightened through the use of the I Ching: progressions, transits, composites, new Moons, eclipses, etc.

To find out about the I Ching hexagrams for your own personal horoscope there are two options:

1. You can order the computer printouts from me (like the ones used in this article).

2. You can order back issues of "News By Degrees" V.2 #1, 2, 3, & 4, and V. 3 #1. These issues give the correspondences of the I Ching to each degree of the Zodiac. You will need your own horoscope and planet positions to look up which hexagrams apply. The correspondences are given for two levels only. (The computer printout gives three levels.) Volume 2 #1 to 4 will give the actual correspondence. V.3 #1 gives an example using Carl Jung's horoscope.[1]

My work with the I Ching and astrology involves the use of the I Ching as a zodiac of 64 divisions instead of twelve. The planets and their energies become the point of focus. The 64 hexagrams become the zodiac and each line of an I Ching hexagram relates to 1 degree of the zodiac on Level 1. The entire system repeats itself within itself as a subsystem, somewhat similar to the idea of duads, but different. I call the subsystem Pentans. In this subsystem, each zodiacal sign occupies a 5-degree section in six different places around the larger zodiac (Level 1). Also in this subsystem, each hexagram occupies 1 degree and each line occupies 10 minutes of a degree. The entire cycle repeats itself six times around the zodiacal wheel to complete Level 2. There is also a sub-subsystem in which the whole cycle of hexagrams (and the zodiac) is repeated 36 times around the zodiacal wheel. In this sub-subsystem,

---

[1]A Windows based computer program "Stars in Sight" is still in developmental stages and will be available at some future date. You can write to me for a price list at Robin Armstrong Enterprises Inc., P.O. Box 5265, Station "A,"Toronto, Ontario, M5W 1N5, Canada.

the I Ching (or zodiac) repeats itself completely every 10 degrees. On this third level, a hexagram occupies 10 minutes of a degree, and each line occupies 1'40" of a degree.

This seems like an extraordinarily small division, but it is nonetheless a very sensitive one that elaborates very significant data. This is most obvious in the study of twins and multiple births, for a small amount of time difference is involved. It should also be noted here that since DNA and the genetic code parallel the I Ching as a language, this work has the potential of validating astrological genetic code research.

So what I have essentially evolved is a system of degree symbols using the I Ching. There are many books on astrological degree symbolism, such as *The Sabian Symbols*, by Marc Edmond Jones.[2] There are also several books published concerning the I Ching and the zodiac, but the correspondences are usually based on numerology, rather than on astrological phenomena.

I use the horoscope and planet positions to tune into the I Ching via the degrees of the zodiac. As the I Ching measures the zodiacal circle on three levels, it can also be applied to an aspect cycle. In short, any position of a planet or sensitive point that is represented accurately in degrees and minutes will yield three hexagram symbols. In each hexagram one line will be accentuated and have special emphasis.

• The Level 1 Hexagram is the Main Theme and the line number (L#1-6) is the special emphasis.

• The Level 2 Hexagram is the Specific Focus and further elaborates the meaning of the line number in Level 1. There is also a specially accentuated line in Level 2.

• The Level 3 Hexagram is the Intimate Emphasis, and further elaborates the meaning of the line number in Level 2, and there is a specially emphasized line in Level 3.

Not only can a zodiac position produce three hexagrams but so can the 1- to 360-degree aspect phase. Any aspect written in degrees and minutes can also yield three hexagrams.

On the computer printout we will work with, the hexagrams and line numbers are printed out for the ASC, MC, DSC, IC, Sun, Moon, planets, and nodes, as well as for each aspect.

---

[2]Marc Edmond Jones, *The Sabian Symbols in Astrology* (Santa Fe, NM: Aurora Press, 1993).

A STUDY OF MICK JAGGER

I chose to study the horoscope of Mick Jagger because he is an exciting person with an incredible lifestyle. I have listened to his music from the very beginning of the Rolling Stones. I appreciate his accomplishments. He has maintained his career and a consistent style of music for over thirty years, outlasting all of his contemporaries. Mick Jagger and The Rolling Stones have become a standard in the music field.

I used two biographies to obtain my historical and personal data. I do not know Mick Jagger personally, but I have followed his career with interest and his music with appreciation. The books I used for reference and personal detail are: *Mick Jagger: Primitive Cool*, by Christopher

MICK JAGGER
Dartford, England

Date: July 26, 1943   LATITUDE   : 51N27
Time: 02:30 A.M. (ZONE −2)   TROPICAL   LONGITUDE: 00 E 14

H10 =	8AQ09		H1 =13GE06
H11 =	4 PI30		H2 = 2CA19
H12 =	17AR54		H3 =19CA11

HEXAGRAMS: HEXAGRAMS:
MC = 8AQ09 = 17L3:26L6:42L6   AC =13GE06 = 14L5:43L6:32L4
IC = 8LE 09 = 18L3:26L6:42L6   DC =13SA06 = 8L5:43L6:32L4

	GEO-TROP	LAT	HOUSE	HEXAGRAMS
SUN	2LE10	0n00	H03	48L3:60L2:43L6
MER	10LE56	1n47	H04	18L5: 9L1:38L4
VEN	13VI34	1s45	H05	29L5:23L3:18L3
MAR	12TA12	1s48	H12	10L1: 8L5:43L5
JUP	5LE30	0n29	H03	48L6:38L3:56L6
SAT	21GE58	1s20	H01	43L3:18L6:34L1
URA	7GE48	0s07	H12	34L5:11L2:27L5
NEP	29VI49	1n21	H05	7L1:13L2:49L1
PLU	6LE43	5n06	H03	18L1:58L5:16L5
MON	23TA58	5s14	H12	26L1:22L1:47L2
NNd	16LE00	0n00	H04	6L3:44L6:39L6

Sandford (London: Victor Gollancz, 1993), and *Mick Jagger: Everybody's Lucifer*, by Tony Scaduto (New York: Berkley Medallion, 1975). The birthdata came from the Arthur Blackwell collection. The time was recorded by the doctor who delivered him. Figure 1 (pages 46–47) has been printed on two pages in order to show some of the detail. Figure 2 (pages 48–49) is also printed on two pages for clarity.

MICK JAGGER'S SUN IS AT 2° ♌ 10' IN H3

The Sun is in Leo, the sign where daylight is predominant but darkness is increasing. This shows a person who has to create his own way in life, and who needs to impress others with what he is doing. The Sun symbolizes one's heart and one's purpose in life. Jagger has a creative playful purpose that loves attention. He is the essential big kid who has to play and be noticed. He is driven to be best; second best will not do. (Who remembers the Beatles anyway?) Jagger did very well in school until, in the higher levels, he realized he could not be number one. He is a born performer. His power is directed to creative expansion and maintaining a leading role.

With his Sun in the 3rd house, Jagger's life focus will be in expressing his ideas and making sure that he is heard. He enforces his ideas dramatically. He will act on his ideas and on whatever motivates him. His Sun rules the IC; Jagger places great importance on his home, his roots, and his mom, but with his Moon being in the 12th house, he rarely feels that it was ever good enough, hence his bluesy angry style.

Jagger's Sun is part of a stellium in Leo. It conjuncts Jupiter, Pluto in house 3 and also conjuncts the IC and Mercury. This emphasizes Jagger's powerful and successful ability to express himself creatively as a songwriter. He really gets into and exaggerates his ideas, acting them out to the hilt. The Jupiter Pluto presence unveils a deep struggle over principles and morals, with a marked tendency to fight against self-righteousness. This stellium also squares Mars in house 12, revealing his sarcastic wit, aggressive agility, and excessive but self-isolating concerns over sex. A parallel would be how most prostitutes have a blatant contempt for their johns. Yes, Mick has always been very concerned over violence and control, a concern that multiplied after Altamont. His performances are vital, energetic, and exaggerated. In close quarters, however, Mick would have

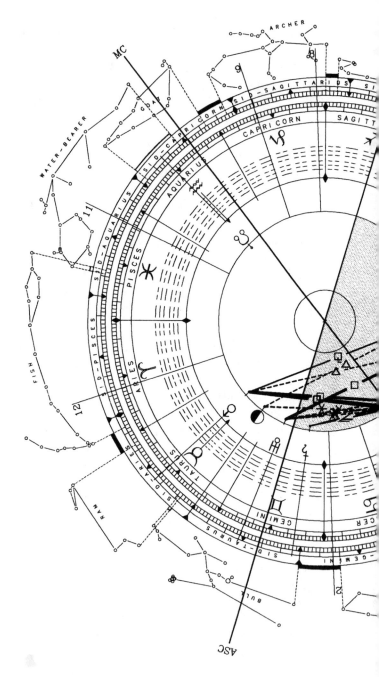

Figure 1. Mick Jagger's chart. Chart printed using the "Stars in Sight" astrology program.

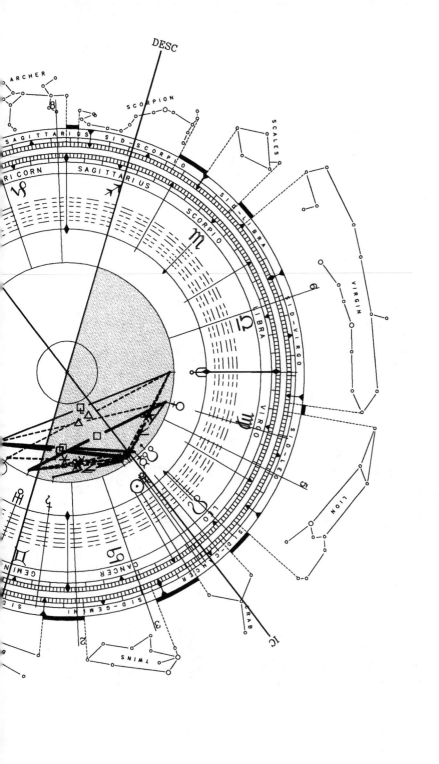

GEO/GEO	SUN H03	MER H04	VEN H05	MAR H12	JUP H03	SAT H01	URA H12	NEP H05	PLU H03	MOM H12	NEd H04	ABC H01	MC. H10
SUN H03		8°46 CNJ-A	41°24 SSQ-S	79°58	3°20 CNJ-S	40°12 SSQ-S	54°22 SXT-A	57°39 SXT-S	4°33 CNJ-A	68°12 SXT-S	13°50	49°04 SSQ-S	174°01 OPP-A
HEX1		27L3	17L6	31L5	24L4	45L5	39L6	63L3	24L5	62L4	3L2	52L5	44L6
HEX2		45L2	34L4	9L6	62L2	51L5	39L4	29L3	53L4	18L5	23L2	16L1	39L6
HEX3		36L3	26L4	19L2	57L6	58L2	62L5	24L6	29L5	9L2	6L1	38L4	39L6
MER H04			32°39 SSX-A	88°43 SQR-A	5°26 CNJ-S	48°57 SSQ-S	63°08 SXT-S	48°53 SSQ-A	4°13 CNJ-S	76°58	5°04 CNJ-A	57°49 SXT-A	177°13 OPP-S
HEX1			21L3	33L2	2L4	52L6	53L3	22L6	2L5	56L2	24L6	39L3	1L3
HEX2			60L4	41L2	59L2	20L6	32L6	32L6	40L2	43L6	39L1	56L2	29L5
HEX3			44L6	11L2	16L6	21L3	22L4	22L4	53L5	32L2	33L3	43L6	23L4
VEN H05				121°22 TRI-S	38°05	81°36	95°46 SQR-S	16°15	36°51	109°36	27°34 SSX-A	90°28 SQR-S	144°35 BQT-A
HEX1				64L2	45L3	31L3	7L6	3L5	45L1	59L2	16L4	7L1	5L6
HEX2				4L3	17L6	26L4	63L5	27L2	22L6	16L4	60L3	13L3	63L3
HEX3				17L5	34L3	21L3	40L4	15L3	32L6	60L3	1L3	30L5	29L4
MAR H12					83°17 SQR-S	39°46 SSQ-A	25°36 SSX-A	137°37 SES-S	84°30 SQR-S	11°45	93°48 SQR-S	30°54 SSX-A	94°03 SQR-S
HEX1					49L1	17L4	51L2	11L1	13L6	27L6	19L4	21L1	7L5
HEX2					22L5	5L2	37L3	3L4	63L3	20L2	61L5	19L6	37L1
HEX3					57L5	49L3	62L4	24L5	29L6	9L3	6L2	38L3	39L5
JUP H03						43°31 SSQ-S	57°42 SXT-A	54°19 SXT-S	1°13 CNJ-A	71°32 QNT-A	10°30	52°23	177°21 OPP-A
HEX1						12L2	39L3	63L6	24L2	62L1	27L5	52L2	44L3
HEX2						27L3	56L2	64L5	31L2	32L3	16L3	12L3	56L4
HEX3						45L1	43L2	40L1	10L2	2L5	61L1	24L5	44L6
SAT H01							14°10	97°51	44°44 SSQ-S	28°01 SSX-A	54°02 SXT-S	8°52	133°49 SES-A
HEX1							8L3	41L2	25L3	16L5	63L6	23L3	6L2
HEX2							44L5	11L1	1L2	41L6	64L6	18L1	28L2
HEX3							53L6	3L1	4L4	34L1	64L6	58L5	15L1
URA H12								112°01	58°55 SXT-S	13°50	68°12 SXT-S	5°18 CNJ-A	119°39 TRI-A
HEX1								61L5	63L2	8L2	55L4	24L6	40L6
HEX2								46L1	4L1	28L1	45L5	39L2	33L3
HEX3								14L6	22L4	52L6	51L2	31L6	60L1

Figure 2. Mick Jagger's hexagrams.

	SUN (H03)	MER (H04)	VEN (H05)	MAR (H12)	JUP (H03)	SAT (H01)	URA (H12)	NEP (H05)	PLU (H03)	MON (H12)	NNd (H04)	ASC (H01)	MC. (H10)
NEP H05	57°39	48°53	16°15	137°37	54°19	97°51	112°01		53°06	125°51	43°49	106°43	128°20
	SXT-A	SSQ-S		SES-S	SXT-A				SXT-A	TRI-S	SSQ-A		
HEX1	39L3	52L6	8L5	46L1	39L6	4L2	59L5		52L1	64L6	12L2	29L5	58L3
HEX2	56L3	20L6	43L2	14L4	39L5	25L1	12L1		52L6	64L6	27L2	23L5	45L4
HEX3	1L6	58L4	6L3	1L5	53L1	14L1	3L6		20L4	64L1	15L1	57L5	21L1
PLU H03	4°33	4°13	36°51	84°30	1°13	44°44	58°55	53°06		72°45	9°17	53°36	178°34
	CNJ-S	CNJ-A		SQR-A	CNJ-S	SSQ-A	SXT-A	SXT-S		QNT-S		SXT-A	OPP-A
HEX1	2L5	24L5	17L1	33L6	2L2	12L3	39L2	22L1		56L6	27L4	52L1	44L2
HEX2	40L4	53L2	58L6	38L3	4L2	24L2	31L1	47L6		50L2	35L5	52L3	31L3
HEX3	56L5	40L5	20L6	56L6	36L2	31L4	58L4	32L4		23L3	37L2	45L4	26L3
MON H12	68°12	76°58	109°36	11°45	71°32	28°01	13°50	125°51	72°45		82°02	19°09	105°49
	SXT-A			QNT-S	QNT-S	SSX-S		TRI-A	QNT-A		SQR-S		
HEX1	55L4	30L2	61L2	23L6	55L1	51L5	3L2	38L6	30L6		49L2	42L2	29L4
HEX2	45L5	27L6	57L4	32L2	20L3	49L6	23L1	39L6	8L2		25L1	51L1	2L5
HEX3	51L2	20L2	30L3	51L3	5L5	42L1	47L6	39L1	28L3		14L5	63L1	40L6
NNd H04	13°50	5°04	27°34	93°48	10°30	54°02	68°12	9°17	82°02			62°54	172°09
		CNJ-S	SSX-S	SQR-S		SXT-A						SXT-S	
HEX1	8L2	2L6	51L4	7L4	23L5	39L6	62L4	23L4	31L2			53L4	43L2
HEX2	28L2	64L1	30L3	55L5	57L3	39L6	18L5	48L5	11L1			29L6	46L1
HEX3	15L1	7L3	24L3	15L2	55L1	39L6	9L2	54L2	3L5			8L3	14L1
ASC H01	49°04	57°49	90°28	30°54	52°23	8°52	5°18	53°36	19°09	62°54		124°57	
	SSQ-A	SXT-S	SQR-A	SSX-S			CNJ-S	SXT-S		SXT-A		TRI-S	
HEX1	22L5	63L3	19L1	35L1	22L2	27L3	2L6	22L1	20L2	37L4		64L5	
HEX2	57L1	29L2	19L3	13L6	46L3	45L1	64L2	47L3	9L1	56L6		40L6	
HEX3	63L4	27L6	60L5	63L3	1L5	22L5	4L6	18L4	38L1	50L3		33L2	
MC. H10	174°01	177°13	144°35	94°03	177°21	133°49	119°39	128°20	178°34	105°49	172°09	124°57	
	OPP-S	OPP-A	BQT-S	SQR-A	OPP-S	SES-S	TRI-S	CNJ-S	OPP-A			TRI-S	
HEX1	1L6	44L3	48L6	19L5	1L3	10L2	54L6	47L3	1L2	60L4	28L2	38L5	
HEX2	64L6	56L5	38L3	54L1	29L4	23L2	7L3	18L4	4L3	44L5	12L1	53L6	
HEX3	64L6	28L4	56L4	64L5	2L6	6L1	30L1	5L1	17L3	53L6	3L1	7L2	
GEO GEO	SUN H03	MER H04	VEN H05	MAR H12	JUP H03	SAT H01	URA H12	NEP H05	PLU H03	MON H12	NNd H04	ASC H01	MC. H10

trouble with intimacy and sexuality. He is a determined man who can put out, but who will struggle with his own receptivity. His Pluto conjunct the Sun, with Mars and the Moon in Taurus in house 12, and Venus afflicted by its square from Uranus, all contribute to a common theme in his songs, in hits, such as "Heart of Stone," and "Can't Get No Satisfaction."

The I Ching Hexagrams that relate to this position of Jagger's Sun are as follows:

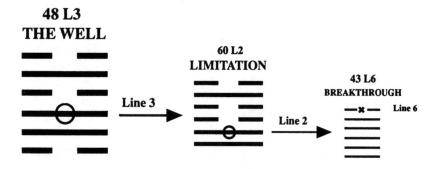

The MAIN THEME (Level 1) is THE WELL, Hexagram 48, Line 3.
The SPECIAL FOCUS (Level 2) is LIMITATION, Hexagram 60, Line 2.
The INTIMATE DETAIL (Level 3) is BREAKTHROUGH, Hexagram 43, Line 6.

THE MAIN THEME OF THE SUN (LEVEL 1 HEXAGRAM) IS
THE WELL
Water is above. Wood is below.
    This symbolizes the bucket that goes down into the well and brings the water up. One idea here is the ability to draw nutrition from an inexhaustible source of water. This also implies the ability to draw meaning and inspiration from the depth of life: the psyche, the unconscious, *and perhaps even from the music and the blues.* Another idea implied is that of dangerous gentleness, or the danger surrounding gentle penetration. *This image is readily given to Jagger by his fans who see a gentle side to him.*

The Judgment
Everyone comes to the well and draws from it.
But those whose bucket breaks do not find nourishment, but rather misfortune.
A theme is brought out here that has significant relevance to Jagger and his creativity.
The well is one of those social structures that go down to the very foundations of life.
It answers our most primitive needs.
For a political or social organization to survive it must take care of deep and basic needs.
If the order is superficial, deep needs will be ignored.
Violence and disaster would likely follow.
Much of Jagger's personal life as well as his songwriting is obsessed with injustice and blues.
The hexagram talks about the foundations of human nature and of spiritual depth. It highlights two problems:

1. A failure to penetrate to the real roots of life and to thus get fixed in convention;

2. A capacity to collapse and neglect self-development.

The Image
The roots of a plant suck water up to keep the plant active and healthy.
Jagger with his blues traditions and concern over health (or to be exact aging), would hold the band together. The operation of the Rolling Stones requires team work which every player must adjust to. The needs of the group predominate. Jagger did hold to his roots and to his band.

Line 3: The Special Emphasis line
No one drinks from this well even though it is clean.
Sorrow because it could be used.
If the leader is clear-minded, everyone will benefit.
A capable man is at hand but no use is made of him. All who know him are sad.
If only the leader could see this!

Brian Jones felt tremendously isolated and left out of the Jagger/Richards writing team. Keith Richards also felt alienated from Jagger in later years. Jagger has the ability to aggressively put out his ideas, but he is not always receptive nor considerate of those around him. At times he can't see it!

THE SPECIAL FOCUS OF THE SUN (LEVEL 2 HEXAGRAM) IS
LIMITATION
Abysmal water over the lake.
Dangerous pleasures can get out of hand if they are not limited or restrained.
This pictures a flooding lake and highlights the need to establish limits.
Applied to life this means limits on finances and limits on loyalty.

These are major Jagger issues. He has consistently worked to limit expenses, to control the band and it's business. When the limits were not there they got ripped off!

Limitation brings success,
but exceptional limitation will cause harm.
Extreme limitations will damage the body.
Imposing excessive limitations on others
will cause rebellion and failure.

Jagger is very concerned about his health. He has always maintained far better self-control than those around him. Restricting the group and controlling it has caused rebellion and "exile." Witness Brian Jones' isolation and Keith Richards' drug busts. Jagger even built a moat around his home for defense.

The Image
Water over the lake.
The superior man generates great abundance.
He must measure what he does.
This creates the need to study what is virtuous correct conduct, and what is not!
A lake can only hold so much water.
A person must be discriminating and self-restrained if he is to become prominent.
The challenge lies in the ability to define the essence of morality.

Unlimited possibilities would dissolve the meaning of a person's life.
To be strong and creative requires restraint and acceptance of duty.

The issue of morality has certainly dominated Jagger's writings and perfor-mances. Witness his exaggerated emphasis on sex and drugs. He even developed a bisexual identity by cross-dressing. His saving grace has been his dedication and duty to the band—his band of course!

Line 2: The specially accentuated line
If one does not go out of the gate or the courtyard,
it brings misfortune and loss.

Jagger grew up dreaming of living in the USA. Certainly the band would not have made it big if they had not gone to Europe and America. Jagger even moved out of England to avoid the excessive taxes.

When the moment for action comes,
it must be embraced quickly.
Some hesitation can be valuable,
but when the way clears, action is imperative for success.
Missed opportunity will lead to disaster.

This was a rule of thumb for the band. When ever an audience got unruly, they would await for the right time or moment to disappear. It may have saved their lives at Altamont. The audience filled with Hell's Angels got violent. A young man was killed in front of the stage. The band hung in and played, until in the nick of time, they were able to get away by helicopter.

THE INTIMATE DETAIL HEXAGRAM OF THE SUN (LEVEL 3) IS
BREAKTHROUGH
Water in the heavens.
A breakthrough is like a cloudburst. It releases tension.
The superior man can breakthrough the effects of inferior or weak
people.
Resolute action creates breakthrough.

The Judgment
Breakthrough. One must be truthful at the court.
There is danger here.
One must inform one's own city.

This is not a time to use weapons.
It is better to undertake something.
Inferior people can oppress superior men.
A passion in one's heart can diminish reason.
There is a struggle here between good and evil.
Regulations and rules must not be ignored.
If one fights evil on its own level, hatred and passion ensue, and misfortune will occur.
Concentrating on one's faults will increase the fault.
Dedicated working towards the good will diminish the bad.

The Image
The lake in the heavens.
Creative joy. Breakthrough.
The great man gives out his riches to those less fortunate or beneath him.
He does not rest on his laurels.
Selfish accumulation of wealth will lead to collapse.
It is important to spread it around and help others.

This was Bianca's challenge to Mick. The Nicaraguan cause was the first major one that he publicly supported. Until then he had avoided the issue. There were many radical causes he refused to help, perhaps to his credit.

He must examine himself continuously to keep his character growing.

He certainly did this musically.

MICK JAGGER'S MOON IS AT 23° ♉ 58' IN HOUSE 12

Jagger's Moon is in Taurus, the sign where daylight predominates and is also increasing. This reveals an instinct to live his own way and to follow his own independent desires. His song, "Hey! You! Get Off My Cloud!" says a lot. This is a fixed earth sign, implying that Jagger likes his comforts, and is consistent in his life style and habits. It shows someone who is physically sensitive but not very sympathetic. Taurus is a reflective sign, ruled by Venus, bringing a slow-to-change sense of self-worth and a strong need for satisfaction. Jagger has an ability to measure and assess tactile quality. He will have strong likes and dislikes,

THE DEGREES OF THE ZODIAC AND THE I CHING / 55

with the accompanying strong tides of attraction and repulsion. The expression of this contrast in his life permeated his creativity. Ruled by Venus, his Moon reveals an instinct for music and the voice.

Jagger's Moon is in the 12th house, above the horizon and rising, implying a need to project his feelings and to influence or impress others, making his personal mark on society. Being in the 12th house also implies a sense of emptiness and isolation. To himself he does not feel that he belongs, nor that he is good enough. This implies that Jagger has difficulty with closeness, and is likely to have his share of isolating habits. He wants attention and wants to make an impression, but he does not like to get too close. The stage is the almost perfect vehicle for him. This 12th-house Moon can bring feelings of despair and emptiness. Satisfaction is important but evasive. Witness "Heart of Stone," "Out of Reach," "I Can't Get No Satisfaction," and "All My Lovin's Been in Vain." This explains his basic identification with the "blues" as well as his, at times, contempt for women. He can get physical and even sensational, but he cannot get truly intimate. Once Jagger identified with the blues it became a consistent theme in his life. He was brought up to be a businessman or an athlete. He has not lived in the manner he was brought up, but has used both his athletic and business abilities. Jagger always wants more. We hear the echo of his song "You Can't Always Get What You Want." Remember that even his songs are not his own, they were for the most part co-written with Keith Richards.

Jagger's adult lifestyle has always been in question. His homes in England ranged from filthy to neglected, and almost non-existent when on the road: "Grown Up All Wrong." His closest associates and friends have had excessively bad habits and addictions. Jagger is often concerned about personal security and not without reason, for his association with sex, drugs, Hell's Angels, and police has been less than harmonious.

This is a difficult house position for the Moon, but it is not afflicted by dire aspects. Jagger has been able to maintain a consistent musical genre throughout his life. He is talented and has been able to live surrounded by corruption and isolation, while maintaining a dedicated creative life. Jagger, with the Blue Boys, and then the Rolling Stones, lived in the shadow of the Beatles. His band, however, has survived, where the Beatles have not. By his consistent effort Jagger was able to make his career and reputation go well beyond the Beatles.

The I Ching Hexagrams related to this position of Jagger's Moon are as follows:

26 L1
GREAT TAMING POWER

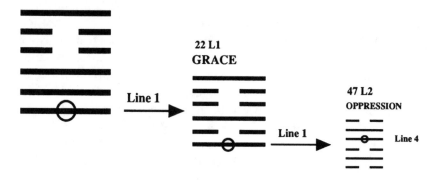

The MAIN THEME (Level 1) is GREAT TAMING POWER, Hexagram 26, Line 1.

The SPECIAL FOCUS (Level 2) is GRACE, Hexagram 22, Line 1.

The INTIMATE DETAIL (Level 3) is OPPRESSION, EXHAUSTION, Hexagram 47, Line 2.

THE MAIN THEME OF THE MOON (LEVEL 1 HEXAGRAM) IS
GREAT TAMING POWER

Above the mountain. Below the heavens.

The mountain in the heavens, Olympus, the mountain of the Gods.

The attribute of this association is the ability to keep still or restrain creative power.

In another way it implies the ability to hold it all together, to hold back, and to hold steady in nurturing those who are close.

Mick did hold his band together in spite of their lifestyles.

The Judgment

It is constructive for great creative power to persevere.

Good fortune comes from not eating at home.

It furthers one to cross the great water.

Jagger spent much of his life and certainly his tours, not eating at home. As he grew up, he constantly dreamed of living in America, the land of luxury and freedom. Whenever he did cross the Atlantic, his North American tours were always a great success.

To secure and maintain great creative powers, a strong clear headed man is required.

Jagger is the strong leader who has held the Rolling Stones together. He, for the most part, held together with the group without going on to his own solo career. He did make a brief solo attempt but returned to the greater success of the band. In general he could hold his creativity back to align with the band.

Normally consistent habits can maintain order, but whenever a great amount of energy is being stored up or accumulated, order depends upon the power of the personality.

The worthy are honored, and the strong are entrusted with leadership. Under such conditions great undertakings become possible.

The Image
Heaven within or beneath the mountain.
Creative power within the mountain.

Jagger has an instinctive ability to control his energy, then erupt volcanically, and still keep things in control. His eruptive erotic performances stop at the edge of the stage. They are controlled.

The superior man learns the sayings of antiquity and the actions of the past.
This enables him to strengthen his own character.

Jagger did learn all the old blues songs of the 1930s and 40s. He kept them as ideals to musically strive toward.

The image of heaven within the mountain suggests the presence of hidden treasures.
If one knows the past and can apply these teachings to the present, much can be accomplished.

Well, Jagger was able to pass on a new sense of an old blues in songs such as "Down Home Girl," which he did not write but embellished well. This sense surfaced emphatically in the albums "Sympathy for the Devil" and "Let It Bleed."

Line 1: This line gives a special emphasis within the main theme.
There is danger close by.
It is appropriate to desist.

Here a man wants to advance aggressively but encounters obstacles.
If he insists on pushing forward misfortune would result.
He must maintain composure and hold back his creative energy
until the right time arises.

*Jagger stayed in school while the band grew, in spite of pressures to let go.
His problems with the drugs, customs, and the law also required him to hold back
and desist.*

The second hexagram, the special focus, highlights or elaborates
the implications of Line 1 of the Main Theme Hexagram.

GRACE

Here the fire is within the mountain.
Keeping still is above and the fire is below. Can one hold back the fire?
The image is of keeping still on hot coals.
One must be graceful indeed to accomplish this. This is no easy nor
comfortable task.
We have here the image of a fire walk, or of an ancient God dancing in
flames.

*This seems an appropriate parallel to Jagger gyrating and dancing on stage,
full of passion and sensuality, on the edge of an audience burning with desire. At
Altamont the fire got out of control: "Dancing, Dancing, Dancing with Mr. 'D'."*

Line 1: The specially accentuated line gives intimate detail within
the Specific Focus of Grace.
He has grace in his toes.

*This points to Jagger's agility and brings to mind his very effeminate style
of dancing in little seemingly high-heeled steps.*

The third hexagram, the Intimate Detail elaborates the previous
line in the Special Focus.

THE INTIMATE DETAIL HEXAGRAM IS CALLED
OPPRESSION or EXHAUSTION
The joyous lake is above the abysmal water.
The implication here is that of Dangerous pleasure,
or of pleasure that overrides discrimination.
Who knows what too much pleasure can lead to?

This is fascinating as the danger of drug and alcohol dependency pervades the musicians around Mick. Brian Jones drowned in his own pool during a party. Even at Altamont the pleasure took a dangerous turn. Jagger's agile and powerful energies have always been surrounded by the lethargy and sloth of the drug-induced musicians around him.

The Judgment
Success in spite of oppression.
The great man creates good fortune.
No guilt.
His words are not believed.
Periods of adversity can be turned to success if the right person is at hand.
Good will in the midst of danger can create stability and survive the adversities of fate.
Failure will come if your spirit is broken by exhaustion.
To overcome adversity it is important to bend rather than break.
Brian Jones broke. Keith Richards lost it through exhaustion. Jagger was able to adjust and bend (Gemini Rising).

The Image
A lake with no water.
Exhaustion.
The superior man's life depends
on following his own will!
Jagger has no water in his chart. Pleasure with no sympathy. Sensation with no satisfaction, "A Heart of Stone."
When adversity surfaces,
one must acknowledge the vulnerabilities,
and remain true to himself.
What can a poor boy do, but to play in a rock and roll band.

Line 2: Is the specially accentuated line in the Intimate Detail Hexagram
Oppressed while eating.
A prince is coming.
Offer a sacrifice.
Going leads to misfortune.
No guilt.

This line criticizes diet and nutrition, something that Jagger places great importance on. He doesn't want to get old! Who does! The other band members ate and drank abysmally. This whole line seems to point to the album "Goat's Head Soup."

The implication of being prepared surfaces.

After Altamont, Jagger became much more concerned with security and potential lapses, partly because of the threat of being murdered.

MICK JAGGER'S MERCURY IS AT 10° ♌ 56' IN HOUSE 4

Jagger needs to be applauded for his ideas. He wants to impress and even shock people with his thoughts. His determination and artistic expression contributed in a major way to his creative songwriting. Being in the 4th house and conjunct his IC, Jagger is deeply motivated to build security around his ideas and his writing. He has never been much of a musician but he certainly has a way with words—his words! He puts power and flare into his ideas, a quality which shines most evidently in his songwriting and singing.

With the multiple conjunctions to the Sun, Jupiter, Pluto, and the IC, he is dramatically expressive and tends to challenge concepts of morality. Pluto adds the darkness as in "Sympathy for the Devil," or "Dancing with Mr. D." With Mars square his Mercury, Jagger is witty, agile, and sarcastic. He punctuates his words with blatant sexual and physical moves. His songs are consistently concerned with sex, and they are successful for that very reason. He has a personal dialog over whether the singer or the song is more important. With his Sun in Leo "It's the Singer Not the Song," but deep down inside it is the song and the idea!

The I Ching Hexagrams related to Jagger's Mercury are as follows:

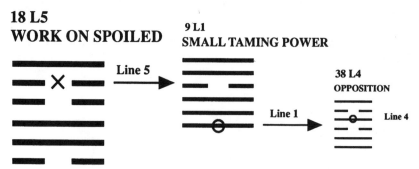

The MAIN THEME (Level 1) is WORK ON WHAT IS SPOILED, Hexagram 18, Line 5.

The SPECIAL FOCUS (Level 2) is SMALL TAMING POWER, Hexagram 9, Line 1.

The INTIMATE DETAIL (Level 3) is OPPOSITION, Hexagram 38, Line 4.

THE MAIN THEME OF MERCURY (LEVEL 1 HEXAGRAM) IS
WORK ON WHAT'S BEEN SPOILED (DAMAGE CONTROL)
Here is a bowl filled with worms.
There is decay and guilt.
There is a need to find and remove the cause of guilt.
Perhaps this is echoed by Jagger in "Pain In My Heart."

Corruption through the abuse of personal freedom.
Work is needed to fix what has been spoiled.
This summarizes a great deal of Jagger's concerns: junkies in the band, drug busts, immigration problems, agents and recording companies ripping him off. Even though Altamont started as an ideal of freedom—give a free concert in California—it got corrupted by Hell's Angels and murder!
This could be summed up as damage control. The work though dangerous must be embraced energetically even though it means crossing the great water. Inertia and indifference must be replaced by energy and decisiveness.

The Image
The wind is mild at the foot of the mountain.
There is much decay and rot here.
The superior man will arouse the people
and strengthen their spirits.
It seems that good music can stir the masses and strengthen their spirits. This is an excellent expression of Jagger's songs and dances, and of the Rolling Stones' popularity. They are a breath of fresh air in the rot and sewers of life!

Debasing attitudes lead to corruption.
The superior man must renew society by stirring up public opinion reinforcing the confidence and strength of those who hear.

The decay at the foot of the mountain could be considered as the fans at the edge of the stage, or even the musicians at the foot of the band's mountainous status.

Line 5: This line gives a special emphasis within the main theme.
Fixing what was spoiled by the father brings praise.
Corruption springs from early neglect.
On his own nothing can be done,
But in a group with helpers,
reform can be accomplished and lead to success.
Perhaps it was Mick himself that got spoiled?

THE SPECIAL FOCUS (LEVEL 2 HEXAGRAM)
SMALL TAMING POWER
This is the power of the shadow.
It can restrict or impede.
Strength is held in check by weakness.
Gentleness will lead to success.

The Judgment
Dense clouds but no rain.
"Hey, Hey, You! Get Off My Cloud"

The problem is how to keep a tyrant in check.
Obstacles prevent immediate success.
Be prepared.
Inner firmness and outer gentleness will win the day.
This reveals Jagger's attitude toward the band, its members, and himself. There is room to argue who the tyrant might be!

The Image
Here the superior man improves
and develops the outward aspect of his nature.
Jagger painstakingly cultivated his image and its effects.

Line 1: The specially accentuated line
No blame in returning to the way.

In pressing forward a strong man runs into obstacles.
Returning to his way or his roots will increase his options.

Whenever lost or obstructed, Jagger and The Rolling Stones returned to their blues/rock roots. Witness "Let it Bleed," "Honky Tonk Woman," "Love in Vain," and "Midnight Rambler."

THE INTIMATE DETAIL HEXAGRAM (LEVEL 3) IS CALLED
OPPOSITION (CONTRAST)
Fire above water.
Clarity versus pleasure.
Fire burns up and water flows down.

The Judgment
Opposition.
Success in small matters.
People living in opposition and estrangement are handicapped.
Great achievement is blocked.
Avoid great judgments and avoid subsequent action.
Success in times of contrast comes slowly in small matters.

Sex, drugs, alcohol, junky's inertia, and a depressed environment provided enough opposition for Jagger to shine. The contrast made him look great!

The Image
Amidst fellowship
The great man can retain his individuality.

Jagger has been able to avoid the addictions and subsequent debasing habits of the rest of the band. At least he did not let himself deteriorate to the same degree.

Line 4: The specially accentuated line in the Intimate Detail Hexagram
Isolated because of opposition.
In the midst of danger one finds a like minded companion that can be trusted.
No guilt in this!

This highlights the way that Mick met Keith Richards, which led to the formation of the Rollin' Stones. Mick would even write his songs in collaboration with Keith at the isolation of the others. This did indeed cause opposition and contrast.

MICK JAGGER'S VENUS IS AT 13° ♍ 34' IN HOUSE 5

Venus symbolizes the need to be loved. It is in Virgo. Jagger has always been critical about his talents and self-worth. With Venus in an earth sign, he is sensitive about his appearance and his health, and it is this concern that kept him from going too far with drugs. Jagger has a love of sports as well as the creative arts. The Mercury rulership points to his needing appreciation for his ideas and songwriting.

Uranus squares Venus from house 12, making Jagger eccentric in his tastes and unstable emotionally. His ability to receive love and be satisfied is afflicted. Unstable love is one of his creative themes. Jagger has difficulty being close and vulnerable to others. "I Can't Get No Satisfaction," "Love in Vain," and "You Can't Always Get What You Want," are good examples. In truth he is insecure about his musical talents, hence a songwriting partnership with someone who is more capable musically.

The I Ching Hexagrams related to Jagger's Venus are as follows:

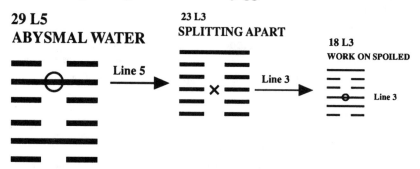

29 L5
ABYSMAL WATER

23 L3
SPLITTING APART

18 L3
WORK ON SPOILED

Line 5

Line 3

Line 3

The MAIN THEME (Level 1) is ABYSMAL WATER, Hexagram 29, Line 5.

The SPECIAL FOCUS (Level 2) is SPLITTING APART, Hexagram 23, Line 3.

The INTIMATE DETAIL (Level 3) is WORK ON WHAT'S BEEN SPOILED, Hexagram 18, Line 3.

THE MAIN THEME OF VENUS (LEVEL 1 HEXAGRAM) IS
ABYSMAL WATER
The abysmal water.
Dangerous water is doubled.

The heart is locked up within the body.
Light is enclosed in darkness.
Danger on top of danger.
Danger here can be overcome.
One can escape if he behaves properly.

Songs like "Let It Bleed," "Midnight Rambler," and "Sympathy for the Devil" come to mind. Jagger always wanted to live across the ocean in America, but danger upon danger piled up. He built a moat around his house for protection, and Brian Jones drowned in his backyard pool. He was swimming at night and stoned! Jagger is surrounded by danger, on and off the stage.

The Judgment
Sincerity brings success.
Accustomed to danger but not attached to it.
Keep true to yourself and do not wait in danger.
You've gotta move on.
The protection comes from being alert to danger.

Jagger's traveling agenda and concert touring kept him on the move and out of danger. Keeping still would attract police and problems.

The Image
As water flows on to reach its goal,
The superior man must walk in virtue and teach the same,
Otherwise danger and guilt will increase.

Line 5: The Special Emphasis
The abyss is filled to the rim
but it is not overflowing.
No guilt.
Excessive ambition creates danger.
Do not reach beyond your limits.
The line of least resistance will get you out of danger.

Here we have Jagger's driving ambition. Even when he tried to go out on his own he did not do as well as when he was with the band. In spite of the dangers he basically held to the band.

THE SPECIAL FOCUS (LEVEL 2 HEXAGRAM) IS
SPLITTING APART
The dark lines push out the last light line.

Inferior and dark elements undermine the strong light element,
and cause a collapse.
The roof is being shattered.
The house collapses.

Jagger bought a mansion in England. He lived in it occasionally, but it was always in repair. In fact many of the houses he purchased were kept in ill repair. You could say he brought the roof down on himself as the police often busted into his home searching for drugs. Songs like "Gimme Shelter," "Sitting on a Fence," and "Gotta Get Away," did not arise out of coincidence.

The Judgment
Splitting apart.
To go somewhere leads to misfortune and loss.
When weak or inferior people are in the majority, it is not the time to start anything.
It is wiser to submit to the time and avoid taking action.

The Image
The mountain on the earth.
The only way for the superior man to maintain his position,
is to give generously to those below.
If the mountain is too steep it will collapse.
Secure your foundations and you will become as secure as a mountain.

Jagger's holding to the roots of blues and rock, and to the passions of the common man has secured his fame. Even the gift of a free show at Altamont had some positive side effects. His records continued to sell.

Line 3: The specially accentuated line
He splits with them.
No Blame.
An individual is committed to an evil or dark environment.
With the help of a man with inner light
he can and must move away from the darkness.
There is no blame in this.

There were many splits within the band. Mick had to split with Brian Jones who was the early leader of the band in everybody's mind but Jagger's own. There were many splits with Keith Richards and they were repaired. This goes further to cover the many bridges that had to be burned behind him—agents, recording companies, and cling-ons in general.

THE INTIMATE DETAIL HEXAGRAM (LEVEL 3) IS CALLED
WORK ON WHAT IS SPOILED (DAMAGE CONTROL)

How to get rid of rot, corruption and inertia.
Decisive energy must overcome inertia and indifference.
Correcting what has been spoiled by the father.
Some remorse. No great guilt.
Proceeding with excess energy can be embarrassing but it is needed,
and it is the lesser of evils.

Once again this hexagram surfaces with the hint of Jagger being spoiled.

MICK JAGGER'S IC IS AT 8° ♌ 09'

The IC is the point of personal motivation and inner integrity. It reveals
the backbone of a person, where he is coming from, and basically what
makes him tick. We see it in the home or family we come from and the
point of security within ourselves. It shows the influence of our dreams
and our past on our present sense of reality and security.

Jagger's IC is in Leo, conjunct Pluto, Jupiter, Sun, and Mercury, all
in Leo. It is sextiled by Uranus and squared by Mars from the 12th
house. Primarily Jagger is motivated to be the best child of his mother,
to get attention, and to impress mom. What starts out in youth as "Hey
Mom look at me. See how good I am!," becomes in adult life, "Hey
babe, here I am! I was great for you wasn't I?" Jagger is motivated by the
need to be noticed and applauded. As he grew up, he wanted to be the
best in school and worked hard for it. When he was no longer able to
be best, he joined a band where he could shine, and then left school for
more glamorous adventure.

The multiple conjunction in Leo shows the importance he placed
on creative thinking and writing. It is essential for Jagger to make his
point and impress others with his ideas. His sarcastic wit and excessive
competitiveness reinforced his need to perform. There are elements of
darkness in his understanding and his environment. He would fight injustice as he saw it: "Play with Me and You Play with Fire." In truth
Jagger is more of an idea man and songwriter than a passionate beast.

His passionate, seemingly evil persona is more performance than
substance. His motivation is to perform and write, and see his name in
lights. The astounding thought here is that he would do this through
a band rather than independently, and that he would hold together

with the band for as long as he has. Of course from his eyes it would be his band.

The I Ching Hexagrams related to Jagger's IC are as follows:

18 L3
WORK ON SPOILED

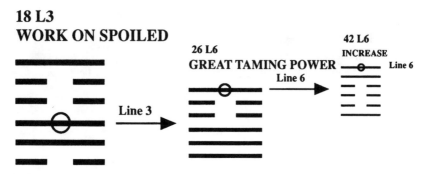

The MAIN THEME (Level 1) is WORK ON WHAT'S SPOILED, Hexagram 18, Line 3.

The SPECIAL FOCUS (Level 2) is GREAT TAMING POWER, Hexagram 26, Line 6.

The INTIMATE DETAIL (Level 3) is INCREASE, Hexagram 42, Line 6.

THE MAIN THEME OF THE IC (LEVEL 1 HEXAGRAM) IS
WORK ON WHAT'S SPOILED (DAMAGE CONTROL)
This hexagram and line also appeared for Venus on Level 3. The symbol is an unclean bowl so dirty that worms are breeding in it. The challenge is how to remove the rot.

This leads to the idea that Jagger's need to be best is underscored by a sense of being spoiled or not good enough. He wrote, sang, and danced, but only learned a musical instrument as time went by. He learned the blues harmonica. Jagger has to prove that he is better than he is or was. He has to be larger than life.

What has been spoiled by man can be repaired with effort.
Abuse of personal freedom leads to decay.
One must take an energetic stand against the source of corruption.
The fight is against inertia and indifference.

Jagger's energy is enhanced and exaggerated by the drug drained back up of the band. The worse they are, the better they make him look, better than he really is.

Here the superior man stirs up the people and strengthens their spirit.

If nothing else Jagger and the Rolling Stones have certainly stirred up many a can of worms in their lives. Aaaahh! The attention!

Line 3: The Special Emphasis
Correcting what has been spoiled by the father.
Some embarrassment. No great guilt.

Here Jagger is motivated to energetically repair the fact that he did not live up to his father's expectations. In a way he did become a businessman and also an athlete. Witness his athletic dancing. His dad wanted an athlete, but got a ballerina with an attitude. Jagger did take care of his family financially, and provided better security for them. No guilt will come from this.

THE SPECIAL FOCUS (LEVEL 2 HEXAGRAM) IS
GREAT TAMING POWER
Jagger's (IC) motivation and sense of security is aligned with the Moon which also resides in this hexagram at level one.

Here we have keeping still like a mountain above and the heavens, or creativity, below.

Jagger has a unique quality to his dancing. In performance he will energetically dance and strut around the stage, and just at a peak moment he will stand still—enhancing the tension and excitement of the moment. He can restrain himself at a very powerful moment. It has become his style.

This hexagram talks about holding firm in three ways: holding together, holding back, and holding steady.

He did hold the band together. He can hold back when necessary. He holds to the stage and is cautious most of the time. He holds steady with the group and its blues roots. These are strong motivational concerns. Jagger has been motivated by the songs and creative blues musicians of the past. He vitalized the blues in a rock genre.

This hexagram encourages one to avoid eating at home and to cross the great water.

Jagger has lived much of his life on the road and eating out! He has always wanted to live in America.

Line 6: The specially accentuated line

He accomplishes the creative way.

Heaven smiles.

Great success.

Repressed energies are released and lead to success.

The superior man attains honor and can shape the world.

This implies that Jagger is motivated to succeed and become great. That his Leo Sun in house 3 rules the Leo on his IC further establishes his power in writing, traveling, and expressing himself.

THE INTIMATE DETAIL HEXAGRAM (LEVEL 3) IS CALLED
INCREASE

With his IC in Increase Jagger is motivated to consistently increase his security and his fortunes. He has bought many homes and mansions in several countries.

Aroused gentleness: Wind and thunder.

These forces increase each other.

Sacrifice of the elevated elements to the advantage of the lower brings increase.

Jagger certainly has the ability to stimulate and excite through gentleness. Performing on an elevated stage to the audience below also fits this idea.

It is important to do something and accept a challenge.

Crossing the great water is fortunate.

With devoted followers a leader will succeed

even amidst obstacles and danger.

When the time is right

one must go with it or the increase will be lost.

Jagger and the Rolling Stones rode the tide of British musical fortune across the ocean to America and back. They went on extensive tours and worked hard to keep up and secure their fame and success. Keeping up with the tide of increase and advancement is a deeply motivating theme for Jagger.

The Image:

Imitate the good

and get rid of personal faults.

This requires an ethical standard.

Jagger from childhood had a remarkable sense of mimicry. He could sing a song after hearing it once on the radio.

Line 6: The specially accentuated line in the Intimate Detail Hexagram

He does not increase anyone.

Someone strikes him.

He doesn't keep his heart steady.

Misfortune.

If you don't help others, no one will care.

If no one cares, enemies will approach and harm will result.

If a man is abrupt in his movements no one will assist him.

If he is irritated in his words, no one will be inspired.

If he asks for something without securing relations first, he will be denied.

Danger will then draw near.

Witness "Gimme Shelter." In his attempt to give a free concert at the Altamont racetrack in California, The Hell's Angels were foolishly enlisted as security guards for the event. Four people died and one of them was murdered in front of the stage. This was not exactly a well-secured relationship or performance. With a now enhanced enthusiasm, Jagger is motivated by security and a fear of violence on and off the stage.

MICK JAGGER'S MC IS AT 8°♒09'

The Rolling Stones provided the Aquarian group that would be so important to Mick Jagger and his career. He put a serious emphasis on the demands of the group and its status. The MC conjuncts the South Node and opposes Mercury and Pluto. This shows that the group members had bad habits and attitudes which profoundly affected the social status of the group. This manifested in their association to drugs, alcohol, violence, civil unrest, and police arrests. Some people seem to be at their best when they are bad. Band members consistently had trouble with authority both within and without the band.

The MC opposition to the Sun and Jupiter generated great competitiveness about who was the leader. This tension was and is a big part of the Rolling Stones. Some cities and even countries did not want them and refused them entry. They were often hassled at borders. They may have grown in the shadow of the good-boy Beatles, but the Rolling Stones and Mick Jagger survived to become the longest running rock band rising into the realm of myth. In fact Jagger and the Stones capitalized on their own shadowy reputation.

The I Ching Hexagrams related to Jagger's MC are as follows:

17 L3
FOLLOWING

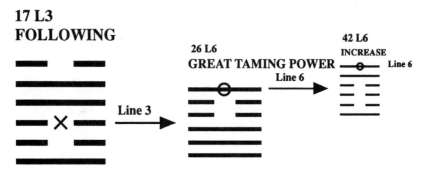

The MAIN THEME (Level 1) is FOLLOWING, Hexagram 17, Line 3.
The SPECIAL FOCUS (Level 2) is GREAT TAMING POWER, Hexagram 26, Line 6.
The INTIMATE DETAIL (Level 3) is INCREASE, Hexagram 42, Line 6.

THE MAIN THEME OF THE MC (LEVEL 1 HEXAGRAM) IS
FOLLOWING
The lake above, thunder below.
Joyous arousal or stimulated pleasure.

Sex and shock is what made Mick Jagger and the Rolling Stones famous. His songs are about sex, pleasure, and satisfaction. His ability to generate shock and sexual tension is what he is recognized and applauded for. You never know what Jagger will wear or how far he will go, when on stage. This includes dressing in drag for a concert filled with Hell's Angels, and ripping off Tina Turner's dress on stage. This is entertainment at its shocking best! It commands attention and generates hysteria. It sells records! Jagger and the Rolling Stones woke up the desires and passions of the audience. Fans loved it. They became hooked on dangerous excitement. It's fun! Who wants a safe relationship anyway? Certainly not teenagers! The Stones generated a following. Once you heard or saw them perform, your sense of music changed. It came alive. It was and is gutsy and real.

An older man gets a young girl or girls to follow him.

This is Mick! This is the "Little Red Rooster" strutting on the stage, squawking, screaming, taunting, singing, "Let's Spend the Night Together" and promising "Good Times."

To obtain a following it is necessary to adjust to the demands of the time and place.

If one is consistent at this, great following results.

The Stones toured relentlessly from city to city, riding the wave of the British invasion as it grew, and then going beyond the wave. They sweat for their following.

The Image
Thunder in the lake implies a time of unsettled darkness.

It could be argued that the main social power of Jagger is his ability to stimulate darkness, hidden desires, and wet dreams!

Line 3: The Special Emphasis
If you cling to the man
you lose the little boy.
Through following you are able to find what you are searching for.

The little boy blue encountered puberty and became known as a Rolling Stone! (The Blue Boys was Jagger's original band name before the Rolling Stones.)

The Special Focus and the Intimate Detail Hexagrams are identical for the MC and the IC. In fact this is so in the I Ching for every exact opposition.

MICK JAGGER'S ASC IS AT 13° ♊ 06'

The Ascendant shows how someone projects his image out into the world of strangers, friends, status, relationships and deals. It is his identity or persona, his mask.

The Gemini Ascendant suggests a double identity which is quick-witted and curious. It shows someone who sees himself putting his own ideas into action. This Ascendant often endows a person with agility and speed. This points to someone who might try anything once! Certainly

Jagger does have a double identity. On the one side he is a freewheeling radical, and on the other, a very controlling business tycoon. Jagger has always identified to contrast, and he has maintained a personal double standard. He thrives on being different or contrary. Even in his cross-dressing role, challenging everyone to notice, he makes a very powerful Gemini statement—I can go both ways. Go figure. He likes to think that he does not fit into pigeonholing or easy labeling. He is different and unique.

With his Ascendant conjunct Uranus, Jagger projects to shock or shake up others. He identifies with excitement and hates boredom, even if the excitement leads to trouble, especially if the excitement leads to trouble.

Unfortunately this Uranus Ascendant conjunction squares his Venus, implying that Jagger is very insecure about satisfaction. He could worry about falling in love until he does, and then he could worry the relationship away by keeping aloof, excited, and distant!

The I Ching Hexagrams related to Jagger's Ascendant are as follows:

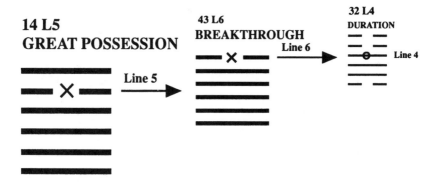

The MAIN THEME (Level 1) is POSSESSION IN GREAT MEASURE, Hexagram 14, Line 5.

The SPECIAL FOCUS (Level 2) is BREAKTHROUGH, Hexagram 43, Line 6.

The INTIMATE DETAIL (Level 3) is DURATION, Hexagram 32, Line 4.

THE MAIN THEME OF THE ASC (LEVEL 1 HEXAGRAM) IS
POSSESSION IN GREAT MEASURE
Fire in the heavens. Burning creativity.
Great light on great light.
Fire on the stage, in the spotlight, and in the star.
Everyone notices fire in the heavens.
Fire is dependent on its fuel.
> *This points to the drug and alcohol use of the band.*

Creative fire brings great success.
Inner strength coupled with outer clarity and culture,
brings success and wealth.
> *Witness "If You Play with Me, Then You Play with Fire!" "High and Dry," "Star, Star," and "Its the Singer Not the Song."*

Fire in the heaven
brings light to good and evil.
The Sun shines on all.
The question: Is creativity good or evil?
> *This is a personal concern for Jagger, being caught in the shadow of the good guy Beatles, and being one of the bad guy Stones.*

Lightning in the sky creates ominous feelings
that in the end releases built up tensions.
> *Never mind "Lucy in the Sky with Diamonds," Jagger is "Lightning on the Stage with Excitement" and danger all around him.*

Line 5: The Special Emphasis
If his truth is reachable
it brings good fortune.
Sincerity brings honor and dignity.
> *Jagger's message is human. It's about passion and sex and SEX. His message is reachable, just beneath most people's facade. He sings desire. He sounds real—real exciting. Everyone hears the message whether they like it or not!*

THE SPECIAL FOCUS HEXAGRAM (LEVEL 2) IS
BREAKTHROUGH
Creative joy.

Here pleasure and happiness are held in high esteem.
A cloudburst breaks the tension.
Creative pleasure breaks through repression
to dance for joy or pleasure.

> *Jagger loves to dance and shock.*

Breakthrough.
One must talk to the courts.
Honesty is essential.
Danger.
This is not the time to fight.
Call for support from within.
Undertaking something leads to increase.
Weak people in authority can oppress superior men.
Passion fights reason. Good fights evil.
If evil is accentuated it leads to violence and greater evil.
Fighting faults directly makes them worse.
Accentuate the good and evil will fall away.

> *This has been a strong lesson for Jagger. It shows clearly in his acceptance of and ability to work with stoned or addicted musicians. It is also the teaching to be gained from Altamont where several fans were killed, one directly in front of the stage. Jagger, after that, began to distance himself from the Hell's Angels.*

The Image
Breakthrough.
The lake in the heavens.
The great man showers his riches down to the people.
He does not rest on his virtue.
Selfishness can lead to collapse.

> *One thing is certain and that is that Jagger is not known for his virtue, much less resting on it. For years Jagger refused to support any special causes. After his marriage to Bianca, he did champion the cause of the Nicaraguans.*

**Line 6: Is the specially accentuated line
in the Intimate Detail Hexagram?**
No Crying.
In the end misfortune.
Even in success darkness comes.
No remorse, no tears, no sorrow, no compassion.

Without a change of heart, evil will reoccur.

There is a healing value for tears.

Jagger attracted much darkness during his tours, but they were still success-
ful business adventures. Even Altamont, his free concert, brought much attention
and sold records. Jagger is constantly on guard for his life because of the environ-
ment that grew around him. Does what you put out always come back? Sooner
or later, yes it does!

THE INTIMATE DETAIL HEXAGRAM (LEVEL 3) IS CALLED
DURATION

Thunder in wind will endure.

Here we have shocking penetration and gentleness.

This is how many of his female fans see Jagger. They sense that he is gen-
tle behind the shocking masks.

The superior man holds firm and does not change direction.

Jagger held on to his blues roots and his band. He kept in touch with time
and rode the wave of destiny, touring on the wave of the British invasion.

Line 4: Is the specially accentuated line
in the Intimate Detail Hexagram?

No game in the field.

Searching correctly is important.

You cannot be shot if you cannot be found.

Jagger's traveling and erratic time schedule would prevent a predictable rou-
tine from developing. No one would know for sure which door of the theatre they
would enter through nor by which exit they would leave. A moving target is
harder to hit. John Lennon's movements were predictable; Mick Jagger's were not!

MICK JAGGER'S DESCENDANT IS AT 13° ♐ 06'

The Descendant shows how we react to others. It represents the reaction to our projections (ASC). The most obvious association is that of
multiple marriages, and marriage to someone from another culture.
Both of which are true for Jagger. The Descendent opposes Uranus and
squares Venus. Jagger is unstable in his relationships. This is not a comfortable area. Shocking upsets have come from most of his partnerships.

The I Ching Hexagrams related to Jagger's Descendant are as follows:

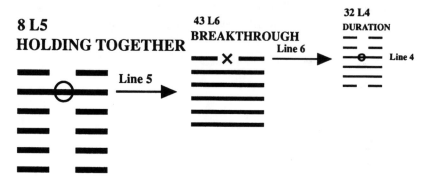

The MAIN THEME (Level 1) is HOLDING TOGETHER, Hexagram 8, Line 5.

The SPECIAL FOCUS (Level 2) is BREAKTHROUGH, Hexagram 43, Line 6.

The INTIMATE DETAIL (Level 3) is DURATION, Hexagram 32, Line 4.

THE MAIN THEME OF THE DESCENDANT (LEVEL 1 HEXAGRAM) IS
HOLDING TOGETHER

Above is the abysmal dangerous water.

Below is the yielding receptive earth.

The weak lines hold together because of the influence of a strong willful man who is the leader and the center of the union. The strong line holds the others together.

Jagger held the band together and he held together with the bands members.

Those who are unsure will eventually join.

Whoever comes too late encounters misfortune.

Jagger and Richards were the writers. The others were, for the most part, left out of the songwriting credits and royalties.

The Image

Holding people together is dangerous and mired with great responsibility.

The central figure must have great spirit,

Be consistent and strong.

The leader must have a real calling,
or the group would not survive,
and members would end up in horrible circumstances.
Each person must know that his best interests lie in holding together as
a group.
  This is true. Even for Jagger, it is better to hold to the group.

Line 5: The Special Emphasis
In the hunt animals are chased from three sides.
All are not killed.
Those that run off are free.
All members come of their own free will.
The leader is accepting.
He invites none and flatters no one!
True leadership will attract those who are meant to join.
  *Jagger is certainly known to be unflattering at times, yet everyone held to-
gether around him.*

  The special focus of Breakthrough, and the Intimate Detail of
Duration are the same for the Descendant and the Ascendant.

MICK JAGGER'S MARS IS DETRIMENT AT 12°♉12' IN HOUSE 12

This earthly Mars reveals Jagger's physical sensuality. Jagger is extremely
tactile. His body movements command appeal. His presence on stage is
tangibly physical-sexual. He does things the way he wants. His actions,
if anything, go overboard on the decadent side. Mars is somewhat self-
centered and vain in Taurus. Jagger has a forceful determination that is
often misunderstood and it generates animosity and enemies.

  In house 12, Mars implies danger due to aggression, and also an isolated sexuality. He shouts about how he "can't get no satisfaction," and
struts tauntingly on the stage. His physicality is quite feminine. With the
sequi-square to Neptune, and the squares to Jupiter, Pluto, Sun, Mercury,
and IC/MC, Jagger has many difficult lessons to learn around his confused sexuality. Yes, it is confused. He puts out feminine energy. This can
be seen in his cross-dressing. Blouses, tutus, dresses, you name it!

  The Venus-ruled Taurus position of Mars in house 12 also accounts
for his lack of refinement and taste. On stage Jagger goes beyond bad
taste to crassness and vulgarity. It is these vulgar actions that have made

Jagger infamous. It brought him plenty of rewards financially through the band, and it created a bisexual following and its subsequent large market. He has consistently been one giant step beyond quality in visual tastes, but that is true of many musicians. Jagger simply over-emphasizes his appearance and movements—enticing, appealing, but vulgar and base. This is the perfect combination for rock and blues.

With all the squares to his Mars, Jagger exhibits a grating manner that increases tension. He is like a child that gets more attention from screaming and throwing a tantrum than from being good. Jagger has a distinct fear of violence. He also has a clear division between on stage performance and personal reality. On stage he is exceptional. In the bedroom, the story is not likely the same.

By forcing issues to get what he wants, Jagger loses the ability to surrender control or to be personally satisfied for any sustainable period of time. He has an obsessive drive to make money and will do almost anything to get it. On the stage this works. Unfortunately his performances generate gross and dangerous reactions. Even from the early days of the Blue Boys, he would intimidate the crowd. It is amazing that there was only one lethal performance (Altamont). He is probably lucky (Sun conjunct Jupiter) that he was not the victim.

The I Ching Hexagrams related to Jagger's Mars are as follows:

10 L1
TREADING

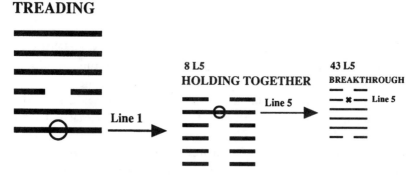

The MAIN THEME (Level 1) is TREADING, CONDUCT, Hexagram 10, Line 1.

The SPECIAL FOCUS (Level 2) is HOLDING TOGETHER, Hexagram 8, Line 5.

The INTIMATE DETAIL (Level 3) is BREAKTHROUGH, Hexagram 43, Line 5.

The Main Theme of Mars (Level 1 hexagram) is
TREADING (CONDUCT)
The creative heaven above, the joyous lake below.
This image is about strong pleasure.

The 12th house puts an obvious shadow on this, however the idea is bang on!

Here the superior man is relating to the fun seeking young woman, or someone's youngest daughter.

The question is: Would you want this man, even with all his money, to marry your daughter?

The idea of treading emerges as well as that of proper conduct.

Well Jagger had it half right, he struts and treads sexuality on the stage in front of all. He flaunts and ridicules proper conduct. In fact he often appears to be the old man trying to look like a young and beautiful woman. With Mars in his 12th house, he falls embarrassingly short of this reality. He does, however, feed the fantasies of the frustrated, the underprivileged, and the vulgar.

The Judgment
Concern comes from treading on the tail of a tiger,
which does not bite him.
This brings success.

Here we see Jagger on the stage, in front of thousands, treading on the tails of both society's inhibitions and its laws. The tail of the tiger could refer to the rampant use of drugs in the band. It could also apply to singing about sex and violence to the oversexed and the violent! He has achieved fame, notoriety, and financial abundance.

The judgment pictures one who is dealing with wild intractable people. This is dangerous, but it can bring success if one behaves with decorum.

I'm sure that Jagger's dramatics and decorum are not what was suggested, but nonetheless it has led to success.

The Image
Heaven above the lake.
Here the strong man must discriminate between the highly placed and the lowly.
This fortifies the common man.

Certainly his earthy blues-rock fortified the fans and reinforced their feelings.

The image continues about unjust class struggles and unfair differences in rank.

If these differences are based on a difference of real worth then it is correct.

Well, Jagger has literally forced himself to the head of the band. It can be argued that he deserved to be there, and that it was his superior worth that held the band together. His bond with Keith Richards as a writing team, and the mainstay of the Rolling Stones repertoire, is an undeniable special worth.

Line 1: The Special Emphasis
It is important to progress without blame.
One can do his own thing as long as he is content,
and makes no demands on others.
When a man is dissatisfied, he becomes ambitious,
and tries to get away from poverty and lowliness,
by way of his own personal actions.
Once he attains success
he is certain to become arrogant and luxury loving
at the expense of others.
Unfortunately this causes worthwhile deeds to remain undone,
and leads in time to guilt and remorse.

THE SPECIAL FOCUS (LEVEL 2 HEXAGRAM) IS
HOLDING TOGETHER
The abysmal water above the receptive earth.
Danger is above, like a storm.
Weakness is below.
To the strong man everyone seems like a weakling.
This leads to the idea of dangerous weakness.

It does not take much to think of Jagger and the band as dangerous weaknesses, with its known addictions, drug abuse, and even suicidal tendencies of band members. They have a remarkable capacity for self-destruction.

The image goes further to suggest the coming together of different streams or rivers. Water has the ability to hold together or join with other water. Here there are five weak lines held together by the power of the ruling fifth line. The group holds together because of a strong man in a leading position, who finds that his nature is complimented by the others.

This hexagram is unique in that it questions whether the person has the sublimity, consistency and the perseverance necessary to lead.

If he has the ability there is no blame.
The uncertain will eventually join.
But if anyone comes too late, they will meet with misfortune.
The accepted rule of the band was that the band came first.
Everyone is benefited by holding together in a complimentary manner.
A strong central figure is needed around whom the others can unite.
If the leader is not up to the task, and does not have a real calling,
then confusion and disaster will follow.
The leader of such a group must make sure that each member sees that
his best interests lie in holding together with the group.

Line 5: The specially accentuated line

Holding together is made real.
Good fortune.
Here there is an influential man to whom the others are attracted.
He flatters no one.
They must come of their own accord, then they will be accepted.
This creates a voluntary dependence on the leader.
Police measures are not necessary.
Jagger is known to be unflattering, but he can accept the dangerous weaknesses of the other band members in order to hold the musical talent together, to play their own special form of blues-rock.

THE INTIMATE DETAIL HEXAGRAM (LEVEL 3) IS CALLED
BREAKTHROUGH

The joyous lake is above the creative heaven.
Pleasure is in the heavens *(or in the spotlight)*.
The strong creative man relates to the pleasure-seeking girl.
"Hot Stuff," "Angie," "Brown Sugar," "Honky Tonk Woman."
After a long build up of tension, comes a breakthrough.
It seems as if Jagger forces tension to build, so that he can break through the atmosphere and draw attention to himself. This form of contrast for effect is a common theatrical maneuver that Jagger uses constantly. Make the bad guys look really bad and it will make the good guy appear really good.

The Judgment

Breakthrough.
It is important to make the matter known in the court.

Truth is essential.
Danger comes from the use of weapons.
It is important to work towards an accomplishable goal.
One inferior person in a position of municipal power
can oppress the creative and superior people.
There is a fight here between passion and reason, and between
good and evil.
To accentuate the evil will increase it,
then one will become attached to hatred and passion.
The best way to fight one's faults is to actively pursue one's
good qualities.

This is an uncanny epilogue to the actions and desires of Mick Jagger. It points to a lesson he must learn. Mars in the 12th house suggests the need for spiritual initiative, instead of a hopeless pursuit of eternal youth and health. As he gets older, the repercussions of the above mentioned principles will begin to dawn on him.

Line 5: Is the specially accentuated line in the Intimate Detail Hexagram?

When dealing with weeds, it is important to be firm.
Hold to the middle way and no guilts will develop.

Weeds grow easily. They are uninvited and cannot be exterminated easily. One must hold to his true way, or he will be brought down by lesser elements. Keeping on course will avoid guilt and bring success.

The association of Jagger and the Rolling Stones to weeds is appropriate in many ways. It could be argued that the Rolling Stones themselves are the weeds, possibly killer weeds! They certainly smoked their share of weeds!—one more pleasant, but illegal, activity (Mars in Taurus in house 12).

MICK JAGGER'S JUPITER IS AT 5° ♌ 30' IN HOUSE 3

Jupiter is the planet of opportunity and principles. It reveals your ability to learn from your life experiences and to benefit from the comprehension thus gained. The difficulty with Jupiter is that wrong understanding can lead to dangerous excesses.

With Jupiter conjunct the Sun and in house 3, Jagger has the ability to communicate successfully and to increase his own creative will and glory. Jupiter increases Jagger's ego and pride. It allows him to mimic and exaggerate for effect and attention. It implies that he is able to see the path to personal glory and quickly move along its steps. The more applause he gets, the further he will go. Touring is easy for Mick. Each performance is a step to glory and fame.

Jupiter is also conjunct the IC, Pluto, and Mercury. This creates a deep dark Faustian battle over principles and morals. His understanding easily moves toward the realms of darkness. His deepest sense of security is somewhat fearful. Anything that diminishes his expansion could be considered the enemy. This highlights his ability to champion the blues, the underdog, and the villain. Anything or anyone going against his will or momentum must be fought. He can creatively exaggerate injustice. Ponder a while on the implications of this. Misunderstanding and legal battles surround Jagger's life, both at home and at work. With the opposition to the MC, he would be inclined to go against the system, and he would know how to get around it. Unfortunately the influence of the Pluto conjunction and the square from Mars in house 12 implies that he could set dangerous and isolating energies in motion.

His charisma far outweighs his reality. It would be difficult to live with Mick, as he can detach to prove a point, even when he is wrong. This man is not likely to grow old gracefully. Although he is already into his 50s, Jagger will always be the big kid. He will probably still be kicking when they lower him into his grave!

The I Ching Hexagrams related to Jagger's Jupiter are as follows:

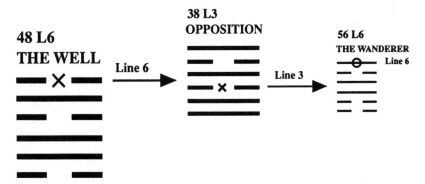

The MAIN THEME (Level 1) is THE WELL, Hexagram 48, Line 6.
The SPECIAL FOCUS (Level 2) is OPPOSITION, Hexagram 38, Line 3.
The INTIMATE DETAIL (Level 3) is THE WANDERER, Hexagram 56, Line 6.

THE MAIN THEME OF JUPITER (LEVEL 1 HEXAGRAM) IS:
THE WELL
This is the same hexagram that the Sun is in.
He knows how to go to the well and tap it!

The challenge here is to understand the circumstances of nutrition, thirst, poverty, and misfortune. The superior man learns how to encourage people at their work so that all the parts are in sync with each other.

Jagger is obsessed with the nutrition needed to keep him young forever. The thirst and misfortune implies losses and perhaps addictions. (Refer to this hexagram under the Sun.)

Line 6: The Special Emphasis
An abundant well with enough for all.
There is a well of energy here that one can draw from, almost a fountain of youth!

Here a person has great inner wealth, and as people are naturally attracted to him, his wealth increases.

THE SPECIAL FOCUS (LEVEL 2 HEXAGRAM) IS
OPPOSITION
The clinging fire above the joyous lake.
Clarity versus pleasure.
People who live in opposition to each other usually cannot undertake great tasks.
Confrontation is not the solution.
One's influence is limited to steady effects in small matters.

Jagger is known to have applied this approach to the dealings with band members and their addictions. He did not force a confrontation.

Opposition or contrast as a polarity within a group can be very useful.

Jagger let the corruption of band members go on because it made him look better! The insights about sexual relations between man and woman provide the major contrast expressed in Jagger's songs. There is an opposition in his own sexuality as to which side of the fence he is on.

The image is Opposition.
Even in the midst of fellowship
the superior man maintains his uniqueness.
This implies that a cultured man never falls into vulgarity.

It could be argued that a vulgar man rarely manifests refinement or culture.

Line 3: The specially accentuated line
The wagon is dragged back.
The oxen are stopped.
A man's hair and his nose are cut off.
Not a good beginning but a good end.

Everything seems to conspire against him. He is held back and delayed. He is insulted and dishonored. In spite of this opposition, if he holds to the man with whom he really belongs, good fortune will result. From a bad start can come a good end.

Jagger and the Rolling Stones were continually harassed and busted. Whenever he traveled the band got into trouble—sex, drugs, violence. Jagger was, however, still able to hold it together sufficiently to profit from his tours. When the band seemed to have split up, and Jagger did three years of his own recording, he came back to his connection with Keith Richards, and the band played on.

THE INTIMATE DETAIL HEXAGRAM (LEVEL 3) IS CALLED
THE WANDERER
Fire on the mountain.
It burns quickly for all to see, but it does not last.

Perhaps it is Jagger's Jupiter here that taught him how to keep on burning to last longer than any other big rock group.

Strange places and separation fill the life of the wanderer.
The stranger in a strange land must be cautious.
Only small things can be achieved by a wanderer.
If he attracts bad elements he will be molested and maligned.

The Image
Fire on the mountain.
The strong man must be clear minded
and cautious in his decisions of discipline,
or else he will attract lawsuits.
Legal matters should be dealt with quickly.
Prison should not become a home.

Jagger, with his stellium in Leo, is the fire on the mountain! He did make and break contracts quickly and completely once he made the decision. However, decision-making did take Mick a long time.

Line 6: Is the specially accentuated line in the Intimate Detail Hexagram?

The bird's nest is destroyed by fire.
At first the wanderer laughs
but then he cries and laments.
Through carelessness his cow is lost.
This is unfortunate.

A reckless traveler has no place to sleep. Uncontrolled partying will lead to sorrow and remorse. Carelessness can lead to evil.

The songbird, Jagger—more like a crow or a blackbird—has lost several homes or places of rest due to carelessness. His homes were generally in poor repair. Sex, drugs, and rock and roll does not a good marriage make. The cow is lost—whether this refers to his wives, his women, or even Brian Jones, is a consideration. There have been many casualties on the path of the Rolling Stones which were caused by arrogant recklessness. This was expected in the 60s!

MICK JAGGER'S SATURN IS AT 21° ♊ 58' IN HOUSE 1

With Saturn in Gemini, Jagger wants to be his own authority. It simply makes sense to him. He continually moves toward more and more individual power. This makes him ambitious, very controlled, and inhibited on a personal basis. His first impression is serious. Being in Gemini there are two sides to his image, and Jagger does thrive in a contrasting image. On the one hand, he appears to be free and radical, while on the other, he is a very conservative, middle class, businessman. Image control gives him his stage presence. Jagger is a serious strategist. He has to manage everything.

Even on stage in the middle of a dance, he has the power to stop dead in his tracks. Music without restraint is simply noise. Jagger in his blues/rock genre has restraint. If we go so far as to give Saturn its older association of being the grim reaper or even the devil himself, the goat-headed god, then the 1st house position of this old devil is blatantly confirmed by Jagger's songwriting. Many of his songs were written in collaboration with Keith Richards, a junkie! Works of the devil? Who knows? The devil does play a big part in Jagger's image and songs. Witness his albums: "Their Satanic Majesties Request," and "Goat's Head Soup," with songs like "Sympathy for the Devil," and "Dancing with Mr. D." Even the fact of two writers working together is reinforced by the image of Saturn in Gemini. Some other related songs would be "Coming Down Again," "Dear Doctor," "Salt of the Earth,"

"Respectable," "Beast of Burden," Under Cover of the Night," and "Mean Disposition." In fact, blues-rock is about the "down" side of music and life. It's about the underdog and the underprivileged. Jagger sees the high and low contrast in things. He revels in the contrast. Misery can make him look better!

The wide square to Neptune can easily be acknowledged by witnessing the corrupt and sleazy side of Jagger's ambition and stardom. How far is he prepared to go to express depravity?

The I Ching Hexagrams related to Jagger's Saturn are as follows:

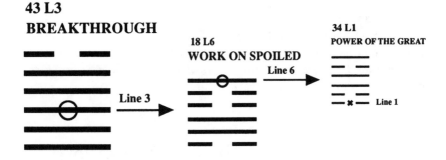

43 L3
BREAKTHROUGH

18 L6
WORK ON SPOILED
Line 6

34 L1
POWER OF THE GREAT

Line 3

Line 1

The MAIN THEME (Level 1) is BREAKTHROUGH, Hexagram 43, Line 3.
The SPECIAL FOCUS (Level 2) is WORK ON WHAT'S SPOILED, Hexagram 18, Line 6.
The INTIMATE DETAIL (Level 3) is POWER OF THE GREAT, Hexagram 3, Line 1.

THE MAIN THEME OF SATURN (LEVEL 1 HEXAGRAM) IS
BREAKTHROUGH
This is the Intimate Detail hexagram of Mars. Once again, the theme of strong pleasure or desire surfaces, as does the association of a strong man to a pleasure-seeking young girl. Again this accentuates an ability to breakthrough to release built up tensions. It points to trouble with the courts and inferior people in authority.

Line 3: The Special Emphasis
Power in the cheekbones.
Misfortune.

The superior man holds firm.

He walks in the rain, alone.

He gets wet, and others gossip about him.

No guilt.

He maintains a relationship to an inferior man.

Outer strength is not the way.

If he turns against this inferior man, danger will threaten everything.

The superior man must stay firm even though he will be maligned.

Relationships with inferiors cause isolation and scandal.

If he is true to himself, the superior man will endure.

This obviously points to members of the band with their addictions and bad energy. Jagger had to hold steady, even through the arrests and scandals. Jagger held the band together through many dubious and dark crises. Not only did he endure, but the bad elements of the band made him look great. No one else could have held the Rolling Stones together. Even the name "Rolling Stones" is indicative of Saturn in Gemini in the 1st house.

THE SPECIAL FOCUS HEXAGRAM (LEVEL 2) IS
WORK ON WHAT'S SPOILED (DAMAGE CONTROL)

Worms in decaying food.

Stagnation and guilt.

The situation must be repaired.

In the early days of the band, their house was a rotten disaster. On the road it was not much cleaner. Jagger has certain guilts about not following the career of his father's choice—accounting or even sports.

The superior man excites the people and reinforces their spirit.

It is important to get rid of corruption.

Jagger had to work hard on damage control. Jones' and Richards' addictions to heroin and alcohol caused much inertia and stagnation. Jagger had to fight this continually to keep his band alive and functional.

Line 6: The specially accentuated line

He doesn't serve kings or princes,

but sets higher goals for himself.

Jagger's stage and international acclaim was more important than serving royalty. He had to be Number One.

THE INTIMATE DETAIL HEXAGRAM (LEVEL 3) IS CALLED
POWER OF THE GREAT
The arousing thunder above, the creative heaven below.
Here we have shocking creativity and a stimulating individual.
The coming together of strength and movement brings about the power
of the great.

*At a glance at Jagger dancing, we see movement and strength. At least we
see in the movement of his muscles, agility, and fitness!*

Here inner worth rises forcefully to power.
There is the danger of too much self-reliance,
and the abandonment of principles or morals.

Did Mick Jagger really sell his soul to the devil?

Too much force leads to poor timing.
In times of great power the superior man must hold to what is right,
and avoid going against the established order.

*Jagger constantly felt the long arm of the law and of border guards. He was
able to avoid the worst repercussions by virtue of his lucky Sun Jupiter conjunction.*

Line 1: Is the specially accentuated line
in the Intimate Detail Hexagram?
Power lies in the toes.
To push forward will bring misfortune.
Great power in a lowly position could misuse its force.

*There is no doubt that the misuse of power surrounded Jagger. However, his
control and power to dance is highlighted here. His short-step-tippy-toed effeminate dance comes to mind. Jagger's power is indeed in his toes.*

NATAL HEXAGRAM TOTALS

While the chart with hexagram positions is printed out, the hexagram
accentuations are totaled. This results in a special printout that takes all
513 hexagram horoscope accentuations and presents them as a study

---

[3]C. F. Baynes and Richard Wilhelm, trans. *I Ching or Book of Changes*, Bollingen Series
No. 19 (Princeton: Princeton University Press, 1967).

guide to the I Ching. All the 64 hexagrams are listed by their number in the Wilhelm/Baynes version of the I Ching.[3] They are listed in zodiacal order down both sides of the page. The lines are 1 to 6 from the bottom to the top of the hexagram. The number of accentuations on each line of a hexagram are totaled and presented from left to right for each level. These three levels are then added together and totaled with a percentage of emphasis (given in decimal form) and a grand total of accents for each line. Certain hexagram themes stand out—the most and least accentuated. What is most accentuated will appear very familiar and the lessons pointed. What is least accented will be somewhat unfamiliar and at times obscure.

The maximum hexagram accentuation for Mick Jagger is Hexagram 39, OBSTRUCTION. Out of all of the horoscope accentuations this hexagram appears 20 times, or close to 4 percent. Line 6 has been activated 9 times, followed by Line 3 with 4 accents (see Table 1 on pages 94, 95).

OBSTRUCTION

Danger on the mountain.
Obstacles arise.
A dangerous crevasse in front, an extremely steep mountain behind.
Trouble ahead, trouble behind!
The solution lies in keeping still and maintaining a positive attitude.
Negative thoughts will lead to severe repercussions.
If the obstacles are too great, retreat,
Join forces with friends who think alike,
and put yourself in the hands of an able leader.
The value of such adversity is that it can help in self-development.
Do not cast blame on others.
It is time to improve oneself.

The mountain could easily be the stage or Jagger's career. It has always seemed to be surrounded by danger. He dances in front of the dangerous audience, with the ominous power of the band and the music industry behind him. This danger could also refer to the drugs and illegal activities on the stage.

Each line of this hexagram has some activity in it, and is worth reading. However the sixth line is the most active. This line refers to a man who is blocked from retiring, and who must return into the life's turmoil. Because he returns, great deeds can be accomplished.

39 L6
OBSTRUCTION

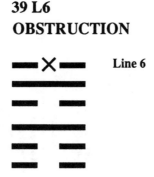 Line 6

This suggests that we can expect to see Jagger returning to the turmoil of the stage even when he is 70. Just one more performance, to hell with the obstacles!

There are two hexagrams that stand out for being the least accentuated and they are Hexagram 50: THE CALDRON, and Hexagram 36: THE DARKENING OF THE LIGHT.

These are the themes least likely to be prominent in Jagger's character. However they are distinctive because these are the lessons he is least likely to have learned.

In THE CALDRON, one is warned about carelessness in preparing food. If the food spills or the pot breaks—misfortune. IN THE DARKENING OF THE LIGHT, the superior man is surrounded by inferior people. He must learn to keep his light within. These are not necessarily negative themes, but they are conspicuous in his life. Where and what Jagger would eat on the road probably implied little discrimination. Also Jagger is known for showing off all his light. He has rarely given up an opportunity to shine.

Table 1. Mick Jagger. Natal hexagram totals.

GEOCENTRIC SYSTEM / TROPICAL   M = Maximum hits, m = minimum hits

HEX #	LEVEL 1 1 2 3 4 5 6	SUM =A	LEVEL 2 1 2 3 4 5 6	SUM =B	LEVEL 3 1 2 3 4 5 6	SUM =C	TOTAL=% A+B+C	LNE TOTALS 1 2 3 4 5 6	HEX #	HEXAGRAM NAME
CP 24:	0 1 0.1 2 3	=7	0 1 0.0 0 0	=1	0 0 1.0 2 1	=4	12=.023	0 2 1..1 4 4	:24	Turning Point
CP 27:	0 0 2.1 1 1	=5	0 2 1.0 0 1	=4	0 1 0.0 1 1	=3	12=.023	0 3 3..1 2 3	:27	Providing Nourishment
CP 3:	0 2 1.0 1 0	=4	0 0 0.1 0 0	=1	2 0 0.0 1 1	=4	9=.018	2 2 1..1 2 1	: 3	Difficult Beginning
CP 42:	0 1 0.0 0 0	=1	0 1 0.1 0 0	=1	1 0 1.0 0 2	=4	6=.012	1 1 1..1 0 2	:42	Increase
CP 51:	0 1 0.1 1 0	=3	1 0 0.0 1 1	=3	0 2 1.0 0 0	=3	9=.018	1 3 1..1 2 1	:51	Arousing Force
AQ 21:	1 0 1.0 0 0	=2	0 1 0.0 0 0	=1	1 0 1.0 1 0	=3	6=.012	2 1 2..0 1 0	:21	Biting Through
AQ 17:	1 0 2.1 1 1	=6	0 0 0.1 0 1	=2	0 0 1.1 1 0	=3	11=.021	1 0 3..3 2 2	:17	Following
AQ 25:	0 2 1.0 0 0	=3	2 0 0.0 0 0	=2	0 1 0.0 0 0	=1	6=.012	2 3 1..0 0 0	:25	Unexpected
AQ 36:	0 0 0.0 0 0	=0	0 0 0.0 0 0	=0	0 1 1.0 0 0	=2	2=.004	0 1 1..0 0 0	:36m	Darkening of the Light
AQ 22:	2 1 0.0 1 2	=6	1 0 0.0 1 1	=3	0 1 0.2 1 0	=4	13=.025	3 2 0..2 3 3	:22	Grace
AQ 63:	0 1 3.0 0 3	=7	0 0 2.0 1 0	=3	1 0 1.1 0 0	=3	13=.025	1 1 6..1 1 3	:63	After Completion
PI 37:	0 0 1.1 0 0	=2	0 0 1.0 1 0	=2	0 1 0.0 0 0	=1	5=.010	1 1 2..1 0 0	:37	Family
PI 55:	1 0 0.2 0 0	=3	0 0 0.0 1 0	=1	1 0 0.0 0 0	=1	5=.010	2 0 0..2 1 0	:55	Abundance
PI 30:	0 1 0.0 0 1	=2	0 0 1.1 0 0	=2	1 0 1.0 1 0	=3	7=.014	1 1 2..1 1 1	:30	Clinging
PI 49:	1 1 1.0 1 0	=4	0 0 1.1 0 0	=2	2 0 1.0 0 0	=3	9=.018	3 2 2..0 1 1	:49	Molting
PI 13:	0 0 1.0 0 1	=2	0 1 1.0 0 1	=3	0 1 0.0 0 0	=1	6=.012	0 3 1..0 0 2	:13	Fellowship With Men
AR 19:	1 0 0.1 1 1	=4	0 0 1.0 0 1	=2	0 1 0.0 0 0	=1	7=.014	1 1 1..1 1 2	:19	Approach
AR 41:	0 1 0.0 0 0	=1	0 1 0.0 0 1	=2	1 0 1.0 0 0	=2	5=.010	1 2 1..0 0 1	:41	Decrease
AR 60:	0 0 0.1 1 0	=2	0 1 1.1 0 0	=3	1 0 1.0 1 0	=3	8=.016	1 1 2..2 2 0	:60	Limitation
AR 61:	0 1 0.0 1 0	=1	0 0 0.0 1 0	=1	1 0 0.0 0 0	=1	4=.008	1 1 0..0 2 0	:61	Inner Truth
AR 54:	0 0 0.0 0 1	=1	1 0 1.0 0 0	=2	0 1 0.0 0 0	=1	4=.008	1 1 1..0 0 1	:54	Marrying Maiden
TA 38:	0 1 0.0 1 1	=3	0 0 3.0 1 0	=4	1 0 1.2 0 0	=4	11=.021	1 1 4..2 2 1	:38	Opposition
TA 58:	0 0 1.0 0 0	=1	0 0 0.0 2 1	=3	0 1 0.2 1 0	=4	8=.016	0 1 1..2 3 1	:58	Joy
TA 10:	1 1 0.0 0 0	=2	0 0 0.0 0 0	=0	0 1 1.0 0 0	=2	4=.008	1 2 1..0 0 0	:10	Treading
TA 11:	1 0 0.0 0 0	=1	2 1 0.0 0 0	=3	0 1 0.0 0 0	=1	5=.010	3 2 0..0 0 0	:11	Peace
TA 26:	1 0 0.0 0 0	=1	0 0 0.1 0 3	=4	0 0 1.1 1 0	=3	8=.016	1 0 1..2 1 3	:26	Great Taming Power
TA 5:	0 0 0.0 0 1	=1	0 1 0.0 1 0	=1	1 0 1.0 1 0	=3	5=.010	1 1 1..0 1 1	: 5	Waiting for Nourishment
GE 9:	0 0 0.0 0 0	=0	2 0 0.0 1 1	=4	0 2 1.0 0 0	=3	7=.014	2 2 1..0 1 1	: 9	Small Taming Power
GE 34:	0 0 0.0 1 0	=1	0 0 0.1 0 0	=1	2 0 1.0 0 0	=3	5=.010	2 0 1..1 1 0	:34	Great Power
GE 14:	0 0 0.0 1 0	=1	0 0 0.1 0 0	=1	2 0 0.0 1 1	=4	6=.012	2 0 0..1 2 1	:14	Great Possession
GE 43:	0 1 1.0 0 0	=2	0 2 1.0 0 3	=6	0 1 0.0 1 2	=4	12=.023	0 4 2..0 1 5	:43	Breakthrough
GE 1:	0 1 2.0 0 1	=4	0 1 0.0 0 0	=1	0 0 1.0 2 1	=4	9=.018	0 2 3..0 2 2	: 1	Creative

Table 1. Mick Jagger. Natal hexagram totals (cont.).

CA	44:	0 1 2.0 0 1 = 4	0 0 0.0 2 1 = 3	0 0 0.0 0 0 2 = 2	9 = .018	0 1 2.0 2 4	:44 Coming to Meet
CA	28:	0 1 0.0 0 0 = 1	1 2 0.0 1 0 = 4	0 0 1.1 0 0 = 2	7 = .014	1 3 1.1 1 0	:28 Great Preponderance
CA	50:	0 0 0.0 0 0 = 0	0 1 0.0 0 0 = 1	0 0 1.0 0 0 = 1	2 = .004	0 1 1.0 0 0	:50m Caldron
CA	32:	0 0 0.0 0 0 = 0	0 1 1.0 0 2 = 4	0 1 0.3 1 1 = 6	10 = .019	0 2 1.3 1 3	:32 Duration
CA	57:	0 0 0.0 0 0 = 0	1 0 1.0 0 0 = 3	0 0 0.0 2 1 = 3	6 = .012	1 0 1.1 2 1	:57 Gentleness
LE	48:	0 0 1.0 0 2 = 3	0 0 0.0 1 0 = 1	0 0 0.0 0 0 = 0	4 = .008	1 0 1.0 1 2	:48 The Well
LE	18:	1 0 1.0 1 0 = 3	1 1 0.1 2 1 = 6	1 0 1.1 0 0 = 3	12 = .023	3 1 2.2 3 1	:18 Work on What's Spoiled
LE	46:	1 0 0.0 0 0 = 1	2 0 1.0 0 0 = 3	0 0 0.0 0 0 = 0	4 = .008	3 0 1.0 0 0	:46 Pushing Upwards
LE	6:	0 1 1.0 0 0 = 2	0 0 0.0 0 0 = 0	3 1 1.0 0 0 = 5	7 = .014	3 2 2.0 0 0	: 6 Conflict
LE	47:	0 0 1.0 0 0 = 1	0 0 1.0 0 1 = 2	0 1 0.0 0 1 = 2	5 = .010	0 1 2.0 0 2	:47 Exhaustion
LE	64:	0 1 0.0 0 1 = 3	1 1 1.1 3 = 8	1 0 0.0 1 2 = 4	15 = .029	2 2 1.1 3 6	:64 Before Completion
VI	40:	0 0 0.0 0 1 = 1	0 1 0.1 0 1 = 3	1 0 0.1 1 2 = 5	9 = .018	1 1 0.2 1 4	:40 Deliverance
VI	59:	0 1 0.0 1 0 = 2	1 1 0.0 0 0 = 2	0 0 0.1 1 0 = 2	6 = .012	1 2 0.1 2 0	:59 Dispersion
VI	29:	0 0 0.1 2 0 = 3	0 2 1.1 1 1 = 6	0 0 0.2 1 1 = 4	13 = .025	0 2 1.4 4 2	:29 Abysmal
VI	4:	0 1 0.0 0 0 = 1	1 1 2.0 0 0 = 4	0 0 0.1 0 1 = 2	7 = .014	1 2 2.1 0 1	: 4 Youthful Folly
VI	7:	2 0 0.1 1 1 = 5	0 0 1.0 0 0 = 1	0 1 1.0 0 0 = 2	8 = .016	2 1 2.1 1 1	: 7 The Army
LI	33:	0 1 0.0 0 1 = 2	0 0 1.0 0 0 = 1	0 1 1.0 0 0 = 2	5 = .010	0 2 2.0 0 1	:33 Retreat
LI	31:	0 1 1.0 1 0 = 4	1 1 2.0 0 0 = 4	0 0 0.1 0 1 = 2	6 = .019	2 3 3.1 1 1	:31 Wooing
LI	56:	0 1 0.0 0 1 = 2	0 2 1.1 1 1 = 6	0 0 0.2 1 2 = 5	13 = .025	0 3 1.3 2 4	:56 The Wanderer
LI	62:	1 0 0.2 0 0 = 3	0 1 0.1 1 0 = 2	0 0 0.1 1 0 = 2	7 = .014	2 1 0.3 1 0	:62 Small Preponderance
LI	53:	0 0 1.1 0 0 = 2	0 1 0.1 0 1 = 3	1 0 0.1 1 2 = 5	10 = .019	1 1 1.3 1 3	:53 Gradual Progress
SC	39:	0 1 3.0 0 3 = 7	1 1 1.1 1 3 = 8	1 0 0.0 1 3 = 5	20 = .039	2 2 4.1 2 9	:39M Obstruction
SC	52:	2 1 0.0 1 2 = 6	0 0 1.0 1 0 = 2	0 0 0.0 0 1 = 1	9 = .018	2 1 1.0 1 4	:52 Keeping Still
SC	15:	0 0 0.0 0 0 = 0	0 0 0.0 0 0 = 0	3 1 1.0 0 0 = 5	5 = .010	3 1 1.0 0 0	:15 Modesty
SC	12:	0 2 1.0 0 0 = 3	2 0 1.0 0 0 = 3	0 0 0.0 0 0 = 0	6 = .012	2 2 2.0 0 0	:12 Standstill
SC	45:	1 0 1.1 1 1 = 5	1 1 0.1 2 0 = 5	1 0 0.1 0 0 = 2	12 = .023	3 1 1.3 3 1	:45 Gathering Together
SC	35:	1 0 1.0 0 0 = 2	0 0 0.0 1 0 = 1	0 0 0.0 0 0 = 0	3 = .006	1 0 1.0 1 0	:35 Progress
SA	16:	0 1 0.1 1 0 = 3	1 0 1.1 0 0 = 3	0 0 0.0 3 1 = 4	10 = .019	1 1 1.2 4 1	:16 Enthusiasm
SA	20:	0 1 0.0 0 0 = 1	0 1 1.0 0 2 = 4	0 1 0.1 1 1 = 4	9 = .018	0 3 1.1 1 3	:20 Contemplation
SA	8:	0 2 1.0 2 0 = 5	0 1 0.1 0 1 = 2	0 0 1.0 0 1 = 1	8 = .016	0 3 2.0 3 0	: 8 Holding Together
SA	23:	0 0 2.1 1 1 = 5	1 2 1.0 1 0 = 5	0 0 1.1 0 0 = 2	12 = .023	1 2 4.2 2 1	:23 Splitting Apart
SA	2:	0 1 0.1 2 3 = 7	0 0 0.0 2 0 = 2	0 0 0.0 0 2 = 2	11 = .021	0 1 0.1 4 5	: 2 Receptive

ABOUT THE AUTHOR

Robin Armstrong is an astrological consultant and teacher. He runs the Robin Armstrong School of Astrology in Toronto, where he teaches both Astrology and I Ching. He's been a founding member of several organizations: the Canadian Independent Astrologers' Order; the Fraternity for Canadian Astrologers; Astrology Toronto; AFAN, the Association for Astrological Networking; and the Toronto NCGR chapter. From 1971 to 1992 he was founder and president of the IAO Research Centre with its Library of Divine Sciences and the Healing Arts.

Robin invented the "Celestial Harp," a musical instrument based on astrology and the I Ching. In 1976 he wrote a two-book treatise called *Astro-logic*, correlating Astrology and I Ching. He was editor of Northern Lights, and the *AFAN 1995 Astrologers Guide*, and presently edits *News By Degrees*. He is president of the Star Centre Library, and is past president of the Toronto NCGR chapter. He was re-elected to the AFAN Steering Committee in 1994, where he held the Education portfolio. Robin is an advisor to the Heart Center Library, and is active in the Astrological Library Association (International).

The printouts and chart form used in this article came from Robin's Windows-based astrology program, "Stars In Sight" which integrates the I Ching with astrology. This program will be available for sale in the near future. Write for details:

Robin Armstrong
Box 5265 Station A
Toronto
Ontario M5W 1N5
Canada
E-Mail: robin.armstrong@sympatico.ca
Website: www.sympatico.ca

CHAPTER 3

CHINESE FIVE-ELEMENT
(TZU P'ING) ASTROLOGY

A STROLOGERS OF EVERY culture believe that there are no accidents—things happen according to a larger plan. Rob Hand once noted, "Events don't happen to people; people happen to events." I "happened to an event" in Taiwan in early 1990, when I accepted an invitation to lead a public seminar on management and creativity in Taipei. At that time, I had been a student of martial arts and Chinese philosophy for a dozen years; I also had ten years' experience integrating Western astrological theory into a management consulting practice, mainly as an executive coaching and team development tool.

Most of the Chinese seminar participants were entrepreneurs or managers from private sector business; however one group member, a woman named Ana Lo, had a clerical job with the government. On the last day of the course, Ana told me privately that she had very little interest in the seminar content and no way to apply much of it in her work; she had come to the course because she had heard that I was a Western astrologer, and she had been studying Western astrology and psychology from books and audiotapes. Further discussion revealed that she had taken vacation time from her job and paid out of pocket for the seminar because she wanted to establish contact with me.

Naturally, I was flattered and pleased that she had made such an effort; as we talked, it came to light that over a twenty-year period, Ana had been a student of three great masters of Chinese Five-Element systems: Dr. Chen Yi Kuei, traditional Chinese medicine and bioenergetics; chi gong master Yü Shueh Hong; and an astrologer with credentials in both the "Ancient" *(Chi Zheng Sz Yü)* and "Five Element" *(Tzu P'ing)* systems known as Shi Lin San Ren (the Western Forest Mountain Hermit). She is a living example of the traditional scholar class in China—one who earns a modest salary in a government job and devotes free time to studying the classics and the pursuit of traditional hobbies. She is a *Tzu P'ing* and *Feng Shui* master in her own right.

I could scarcely believe my good fortune—she was willing to trade information. *Tzu P'ing* is the technique of "fate calculation" that has ancient origins, and continues to this day to be the most widely used and respected system among Chinese people. This was the beginning of what has become a great friendship, one which has deepened my understanding of traditional Chinese customs, and given me access to information which is rarely shared outside of the culture. I would like to express my gratitude to Master Lo, for it is by her permission that I am able to share this information with you.

The attitude of Chinese astrologers toward the open sharing of information is quite different from ours in the West. There are no conferences, and very few workshops that are open to the public. If Western astrology is Aquarian in nature, with active networking of practitioners, Chinese astrology is Scorpionic, with carefully guarded secrets, interpersonal rivalry, even occasional vendettas. Knowledge of how to apply the Five Element theory to individual fate is considered a form of great wealth; individuals who have mastered a system will carefully guard their professional knowledge. There is an old saying in the Chinese language which literally translates, "I'm Chang, the Tutor of Heaven, with my hands over my mouth," the implication being that the secrets of Heaven must not be revealed.

Tzu P'ing is a very ancient practice which has been passed on orally, from teacher to student, for more than 2000 years. It is an initiate tradition; no one gets handed a book that contains all of its secrets. It may be technically incorrect to call *Tzu P'ing* an astrology, because the planets are not considered, fixed stars are used only to identify the horizon direction, and there is no time zone correction. All of the essential astronomical calculations have been computed in the Chinese ephemeris. Nonetheless, it is considered to be a form of astrology by millions of Chinese people, and its practitioners are commonly referred to as astrologers. Within the wide range of Chinese mantic beliefs and practices, *Tzu P'ing* is known as a "Fate and Fortune" technique, one of five kinds of "practice" (*wu shu*, lit. five techniques, or technical philosophies). These are: Energetic, Chinese Medicine, Fate and Fortune, Divination, and Observation. Each of these techniques meet in the liminal space between the secular and the sacred, mediating between the worlds of the known and the unknown.

Of the three main Fate and Fortune techniques, *Tzu P'ing* is the foremost; it is popularly known to Chinese people as *ba tze*, meaning eight characters. It is an altitude and azimuth system, based on direction and the seasonal relationship of the Earth to the Sun. However, it is not an "intuitive" approach to knowing the quality of time, as, for example, are most divination techniques, Eastern or Western. As Western astrologers, we may have discomfort with the terms "fate" and "fortune," but I believe that information obtained from calculating the position of planets is qualitatively no different from that obtained by a Chinese *Tzu P'ing* practitioner calculating an eight-character structure from the Earth's seasonal relation to the Heavens. The essence of both practices involves forecasting both opportune and challenging periods from astronomical and birth data.

All traditional Chinese astrologies appear formidably complex; masters typically recruit students for life, then parcel information into bite-sized chunks in weekly classes—for years! To become an "insider" and learn the master's secrets typically requires a very substantial one-time, up-front payment. Chinese people will seldom attempt to learn a system from books alone; the intricacies require the skillful guidance of a master. As it is in the martial arts *(wu shu)*, so it is in the occult arts: masters do not teach students everything they know; they hold back a few tricks to prevent being eclipsed by a younger, possibly stronger and more aggressive student.

I recently returned from my nineteenth trip to Taiwan in the past five years; during this period of time, I became completely absorbed in Chinese astrology. Reflecting on this remarkable learning experience brings back memories of many hours spent as a child·trying to open my grandmother's marvelous Chinese puzzle box. It had secret interlocking pieces that were barely visible, even on close inspection. I can recall the feeling of elation at finding a piece that moved in this apparently seamless wooden box. The study of *Tzu P'ing* has a similar quality; it is truly an "eight-character puzzle."

I have become familiar with the cultural style of the Chinese through doing client readings on Taiwan. As a way to defray a portion of my travel costs, Ana made arrangements for me to give Western astrology readings to some of her clients. We agreed to do the readings jointly; she would contribute information from a Chinese astrological perspective where appropriate, and translate as needed. I wanted to be as impressive as possible, and give as thorough and detailed a reading as I could with these first Chinese clients, so I worked far into the night preparing for them. I printed natal, progressed and solar return charts, transit runs, and midpoint sorts for each, and used every analytical technique in my toolkit. By the time I had finished, there were eight computer-generated pages of data for each client, along with two pages each of handwritten notes. The next morning, my teacher arrived with a small Chinese ephemeris and a slip of paper for each of the clients, inscribed with their eight characters and ten progression steps. In spite of all of my work the previous evening, I was not prepared for what happened.

I had decided that I would take some time at the beginning of a reading to explain to each client what they were looking at. This was based on prior experience with Western clients, many of whom have either been skeptical about astrology, or convinced of its value but curious about how and why it works. However, I hadn't been talking for more than three minutes when they began to show impatience with my explanation of the glyphs and the archetypal meanings of the planets. I rapidly found out that they were not the least bit interested in the system, *per se*; they had come to hear me discuss their future.

I found these new clients very demanding, and a bit unnerving. They asked very pointed questions: did I see a man in their life next year? Is building a factory on the mainland a good idea? If so, what is the best time to do it? Would their mother's operation be successful? This type of question sent me scrambling in my stack of charts, but Ana would save my face every time, answering directly and without hesitation. She read from only eight Chinese characters, arranged in four columns, or "pillars." I was impressed.

From the beginning, our process has been a comparative study. We have given joint astrology readings to more than one hundred clients over a four year period. In our break between client readings, we would compare notes: "How did you know this?" How can you get that bit of information so quickly?" In spite of all my preparation, I think that she made a far greater contribution to those early readings.

Although *Tzu P'ing* and Western systems have different foundations, we discovered that we could consistently cross-validate highly detailed information about a client's character and current life issues. For this reason, I consider the Chinese system to be equal in accuracy to traditional Western astrology. Reflecting on our process, it became apparent to me that the Chinese astrologer had several advantages—

• The *Tzu P'ing* system is far more portable. All of the essential data is contained in the ephemeris, and erecting a chart by hand takes about three minutes for an experienced astrologer. Because the Chinese system requires accuracy only to the "double hour" (i.e., a two-hour increment of time), it eliminates the need for a precise birth time or a lengthy rectification process. Calculating and displaying a Western chart is a cumbersome process by comparison, even with a notebook computer.

• It is necessary to establish personal credibility with clients, but not to defend the credibility of the discipline. This comes from the fact that Chinese astrologers have enjoyed respect and social legitimacy in their culture since ancient times. They have never experienced ridicule or persecution for their practice or beliefs (only for inaccuracy), and they are given status and prestige in every Chinese community. In Taiwan, a typical professional astrologer's hourly fee is two or three times that of a psychotherapist.

• Prescriptive counseling is expected. The culturally appropriate style when dealing with Chinese people is to be considerate of their privacy, but to be task-oriented and directive with advice. This is what they want, and expect, from counselors and healers. The reading is less about psychological issues than external affairs and issues of personal fortune; it is not necessary to beat around the bush when you see something difficult, or re-frame everything you see in personal growth terms.

• Perhaps the system's most impressive advantage is the ability to provide a clear and rapid *gestalt*. The four pillars provide an excellent overview of the client's character, progressions show the ups and downs of the entire life in ten year increments, and the stem and branch of the current year is the functional equivalent of a solar return. It requires only a short time to arrive at this overview; a skilled *Tzu P'ing* astrologer can begin a reading from the moment he or she writes the characters down.

I also learned that Chinese and Western astrologers examine the client through different lenses. Chinese fortune tellers work in the ancient tradition of the shaman, who intervened for the good of the community. Readings are often contextualized to include the extended family. The Chinese self is defined by its web of relationships; individuals raised in Asian cultures tend to be more concerned with how they can function more effectively as a group member. Those of us raised in a Western culture tend to have a stronger sense of personal autonomy and mobility; we are more likely to ask about how we can grow and develop as individuals. In Western culture, particularly America, relationships are voluntary and often ephemeral. There are no clear-cut answers to questions of what to do with one's life, because lives are not circumscribed by familial obligations; there is more freedom to chase opportunities than there is in the East. It is important to realize this when learning an Eastern system, because interpretations have been developed in the context of cultural values, and it is necessary to have at least a modest understanding of those values to give clients an accurate and useful reading.

Chinese Five-Element and Western astrological systems appear to be thoroughly different, but there are a number of important similarities at the core. For example, both systems identify correspondences between a higher "implicate order" and individual character; they are in basic agreement that one of the highest uses of astrology is to provide the client with information that leads to character development. The more traditionally-oriented Chinese client will expect the astrologer to do this in a prescriptive manner; however, a small number of professional astrologers have started to integrate Western psychological concepts with the traditional values of Chinese society in their counseling practice.

There is also substantial East-West agreement about the concept of time, particularly cyclic time as a universal structuring factor. Einstein once said, "Time is simply what the clock reads." For "clock," you can substitute any physical mechanism with a natural cycle, such as a pulse, the seasons, or a planetary cycle. Although the Chinese use measurement techniques different from ours, both systems can describe a given moment in time in detail.

This raises the important question of accuracy. To the technically-minded Western astrologer, *Tzu P'ing* may seem a rather crude instrument, indeed. Although the Western system of astrology requires more precise timing, it is unwise to use this as a yardstick by which to measure other systems.

I have serious doubts about whether any astrological tool—ancient or modern—can be considered "precise" in the modern scientific sense of the word, but I consider it essential to take a systems approach to any discussion of precision because in the final analysis, the need for accuracy in time and space is a relative concern. For example, I have personally sailed a small yacht across the Pacific Ocean several times, using sextant, chronometer and air navigation tables (HO 249) to determine my position. When you are looking for a small island in a vast expanse of water, it is a comforting feeling to see that speck of land appear on the horizon just where it is supposed to be.

While this process requires considerably more skill than does navigation with the latest electronic satellite tracking equipment (GPS), it pales in comparison to those navigators, ancient and modern, who determine their approximate location at sea from a bamboo gridmap, the heliacal rising of stars, and the size and direction of the sea wave under their canoe. In each case, the navigation "system" provides the user with correct information, relative to the input data. It is arguable that the *Tzu P'ing* calculation system, using the combination of "double hour" and "local space," is ideally suited to the level of precision attainable by its users. For example, some of my clients have told me that their mother came in from working in the fields to give birth, and the double hour was the greatest accuracy possible under the circumstances.

To dispute the validity of *Tzu P'ing* on the criterion of imprecision is to miss the point entirely: it doesn't have to be a tool of the stars and planets to give an explicit and reliable character interpretation, or an accurate forecast of events. The system gives excellent results without the aid of computers and chronometers because of the tolerances in the system, and the fact that you won't find many of these high-tech items in rural China, even today.

In my experience as a Western astrologer, about four clients in ten will know (or have access to) their birthtime to the minute. (Then we have to trust that the clock was showing the correct time, and those in attendance recorded it accurately.) Another three in ten will know their birthtime to the half-hour, and there will be two that only know that it was morning, afternoon, evening, or between midnight and dawn. One in ten either does not know the birthtime at all, or there is no record of the event. Given the likelihood that half of your clients are providing rough or inaccurate input data, do the tolerances in the system increase or decrease the chances of an accurate reading? How often do you begin a reading with rectification questions?

These figures have been significantly different for my Chinese clients. Less than two in ten know their precise birthtime, but at least six in ten know their birthtime to the double hour. To the Chinese astrologer, that is enough; *Tzu P'ing*'s long-standing popularity is due in part to the fact that it does not require a precise birth moment or knowledge of coordinates to calculate a birth or event chart.

To elaborate on the problem of place, China spreads across 2,700 miles, roughly 45° of the eastern portion of the globe; however, 95 percent of her population is contained within 1,200 miles, or 20° of longitude, from the Eastern offshore islands to the foothills of the Tibetan plateau. Most *Tzu P'ing* astrologers deny that time zone calculations are necessary to calculate a chart, claiming that the date is whatever the local calendar reads. Theoretically, the date and time present the greatest potential problem of accuracy when the location is other-than-China: the date because of the International Date Line (IDL), and the time because the time stem is determined from the relationship between the Day Master (date stem) and the time branch. This issue is raised here because some authors (cf. Sherrill & Chu, 1977, p. 74) have challenged the theoretical foundations of *Tzu P'ing*, and recommended calculating for the meridian of the time zone and adjusting to match the ST of the zone (120° E is the Chinese "Prime Meridian").

My approach is strictly empirical: which practice produces the most accurate chart? Fortunately, there is a way to test this, and the differences in outcome are significant. Because of the alternation of Yin and Yang, not only are three out of eight characters directly affected by a change of day, *every relationship in the structure changes*, because one of the three characters is the date stem, or "Day Master." This not only changes the essential character of the chart, it also changes the timing and interpretation of progressions and solar returns. A *Tzu P'ing* interpretation of the charts of famous non-Chinese historical and contemporary personalities born in the Americas and Western Europe demonstrate the effectiveness of this local space system. An analysis of President Clinton's eight-character structure will be used to illustrate.

Beyond the apparent technical differences, the contrast between the Chinese and Western horoscope systems can be reduced to a few general arguments:

• *They are based on different cosmologies, primary archetypes, and symbols.* What has evolved in the Western cultural tradition has nothing in common with the Chinese cultural tradition. The symbolic associations of Western astrology come primarily from Greek mythology. They have archetypal meanings which are alien to the Chinese psyche, perennialist philosophy notwithstanding. The structuring principles and symbols that delineate the Chinese understanding of the cosmos is clearly expressed in the *I Ching*. Although there are some Chinese myths, an elaborate mythic structure doesn't play a vital role in expressing cultural archetypes, as it does in the West.

• *They reflect important differences in psychological and cultural orientation.* Chinese astrological systems provide highly accurate, but in most cases less detailed information about character than do Western systems. This is because in the Chinese culture, individual personality is deemed unimportant, *except in the context of relationships.* The notion of a collective identity overshadowing the individual is a common feature of all Asian cultures, and runs contrary to the individualistic nature of Western society, which has its roots in Greek civilization. The web of familial relationships and how the client interacts with them is a primary consideration in a reading, because lives are more circumscribed by obligations and there is generally less freedom to chase opportunities than there is in the West, where individuals have a stronger sense of personal autonomy and mobility, and the bonds of relationship are more easily broken.

• *They use different systems to represent the passage of time.* The Western year is of fixed length, varying by only one day every four years; the length of each Chinese year varies considerably. This structural difference presents a real challenge for the Western novice, because of anomalies in the lunar system and the necessity of learning a minimum of 32 Chinese characters to obtain data directly from the ephemeris, euphemistically known as the "Ten Thousand Year Calendar" *(Wan Nien Li).* Once the process is mastered, however, there are no further calculations necessary to produce the four pillars, which form the basis of the interpretation. Several Western authors have attempted to develop a process using tables and procedures to circumvent the ephemeris problem; however, these have the simplicity of an IRS form. Such calculations typically result in considerable frustration and a roaring headache, discouraging all but the most motivated students.

• *They have different understandings of the meaning and value of personal integration.* In the West, much emphasis is placed on healthy ego development. The Sun in its natal and progressed signs is related to the concept of individuation and the hero's journey. It is considered to be a major determinant of our life goals and our ability to achieve them. In Asian culture, it is exactly the opposite: the Sun represents your *weakness*, because it is already a strong part of character, and can easily create an imbalance that results in narcissism or too much self-orientation and attachment to personality. Chinese people are not encouraged to "become all that your Sun sign promises," or "do your own thing"; that's considered to be the worst possible thing for society. They devise strategies to moderate the Sun sign, because the goal is to not to be unique, but to become more adapted and useful to one's society. In fact, one's birth month (the equivalent of the Sun sign) is considered the worst time of year, because in Chinese Five-Element astrology, *the month is what makes one weak or strong.*

Perhaps the most common misconception about Chinese astrology is the notion that the animal signs themselves represent character types. This misunderstanding began two centuries ago in Ch'ing dynasty China, when authors of vernacular literature used the animals to create personality sketches in works of fiction that could be easily recognized by the common reader. As part of the technical philosophies, astrology was the realm of scholars, but astrological folklore circulated among the common folk in both cities and rural villages. This popular knowledge eventually migrated to the West via the mass market press and restaurant placemats. It has since become the basis for many books on Chinese astrology, whose authors have created an elaborate mythology around the twelve animals as descriptors of character. This in itself is harmless, except that Western readers take it for the genuine article.

Food awareness provides a useful analogy. Earlier this century, the average Westerner had little knowledge or experience of the rich variety of regional Chinese dishes. What they knew about Chinese food was Chop Suey, fast food prepared for the Western palate. Chop Suey gradually disappeared from Chinese restaurant menus as Western people developed more sophistication in the fine art of Chinese cuisine.

Although we cannot know precisely how and when the Chinese first developed the theory of the twelve animal signs (also known as branches), we do know that it is an integral part of a fully functioning calendric and predictive system today, one which has been verified by experience for many centuries. No professional Chinese astrologer would dream of reading someone's character from a single animal sign, particularly the animal representing the *year of birth* (year branch), which has very limited interpretive value in isolation from the eight-character structure. The year branch must be understood and interpreted in relation to the seven other characters in the chart, particularly the "Day Master" *(Zu Chu)*, the stem of the date pillar. (Stems and branches will be explained in detail later.)

Also, there is a "hierarchy of strength" in the eight characters—just as, for example, in a Western chart, an angular planet in its dignity is generally considered to be stronger than a planet in detriment in a cadent house. Physical proximity of a stem or branch to the Day Master in the eight-character structure is one important criterion of relative strength, which means that the month pillar is the most powerful, then the hour pillar; *the year pillar, particularly the animal sign (i.e., the branch), has the least influence.* It refers to one's female ancestors, and when used for purposes of chart comparison, it is the determinant of how the *families* of the couple will get along.

Another commonly held misconception is that direct correlations may be made between Chinese animal signs and Western Sun signs—e.g., Dragon is like Aries. While there is no basis whatsoever for such a connection, there is a practical way to understand the actual relationship that exists between a Chinese month and a Sun sign. Master Lo devised this simple technique, which combines ancient Western rulerships with a step in Five-Element astrology analysis traditionally used to identify a special type of relationship between the four branches in an eight-character structure.

Certain pairs of animal signs share a common rulership—for example, Dragon and Rooster. As we can see from the Table 1 (page 108), they correspond to Libra and Taurus, both ruled by Venus. This planetary co-ruler is the link between the Sun sign and the Chinese month—*minus 15 days.* If you are born in a Dragon month, your Sun is in the opposite sign of Taurus. However, it is not correct to say that Dragon energy is like Taurus (or Leo, or anything else).

There are primary and secondary sources of these misconceptions. A primary source is the Chinese language itself, which is very subtle and (like the puns or poetry of most languages) does not always translate easily into English. Chinese is a tonal language—each character may be

Table 1. Rulerships

♌ Horse—☉	☽—Sheep ♋
♍ Snake—☿	—Monkey ♊
♎ Dragon—♀	—Rooster ♉
♏ Rabbit—♂	—Dog ♈
♐ Tiger—♃	—Pig ♓
♑ Ox—♄	—Rat ♒

pronounced four different ways—which produces four different words, some with as many as twenty shades of meaning, depending on context. This makes the Chinese language a comfortable container for paradoxical statements. For example, a Zen master might say, "Tell me, is Chinese astrology any more than an endless parade of animals? If you say it is, you are wrong. If you say it is not, you don't comprehend the system. *What will you say?* Speak!" For centuries, such subtle, enigmatic verbal challenges have awakened Rinzai Zen monks to the oneness of the phenomenal world and the essential world.

This subtle quality also makes the language vulnerable to both mistranslation and to missing the intended meaning; astrological interpretation is particularly vulnerable, because it requires the use of language at the highest metaphoric level. This vulnerability is amplified by changes to the written language which have occurred over the centuries—to the point where very few Chinese people can read a text in classical script, which is as different from modern Mandarin as Old High German is from English.

The suggestive nature of the Chinese language no doubt helped in the development of such elegant interlocking theoretical structures as Five-Element theory; however, elasticity of keywords has left ample room for authors of popular Chinese astrology texts to freely interpret what is written and lift pieces out of their traditional context. With no grounding in the principles upon which the Chinese system is built, some have created their own simplified versions and presented it as an entire system. Others have created syncretized versions, combining aspects of Western astrology and psychology with Chinese animal signs in an attempt make it more understandable to Western readers.

Adrift from its holistic moorings, the power of Chinese astrology cannot be fully understood and appreciated; it becomes a mere consumer commodity. Some Chinese astrology books by Western authors are collections of useless facts and anecdotes, others are opinions not backed with careful research and field work. Chinese astrology is a living tradition; if it is to be understood in light of its own categories and values, it is necessary to know what still has currency *with the Chinese practitioners themselves.*

THE BALANCE
BETWEEN COMPETING FORCES

The concept of fate *(ming)* has been part of the Chinese worldview for all of recorded history, and in the late 20th century it continues to be a powerful influence on attitudes, values, and behaviors at every level of Chinese society. Of the many differences between Chinese and Western culture, I consider the attitude toward fate to be one of the most striking and profound. The master of Beijing Opera in the film, "Farewell, My Concubine" stated the Chinese position powerfully when addressing his students:

> "The opera ... tells the story of the struggle between the Chu and Han kings. What sort of man was the King of Chu? A peerless and invincible hero. A bold and resourceful general capable of defeating vast armies. But fate wasn't on his side; at Gai Xia he was outwitted by the Han king.
>
> "As they prepared for battle, Han troops sang victory songs which carried on the wind and echoed through the valley. Fearing the rest of their land was already conquered, the Chu warriors fled in a great panic. Even the king was weeping.
>
> "There is a lesson in this story for all of us: no matter how resourceful you are, you can not fight fate. The king had once been all powerful, but in the end all he had left was one woman and one horse. He tried to get his steed to run away, but it wouldn't go. He wanted the concubine to flee, but she stayed, too. For the very last time, concubine Yü poured wine for the king and danced for him with a sword, then cut her throat with it ... faithful to the king even unto death."

Tzu P'ing astrologer Michael Lin has written several books on astrology and divination, and writes a regular column for a Taiwan newspaper; one afternoon over tea, he discussed with me his personal understanding of fate, and the astrologer's role in interpreting it for clients:

> "There are five different planes or dimensions of existence: the first dimension is like a straight line, on which one can only go forward or backward. It is not possible to turn or cross over. The second dimension is a plane, like the ant's world. In this reality, we are contained to the surface of experience, it is not possible to jump or fly, only to move on one level.
>
> "Most of us live in the third dimension; we can sense, feel, express, organize, think, make plans, fly from San Francisco to Taipei, etc. Most psychologists work on the third dimension, at the head level; however, when people really connect, it is on an energetic *(ch'i)* level. On this level, things are mainly subjective; we use our heads to evaluate, make decisions with the rational mind. It is a third dimension tendency to say, 'Why do I have to experience this? I give it my best and I still don't succeed.'
>
> "The fourth dimension is 'value free'; there are no socially imposed values or conditions. Many things appear to be in conflict on the third dimension, but once we take it to a higher plane, the conflict is eliminated. On this plane, we step outside of life. The concept of time is different, it's a bridge between the third and fifth dimensions. Past, present and future can be discerned; whatever the fortune, we can understand what's coming and prepare for it. Here, we can understand our karmic mission, and know the working of *Tao*.
>
> "The fifth dimension is not a world we are familiar with; it is eternal time, and holds the key to our life purpose. From this higher order, we act on past karma; maybe we have a strong attraction to someone, a love or hate relationship with a parent, a partner, or a good friend. People with an 'active third eye' can see this; however, these things can be explained on the fourth dimension.
>
> "Through an understanding of the nature of each moment of time you can evaluate any relationship. The principles

are expressed in *I Ching*; political and strategic astrology are based on *Tao, Yin-Yang,* and Five-Element theory. This is because *Tao reveals the correct time for everything.* This is my consulting style, to reach into the higher plane and offer the client a philosophical explanation that helps to put his or her experience into karmic perspective, because understanding what happens on the fourth dimension can help us to be more effective on the third.

"Reality can best be bridged through a fourth dimension system; the key question is, how can we use this fourth dimension intelligence to resolve a fifth dimension past life problem and bring happiness to this life? This is what people in the West come to a psychologist for. Chinese people come to an astrologer. The New Age movement spends energy exploring the mind and spirit connection, but it is overly theoretical and the focus seems too far away from real life. Transpersonal psychology is exploring the fourth dimension, but Western ethics may be different, there are different expectations around the nature of the client relationship."

What influences the Chinese attitude toward fate? Based on our experience, we adopt one of two views of the world: either the control over our individual lives resides within us, or with some external force outside of us. In psychological terms, this axis is known as the "locus of control"; both individuals and cultures can be measured on this axis. By emphasizing individual responsibility, Western culture makes strong connections between ability, effort, and social success. From the Western perspective of a moderate internal locus of control, it is considered reasonable to say, "I am the captain of my fate. When things go wrong in my life, it is for a reason: there is a lesson that I must learn to move toward wholeness." At the extreme end of the continuum, the mentalists and hard-core New-Agers make narcissistic assertions that the only limitations on human potential are mind-imposed, that each individual has the ability to create his or her own reality.

Clearly, the Chinese believe that *there are other factors in the equation,* particularly in the interpersonal sphere, over which we have little control. When things go wrong, they are more attuned to the possibility that the reason is "out there," with external forces in the cosmos or the culture that hold power over their self-determination. With regard to cosmic forces, chance and luck are mirrored in the eight-character structure; they are allotted according to individual destiny.

The Buddhist term *yuan* means fate or predestination. *Yuan* serves a protective function by explaining away negative interactions with others, since the individual does not blame himself or herself for the outcome. By providing an external explanation for any unexpected outcome, whether it is considered highly fortunate or disastrous, *yuan* protects Chinese people from intense feelings of elation or regret.

For most Chinese, cultural and social forces are very influential in determining the outcome of events. Tight classroom control, heavy family responsibilities and stern political authority are the social realities. This is particularly true in modern mainland China, where most people are held firmly in place by strict administrative controls, and subject to the whim of bureaucrats. Further, an individual is not defined apart from his or her family or birthplace; each is part of a complex web of rules, obligations and expectations. Chinese children are taught to suppress their feelings in the interests of social harmony. The culture actively discourages social risk taking—in fact, to the Chinese, Saturn ($\hbar$) is the best planet, because of the high value placed on social order and hierarchy. Individuals have little personal control over destiny unless they occupy a social position of considerable power.

How are fate and freedom connected? To a greater or lesser extent, cultural conditioning dictates our individual response to this question. At the level of the individual, we choose between either "tempting fate" by acting on powerful impulses that come to our conscious mind, or suppressing them. Regardless of cultural sanctions, there is a third possibility that comes with self-cultivation—to accept the fated nature of an experience, but to understand it as an opportunity to exercise a moral choice. Self-cultivation is a process through which we come to understand our personal "Mandate of Heaven," and learn to accept changes in fortune, for better or worse, with equanimity. In the Chinese culture, the process of balancing and harmonizing elements is considered to be the very essence of spiritual practice. Accordingly, professional Chinese astrologers are likely to encourage "spirit practice" *(shou tao)* when a client's fortune is ebbing. The task is to moderate character, to transform the stone into jade.

The philosophical foundations of the great Eastern traditions—Confucian, Buddhist, and Taoist—offer different insights into how to deal with fate; for Confucians, it is perfection of *li*, maintaining perfect harmony with surroundings. For Buddhists, fate is *karma*, and its effects are overcome by accumulating merit through wisdom and compassion.

The Confucian philosophy is akin to the ancient Greek Stoics: to be happy, one must understand fate and be willing to work with it—simply do their best, and not be upset by the consequences. There is an awareness of the impersonal nature of the cosmos, and of the need to humbly and quietly make adjustments to relationships and lifestyle in order to cope with changes in circumstances. Michael Lin says of this, "Confucian values are third dimension; in peaceful times, the socially imposed values and conditions of Confucianism dominate our lives. It is a philosophy of order and stability. In good periods, many of the intelligentsia are Confucian, and work within the system; however, in hard times, when government is repressive, when disorder comes, a different ethic takes over, a more spiritual, change-oriented Taoist philosophy. The two systems compensate for each other."

Taoists emphasize personal freedom, believing that freedom from the bondage of fate comes from abandoning material ambitions and seeking to understand both inner and outer worlds. The ideal is a state of equanimity and inner contentment with whatever our circumstances happen to be. From the Taoist point of view, there is an essential unity between man and the various forces of nature. Living in accord with Tao therefore means *embracing simplicity*, and not having egoic attachment to the fruits of one's actions. How does one achieve this state? Taoists believe that the union of Heaven and Earth produced mind, which is the essence of humanity. Our minds are a composite of Heaven and Earth, the Divine and the animal nature, and in this mix there is always a struggle. The mind struggles in one direction and then in another; it holds one attitude and then another, and does not even recognize the conflict. The result of the struggle is loss of peace.

When this struggle is resolved, it is like living in the center of the cyclone. Establishing a quiet zone within consciousness gives a strange sense of fulfilling by non-action, and stress drops away. Every problem that demands solution is considered, and yet there is no strain, no internal dialogue, because there is no longer conflict between what is desired and what is required. When that pressure is gone, the total expenditure of energy is infinitely reduced, not only in the action, but in coping with the reaction from it. There is complete efficiency, because everything is ruled by consciousness, and not by ulterior motives, which inevitably lead to complication.

This does not mean that a Taoist adept becomes withdrawn and anti-social; rather, it means that everything that he or she does is moved by quietude within, rather than by stress or urgency. All actions are performed with complete and total disregard for the personal equations that make action happy or unhappy. Everything is done directly, with a full sense of security. These individuals know that as long as they act in this manner, they will not suffer, because when the elements work in harmony and external forces cooperate, then success is predicted; *the degree of success can be determined by the nature of the interaction of elements.*

Astrology and divination practices were therefore resonant with all of the great Eastern religious traditions. The role of of these technical philosophies was firmly established as a way to help individuals realize their true place in the cosmos, and live in proper balance and harmony between Heaven and Earth.

AT ONE WITH THE NATURAL ORDER OF THINGS

All phenomena can shrink to ten characters (stems) and expand to infinity, to fill the universe.

—Michael Lin

Chinese astrological systems, like those of the West, are based on an understanding of the created universe as an organic whole, unfolding in space and time. Because there is no absolute separation between events and objects in the space-time continuum, human consciousness and experience is entwined in co-evolutionary development with the natural world and all other parts of the cosmos. The changing relationships between its component parts create cyclic patterns, which can be observed and measured.

The monad *(T'ai Chi T'u)* represents the metaphysical principle of unity-in-duality in a world of opposites. This primary symbol of wholeness is composed of *Yin* and *Yang*, described by Chuang Tzu as "The Two Powers of Nature." They represent the polar aspects of all interrelated phenomena. The alternation of these two forces *produces* the processes of nature and the entire universe, visible and invisible. The great sages called the Yang force the movement of the Heavens, and the Yin force those energies generated within and by the Earth. From observation and intuition, they came to believe that these forces exerted an influence on the earth and all terrestrial life. The Heavenly forces were given the symbolic names Wood, Fire, Earth, Metal and Water.

These five forces came to be known as Elements *(shin)*. This unfortunate choice of word is actually meant to describe *a system of correspondences based on movement*, and does not reveal the dynamic character that was implicit in ancient usage. However, a more meaningful translation of *shin*, taken from ancient classical texts, is "crossroads" (Matsumoto, 1973), a term which implies energetic coordinates, and provides a deeper and more useful understanding of the interactive nature of these forces. Like the planets in Western astrology, the elements also represent energy in the psyche.

What have been known since earliest times as the Five Cardinal Points are the Four Directions (East, South, West and North), and the Center. The Chinese correlated the four compass points to the four seasons *at least four thousand years ago*. See figure 1.

Only the element of Earth has no specific direction or season. The problem of how a fifth element can be integrated into an obviously four-season year is resolved by *Tzu P'ing* astrologers by considering Earth to be an interactive element. Through the self-renewing power of the center, the stabilizing and harmonizing influence of Earth mediates the change between each of the seasonal energy states at the four transition times of the year. The four directional elements appear twice each year, earth signs appear four times, as shown in figure 2 (page 117). (Numbers represent months; the first month of the lunar year is Tiger, representing the beginning of Spring, the element Wood, and the Eastern direction.)

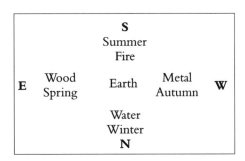

Figure 1. Relationship of Elements, Directions and Seasons.

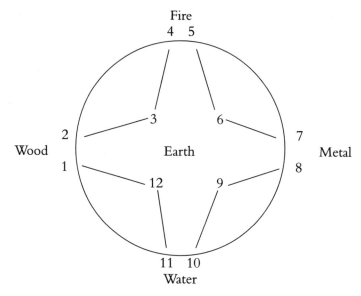

Figure 2. The four directional elements.

Visualizing the Earth element as a container for other elements helps to understand its role and function in the seasonal cycle: the composition of Earth is rocks and soil. Some rocks contain metallic deposits; some soils have plant or vegetal matter (Wood) within. Fire in the earth is volcanic, and Water in the earth is damp soil and mud.

The foundation of the Five-Element theory is the production or generating sequence, so-called because in this clockwise order, beginning at any point on the cycle, the elements "produce" or nourish each other. It is a beneficial (Sheng) cycle, a "parenting" function, which promotes life and growth.

Wood gives birth to Fire; through the burning process Fire, the mother of Earth, produces ash (and fiery lava, which coagulates into rock). Earth is the primary source of Metal, which melts and becomes a liquid. Metal "nourishes" Water (mineral-rich water provides essential nutrients). Seeds and tender shoots nourished by liquids grow into Wood.

It is important to note that if Wood "gives birth" to Fire, it means that the *potentiality of Fire is in the Wood itself*; likewise, if Fire gives birth to Earth, the potentiality of Earth is in the Fire, etc. Therefore, the five elements are not five separate and distinct things, but a *single cosmic force, differentiated into five appearances by time and space.*

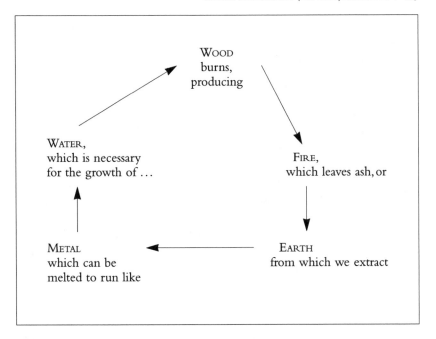

Figure 3. The Elemental Cycle.

Five Elements can be divided into two halves. Metal and Water represent Yin; they are energies which are intense and withdrawing, cold and wet. Wood and Fire represent Yang. They are the energy which is expanding and enthusiastic, growth oriented and warm. Earth stands between these two extremes. Those who were born in Autumn and Winter have more Yin energy, and those who were born in Spring and Summer have more Yang energy. Between seasons, those who were born in March, June, September and December of the Chinese calendar year acquire their energy from Earth.

If we choose the element Wood as a way to examine the nature of elemental relationships, we can see that five different relationships are possible, including Wood's relationship to itself. Each of these five relationships has its own unique quality. It is logical that the relationship illustrated in the "production sequence" in figure 3. Water to Wood, *adds* energy to the Wood; so does the same element relationship, Wood to Wood. To varying degrees, any other relationship *takes* energy from the Wood (Fire burns it, Metal chops it; Wood can control Earth, but it requires much energy to do so).

The presence of certain elements in a chart and the nature of their relationships to each other will determine their function in the psyche and character of an individual. However, an element cannot be accurately described without reference to its gender, which is an essential factor in determining the quality of each elemental relationship. For example, a comparison of Yang and Yin Wood shows that they have quite different characteristics:

Chia (lit. the first) is the Chinese word that represents Yang Wood, a large tree. The characteristics ascribed to Yang Wood *(Chia)* are kindhearted and virtuous; moderate and conservative; calm outside but firm and resolute inside (unyielding); sensible but suspicious, good at planning, and fond of money. In relationship to other elements in an eight-character structure, *Chia* needs to be carved and chiseled by Metal in order to become useful and effective (i.e., it is strong, so it needs to give away its energy to something stronger in order to balance). The best kind of Metal for this purpose is Yang Metal, *Geng*, which represents cutting tools, such as a knife or axe.

Yi (lit. the second) represents Yin Wood, such as parasitic fungus, orchid, wicker and rattan. Its character is gentle and delicate; clever and tolerant; stubborn, but flexible. Because Yin Wood does not have a firm and strong trunk, it cannot be carved or chiseled by sharp knives or axes. Like the grasses on the prairie, it only requires water and sunlight in order to flourish, so in relationship to other elements in an eight-character structure, it needs Yang Fire, *Bing* (sunshine), and Yin Water, *Kwei* (nourishing raindrops and dew). Note the difference: Yang Wood benefits from *giving* (to Metal), Yin Wood benefits from *receiving* (from Yang Fire and Yin Water).

No single element, regardless of gender, can be called the strongest or weakest; can you say that the cat is stronger than the dog? Linked by a complex chain of cause and effect, each has its own place and function.

BASICS OF THE SYSTEM

A *Tzu P'ing* birth chart is made up of eight characters *(ba tze)*, two for each category of year, month, day and time, reading right to left. These are found in the Chinese ephemeris *(Wan Nien Li)*. The interplay of these eight symbols form the basis of a character analysis; to return to the ancient concept of element as "crossroad," each relationship in the four pillars can be expressed as a facet of an individual's character, an interplay of energies that produces the complexity inherent in the human psyche. As a natal or event "chart," it has a deceptively simple appearance when compared with a Western horoscope. Reading right to left, as do the Chinese—

TIME	DATE	MONTH	YEAR	
庚	乙	丙	丙	STEMS
辰	丑	申	戌	BRANCHES

• The first column (year) is the "root" *(gen)* of the chart. It is about one's ancestors, particularly grandparents, and the general (larger) environment.

• The second column (month) is the "sprout" *(miao)*—your parents, family, and immediate environment.

• The third column (day) is the "blossom" *(hua)*, which represents your partner or spouse; the reference is to one's generative potential.

• The fourth column (hour) is the "fruit" *(guo)*. Children and career are fruit, both things you are involved in creating (they are the seeds of the future).

Each of the four "pillars" has a stem above and a branch below. The stem represents one element only; the branch may "contain" from one to three elements, in varying proportions.

The dominant element in all Chinese animal signs comes from their *direction* (e.g., Tiger is Wood because it is located in the East). To use a Western astrological analogy, "Cardinal" signs at the beginning of a season (analogous to Tiger, Snake, Monkey, Pig) contain two elements, one for direction, the other for the trine to the "pure" element. The sign at the height of each season (Rabbit, Horse, Rooster, Rat) is "Fixed," and contains only the element of the direction. "Mutable" signs occur at the end of each season (Dragon, Sheep, Dog, Ox) and contain three elements: Earth, along with the directional element, and a small amount of the trine to the pure element. Because each elemental relationship adds shades of subtlety to the reading, Chinese astrologers express different opinions over the amount of each element contained in the branches, just as Western astrologers will occasionally dispute the width of an orb of influence between two planets in aspect.

Think of characters on the bottom row (branches) as material substance, and those on the top row (stems) as energy, or spirit. The energy above requires a resource base below to be utilized. Also, the presence of special relationships between branches can alter the content of the bottom row, with the potential effect of either strengthening or weakening the overall chart. These special relationships between branches may be simply alliances that strengthen a single element, or they may involve an alchemical transformation to a third element.

Within the four pillars, the date stem (top of the date pillar) is said to represent one's "fate." Known as the "Day Master" (*Zu Chu*), it is the pivot of the chart, to which the astrologer will frequently refer throughout the reading. The Day Master represents the ego, the authentic self; it is the life force, the source of capability. One is said to *belong to* the element of the Day Master, which forms paired relationships with the seven other characters in the structure, each with its own significance.

The relationship between each pair can be only one of ten possible combinations, illustrated below. Each of these ten energetic relationships has a Chinese name, but they can also be expressed symbolically, since their meanings are *roughly* equivalent to those ascribed to the planets by a consensus of Western astrologers.

Master Lo used her growing knowledge of Western astrology to develop many innovative teaching techniques. These do not in any way combine the two systems, but they certainly make learning the Chinese system much easier for anyone with a background in Western astrology. Together, we have spent many months working out planetary correlations with elemental relationships so that they would be more illuminating than confusing. It is essential to understand that *there are no straight, one-to-one correlations*; just as Western sun signs and Chinese animal signs cannot be properly aligned, there always seems to be a twist on the Chinese meaning that makes the description around 10–20 percent out of alignment. However, the planets serve quite effectively as a guidance technique and a memory aid. As an example, figure 4 shows all possible relationships of President Clinton's Yin Wood Day Master to other Yin and Yang elements.

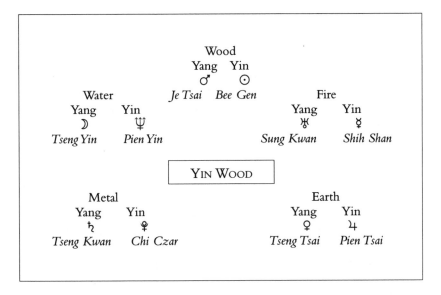

Figure 4. President Clinton's Yin Wood Day Master.

Two significant words among these are *tseng* and *pien*; *tseng* denotes a mild and stable personality, so planet symbols are used to represent *tseng* characteristics that suggest mildness or stability, reflecting a "normal," balanced (i.e., *Yin/Yang*) relationship; *pien* means not ordinary: a more intense, active, serious, strong personality, with a potential for excess. For *pien* relationships, we used planet symbols that suggest unbalanced, abnormal or extreme situations (*Yang/Yang* or *Yin/Yin*). Bear in mind that what is considered to be a "normal" relationship comes from the Chinese, not the Western cultural perspective.

While ability to understand how the system works is not culturally dependent, there is a certain "spirit" of a *Tzu P'ing* reading. The ability to describe what is seen in an accurate, yet poetic way depends largely on one's depth of understanding of the interplay of cosmic and terrestrial forces. For instance, the Taoist perspective on spirit and matter is helpful for understanding the interplay of the top and bottom lines. Lao Tze believed that spirit was a mysterious active agent that held the body together, made it alive, manifested through it and was endowed with all the potential or power necessary for the attainment of the a harmonious life. This spirit, operating upon and through body, produced what we call the human character, for character is nothing but the relationship of spirit to the instrument through which it must function. A person of good character is therefore one in whom harmony between body and consciousness (*yin* and *yang*) is evident.

All the different states of human intelligence may be determined simply as relations between spirit and matter in their operations in the human organism. If there is lack of order, adjustment, and harmony between body and spirit, then the person is less good, his or her works are less virtuous, happiness is less consistent, and illnesses of the body increase. The ancients believed that every type of energy is born of a corresponding type of relationship established and fulfilled. The greater the fulfillment, the greater the energy generated.

You will see how these principles apply in the following reading of President Clinton's eight-character structure. I am aware that this analysis is far from poetic, but my main purpose is to demonstrate the way in which the *Tzu P'ing* astrologer is able to extract an abundance of good information from what appears to be a very meager amount of data. Before beginning the analysis, I should mention that there are many tools in the Chinese astrologer's kit, some that have a Western counterpart, such as progressions and solar returns. With far more techniques to a full eight-character structure analysis than the scope of this paper permits me to cover, it is not possible to present a full explanation of all the steps used to obtain chart information.

SAMPLE CHART: PRESIDENT BILL CLINTON

President Clinton's chart is calculated for August 19, 1946, 7–9 A.M., LMT, which corresponds to the 23rd day of the seventh lunar month, hour of the Dragon. Figure 5 shows the eight characters the astrologer locates in the ephemeris and writes down.

GAINING AN OVERVIEW OF THE CHART:
STRONG OR WEAK, YIN OR YANG, BALANCE

1. IS HE STRONG OR WEAK?

The single most important determination in any analysis of an eight-character structure is whether the chart is strong or weak. It is essential

TIME	DATE	MONTH	YEAR	
庚	乙	丙	丙	STEMS
辰	丑	申	戌	BRANCHES

This is what the astrologer "sees" within those characters:

TIME	DATE	MONTH	YEAR	
Yang Metal	Yin Wood	Yang Fire	Yang Fire	(STEMS)
♄		♅	♅	(Relationship to Day Master)
Dragon	*Ox*	*Monkey*	*Dog*	(BRANCHES)
Yang Earth	Yin Earth	Yang Metal	Yang Earth	(Dominant Element)
♀	♃	♄	♀	(Relationship to Day Master)
Wood/Water	Water/Metal	Water	Metal/Fire	(Other Elements Within Branch)
♂ ☽	♆ ♀	☽	♄ ♅	(Their Relationship to Day Master)

Figure 5. President Clinton's Chart.

to establish this first, because it becomes the foundation of all further interpretation. There are shades of strong and weak; generally, neither too weak nor too strong is best, because it means there is balance between the individual and the environment. Too weak means no positive relationships can be found within the chart; too strong means there is no outlet for the Day Master's energy. This may be easy or difficult to determine, depending on the chart in question; in Mr. Clinton's case, it is complex and difficult.

President Clinton "belongs to" the element Wood; all relationships between his Yin Wood Day Master and other stems and branches must be carefully examined. The first indication that Clinton's Day Master is not strong is the fact that it has no substantial "roots" (note that among the branches there is only a very small amount of Wood—a *Je Tsai* (♂) relationship from within the Dragon on the time stem).

The month and date of birth have the strongest influence on character, so the most significant factor in the eight-character structure is the relationship between the date stem and the month branch. The month pillar represents family of origin and relative ability to cope with the immediate environment—is he overwhelmed by it, does he handle responsibilities with ease, or somewhere in between? The month branch-to-Day Master relationship counts for 60 percent[1] of the main character type; therefore, we can provisionally say that Mr. Clinton is mainly *Tseng Kwan*, (lit., genuine, legitimate/official), represented by the glyph for the planet Saturn ($\hbar$). This is determined by noting that Metal controls or dominates Wood; since Wood is the ego, it is therefore weakened because the Metal (environment) takes energy from it. We also notice that it is an opposite gender relationship (Yin Day Master with a Yang month branch), which is considered a milder, less intense kind of relationship than same gender.

The character of *Tseng Kwan* is considered to be the best in China; it is thought to be ideal for government officials. Responsible and disciplined, with an aptitude for leadership and the ability to turn ideals into practical goals, this character tends to be strict with himself but generous to others. For example, in the aftermath of the 1968 Washington, D.C. riots, a young Clinton pasted a Red Cross on the side of his white Buick and ferried groceries to people in riot-torn areas.

Tseng Kwans have a healthy respect for tradition and an innate understanding of propriety. They are neither arrogant nor obsequious, but have a kind of gentility—modest and polite, with regard for formal rank and status. Mr. Clinton has consistently demonstrated that he can display the dignity of office, and maintain his self-control under fire. *Tseng Kwans* consider a good reputation very important; they will show due respect to parents and superiors, and deference to authority. They are usually cautious and prudent, valuing gradual progress over radical change; they tend to think in conventional ways.

Tseng Kwan ($\hbar$) on Mr. Clinton's month branch cannot be called a supportive relationship to his Day Master, which means his overall energy is not strong. However, because he can draw energy from other elements in the structure, a careful analysis is necessary to confirm this early hypothesis. His *Tseng Kwan* ($\hbar$) gains additional strength because it is also the relationship between the time stem and the Day Master, and Monkey is the "fourth step" of Metal (steps will be explained later in the analysis). This adds to his fitness for government service, indicating that he was raised in an environment that prepared him, through dedication and hard work, for great career achievement. High position comes to

---

[1]This is an average of Chinese astrological opinion; the amount of influence ranges from 50 percent to as much as 80 percent.

Bill Clinton with relative ease because of the harmonizing relationship between his Yang Metal month branch and Yin Wood Day Master. His election success in 1992 was considered by *Newsweek* to be an "abrupt, improbable rise to power."

As you may recall, a Yin Wood (grass) Day Master benefits from receiving—sunshine from Yang Fire and raindrops and dew from Yin Water. Clinton does not handle large amounts of responsibility with ease because his Day Master is not strong; his ongoing success is made possible by the small amounts of Water hidden in the branches that nurture the Day Master (notice that all of his branches contain more than one element). His Water cannot be considered strong either, because it does not show on the stems (i.e., there is no Water in the Heavens, it is a cloudless sky).

Recall that the branches represent matter, substance; in Clinton's chart, every single relationship from a branch saps the Day Master's strength. The element of Earth dominates the branches; if he had lots of Earth in his Western chart, it would be considered a grounding influence, adding to his stability and reliability; in a Chinese chart, the element *only has meaning in the context of its relationship to the Day Master*, and the relationship of the Earth element to Yin Wood is ♀ *(Tseng Tsai)* and ♃ *(Pien Tsai)*. Tsai planets are full of desire, they are major destabilizing influences. ♄ *(Tseng Kwan)* represents fame, ♀ and ♃ both represent wealth *(Tsai);* Mr. Clinton burns up lots of energy striving for fame and wealth.

To the Chinese, "wealth" *(Tsai)* is money and women (plural). *Tseng Tsai* ♀ (lit., legitimate/possession, wealth) represents the wife; *Pien Tsai* ♃ (lit. illegitimate, on the side/possession) represents both monetary gains from speculation and lovers or concubines. *Pien Tsai* (♃) is also to do with generosity, but it does not imply any deep attachment. The Chinese believe that when ♃ comes to a man's "spouse house" (day branch) it means he will bring women to his bed, that he is likely to be more generous to a lover than to his wife. One of the cultural differences that must be noted is that the Chinese do not judge such behavior from a late 20th century Western feminist perspective; the social structure and the rules definitely favor men, and such behavior is considered normal for men of wealth and power. Some of the core concepts and much of the analogy and metaphor are based on assumptions of gender inequality. Note that in Clinton's eight-character structure there are distinctly two *Tseng Tsai* (♀) and one *Pien Tsai* (♃), which implies that he will have "concubines" or mistresses, or at least that he will experience many love affairs in his lifetime. Since this also means gains from speculation, it might also account for involvement in Whitewater, as well.

Allegations of poor character have been Clinton's political Achilles' heel. He was attacked on his character and the quality of his marriage by the opposition party in four gubernatorial races from 1984 to 1990. In 1985, he declined to make a bid for the presidency, claiming that his daughter Chelsea was too young to understand the media attacks. Accusations of marital infidelity surfaced early in the 1992 presidential campaign, including an alleged twelve-year affair with Gennifer Flowers; this led only to an admission that he had "caused pain in his marriage."

Mr. Clinton's chart suggests many opportunities to act on his abundant *Tsai* energy, even in a bad progression period; however, he cannot afford to risk having an affair. All of the *Tsai* ($\mathcal{Q}$, $\mathcal{2f}$) are "underground" (on the branches) and his $\hbar$ government position and high status forbid him to do anything openly that would violate American moral or social convention. The source of trouble is simply that he is not strong enough to handle this energy. According to Chinese cosmology, as soon as something reaches its extremity, it reverses its course. With a weak Day Master and an abundance of *Tsai* (wealth) planets, Mr. Clinton still may have strong desires, but they can only bring him trouble, because every time he acts on them he will get caught—sooner or later.

What are known as *empty branches* in the eight characters have an effect in the natal structure and solar return similar to, but stronger than, the Western concept of interception. Since there are twelve branches but only ten stems, in any chart there will be two "extra" animals that are not paired with a stem. These are found by starting from the date pillar (in this case, Yin Wood/Ox), and adding stems and branches in sequence, both directions from the date pillar.

Clinton's "empty branches," with no corresponding stems, are Dog and Pig (see figure 6). Each of the four pillars in the eight-character structure represents a field of experience, and with an empty year pillar (Dog on the year branch), Mr. Clinton lost direct contact with his paternal ancestry, his Clinton roots. The effect of the empty branch on his chart was to erase that part of his life. He never knew his own father; he was raised in early years by his maternal grandparents, who were poor Red River Valley farmers, while his mother went to back to school so she could support herself and her young son. Empty branches also affect

Figure 6. President Clinton's "empty branches."

our lives when they come in the Solar Return. After completing the natal analysis, we will examine this influence on Clinton's ability to be an effective president.

Earlier I mentioned that Mr. Clinton's *Tseng Kwan* (癸) gains strength because the Monkey is the "fourth step" of Metal, which adds to his fitness for government service. What are "steps," and how do they influence the analysis? The words for step and progression are the same *(ta yuan)*. They are an important part of any *Tzu P'ing* analysis, particularly helpful in providing an overview of where the Day Master's energy is located within the branches. Taken together, the twelve steps represent a complete life cycle, from birth to rebirth (the eighth step is death). They are similar to Western "houses," but they run in a clockwise direction.

Each step has a specific meaning. The first step, called "the beginning," represents birth. The second step is the time when we are very young. The personality is not fully formed, and the nature of reality is not completely clear to the conscious mind. For this reason, the second step (called *tao hua*, peach flower), is always associated with passion and romantic fantasies. The third step has to do with education and study, building the foundations of career. The fourth step is about one's career or profession, having position and status in society. The fifth step is known as "the peak." Its meaning to be literally in the prime of your life and at the summit of your career. The sixth step is called energy getting weak, it relates to disease, getting old. The seventh step is the opposition, it means getting sick; the eighth step is death. The ninth step is called "the tomb," and the tenth step is disappearance from earth, now "only a memory." The eleventh step is conception. This refers to a next lifetime conception, but converse progressions may be applied to this step to discover information about pre-natal issues. The twelfth and final step is in the womb, the fetal stage before taking a new birth. Each step has its own place in a hierarchy of strength and weakness.

Recalling that only the twelve symbols of the animal zodiac are required to represent the year, month, day and hour in Chinese astrology, the process of finding where the Day Master's energy is located within the branches involves placing each branch into the appropriate "step" of the Day Master's element. To begin with, we will get oriented to the animal zodiac, using Mr. Clinton's Yin Wood Day Master as an example. The Beginning of Wood is Pig, from which all steps (1-12) in the Wood progression may be found in a clockwise direction. The fifth step, the Peak of Wood is Rabbit, naturally located at the height of Spring, the season of Wood. The ninth step, the Tomb of Wood, is Sheep.

The numbers in figure 7 represent the branches, in decreasing order of strength (1 being strongest) of—

① his Wood progression (the Day Master, his available energy to achieve)

❶ the Metal progression (his career, and motivation to achieve)

The branches form the power base of the chart, but the power is always relative to the strength of the Day Master; the diagram shows that most of the energy is in the West and North (Metal and Water), so we can see at a glance that his Wood (in the East) is not very strong. His date branch ① is in the 3rd step, which is about education; it is the only step that adds strength to his Day Master. Evidently Clinton was aware from an early age that education is the key to the good life. In order of decreasing strength, his year branch ② is in the 12th step, his time branch ③ is in the 6th step; finally, his month branch, ④ which accounts for around 60 percent of the total, is located in the very weak 10th step of Wood.

How are goals determined? Look first to see what is on the stems; select the strongest element relationship as the goal. Although Clinton has two *Sung Kwan* ☿ among the stems, which gives him a quick mind, *they have no roots among the branches;* a stem has no strength if it is not well supported by a branch. However, the *Tseng Kwan* ♄ on the time stem

N

Snake **fire** *April*	Horse **fire** *May*	Sheep **earth** *June*	Monkey ④ **metal** *July* ❶
③ Dragon **earth** ❹ *March*			Rooster **metal** *August*
E Rabbit **wood** *February*			Dog ②^W **earth** *September* ❷
Tiger **wood** *January*	Ox ① **earth** *December* ❸	Rat **water** *November*	Pig **water** *October*

S

Figure 7. President Clinton's Yin Wood Day Master. The first step (1) is Pig in the lower right hand corner.

has a strong root on the month branch. This means that Mr. Clinton's life goal is to be an official, his only real achievement will come through government. It seems that he was aware of this from his youth. Clinton met President Kennedy in 1963 at age 16, and the following year became an intern with Senator William Fulbright (D-Ark). As a young Rhodes scholar bound for Oxford aboard the S.S. United States in 1969, he was already socializing and networking like a presidential candidate, causing one reporter to comment, "In a boatload of driving ambition, Clinton stood out."

Having identified the time stem (Metal) as the primary motivation for goal achievement, the four branches are placed in the twelve steps of the Metal progression, which begins with Snake. Counting clockwise from Snake, the month branch, Monkey ❶ is now the fourth step, one of the most powerful. This clearly shows the strength and intensity of Mr. Clinton's ambition to be a leader. In diminishing order of strength, his year branch ❷ is the 6th step, date branch ❸ the 9th step, and time branch ❹, the 12th step. To have both the Day Master and the career goals in strong steps is excellent for business and career. Mr. Clinton's goal is found on a strong step, but his Day Master is on a weak one, which means he can be successful, but it will be very hard work, possibly at great personal cost.

2. IS HE YANG OR YIN?

The second factor is harmony between Yang and Yin. Metal and Water, energies which are intense and withdrawing, cold and wet, represent Yin. Wood and Fire, the expanding, enthusiastic, growth oriented and warm energies, represent Yang. Clinton's Yin and Yang are imbalanced because he was born in early Autumn[2] of the Chinese year, a Yin season, when the Earth begins to grow colder. This requires Yang to balance. There are two different Yang elements: Wood and Fire. Because Mr. Clinton is weak Wood, Fire is not good for him; it will absorb his Wood energy. He needs only "Minor Yang" (Wood). For this reason, he would do well on a vegetarian diet. If his Wood were stronger, or he had been born in Wintertime, when Wood is nourished by Water, Fire would be helpful.

3. IS THE OVERALL CHART BALANCED OR UNBALANCED?

The third factor is balance. The Chinese ideal is a balanced personality—neither too strong, nor too weak. People who are too weak or too strong are considered to be "naturally unbalanced." Chinese astrologers call the birth month "the enemy," because it is the main factor in unbalancing the chart. Characters that can balance the month (i.e., strengthen it if it is too weak, weaken it if it is too strong) are known as helpers, and to offer a client useful advice, it is necessary to figure out which element is the helper. The term *Yun Shan* (lit. useful/god, principle) is used to describe whatever element in the chart balances the Day Master's energy. The *yun shan* in this case is according to two principles: one is the element that strengthens the Day Master, which is Water; the other is, that which balances the Yin and Yang, which is Fire.

---

[2]Chinese seasons are similar to those of Northern Europe. Beijing, the center of the Middle Kingdom, is located at 39°N36′ x 116°E25′, 960 miles north of the 23rd parallel; hence, the Sun is always in the South.

A. The Water Imbalance

As previously discussed, Water is weak in the chart, because it is only a small part of the Monkey, and there is even less hidden in the Earth—both Ox and Dragon contain small amounts of Water within—but it is not enough. The Yang Water in the Monkey is not as useful to the Day Master as Yin Water, but it is still some help—maybe 50 percent. Note that there is a trine relationship between the month (Monkey) and time (Dragon) branches, and both contain Water (Monkey is the beginning of Water, Dragon is the "tomb" of Water). Clinton's chart would have an ample supply of Water if the "peak" of the element (Rat) were one of the branches, or if Water could be found among the stems as well for the trine to function. The Dragon and Monkey trine is therefore not a strong alliance, and the Dragon retains some of its Earth characteristics. However, the trine activates when his Rat progression arrives (age 37–47) or by solar return (once every 12 years), which partly accounts for why his career became so successful.

B. Borrowed Energy

The relationship of Yang Water to Day Master is *Tseng Yin*, ☽ . This helps Clinton with "borrowed energy." Others are drawn to support him because he has no self-serving relationships to his Day Master (*Bee Gen* ☉ or *Je Tsai* ♂); his reserves of strength are not deep and self-sustaining. The more people he has around him, the more energy he has. Because *Tseng Yin* ☽ is hidden in the Monkey, kindness, compassion and the ability to forgive is latent in his nature. He is apt to be deeply moved by a touching event, however small. The more he develops his ☽ by being empathetic, developing good will and a forgiving nature, the stronger his Day Master will become. It gives him a natural curiosity about others, makes him a good listener, able to treat each individual, from a school-child to a head of state, as if he or she were the most important person he could be talking with.

C. The Fire Imbalance

Anyone born in the Autumn or Winter needs Fire, so Yang Fire is part of Clinton's *yun shan*. A Yin Wood Day Master cannot be nurtured by

Fire unless it is strong enough; otherwise it will be consumed, it will give away its strength to the Fire. The Yang Fire relationship to Day Master is *Sung Kwan* 丙 (lit. to harm or oppose/official), which is highly intelligent and will always challenge authority, so it helps to balance. *Sung Kwan* 丙 quite naturally conflicts with *Tseng Kwan* 癸; Clinton's mind is razor sharp, and when he is faced with an important decision, he can race far ahead of cumbersome governmental decision processes. On a personal level, 癸 and 丙 can operate as a major source of inner conflict. "Clinton the official" may sometimes feel like being bold, informal, or direct with his opinions, but his *Tseng Kwan* nature attempts to override this, to insist that he behave in a manner appropriate to the office.

In Clinton's case, his Yang Fire serves the useful purpose of both repressing the *Tseng Kwan* 癸 (which is too extreme, the 癸 kills the Yin Wood) and balancing the Autumn weather (taking the chill out of the air). It is actually only a small amount of Fire, because it is not substantially connected to the branches (the Fire in the Dog is not strong enough to support his Fire in the Heaven). The two *Sung Kwans* on the stems mean varied talents—and the natural inclination to use them to entertain. He is not reluctant about bringing his hidden talents out for display, e.g., playing the saxophone. This doesn't mean he has a big ego (that would be a *Bee Gen* ☉ or *Je Tsai* ♂ in his chart); such a confident style is simply part of his "persona."

Clinton also has what is known as *Kwei Gong* on his time column, which gives him a commanding presence, an air of authority; however, he has no *Bee Gen* ☉ and only small *Je Tsai* ♂, so he is not strongly self-oriented. His Monkey on the month branch is called a "Traveling Horse," *(Yi Ma)*, which indicates that he will travel frequently and visit many different countries in his lifetime. Also, Monkey years will always signal important changes in his life, usually involving major travel or a change of residence. In 1980, age 34, he moved out of the Governor's mansion for a two-year period, and in 1992, age 46, he moved into the White House.

Overall, Mr. Clinton is *Fu Kwei* (lit. rich/rank, title). One who is judged *Fu Kwei* has the potential to reach a high position, achieve fame and fortune. This is because he has two *Tseng Tsai* ♀ and a *Pien Tsai* 癸. His interests are focused on practical, worldly, outer-directed interests; knowledge and scholarship are directed toward the material world, rather than toward philosophy or metaphysics. Although the Day Master doesn't really have enough energy to handle the opportunity for fame and wealth by itself, he gets the needed boost during his "Water progressions," ages 27–47. However, we will see that these *Tsai*, ♀ and ♄, are also destabilizing influences in his chart, and may work against his long-term success.

People might look at Mr. Clinton and think that he must be pleased with his high position; however, this is not likely. In actuality, the excessive Metal in his chart brings him more responsibility than he wants to bear. Ambition (♄) put him in the White House, but it is very likely that he has since discovered that the job brings more pressure than he expected, or wanted for himself. Anyone who is envious doesn't understand the amount of strain he bears. This is quite different from former President Eisenhower, who had a very strong chart, was pleased to have the power, and handled it with ease.

PRESIDENT CLINTON'S PROGRESSIONS

Chinese progressions are a series of pillars for successive ten-year periods of life, each with a stem and branch. Progressions are based on the month pillar, and therefore describe environmental changes that set the overall tone of a ten-year period. Sometimes the stem or branch of the progression will harmonize with the eight-character structure; sometimes they will conflict. Through the process of comparison, the Chinese astrologer is able to determine fortunate and unfortunate periods, along with attendant opportunities for personal growth.

There is a simple calculation to determine the year of life (from age 1–9) that the first progression takes effect. It begins from the birthdate of the calculated year and is progressed "forward" or "backward" (depending on the gender of the individual and whether his or her year stem is Yang or Yin) in the Chinese ephemeris to the turning point of the lunar month. The first five years of each ten-year period are represented by the stem; the second five years by the branch. The branch carries more significance for the period than the stem, although the meaning of the stem is considered when evaluating the first five years of the progression period.

This is what the astrologer writes down:

壬　　辛　　庚　　己　　戊　　丁

寅　　丑　　子　　亥　　戌　　酉

The astrologer "sees" the following: (Mr. Clinton's progressions, reading from right to left):

☽	♀	♄	♃	♀	☿
Yang Water	Yin Metal	Yang Metal	Yin Earth	Yang Earth	Yin Fire
57–62	47–52	37–42	27–32	17–22	7–12
—	—	—	—	—	—
62–67	52–57	42–47	32–37	22–27	12–17
Tiger	Ox	Rat	Pig	Dog	Rooster
♂	♃	☽	♆	♀	☿
♅			☉		

Clinton's first progressed period is Yin Fire/Rooster, from age 7–17. The Yin Fire relationship to the Day Master is ♀ *(Shih Shan)*, the Rooster is ☿ *(Chi Czar);* these conflict with each other, which makes the effect on the Day Master milder than it might otherwise appear. Nonetheless, it suggests a difficult early environment, particularly during his adolescence. In fact, his stepfather was an alcoholic, whom young Bill avoided whenever possible.

In the Yang Earth/Dog progression *(Tseng Tsai* ♀, age 17–27) he has the potential to spend more money than he is able to earn. He is living "close to the edge," possibly going into debt for his education. *Tseng Tsai* is wealth; when it comes to a weak chart by progression, it uses lots of the Day Master's energy, which can bring the potential for problems with money (or women).

The Yin Earth/Pig, age 27–37, is possibly his best progression. His marriage to Hillary Rodham in a strong progressed period (and a lucky solar return year: 1975, Yin Wood/Rabbit) bolsters his career prospects. The Pig arrives with lots of Water, giving him a chance to build a big reputation and acquire lots of fame. He is elected Governor of Arkansas in 1978, age 32. Because the Wood in the Pig becomes the root of the Day Master, it builds his career. His successes continue in the Rat progression; the Rat trines his month branch, and the Yang Water ☽ on the branch nurtures the Day Master.Yang Metal on the stem brings continued popularity and more money; from 1982, the Arkansas voters return him to office for ten more years.

The end of the Rat progression moved him into the White House. By the end of November 1992, the entire world knew that Mr. Clinton's luck was running.As a relatively unknown governor of a small Southern state, with no experience in Washington or with foreign policy, he had looked at very poor odds and gambled.

The downside of this period can be best expressed in a Chinese saying that roughly translates, "The good time of life contains the seed of the difficult period, so you had better exercise restraint." If he has done the right thing in a good period, when the bad period comes there will be no problem. Otherwise, it will be an enjoy now, pay later situation.The Rat is also the second, or "peach flower" *(tao hua)* step in his chart, which is particularly dangerous in this respect. It was in this Rat progression that he is alleged to have exposed himself to the woman who has brought a lawsuit against him for sexual harrassment.

His current progression shows that he is facing eight more rough years. His Yin Metal ☿ *(Chi Czar)* period began in 1993 at age 47, the start of a painfully difficult five year period.As we will see, it is offest by a few good solar returns, but overall, the times are demanding, and will put a serious strain on his personal energy resources.The end of 1994 revealed signs of increasing difficulties, as Clinton faced a Republican-dominated Congress for the first time. Of the many extant definitions of leadership, Clinton best fits that of St. Euxpery, author of *The Little Prince*, who said, "A leader is one who has an infinite need of others." If his support network loses strength, if his allies back away from him, if the voters desert him, it will become very hard, indeed.

In the following five years, from age 52, the progression is also not very good.The Ox arrives on the scene, bringing Yin Earth (♃) but also containing Water (♆) and Metal (♀) since the Metal ♀ *(Chi Czar)* is also on the stem of the progression, it is a very tough Ox, and his economic troubles will increase.While this Ox is not too bad for his career (Earth generates Metal), it is not good for his personal life. It will not be an easy time, with the likelihood of lawsuit, and more public attack, all related to *Chi Czar* ♀, but probably not as bad as the previous five years.The Presidential office is *Tseng Kwan* ♄, and the tension and the burden associated with the office taxes his strength severely.When ♄ and ♀ are strongly reinforced in the second half of this

Ox progression (1998–2000), the pressure will become intense. When ♀ is heaped on the ♄, fame draws strong public criticism, attack and possibly disgrace to the Day Master (♀ seeks power over the Day Master: it could even cause him serious harm). He is not having an easy time as President, and when he is out of office he will feel free, relieved of this burden.

At age 57, the Yang Water/Tiger progression arrives, heralding a major change in his life. His Yang Metal (♄) will be "absorbed" by the Yang Water (i.e., the Metal will give up its energy to the Yang Water). The Tiger is the opposite sign to his Monkey, which will shake the structure of his chart; however, it is likely to have positive consequences. The Tiger helps the date branch (spouse house) by repressing his *Pien Yin* ♄, because Wood powers over Earth. It also strengthens his Day Master; ambition is *Tseng Kwan* ♄, desire is *Pien Yin* ♃, these will both be under better control. It is the beginning of major improvements in his personal life. For the first time in many years, he will be out of the public eye and have the time to develop his inner self. The Tiger progression will be Clinton's best ten-year period, if he survives the Ox. Of course, he is likely to make it through to his good years, from age 57— somewhat worse for wear, but relieved.

There is nothing in *Tzu P'ing* astrology that resembles the Western concept of transits, but there is a technique step that approximates solar returns. It is neither solar nor a return, but serves the same purpose as the Western technique of analysis (i.e., to examine a specific year in detail and predict the effects of the incoming energy on the individual). It is as if an animal comes for a visit, bringing a certain energy that blends or clashes with the energy of the eight characters. As a new stem and branch for each successive year interacts with the eight-character structure, it strengthens or weakens the Day Master in the process. In analyzing progressions, the branch dominates; in solar returns, the stem carries most of the significance of the year. Here are the four consecutive years of Mr. Clinton's presidency:

1993	1994	1995	1996	1997
♆	♂	☉	♅	♀
Yin Water	Yang Wood	Yin Wood	Yang Fire	Yin Fire
Rooster	**Dog**	**Pig**	**Rat**	**Ox**
♀	♄♀♆	☉	☽	♆♃♀

Although the same solar return pillar is used for everyone in a given year, the results will be quite different, depending on how its stem and branch relates to their pillars. The standard technique is to examine relationships between the solar return stem and branch and the Day Master, then compare the stem with the other three stems. Finally, look for *aspects* from the year branch to the branches in the eight-character structure (i.e., trines, oppositions, etc. between the four pillars and the solar return branch). For example, The Water Rooster year, 1993 (Ψ / ♀), increases the job pressure. Although Yin Water is good for the Yin Wood, the Rooster is quite difficult, because it forms a sextile with the Dragon, also a trine with the Ox, creating lots of Metal. When the year is a big drain on his energy, he gets added pressure, which decreases his ability to deal with the environment. In those years he will work hard and have few results to show for it. In such a period it is best not to try for immediate results or short-term gains, but to put in effort on projects that will have payoff in future years.

On the surface, 1994 looked good, there is Wood on the stem; however, there was trouble lurking underneath. There was too much Earth, which is not good for him; the Dog formed a T-square with the Dragon and the Ox, which is why the loss of much of his support in Congress was predictable. Also, the relationship of the Dog to the Day Master is *Tseng Tsai* ♀, which suggests worry about finances.

Even with the Yin Metal/Ox progression lurking in the background, the Yin Wood/Pig year (1995) proved to be helpful for Clinton on the personal level. Of the twelve-year animal cycle, Pig is the best year for a weak Wood person (the Water generates Wood, nurtures the Day Master). However, the stem is always the most important influence in a solar return; in 1995, the stem is also Yin Wood. The Pig contains two elements, Water and Wood. By picking up the energy of the element on the stem, the Pig increased the "woodiness" of the year, which gave him extra strength.

Having said all that, let's recall that Mr. Clinton's empty branches are Dog and Pig, and they came to him in 1994 and 1995. During certain years of life, empty branches have the effect of erasing all the usual indicators of success or failure. If they occur in a good period, the positive effects of individual effort are canceled—one's work is in vain; conversely, a difficult period will not be as tough as it might otherwise have been. The potential for both positive and negative results are canceled by an empty branch in a solar return period. An August 1995 New York

Times/CBS News poll showed tremendous voter dissatisfaction with what was perceived by many as a stalemate—nearly 75 percent believed that neither Mr. Clinton nor the Republican-dominated Congress were doing a good job.

Consider that in January 1996, the "tail of the Pig," Democratic congressmen defected to the Republican camp, deserting President Clinton and their party; the latest budget battle between the President and Congress ended without resolution and became a no-win war of nerves; the Bosnian situation intensified; William Safire called Hillary Clinton a " congenital liar"; a court in Kansas City upheld a sexual harrassment suit by Paula Jones; and D.C. was covered with several feet of dirty snow that froze solid. Fortunately for Mr. Clinton, the Yang Fire/Rat year arrived like the U.S. Cavalry in the first week of February. Although his ability to be a catalyst for change was impeded in the 1994–1995 period, Mr. Clinton is clever, and he rises to a challenge. Congress proved to be a foil to his administration, and now that luck is once again running with him, he has turned the situation to his advantage. In May, Mr. Clinton's lawyers successfully argued to the Supreme Court that the Paula Jones sexual harassment lawsuit be deferred until the President leaves office, overturning the January federal appeals court ruling. In fact, the Yang Fire/Rat year has thus far proven to be his best year in office; even after the Republican convention in San Diego, the polls are strongly favoring a Clinton win in November.

Yang Fire is sunlight, which benefits his Wood, and the Water in the Rat nurtures his Day Master, as it did for the ten-year progression that played a role in his 1992 election victory. However, Mr. Clinton is right in the middle of his Ox progression. It will be interesting to see if the Ox will allow him a second term in office. At the time of this writing, the election is three months away; my prediction is that he will be re-elected, but the margin of victory will be smaller than anticipated.

CONCLUSION: WITH BEGINNER'S MIND

It is of little consequence whether President Clinton is innocent or guilty of marital infidelity. His chosen environment of American politics is, at the close of the 20th century, particularly hostile to the notion, a fact which has little to do with his personal morality, and even less to do with his political acumen. The late President Kennedy is known to have been unfaithful to his wife (as were Roosevelt, Eisenhower, and other American presidents of previous generations), yet he is still revered by millions of Americans. Why is it that previous presidents managed to escape the wrath of the forces of the "moral right," but Mr. Clinton has been hammered by them constantly, for the last fourteen years? From the Chinese perspective, *there is a clear mismatch between Clinton's energies and the environment.* Basically, he is out of step with the time, caught in the machinery of a sexual revolution.

To the Chinese, there is no good or bad, no success or failure— only lucky and unlucky, and this comes not only from one's internal resources, but also from their "fit" with the needs of the times and the environment into which they are born. These are equally important factors in determining how one's destiny unfolds. There is, at present, a lot of "house cleaning" going on in America relative to gender issues, and any dirty linen, be they boxers or briefs, will be publicly aired. In Clinton's case, the relationship between his ego and the environment shows clearly in his eight-character structure: he gets the support when he does what he must for his career, but he is punished by the environment when he does what he desires. The environment will always provide the correct amount of Rush Limbaughs, Jesse Helmses, Newt Gingriches and Gennifer Flowers to attack his Day Master and drain his personal resources. That, in a word, is "fate."

Had President Clinton been a Chinese leader, his "fate" would surely have manifested in a different way. Consider, for example the Chinese leader Mao Tsedong, who (although married) is known to have had a fondness for taking anywhere from one to three different young girls to bed with him, sometimes at the same time. Yet to this day, many millions of mainland Chinese consider him to have been a god. Chairman Mao's nationwide ban on astrology and all forms of divination has never been lifted, but he himself was a strong believer, and is said to have consulted a *Tzu P'ing* astrologer for virtually every important decision he made. Why? You could pass it off as peasant superstition, but the Chinese know that Tao regulates everything, both the individual and the environment. Personal change can be in step or out of step with the times. The Taoist way is to match the leader's energies with the environment, and to understand when the energy of the time is correct to proceed on certain issues.

Western astrologers who move away from acknowledging the reality of fate and increasingly toward an alliance with the philosophy of the human potential movement are in danger of losing their roots and mis-representing the fact that many events in life are unavoidable. In *The Astrology of Fate*, Liz Greene writes of this.

> It is not surprising that the modern astrologer, who must sup with fate each time he considers a horoscope, is made un-comfortable and attempts to formulate some other way of putting it, speaking instead, with elegant ambiguity, of poten-tials and seed plans and blueprints. Or he may seek refuge in the old Neoplatonic argument that while there *may* be a fate represented by the planets and signs, the spirit of man is free and can make its choices regardless.... Either fate is merely a trend, a set of possibilities, rather than something more defi-nite, or it is indeed definite but only applies to the corporeal or "lower" nature of man and does not contaminate his spirit. ... I do not pretend to have an answer to these dilemmas ... [b]ut I am left with the feeling that something is being avoided.[3]

A major reason that Western astrologers consider fate the "f--- word" is inherent in the problem of mixing astrology with New Age perennialist philosophies, which ignore the fact that cultural factors can be an influ-ence in personal growth. This inflates the ego to the point where it is prepared to believe that mastering the environment and overcoming all familial, work-related and cultural problems requires that it visualize, af-firm, and change its mindset. To have this understanding is to not be in touch with the Tao, because *Tao is moving everything*, including cultural re-alities and considerations. Individuals *and* cultures are at different stages of growth; we are all cycles within cycles, and to be "strategic" requires a full awareness of the "other." There is nothing in New Age thought that helps to analyze the "other," that helps to realize that a personal improvement plan created in a seminar may not fit within the constraints of time and place. The Scots have a saying, "The best laid plans of mice and men often go astray." I have counseled many people who had placed heavy blame upon themselves when the plan they hoped to implement failed for reasons beyond their control. The simple fact that the "other" is also in a state of evolution suggests certain limitations as well as opportunities.

---

[3] Liz Greene, *The Astrology of Fate* (York Beach, ME: Samuel Weiser, 1985), pp. 4–5.

The notion, "Events don't happen to people, people happen to events," is frequently the decisive factor in determining the course of an individual's life. Nikola Tesla was a great genius, but he failed to match his great gifts with the needs of his environment, and he died in poverty. Through his ability to capitalize on Tesla's ideas, Thomas Edison became immensely wealthy.

As poet and insurance salesman Theodore Roethke expressed it from a position of deep personal knowing, "What's madness, but genius at odds with circumstance?" *It is this matter of circumstance, the relationship between the individual and the environment, that Chinese astrology is so effective at analyzing.* Taking circumstance into account illuminates the destiny of the individual, because it is, in reality, the co-creator of our individual destiny. As a young Hamlet so aptly phrased it, "The time is out of joint. O cursed spite / that ever I was born to set it right." The often quoted Chinese curse, "May you be born in important times," takes on a new meaning in this context.

To anyone who has read this far and still wants to know more, I offer the following advice: Begin with the assumption that the Chinese people are experts on *certain aspects of human experience,* and their reflective consciousness and symbol systems have an internal logic which can be used to reveal hidden dimensions of the self. Try to penetrate that consciousness and understand their worldview and value system. This is called "thinking through others."

Approach the study with "beginner's mind." This may require letting go of some preconceptions, possibly even un-learning a few things you have read in "pop" Chinese astrology books. Don't attempt to merge two different reality models, or mentally reconcile the four and five-element systems. Both are valid symbolic ways of describing reality, each has its own elegance and function. Learning to calculate and interpret an eight-character structure is a conceptual challenge because it requires that you visualize a set of mental models that are likely to be outside the boundaries of your life experience. As we have seen, Chinese astrology is every bit as complex as its Western counterpart, and to learn the discipline requires an equivalent amount of study and practice.

Read the classics. Begin by studying the content and structure of the *I Ching* (Book of Change). This is the fastest way to develop interpretive skill. The greater the understanding one has of *I Ching,* the more accurate interpretations will become, since *Tzu P'ing* astrology is based on the same holographic system. Some *I Ching* translations are better than others; I recommend the Wilhelm-Baynes version (Bollingen Series XIX, Princeton University Press, 1967).

The foundation of *Tzu P'ing* interpretive skill is "mental models," solid networks of association for each of the elements; the better the models, the more accurate, elaborate and finely phrased will be the interpretation. If you have a grounding in Western astrological technique, and are open to exploring how a new system can add structure and focus to your readings, you will discover many simple and effective techniques that will strengthen your analysis of any chart, with only a small investment of time in the calculation process.

ABOUT THE AUTHOR

Bill Watson's Asian perspectives come from years of practice with Taoist adepts and Rinzai Zen masters. He has been a martial artist, and student and practitioner of Asian philosophies for sixteen years; studied Tzu P'ing astrology (one of the technical philosophies) with Masters Lo and Lin in Taiwan, Taoist internal exercises with adept Gia-Fu Feng, T'ai Chi Ch'uan with Malaysian Grandmaster Huang Sheng Shayan and Chi' Kung with Singapore Master Lee Ching Han.

He owns Hwa Shen Associates, a management consulting practice and has been managing director of a career counseling service, corporate counsel to two international venture capital companies, senior consultant with Levi Strauss & Co., and Director of Organization Development for Kaiser-Permanente Medical Care Program. He has conducted management training seminars throughout Southeast Asia. He lectured at the Institute of Transpersonal Psychology in California (three years), and the University of Auckland in New Zealand (eight years); is adjunct faculty at the California Institute of Integral Studies and University of California, Berkeley; he was guest professor of Psychology at South China Normal University in Autumn, 1996, has published articles in both Chinese and English on management training and business forecasting, and trained at San Francisco State University and the University of California, Berkeley. He has dual citizenship in both the United States and New Zealand.

Bill Watson travels a great deal. Readers may write to him in care of Samuel Weiser, Inc., Box 612, York Beach, ME 03910-0612.

MICHAEL ERLEWINE

CHAPTER 4

TIBETAN ASTROLOGY

I must thank Noel Tyl for encouraging me to make this material available. I have been sitting on much of this information for many years, yet I knew that others might like to know something about Tibetan astrology and carry on from there. As you will read, my interest in this subject has been superseded by my interest in the psychology out of which it arises, and I have turned my attention there. My apologies for what is, by necessity, a brief and somewhat fragmented presentation. Astrology awaits a real scholar who will document the intricate details of Tibetan astrology, and who will not just use it as a stepping stone to the Buddhist teachings. For me, the need for what the astrology pointed toward was more important than pursuing the astrology itself. My most sincere thanks to Khenpo Karthar, Rinpoche and the other Karma Kagyu lamas who answered my many questions, and to John Reynolds and Sange Wangchuk.

I FEEL IT NECESSARY TO START this discussion of Tibetan astrology by describing several concepts that readers will need to understand this material fully. Please bear with me. Most valid astrological techniques are the residue of a particular insight or astrological experience. After the initial fire of the original insight is gone (the realization), what remains is a practical technique or method to capture or recreate that experience on paper. Many of us use techniques of which we have never had realization and for which we have never been empowered. We are lucky if we get realization on even several of the many techniques that we use. That's just the way it is.

To realize a technique in the truest sense, we somehow have to become empowered in the actual experience. With the help of a book, or teacher, and a lot of concentration, sooner or later we hope to find our way *to the experience itself* and actually have that experience. Then we can begin to use the technique in something more than a rote or mechanical fashion, for we have realized it. This is even more true when it comes to a whole new kind of astrology, such as that which the Tibetans are using.

Tibet, the so-called spiritual and physical "roof of the world," has been the source for much inspiration to Westerners for over two centuries. More than just an East-West sort of thing, Tibetan astrology is inextricably bound to Tibetan Buddhism. With few exceptions, the primary practicing astrologers in Tibet were and are Buddhist monks. To learn something about one is to learn something about the other. You cannot skim the astrology off the top of the Tibetan Buddhism. So, to get to the astrology, you have to negotiate the Buddhist psychology in which it resides.

Because of this fact, I feel it is important to give readers some idea of how I became interested in Tibetan astrology. Also, since it is impossible to separate Tibetan astrology from Tibetan Buddhism, it may be important to understand something about the Buddhism itself, and how it relates to the astrology.

My interest in all of this stretches back to the 1950s and the beat movement—Jack Kerouac, Allen Ginsburg, etc. These writers helped to introduce Buddhism to many of us at that time. Writers like Allan Watts and D. T. Suzuki, who wrote and spoke on Buddhism, introduced a whole generation to the subject. In the late 50s and very early 60s, Buddhism appeared as one interesting philosophical view among many others, such as Existentialism and the beat movement, itself. Buddhism at that time (of the Allan Watts variety) was very intellectual and philosophical—something to think about. Almost none of us made the connection that Buddhist thought was not just something else to think or philosophize about, but, rather a path or dharma, something to do—to put into action. This came much later.

It is important to make clear that Buddhism is not a religion in the ordinary sense. Although I have worked with it for many years, I have never considered myself as religious. What I *am* interested in is psychology—the human psyche. In fact, my interest in astrology, itself, can be traced to an interest in the psyche—how the mind and its experience work.

In the early 70s, Buddhism took the next step to being understood when the works of the Tibetan lama Chogyam Trungpa became available. His book *Cutting Through Spiritual Materialism* is the chief example of what I am pointing toward—a practical Buddhism. With Trungpa came the end of Tibetan Buddhism of the through-a-glass-darkly variety. Previous to Trungpa, most insight into the Buddhism of Tibet came through writers like Alexandra David-Neal, T. Lobsang Rampa, T. Evans-Wentz, and the writers on esoteric Buddhism like H. P. Blavatsky and C. W. Leadbeater. There was little or no mention of Tibetan astrology. These were Westerners who could not help but put their own spin on the subject. Trungpa ended that.

Chogyam Trungpa made it very clear that Buddhism was not something to think about, but a path, something very practical to do and put into practice. Buddhism was a way of handling our experience and this world—a dharma path. This came as almost total news to those of us brought up through the late 50s and 60s.

I met Chogyam Trungpa early in 1974 when I helped to bring him to Ann Arbor, Michigan to speak. From the moment of meeting him, suffice it to say that I got a very different take on Buddhism. Which leads me to the other main point that I must present before we can discuss Tibetan astrology, and that is meditation.

Prior to meeting Trungpa, I had the (quite common) idea that meditation was a method to relax around, a way to get away from the chaos of day-to-day life—a form of stress management. I had never found the time nor interest for it.

No sooner had I met Trungpa than he took me into a room with him, closed the door, and proceeded to show me how to meditate, although he didn't call it that. At the time, I don't believe I was able to grasp what was going on. It was only much later that I realized what happened on that day. What I experienced then were some real answers to questions that had always tortured me—questions about death, about letting go, things like that. Trungpa pointed out what awareness looked and acted like. I watched him enjoying and using the mind in a multitude of ways that I had never known as possibilities. He demonstrated that the mind and awareness could be developed and practiced. Intuition, or true insight, could be developed.

Meditation has to do with developing intuition, learning to connect with ourselves, and the taking possession or advantage of our current situation—whatever it happens to be. From that day in 1974, I began to connect with myself and then explore the so-called outer world in a somewhat different way.

What I am getting at here is that the primary tool for learning astrology in the Tibetan system is not a set of ephemerides, a series of calculations, and research in books. Instead, it involves establishing this inner connectivity—call it intuition, meditation, mind practice, mind training, whatever.

Here in the West, learning astrology is often centered around learning the various correspondences between terms, such as Aries relates to Mars, relates to the Ascendant, relates to the 1st house, and so on. If you can't get into learning about astrological correspondences, then you are going to have real difficulty grasping classic Western astrology. Well, in Tibetan astrology, the primary educational tool is learning to use your intuition in a direct and practical way. This is called *mind practice* or, most often, just meditation. If you approach the Tibetan lamas, you will not find easy access to their astrological teachings without this very basic mind training.

It is not because these matters are in any way secret, but rather because we may lack the essential tool for grasping them—awareness and an active intuition. In this sense, they are what has been termed *self-secret*. Their sheer simplicity, openness, and directness are closed to us because of our own inherent confusion and complexity. What to do?

I can well remember my own first meeting with a Tibetan lama when I asked about their astrological tradition. I had just driven 800 miles with my entire family during the coldest day of the year. Having arrived at the top of a mountain in the dark of night, I was ushered into a small room for a very brief interview. I explained my interest in astrology, and the fact that I had worked for so very many years in this field. I was hoping somehow to be able to skip "Meditation 101" and enter one of the more advanced practices. What the lama said to me was that, although he could see that I had never harmed anyone with my astrology, still, in this area it was best for me to start at the very beginning point with meditation. He explained what I should do. And then he was gone.

That night my family and myself were sheltered in a tiny motel room with one small wall heater. The night was bitter cold. It was in that moment that I had to decide to accept his advice and start at the very beginning or follow my pride and refuse to admit that, after all my years of spiritual work, I would have to go to that very first step to begin. I am forever grateful that I was able to admit that I knew nothing about mind practice and that I would begin at the beginning.

MIND PRACTICE

As mentioned, mind practice is not much known here in the West. I mean, how many people do you know who practice using their mind anyway? Most of us assume that the mind is perfectly usable just as we find it, and doesn't require any practice. I know very few Westerners who are aware that they are not aware of how to use the mind.

In the East, mind practice is not only acceptable, it is pretty much obligatory. This is true for countries like Tibet, Nepal, much of India, and even parts of China and Japan. Over there, the mind is considered by nature to be unruly and hard to manage. No one would think of trying to do much with it without considerable practice. Mind practice, or mind preparation, or training, as it is sometimes called, is standard fare in the Orient.

We might wonder why this style of mind practice has never caught on in North America. In part, this is due to our whole take on meditation and what we think it is. Meditation in the West has come to mean something almost like relaxation therapy, a way to relax and get away from it all, a way to escape the worries of the world in the contemplation of some inner landscape. Of course this is nothing like the Tibetan or Zen concepts of mind practice or mind preparation, which involve the intense use of the mind. It is unfortunate that this very active mind practice has also come under the general label of meditation here in the West.

Having pointed this out, it may be helpful to clarify and describe what it is that the Tibetan Buddhists (and other groups, too) do when they sit down on their cushions. In general, if you ask them what they are doing on their cushions, the answer will be that they are "practicing," or they are "sitting." Indeed, that is what takes place. They sit.

There are many Tibetan words for the different kinds of mind practice that are possible (scores of them), while in the West we have just the one word: meditation. What then *is* mind practice?

As pointed out, the most important difference between sitting practice (mind practice) and meditation, as it is understood in this country, is that mind practice is anything but relaxing or passive. It is very active, involves intense concentration and patience, and is not something acquired overnight.

The actual technique is quite simple, taking only a few minutes to learn. And it is worth getting this instruction from someone authorized to give it. In this way, you have an authentic connection handed down in an unbroken line reaching back at least 1500 years. Feel free to write me for a list of centers (Tibetan, Zen, Hindu, etc.) where you can get the instruction.

To wrap up my personal history on this subject: as an astrologer who was also now studying Buddhist psychology, I continued to be fascinated by Tibetan astrology. My reasoning was this: if their psychology was so powerful (which it indeed was), their astrology must also reflect this, as well. I read through all of the various Buddhist scholarly works in which astrology was mentioned, finding only an occasional few words and the odd diagram here or there. There was no sense of any comprehensive understanding.

I then met John Reynolds, an American who was studying Tibetan Buddhism, and who also had an interest in Tibetan Astrology. He spoke and read Tibetan fluently. I set up a workshop here at Matrix, and John came and gave a seminar on Tibetan astrology in the early 1980s. I learned a lot from meeting Reynolds, but most of all I remember John's words to me. He said that, in order to learn Tibetan astrology, you had to learn the Buddhist psychology around which it was based. He confided to me that the Buddhist psychology was much more interesting than the astrology, and that he had become fascinated with that, leaving the astrology somewhat unfinished. "Interesting," said I.

My next step was to invite Nepalese Sange Wangchuk to come and reside at our center in 1985. Wangchuk, a former monk and skilled calligrapher and artist, was fluent in five languages, including Tibetan and even Sanskrit. Today he is director of the National Library of Bhutan. Sange Wangchuk spent $2\frac{1}{2}$ years with us and, during that time, we translated a lot of Tibetan astrology from the original manuscripts. This really helped me fill in many of the blanks. But, like John Reynolds, I was becoming increasingly seduced by the Buddhist psychology at the expense of the astrology.

There is no doubt about the fact that, if it is personal results you are interested in, the Tibetan Buddhist psychological teachings are the very essence of that of which astrologers dream. By this time, our center here in Big Rapids had become one of the primary centers in North America for the translation and transcription of Buddhist texts of the Karma Kagyu tradition. We have maintained a full-time staff on this subject since 1986. Or, as one Tibetan lama put it to me: "Michael, astrology is one of the limbs of the yoga, but not the root or trunk itself." The Buddhist psychological teachings themselves are the root, and these profound teachings deserve the respect they inspire. They have value because they help individuals both to orient themselves within their current situation and to begin to take action of a clarifying and creative nature.

So, there you have my background. I continue to work on the development of clarity and intuition through various methods of mind practice or meditation. Like John Reynolds, I have traced the astrology back to the ground of Buddhist psychology out of which it arose. That psychology is a precious teaching.

I will now try to share with you some of the basic elements of Tibetan astrology. Of course, there is far too little room here to offer more than a brief snapshot of this fascinating subject. I apologize in advance to those scholars (who will one day make this subject very clear to all of us) for any mistakes in presentation that I may make.

TIBETAN ASTROLOGY

The Tibetan system of astrology is a combination of Indian and Chinese methods, the greater and most essential (spiritual) part being taken from the Chinese, with the technical element coming from the Indian system. The Indian or technical part (ephemerides, lunar tables, etc.) is called *Kar-Tsi* and the Chinese or spiritual part, is called *Jung-tsi*.

The Tibetans, who are short on calculation ability, borrow whatever planetary tables they use from the Indians, and don't depend upon these planetary ephemerides for much of their system. They make great use of the 12-year cycle of the animal signs, plus the five-fold element sequence as used in the various forms of Chinese astrology *(Jung-Tsi)*. The *Kar-Tsi* came from the Indian system, along with the Kalachakra system. The quintessential portion of the Indian system of value to the Tibetans is the division of the lunar month into 30 equal parts, called *tithis* in the Indian system.

Tibetan astrology is lunar-based, with the Sun (and all the planets) taking a secondary position to the Moon. As proof of this, witness the fact that your Tibetan birthday is not your solar birthday (or yearly return), but the lunar phase-angle day on which you were born. Thus you would celebrate your birthday on that 25th (or whatever) day of the *lunar* month you were born in.

Astrologers seem to love to manipulate cycles and numbers. The Tibetans, even lacking planetary calculations, make up for it with the manipulation of the various cycles they do use. In Tibetan astrology, numbers are counted forward, backward, and around in many different combinations. It is complicated enough so that not everyone can do it. It requires an astrologer. In fact, it is ironic that astrology, East *and* West, seems to be just complicated enough that most people can't do it for themselves and require some expert to do it for them. Although my experience with the system is not that great, it is enough to assure me that the net result of the Tibetan calculation is quite similar in effect or portent to Western methods. In other words, the amount of information or life direction (if you will) is of the same caliber (and quantity) as similar material here in the West.

The chief exception to this generalization is the use of the lunar cycle in day-to-day life. It is here that the Tibetan system excels and has a great deal to offer Westerners, while here in the West the awareness of the lunar cycle has been lost or trivialized. It is interesting to note that, although few high lamas that I have met make much use of the cycle of the signs, elements, *parkhas,* and *mewas* that I shall present (some do), they all seem to depend upon the cycle of the lunar days for creating their practice and teaching calendars. In other words, much of Tibetan astrology is considered non-essential, or of secondary importance, to the Buddhist practitioner. However, this opinion does not extend to the lunar cycle, which is accorded much attention.

THE LUNAR CYCLE AND LUNAR GAPS

The phases of the Moon have been observed for ages. The Moon, from a Sanskrit term for measure, is still the primary means by which the majority of the people in the world (even in this 20th century!) measure time and the events in their own lives. Although measuring time and life by the Moon is ancient, it is not just some primitive sort of clock. The very sophisticated concept of lunar gaps springs from centuries of painstaking psychological observation by the lamas of Tibet, and the Hindu sages. They practice it today with the same vigor and intensity as they did a thousand years ago. Unlike many other traditions, where the line of successors (lineage) has been broken due to various events, the dharma and astrological tradition of Tibet remains pure and unbroken to this day.

Although much of the Tibetan dharma tradition requires dedication and intense practice, learning to use the Moon's phases and the concept of lunar gaps is easy to get into. The theory is simple. It involves the ongoing relationship between the Sun, the Moon, and the Earth—the monthly cycle of the phases of the Moon. We already know about the Moon cycle, and can even walk outside at night and see which lunar phase we are in.

This is not the place (and I am not the expert) to describe to you either the very complicated astronomical motions these three heavenly bodies produce, or the profound theories of what all of this motion means in a philosophical sense. What is quite accessible, however, is the concept of *lunar gaps*.

As we know, the Moon cycle goes through its phases from New Moon to Full Moon, back to New Moon in a cycle of about one month, some 30 days. This is seen as an ongoing cycle of activity, endless in extent. It goes on forever. However, although the Moon cycle is unending, it does have distinct phases, like the Full Moon, New Moon, quarters, and so on. In Tibet and India, the monthly lunar cycle is divided into 30 parts called lunar days. There are thirty lunar days (cumulative 12-degree angular separations of the Sun and Moon) starting from the New Moon (considered the 30th day), counting through the waxing half of the Moon cycle to the Full Moon (start of the 15th day) and on around through the waning cycle, back to the New Moon again.

What is interesting about how the lamas (and most Hindus, too) view this 30-day cycle is that the 30 lunar days are not considered of equal importance. The monthly cycle has very definite points in it of increased importance—*lunar gaps*. It is at these lunar gaps or openings that it is possible to get special insight into different areas of our own life. In fact, the Tibetans take full advantage of these lunar gaps to perform very specific practices. That is, certain of the lunar days have proven themselves to be auspicious for particular kinds of activities.

In the East, they speak of mental obscurations that tend to cloud our minds, but that can sometimes clear up, just as the Sun comes out from behind the clouds. These moments of clarity are the gaps in the clouds. From a reading of the Eastern literature on this subject, one gets the sense that (in general) life is perceived as being filled with the noise of our own problems (obscurations), making clear insight often difficult. These obscurations can be many and their accumulation amounts to the sum total of our ignorance—that which we ignore.

Therefore, in Eastern countries, these articulation points or windows in time/space (lunar gaps) are very much valued. In fact, the Eastern approach is to analyze the lunar cycle, in minute detail, in order to isolate these moments (gaps in time/space) where insight into our larger situation can be gained. Much of day-to-day practice in Eastern religions amounts to a scheduling of precise times for personal practice or activity built around the natural series of gaps that can be found in the continuous lunar cycle. In its own way, this is a very scientific approach. In the East, they have been astute observers of the mind for many centuries.

Here in the West, we are no stranger to clear days in our mind. We have those too! The only difference is that we tend to believe that these so-called clear days appear randomly every now and then. The more sophisticated (and ancient) psychological analysis of the East has found that these clear days are (for the most part) *anything but random events*. They have their own internal ordering, and often times this ordering can be associated with the phases of the Moon.

In summary, there are times each month when it is more auspicious or appropriate to perform or be involved in one kind (or another) of activity. Gaps come in the general obscuration or cloudiness of our mind, times when we can see through the clouds, when penetrating insight is possible.

As noted, times when one can see without obscuration (see clearly) are very much valued in the Tibetan dharma tradition. These are viewed as real opportunities for insight and the subsequent development such insight generates. Knowing when and where to look for these insight gaps has been the subject of study and research in Tibet for centuries. This is not just academic research: Lunar gaps are used to plan a wide variety of events in the Tibetan calendar, everything from finding a time to perform a simple healing ceremony to full scale empowerments.

Aside from knowing when these lunar gaps can be experienced, the other major thing to know about this subject is what to do when the gaps occur. As you might imagine, there are a wide range of practices, depending on the particular lunar gap (phase) and the personal needs of the practitioner.

However, in general, these lunar gap times are set aside for special observation. Tibetans observe these days with great attention and care. In fact, until recently in many Eastern countries, they didn't have Saturday and Sunday off. Instead, new and Full Moon days were considered holy days (holidays), and normal routines were suspended at these times. These days were set aside for observation.

This word "observation" is worth special mention, for this is what takes place at these times. In the West, we might use the word insight or meditation. In Tibet there are many words that come under the general concept of meditation. The word "observe" is a lot closer to what happens during these lunar gaps. *Observe* the nature of the day. *Observe* your mind at that time. Be alert, present, and set that time aside for just examining yourself, your mind, the time—what-have-you? It is while being present—observing these seed times—that the so-called lunar gap can present itself. Many great dharma teachers have pointed out the existence of gaps in our life, moments when clarity and real insight are possible.

Lest we get too far afield sitting there waiting for a gap in time or space to occur, let me restate: the gap that appears is a gap in our particular set of obscurations, our own cloudiness. When such a gap takes place, there can be an intense insight into some aspect of our situation, the effects of which stay with us for a long time. One moment of real insight or vision can take weeks or months to examine in retrospect. Each time we bring it to mind, its richness is such that it continues to be a source of inspiration. This is what lunar gaps are all about.

At this point, it is hoped that you have some general idea of what lunar gaps are and how you might go about taking advantage of them. It remains to give you a schedule of when they will occur. Below you will find a list of the major lunar days in the Tibetan practice calendar for the coming months. There are still further divisions that we have not included here, to keep this simple. Those of you who are interested can write us for more details. However, these are the days observed by most Tibetan lamas in one form or another.

These lunar opportunities are sometimes referred to as gaps or openings in the otherwise continuous stream of our lives—windows. The lamas conceive of these gaps as articulation points, much like an elbow is where the arm is articulated. They are natural joints or gaps in time/space upon which time and space turn and through which it is sometimes possible to gain access to information about the larger, dynamic life process that already encapsulates us. Among other things, I have made a detailed lunar calendar available for many years. See the end of this article for details about how to obtain one.

SPECIAL LUNAR DAYS

Dharma Protector Days—Both East and West lunar traditions agree that the 2 or 3 days preceding the moment of the New Moon can be difficult ones, which require special observation. In the West, these days have been called the dark of the Moon, or devil's days—days when the so-called darker forces are said to have power. Both traditions affirm that we sort of survive these final days each month. Check it out for yourself. The three days before New Moon can be a hard time. The East is in total agreement on this point, and the days prior to New Moon are set aside for invoking the fierce dharma protectors, those energies that ward off harm and protect us during the worst of times.

In particular, the 29th day (the day before New Moon) is called dharma protector day. It is a time given over to purification and preparation for the moment of New Moon. Ritual fasting, confession of errors, and the like are common practices.

Purification Days—In a similar vein, the days just prior to the Full Moon (the 13th and 14th) are also days of purification, days in which the various guardian and protector deities are again invoked, but in a somewhat more restrained way. For example, the 14th day is often given over to fire *puja*, a ritual purification. In summary, during days prior to Full and New Moons, there is some attempt at purification, both physical and mental, in preparation for those auspicious events.

Full and New Moons—It is clear from the literature that the times of the New and Full Moon are considered of great importance. These days are set aside for special rituals and worship. As pointed out, Full and

New Moon (Full more than New) are times of collective worship and public confession. In many traditions, the monks and priests assemble for a day of special observance. In the East, the Full Moon celebration and the entire waxing lunar fortnight are oriented to the masculine element in consciousness, what are called the father-line deities. The New Moon and the waning fortnight are given over to the mother-line deities and the feminine element. The Full Moon completes the masculine, or active, waxing phase of the cycle, and the New Moon completes the feminine, waning phase of the month. To my knowledge, this kind of analysis does not exist in the West.

It is quite clear from the Eastern teachings that the moments of Full and New Moon are times when the various channels in the psychophysical body are somehow aligned. This is not to say the New or Full Moon days are days of peace and quiet. It is taught in the East that, although a New or Full Moon day may tend to be wild or hectic, any patience or forbearance we can muster at that time will be much rewarded. In other words, there can be deep insights available to us at these times.

Eclipses—According to these same teachings, an eclipse at the Full or New Moon is even more auspicious. In the teachings it is said that, during these very special events, both male and female energies (channels) are in simultaneous alignment—the ultimate opportunity. The lunar cycle and its effects and opportunities have been analyzed in great detail in the Eastern teaching.

Feast Days—Aside from the New and Full Moon, the two most auspicious lunar days in the East are the 10th and the 25th. The 10th day (120° of angular separation), called Daka Day, is considered auspicious for invoking the father-line deities—the masculine. The 25th day (300° of angular separation), called Dakini Day, is given over to the feminine principle and the mother-line deities, in general. These two days, the 10th and the 25th, are formal feast days, days of observation when extra offerings are made and increased attention given to what is happening. There is some sense of celebration at these points in the month. In many respects, these two days even rival the New and Full Moon days in importance. The fact is that these four days (New, Full, 10th, 25th) are the primary auspicious days as practiced in many Eastern rituals.

Healing Days—There are many other days of lesser importance, which might also interest Western astrologers. Health and healing are important in Eastern ritual, and the 8th and 23rd days of the lunar month are auspicious for this purpose. It is these days that straddle the first and last lunar quarters. The 8th day (96° of separation) is often called Medicine Buddha Day. Again this occurs in the male, or father-line, half of the month. The 23rd day (276° of separation), occurring in the feminine half of the month, is dedicated to Tara practice. Tara is the female deity connected to health, long life, and healing in general.

More Protector Days—Earlier I mentioned the days given over to purification, most prominently the 13th and the 29th. In addition, on a lesser scale, the 9th and the 19th days are also noted as days when the protector deities should be invoked and kept in mind. These, too, are days of purification. And there are more, still finer subdivisions that are made.

MAJOR ELEMENTS
OF TIBETAN ASTROLOGY

The manipulation of the animal signs, elements, parkhas, mewas (presented below) takes considerable skill in calculation and, as might be expected, even more expertise when it comes to interpretation. The net result is a somewhat complex system that does claim to explain the status quo, but, like its Western counterpart, allows so much interpretation that hard and fast conclusions can seldom be drawn. As far as I can determine, you can't predict the stock market with it.

In many ways, astrology (East and West) amounts to little more than a grand set of worry beads, the manipulation of which is somehow comforting to those of us who make use of it. One wonders, considering the amount of calculation involved (the work put into it), if the average astrologer gets a profitable return for the time invested. In other words, does the system work for us, or do we, in truth, end up working for the system? I am not at all pessimistic about all of this, but this is an area that has received very little comment. In the last analysis, it is a fact that we astrologers like to do this sort of thing.

There is another factor in Eastern astrology that deserves general comment. It has been the view of Western observers that the East has a tendency toward fatalism and resignation to what fate has delivered to them. I was interested to note that most of the Tibetan lamas and teachers that I met were not all that interested in astrology outside of using the lunar cycle to plan and time events.

To the Buddhist mind, personality makeup is not of great importance. For, no matter what that makeup, good or bad, the remedy remains the same: mind practice of one form or another. In fact, throughout the East, you do not find the interest in personality psychology that we have here in the West. The reason is clear to anyone who has studied Eastern philosophy. They have no need to flirt with the deeper areas of the mind, but have long ago been introduced to them, and take them as a matter of course.

Keep in mind that reincarnation is the accepted belief system in both India and Tibet and, for that matter, the greater part of the world. They have, as a standing belief, what we have as yet to accept: *the continuity of consciousness.*

Here in the West, this awareness of cycles is not self-evident to the majority. As astrologers, we attempt to bring it to the public's attention. Yet as a society, we have yet to come to such a conclusion, much less push toward a solution. Buddhist countries, long trained in the analysis of emotions and desires, have little interest in re-examining emotional and personality issues, which have been clarified in ancient times. Instead, the interest in expanding the awareness of the person (happy or sad) beyond such personal issues, and focusing on the root of our problems and sufferings is assumed. Everyone over there knows this from childhood.

Any Western astrologer can easily check this out for himself by doing an astrological reading for an East Indian. They are not remotely interested in the psychological observations that fascinate us here in the West. Soul, spirit, unity, are already their old friends. Their response to our psychological pap is "Yes, yes, yes ... please get on to something of importance, like exactly how many children will I have, and what will their sexes be." Or, "How much money will I make this year and when."

There is no point in hinting to a Tibetan or Hindu that consciousness may extend beyond this life or that he is one with the creative forces. That is already a given, a fact upon which they have depended all of their lives. The psychological crib out of which we Westerners are just learning to climb (when it comes to the mind), the continuity of consciousness, and all that these thoughts suggest is old news in India and Tibet.

The fact that the whole world is, in reality, our personal mandala and that everything that appears to us as a sign from the cosmos, may be a revelation to a New Yorker, but not so for a resident of Katmandu or Delhi. While here in this country we continue to explore our psychological infancy, this holds little interest for those from the East. With this said, let us look at some of the main elements of Tibetan astrology.

OUTLINE OF MAJOR TIBETAN TECHNIQUES

Here are several of the major calculation techniques used by the Tibetan astrologer. Space does not allow either a more general discussion or a point by point elaboration of many of these. At minimum, I will try to present enough of the bare-bone basics so that those of you interested in exploring the subject can do your own calculations.

Before we launch into the techniques that will be presented, I want to mention an area I won't be presenting here, due to space considerations: the *Nakshatras* or lunar mansions. This technique has been taken directly from the Indian system, and I refer you to one of the many books on that subject.

I use my own birthdate in some examples to follow: it is July 18, 1941.

0. **Cosmic Tortoise Diagram**
1. **The Wheel of the Twelve Signs**
   Century Birth Animal Table
   Sign Polarity
   Triangles (THUN-SUN)
   Opposites (PHUNG-SUN, DUN-ZUR)
   SHI-SEY
   Brief Sign Descriptions
   Sign Power
2. **The Five Elements**
   Relationship Table
   Good, Friends, Filial, Antagonistic
3. **Major Life Factors**
   Life Force
   Power
   Bodily Health
   Luck
   Soul
4. **Tibetan Yearly Calendar**
   Months of the Year
   Days of the Month
   Hour of the Day

5. **The Eight Parkhas**
  Four Good Directions
  Four Bad Directions
  Month's Direction
  Descending Parkhas
  Birth Parkha
  Gu-Mik (9th Spot)
  Dur-Mik (Death Spot)
6. **The Nine Mewas**
  The Magic Square
  Birth Mewa
  Descending Mewa
  Daily Mewa
  Nine Mewas Described
7. **Log Men** (not turning back)
8. **Deu**
9. **Day of the Week Cycles**
10. **Lunar Related Data**
  Lunar Day of the Month
  Lunar Days for Travel
  Losar
11. **Dar-Ghe**
12. **Lo-Khak**
13. **Shi-Shey**
14. **The Seven Obstacles**
15. **The Four Mewa Obstacles**

Illustrations, like figure 1, are common in writings on Tibetan astrology. Often this illustration is shown drawn on the underside of what is called the Celestial Tortoise. This tortoise represents the universe of both China and Tibet. The upper shell is the dome of Heaven, while on the underside is inscribed the essential elements of the astrological mandala. Figure 1 contains the wheel of animal signs, the elements, directions/colors.

Yellow			*South*	*South*			Yellow
	Earth		Fire	Red		Earth	
		Dragon	**Snake**	**Hare**	**Sheep**		
East	Wood	**Hare**			**Monkey**	Iron	*West*
East	Green	**Tiger**			**Bird**	White	*West*
		Ox	**Mouse**	**Pig**	**Dog**		
	Earth		Water	Blue		Earth	
Yellow			*North*	*North*			Yellow

Figure 1. The Turtle's Head.

THE WHEEL OF THE TWELVE SIGNS

The wheel of the animal zodiac is ancient, arising somewhere in central Asia, and later incorporated by the Chinese. The calendar used by the Chinese is said to have entered Tibet in the year A.D. 642 by the Chinese Princess Kong-jo, who married the first Buddhist King of Tibet.[1]

The Tibetan wheel of twelve animals, with its twelve-fold division, reminds us of its Western counterpart, the zodiac. Unlike the West, where people's signs are determined by the solar calendar, in the East our sign is determined according to which year we are born in. The cycle of twelve animals rotates in strict succession from year to year. The order of the animals is Mouse, Ox, Tiger, Hare, Dragon, Snake, Horse, Sheep, Monkey, Bird, Dog, and Pig. Each animal sign has its own qualities, which are well-known to the general public. Table 1 shows some examples:

However, please note that these years are not measured from either your birthday or from January 1 of any year. Instead, *they are measured from the beginning of the Tibetan new year,* a fluctuating point that marks the New Moon that is nearest to the beginning of February. It is important to note that on occasion, the start of the Tibetan and Chinese New Years differs by an entire month!

The animal of one's birth year is central to both the Tibetan and Chinese systems of calculation, and is the most common form of counting time. The twelve-year animal cycle repeats itself from year to year. Just as we might inquire about a person's Sun sign, in the East they want to know what animal sign you were born under. There are male and female signs as shown in Table 2, page 161.

TRIANGLES (THUN-SUN),
OPPOSITES (PHUNG-SUN, DUN-ZUR), AND SHI-SHEY

The Chinese call them the three friends, but the Tibetans call them the three destroyers. The triangles or Thun-Sun (three corners) are shown in Table 3 (page 162).

The worst or opposites (DUN-ZUR: which means seventh corner, or opposite) are shown in Table 4 on page 162.

---

[1]John Reynolds, *Astrological Calendar & Almanac,* 1978, p. 6.

Table 1. Find Your Birth Year and Animal Sign.

Mouse	1900	1912	1924	1936	1948	1960	1972	1984	1996
Ox	1901	1913	1925	1937	1949	1961	1973	1985	1997
Tiger	1902	1914	1926	1938	1950	1962	1974	1986	1998
Hare	1903	1915	1927	1939	1951	1963	1975	1987	1999
Dragon	1904	1916	1928	1940	1952	1964	1976	1988	2000
Snake	1905	1917	1929	1941	1953	1965	1977	1989	2001
Horse	1906	1918	1930	1942	1954	1966	1978	1990	2002
Sheep	1907	1919	1931	1943	1955	1967	1979	1991	2003
Monkey	1908	1920	1932	1944	1956	1968	1980	1992	2004
Bird	1909	1921	1933	1945	1957	1969	1981	1993	2005
Dog	1910	1922	1934	1946	1958	1970	1982	1994	2006
Pig	1911	1923	1935	1947	1959	1971	1983	1995	2007

Table 2. Sign Polarity.

MALE ANIMAL SIGNS	FEMALE ANIMAL SIGNS
Mouse	Ox
Tiger	Hare
Dragon	Snake
Horse	Sheep
Monkey	Bird
Dog	Pig

Table 3. Three Friends.

3 Friends =	Pig	Sheep	Hare
3 Friends =	Tiger	Horse	Dog
3 Friends =	Mouse	Dragon	Monkey
3 Friends =	Bird	Ox	Snake

Table 4. The DUN-ZUR.

SIGN	DUN-ZUR (Opposite Sign)
Horse	Mouse
Ox	Sheep
Tiger	Monkey
Hare	Bird
Dog	Dragon
Snake	Pig

Table 5. SHI-SHEY.

SIGN	SHI-SHEY (4th Sign)
Snake	Monkey, Tiger
Horse	Bird, Hare
Sheep	Dog, Dragon
Monkey	Pig, Snake
Bird	Mouse, Horse
Dog	Ox, Sheep
Pig	Tiger, Monkey

Table 5. SHI-SHE *(continued)*.

SIGN	SHI-SHEY (4th Sign)
Mouse	Hare, Bird
Ox	Dragon, Dog
Tiger	Snake, Pig
Hare	Horse, Mouse
Dragon	Sheep, Ox

SHI-SHEY (enemy of the fourth one): in addition, the fourth sign over from any given sign (either way) is called SHI-SHEY and that is bad, too. See Table 5. The rest of the relationships of the signs are okay (such as triangles).

ANIMAL SIGNS

Each of the Tibetan signs, like our Western zodiac signs, has its own qualities. Here is a very brief description of the twelve signs as taken from some of the Tibetan manuscripts. Please note that this is a direct translation of a Tibetan text. The translation has not been altered to make it "gender free" because it was written for a male-oriented world. I feel that women reading this text will understand why I have not altered this text.

Mouse: The mouse is quiet. He is not friendly or outgoing and tends to be stable. He is not rough. Even though he does good to others, others don't seem to respond. On the outside, he is open and relaxed in appearance, but inside he is very strong and critical. Very open-mouthed, he says what he thinks. He is kind, but not generous. He misses the big opportunities, and takes the small ones. He is always searching.

Ox: The ox is a difficult person. He is hard to get to work, and is not obedient. He likes to sleep. He often exhibits bad behavior. While it is hard to change him, he is most often an agreeable person. However his slogan is, "Don't mess with me!" He is very slow and doesn't care much if things are satisfactory or not. He postpones everything. He is good-tempered. He likes to eat, and sleeps like a bull.

Tiger: The tiger is brave, active, and bright. Always proud and loyal to close relatives, he tends to have rough behavior and speech. He does a lot of thinking. He likes gambling and makes a good businessman.

Hare: "I am just for myself." The hare is independent, and does not need or ask others for their help. "I can survive. There is much opportunity in the world to be enjoyed. I am satisfied with that." He tends to be indirect, devious, and possibly dishonest, but always skillful. He is stingy, but smiles and is generous on the surface. Possible diseases include those of the stomach and gall bladder.

Dragon: The dragon is neither brave nor active, but is good. He never does bad. "I am not very powerful, but nobody harms me." He does not make much effort, but also does not procrastinate, or put things off. When the time comes, he does his duty. He has a short temper, but is good minded. He is talkative. He listens to others talk. He has trouble containing himself. He has less disease than some of the other signs, but if he gets sick, it can be serious.

Snake: The snake has a bad temper, and is always burning his own mind-stream. However, he has a good heart and is very optimistic or forward minded. Even if others are jealous of him, no one has the power to put him down. He can, however, destroy himself. He may have a somewhat rough character, and can be mean. Once his mind is made up, he won't change it. He tends to diseases of the stomach and liver.

Horse: The horse is said to have miraculous power and is capable of great effort. Even though 1000 enemies chase him, he cannot be defeated. His older life will be better than his youth. He listens to others. He likes horses. He is a fast walker, and enjoys play. He has a self-sacrificing character and always helps others. He needs little sleep. His life has a lot of ups and downs.

Sheep: The sheep does not talk much and tends not to be too bright. He can be a rough character. He likes to eat. He causes others no harm, but does not sacrifice himself for them either. He is generally good-tempered and good-hearted. Always relaxed, he does not rush. He is not lazy, but can't get things done on time. He does not show either like or dislike. He is a good provider.

Monkey: Monkeys are very smart, very talkative, and tend to have bad tempers. They have lightweight, weak bodies. They are not always open minded and are said to have "small" mind power. Not noted for their sense of responsibility, they like to play and enjoy themselves. Their words are not to be trusted and they talk, gossip and lie too much—surface oriented. They look clean, but tend to eat dirty things. Very ambitious, they always have great plans. They like to praise themselves.

Bird: It is easy for the bird to loose his possessions, legacy, inheritance, what-have-you? They are always advising others, but seldom take their own advice. Possessing a very strong sexual desire, they always need company. They like to be neat and clean, and don't require much sleep. They are prone to blindness. They love style, dressing up and tend to smile a lot. They enjoy walking and stylish movement. Good with friends.

Dog: The dog is proud, mean and somewhat wrathful. He can't seem to get kindness from others no matter how hard he tries. He is self-interested, does only for himself, and never for others. His mind is always filled with lots of thoughts. He tries to do things right, but they tend turn to out bad or wrong. He likes meat. He is a fast walker. Very sexual. A traveler. He is high or good-minded, and elegant people tend to like him.

Pig: The pig is not bright. He likes to eat but is not concerned with what type of food. He eats everything. He likes yoga. He has good self-discipline. Can be greedy and often takes advantage of others. He does not benefit himself. He lies. He has a big stomach. He is good with the good people, and bad with the bad people. He seldom smiles and is often mean. He can be a rough character.

POWER OF THE SIGNS

The signs have different power or importance as shown in Table 6 (page 166). By far, the most important are the first four, which are similar to what are called cardinal signs in Western astrology. These signs rule the

Table 6. Power of the Signs.

SIGNS	POWER
Tiger, Monkey, Pig, Snake	Best
Mouse, Horse, Bird, Hare	Next-best
Ox, Sheep, Dragon, Dog	Lowest

four major directions as follows: Tiger (East), Pig (North), Monkey (West), and Snake (South).

THE FIVE ELEMENTS

The five elements are taken from the Chinese astrological system, for which there are a number of books and articles. Although somewhat similar to elements as used in Western astrology, the five elements of Eastern astrology are much more defined and depended upon. They are a major factor in Tibetan astrology. Like the animals signs, the elements also rotate in strict sequence from year to year, but unlike the signs, each element holds for two years before changing. Thus the elements and signs rotate in combination, the total cycle taking sixty years. See Table 7.

Wood (air): Long-life, beauty, good or increasing energy, mental energy, changeable, not-stable.

Fire: Strong, instant, hot, warmth.

Earth: Stable, strength, ground.

Iron: Strong, cutting, direct, weapon, changing (similar to earth)

Water: Soft, fluid, clear-seeing, flowing, smooth. Often connected to the blood and emotional concerns.

Each year is assigned an element. These elements rotate in a particular order. Each year's element is the son of the previous year's element.

Table 7. Elements and their Correspondences.

ELEMENT	COLOR	BODY	FUNCTION
Wood (Shing)	Green	Veins	Cause to Grow
Fire (Me)	Red	Warmth, Heat	To Burn
Earth (Sa)	Yellow	Flesh	Stabilize
Iron (Chak)	White	Bones	Hardening
Water (Chu)	Blue	Blood	Moistening

In other words, the previous year is considered to be the mother of the following year.

Relationship Table: Table 8 is read as follows: Wood is Mother of Fire, Fire is the Son of Wood and ...Water is the enemy of Fire and Fire is Water's friend. In terms of Mother, Friend, Son or Enemy, the elements are related in the direction of the arrow.

Element Relationship Pecking Order: There are preferred relationships between the elements. Mother is the best because then you are the

Table 8. Element Relationships.

MOTHER ↓	FRIEND ↓	SON ↑	ENEMY ↑
Wood is Mother of Fire	Fire is Friend of Water	Fire is Son of Wood	Water is Enemy of Fire
Wood	Fire	Wood	Fire
Fire	Water	Fire	Water
Earth	Earth	Earth	Earth
Iron	Wood	Iron	Wood
Water	Iron	Water	Iron

Table 9. Element's Pecking Order.

GOOD RELATIONSHIP:	FRIENDLY OR BENEFICIAL RELATIONSHIP:
Water is the Mother of Wood	Earth is the Friend of Wood
Iron is the Mother of Water	Wood is the Friend of Iron
Earth is the Mother of Iron	Iron is the Friend of Fire
Fire is the Mother of Earth	Water is the Friend of Earth
Wood is the Mother of Fire	Fire is the Friend of Water
NEUTRAL OR FILIAL RELATIONSHIP:	ANTAGONISTIC RELATIONSHIP:
Fire is the Son of Wood	Iron is an Enemy of Wood
Earth is the Son of Fire	Fire is an Enemy of Iron
Iron is the Son of Earth	Water is an Enemy of Fire
Water is the Son of Iron	Earth is an Enemy of Water
Wood is the Son of Water	Wood is an Enemy of Earth

Son. Son is the next best. Friend is less important, but acceptable. Enemy is, as might be expected, not so good.

Element Togetherness: Certain elements go (or do not go) well together. Earth and Water are good, while Wood, Iron and Fire (in combination) are not as good. See Table 9.

MAJOR LIFE FACTORS

There are five major factors that are taken into consideration when examining the nature and qualities of a given calendar year. They are listed in Table 10, in order of their importance.

In regard to these major elements, the life force is the most important of them, for both sexes. It represents the life strength or *élan vital*—

Table 10. Tibetan Names of Major Life Factors.

MAJOR LIFE FACTORS	TIBETAN NAME
Life Force (holder of the life)	(SOK)
Power	(WANG)
Bodily Health	(LÜ)
Luck	(LUNG TA)
Soul	(LA)

how you hold your life. Then comes the power element, how you overcome obstacles, and achieve goals. This is of special interest for women. The function of power is spontaneous, instantaneous—you must have it now. Bodily health, physical health or sickness is important for all. The Luck Element, also called "wind horse," is special for men, while Soul, which is somewhat similar to the life force, but more concerned with the emotional or psychological state, is not used very much. Here is how they are determined in relation to the current year:

Life Force: The life force is determined according to Table 11 (page 170). The left-hand column is the animal for the current year, while the right-hand column is the element for that year's life force:

Power Element: The power element will always be identical to the element determined for the current year. For example, 1991 is the year of the Iron Sheep. Therefore the power element for 1991 will be Iron.

Luck Element: The luck element is determined according to Table 12 (page 170). The left-hand column is the animal for the current year, while the right-hand column is the element for that year's luck: Note: there is no Earth element with luck.

Bodily Health: With bodily health, calculation is a little more complicated. First determine the key element using Table 13 (page 170). Next, using this key element, take the Power Element (as calculated in Table 14). This will always be identical to the element determined for the current year according to the rules listed in Table 14 (page 171).

Table 11. Life Force Element and Current Year Animal.

CURRENT YEAR ANIMAL	LIFE FORCE ELEMENT
Snake, Horse	Fire
Hare, Tiger	Wood
Mouse, Pig	Water
Monkey, Bid	Iron
Dragon, Sheep	Earth
Ox, Dog	Earth

Table 12. Luck Element and Current Year Animal.

CURRENT YEAR ANIMAL	LUCK ELEMENT
Tiger, Horse, Dog	Iron
Pig, Sheep, Hare	Fire
Mouse, Dragon, Monkey	Wood
Ox, Snake, Bird	Iron

Table 13. Health Element based on Current Year Animal.

CURRENT YEAR ANIMAL	HEALTH KEY ELEMENT
Mouse, Ox, Horse, Sheep	Wood as Key
Tiger, Hare, Bird, Monkey	Water as Key
Dog, Pig, Dragon, Snake	Iron as Key

Table 14. Bodily Health and Power Elements.

IF POWER ELEMENT IS	THEN: BODILY HEALTH ELEMENT IS
Son of Health Key Element	Water
Mother of Health Key Element	Wood
Enemy of Health Key Element	Earth
Friend of Health Key Element	Fire
Same Element Health Key Element	Iron

Soul Element: The soul element is always the mother of the Life Force Element. Use Appendix (page 195) to determine this.

THE TIBETAN CALENDAR:
THE 12 MONTHS OF THE YEAR

The months always start with the Dragon month, which is the first month or Losar (Tibetan New Year), no matter what the year. Each month has an element, which is calculated by taking the son of the year's element *and making that element go with the first month's sign.* Thus, 1988 is the Earth Dragon year, and the son of Earth is Iron, therefore the first month is the *Iron Dragon Month.* Elements are used twice each, so the second month of the year will also be an Iron month, and then two Water months, and so on in rotation: Iron, Water, Wood, Fire, Earth . . . Iron, Water, etc. The beginning of the next year does not continue the rotation, but starts afresh.

It is interesting to note that in the earlier Tibetan system, which is still observed for certain calculations, the year started with the New Moon *prior to* the Winter Solstice, rather than Losar. That moment began the first month, which always took the sign of the Tiger, with the other signs following in normal rotation. The elements also start (if I get this right) with the calculation of power element for the element of the current year. That power element is then used.

Keep in mind that male signs are Mouse, Tiger, Dragon, Horse, Monkey, and Dog, while female signs are Ox, Hare, Snake, Sheep, Bird, and Pig.

THE DAY OF THE MONTH'S SIGN AND ELEMENT

Each day of the month depends on whether the month is a male (animal sign) or female month. For all months that are under a male sign, take the Tiger for the first day of the month and proceed in strict sign rotation to the end of month. For female months, take the Monkey and precede in sign rotation. Either way, the rotation ends at the end of the month, and the next month's first day takes either the Tiger or Monkey as a starting point. The first day of the next month depends on the gender of animal sign, etc. The element for each day is derived by taking the son of the month's element (as described above). However, in the case of days, elements are used singly and not by twos (as in the case of the months).

THE HOUR OF THE DAY'S SIGN AND ELEMENT

Start at sunrise and go for 12 hours by 2-hour sections. The first two hours after sunrise belong to the Hare and each two-hour section follows in strict animal sign rotation. As for the 2-hour elements, take the son of the element for the day (described above) and use the elements in single rotation (one only, and not two each).

Sunrise: Sunrise is determined, when there are no exact calculations, as the moment when you can see the lines on the palm of your hand.

THE I-CHING PARKHAS

Taken from the *I-Ching* or *Chinese Book of Changes*, each day has a morning and evening *parkha*, or trigram. Combined, these parkhas give a complete hexagram for that day that can be used to consult the *I-Ching*. See Table 15. There are eight parkhas as part of *Jung-tsi*:

Table 15. The Eight Parkhas (Trigrams from the *I-Ching*).

LIE	Fire and South
HON	Earth (South-West)
DOHA	Iron and West
KHEN	Sky and Earth (North-West)
KHAM	Water and North (Earth)
GIN	Mountain & Earth(North-East).
ZIN	Wood and East (Earth).
ZON	Wind and Earth (South-East).

PARKHAS: MONTH'S DIRECTION

The triangle of Tiger, Horse, and Dog start the first day of month with LI. The triangle of Mouse, Dragon, and Monkey starts first day of month with KHAM. The triangle of Bird, Ox, and Snake starts first day of month with DHA. The triangle of Pig, Sheep, and Hare starts first day of month with ZIN. The Parkhas then follow in strict order, one for each day of the month. See Table 16.

Table 16. The Month's Direction.

ANIMAL SIGNS FOR MONTH	PARKHA FOR 1st DAY OF MONTH
Tiger, Horse, Dog	LI, then KHON, DHA, etc.
Mouse, Dragon, Monkey	KHAM, then GIN, ZIN, etc.
Bird, Ox, Snake	DHA, then KHEN, KHAM, etc.
Pig, Sheep, Hare	ZIN, then ZON, LI, etc.

DESCENDING PARKHA (BAP-PAR)

The descending parkha for the current year is counted differently for male and female. For males, start with the parkha LI and count clockwise; for females, start with the parkha KHAM and go counterclockwise.

The count, in either case, is to what we will call the "ageSign" which means the number of years from birth to the current year, starting with the birth year as one. Thus my ageSign for 1988 is 48, and so on. Once the descending parkha for the current year is determined, refer to Table 17 (below) to determine the good and bad directions for that year. A look at the parkha for the current year gives us an idea as to what are the good and bad directions.

Table 17. The Eight Parkhas and the Directions.

CHA-LÖN	PAL-KEY	DRE-GNA	PAL-KEY	CHA-LÖN	LÜ-CHEY	DRE-GNA	LÜ-CHEY	CHA-LÖN
NAM-MEN	ZÖN	LÜ-CHEY	SOG-TSO	LI	DRE-GNA	NÖ-PA	KHÖ-N	PAL-KEY
DÜ-CHÖ	SOG-TSO	NÖ-PA	NÖ-PA	NAM-MEN	DÜ-CHÖ	SOG-TSO	DÜ-CHÖ	NAM-MEN
NAM-MEN	SOG-TSO	NÖ-PA		SOUTH FIRE		LÜ-CHEY	DRE-GNA	PAL-KEY
CHA-LÖN	ZIN	DÜ-CHÖ	EAST WOOD		WEST IRON	DÜ-CHÖ	DHA	CHA-LÖN
LÜ-CHEY	PAL-KEY	DRE-GNA		WATER NORTH		NAM-MEN	NÖ-PA	SOG-TSO
DÜ-CHÖ	NÖ-PA	SOG-TSO	SOG-TSO	NAM MEN	DÜ-CHÖ	NÖ-PA	DÜ-CHÖ	NAM-MEN
LÜ-CHEY	GIN	NAM-MEN	PAL-KEY	KHAM	NÖ-PA	DRE-GNA	KHEN	SOG-TSO
CHA-LÖN	DRE-GNA	PAL-KEY	DRE-GNA	CHA-LÖN	LÜ-CHEY	PAL-KEY	LÜ-CHEY	CHA-LÖN

Note:The descending parkha is counted from solstice to solstice of a given year. For example, I am 46 years old in 1988, so my parkha is GIN until solstice of 1987, at which time it turns into ZIN.

DIRECTIONS

Four Good Directions are as follows:

1) NAM-MEN (sky healer)—The best one. Good for doctors.

2) SOG-TSO (healthy life)—Next best. Good for sleeping; point the head in this direction.

3) PAL-KEY (generating, glorious)—Third best, but a lower good. It is good to buy or obtain things from this direction.

4) CHA-LÖN (bringing auspiciousness, prosperity)—Fourth good, least. Good for traveling.

Four Bad Directions are as follows:

5) NÖ-PA (evil spirit)—Least bad.

6) DRE-GNA (five ghosts)—More bad.

7) DÜ-CHÖ (devil-cutting)—Even worse, strong negativity, cuts us.

8) LU-CHEY (body destroying)—Worst one (avoid this direction).

The four good directions are the good side or ZAN-SHI, while the bad side or four bad ones are GNEN-SHI.

BIRTH PARKHA

Also important is the birth parkha. To find the birth parkha, it is necessary to calculate the descending parkha for the *mother* of the individual for the year of the individual's birth. For example, my mother was born in 1917. Using the method described above, calculate her descending parkha for the year 1941, and that is my birth parkha, which is said to give space directions for the entire life.

GU-MIK (9TH SPOT)

GU-MIK:The GU-MIK or 9th-eye spot is calculated as follows: from the birth sign, every 9th sign is GU-MIK. Thus, with my birth sign as the Snake, the year of the Ox will be my GU-MIK—not so good.

Parkha GU-MIK or 9th spot: with male persons, LI is the 9th spot, or not so good for that year—it marks a transition. With females, the same is true for KHAM.

In addition, Mewa GU-MIK is when the birth mewa is same as current year's mewa. Again, not so good. (Mewa is discussed below.)

DUR-MIK (DEATH SPOT)

DUR-MIK or "death spot" is not as strong as the name suggests. Still, however, it portends a bad year, and is calculated as follows:

Signs Tiger and Hare, use descending Parkha KHON;
Signs Horse and Snake, use descending Parkha KHEN;
Signs Bird and Monkey, use descending Parkha GIN;
Signs Mouse, Pig, Ox, Sheep, Dog and Dragon, use descending Parkha ZON.

If the descending parkha of the current year is any of the above for the particular signs, then those signs have a year that is DUR-MIK—not so good.

THE NINE MEWA

Mewa means "mole" or birth mark, and the nine mewa stem from a system of numerology used for centuries by the Chinese. It indicates a karmic relation from life to life. There are nine mewas, and they are often arranged in a so-called magic square that gives totals of 15, whichever way they are totaled up. See Table 18.

These nine mewa (Table 19) are counted backwards starting with the Wood-Mouse year (1,9,8,7,6, etc.). An entire circle consists of three 60-year cycles. The current major cycle began in 1864 and will end in 2044 (1924 and 1984 were turning points). The 180-year cycle counts backward until the year before the Wood-Mouse year in the third cycle,

Table 18. The Magic Square.

South East		South		South West
	4	9	2	
East	3	**5**	7	West
	8	1	6	
North East		North		North West

which is the Water Pig year. At that point, the mewa for that year is made to be (2) Black thus making ready for the following year to be (1) White, and the start of a new major cycle.

Any number can be put in the center of this diagram and the ascending numbers placed in the corresponding order. See Table 20, page 178. Table 21 (page 178) is an example of how this magic square works for me.

Table 19. The Nine Mewas and the Elements.

NINE MEWAS	ELEMENTS
1 White	Iron
2 Black	Water
3 Indigo	Water
4 Green	Wood
5 Yellow	Earth
6 White	Iron
7 Red	Fire
8 White	Iron
9 Maroon	Fire

178 / EASTERN SYSTEMS FOR WESTERN ASTROLOGERS

Table 20. The Nine Magic Squares

8	4	6		4	9	2		6	2	4
7	9	2		3	5	7		5	7	9
3	5	1		8	1	6		1	3	8
7	3	5		9	5	7		2	7	9
6	8	1		8	1	3		1	3	5
2	4	9		4	6	2		6	8	4
3	8	1		5	1	3		1	6	8
2	4	6		4	6	8		9	2	4
7	9	5		9	2	7		5	7	

Table 21. The Magic Square of Michael Erlewine for July 18, 1941.

ZON	LI _South_			KHON	
	4	9	2		
ZIN _East_	3	**5**	7	_West_ **DHA**	
	8	1	6		
GIN	_North_ **KHAM**			KHEN	

BIRTH MEWA

The birth mewa is calculated by counting backward using the current year's mewa in the center up to your ageSign. For convenience, please refer to Appendix (page 195) to determine your birth year mewa. Please remember that birth year here means the year as measured from the Tibetan New Year, which is (approximately) the New Moon nearest February 1st of the year. The result is the birth mewa. For example, I am (1941 birth) "5 Yellow."

Current Year Mewa = Birth Mewa: If the current year's mewa is the same as your birth mewa, that is said to cause the current year to be a little difficult. This is also true for birth mewa and current year's descending mewa; if the same, then that year is not so good.

DESCENDING MEWA

Another much used calculation is the descending mewa. To calculate your descending mewa, place your birth mewa in the center of the magic square and count from the center to the East (left) one number. Then, count counterclockwise if your birth zodiac animal is a male sign, and count clockwise if your birth zodiac animal is a female animal zodiac sign. I am a Snake animal sign (female), so I would count clockwise. Count to your ageSign with the first count (the center) counting as #1. The result is your descending mewa. When counting, always remember that in the Tibetan system you are one year of age at birth. So, always take your Western age and add one, and then count.

The meanings of the descending mewa for the current year are as follows:

1, 8: Iron, Good

2: Black, Bad (worst one)

3: Blue (not-so-good)

4, 5: Medium (5 is the astrologer)

7, 9: Almost good

Good (in descending order of goodness): 1,8,6,4,5 (1 being best);
Bad (in descending order of badness): 2,3,9,7 (2 being worst).

MEWA DAILY

Readers must place their birth mewa in the center of the square and go
from there.

You can also calculate a mewa for each day of the lunar month.
The following refers to the first day of the zodiac animal month. For example, the first day of the Snake month:

The mewa 2,5 and 8 are ruled by the Tiger, Monkey, Pig, and Snake.
Start counting from (1) White.

The mewa 1,4, and 7 are ruled by the Mouse, Horse, Bird, and Hare.
Start counting from (4) Green.

The mewa 3,6, and 9 are ruled by the Ox, Sheep, Dog, and Dragon.
Start counting from (7) Red.

These mewa always occur with the signs listed above. For the signs mentioned here, start counting with the indicated mewa, and count each day
of the lunar month in a forward (1,2,3) direction. For example, the first
day of a Snake month would start with 1-White, and move forward.

THE NINE MEWAS (KARMIC RELATIONSHIPS)

Here are some very rough translations as to the general meaning of the
nine mewa. It is traditional that there is some birthmark associated with
each mewa, a probable length of life, a specific dharma practice, and
mantra for that mewa. Note: The following copy is a direct translation,
and has not been altered.

1 — White

Length of life: 71 years. There will be four difficult times during the life.
Birthmark: Has a birthmark or mole on the right side; is left-handed.

Practice: The practice involves obtaining a Chenresik statue (loving kindness, compassion) and that you practice this sadhana (the actual, specific practice for this deity).

Mantra: OM MANI PADME HUM

Either an only child, or only one child turns out useful and carries on the generation. He travels a lot. Good in social work, where others are benefited. If a male, then brave. If female, then a strong one. Could have three children. Likes to move about here and there. Snakes are their protector. Difficult with children, meaning not so good for the kids—things happen to them. Possessions and jobs are very unstable. He is bad tempered, but has a good mind. A difficult early life, but the longer the life the better it gets. He is a clean person physically, and likes white things, like milk, butter, etc.

2 — Black

Length of life: 61 years. There will be three bad periods.
Birthmark: There is a birthmark on the right hand or arm, the heart side or the neck.

Practice: The practice is that of Vajrapani, which is strength, and the clearing of obstacles. Become like the vajra—indestructible. Get a statue of Vajrapani or a stupa.

Mantra: OM VAJRA PANI HUM

If the child is first born, it will be easy to care for him, an easy child. Is often sick when a child. He has nice speech, but a bad mind. He has a dark appearance, mean and horrible. Always sad. He tries to do good things, but no one likes him. If a monk or a member of the Bon religion, then he is a very strong practitioner. He likes meat and alcohol. He has many friends, which he loves but seldom has an opportunity to be with them—and thus no result. If sick when an adult, will be hard to cure.

3 — Blue

Length of life: 50 years with three difficult periods.
Birthmark: On the calf of the left leg.

Practice: The suggested practice is that of Vajrasattva (dorje-sempa) practice. Vajrasattva purifies and removes the limitations, obstacles, and imperfections of the mind.

Mantra: OM VAJRA SATTVA HUM

He likes to sleep. He has a strong mind, but there is much instability in his life. He is a little bit greedy. At work, he is not able to concentrate, and tends to skip around. If male, he will talk less, and if female, will tend to be sad. He is difficult to change. Blame comes even if he does good things for others. He may have many wives (husbands) but no children. He will go to and die in another country. He may have paralysis.

4 — Green

Length of Life: 65 years. There are four difficult periods.
Birthmark: On either thigh is a black circle birthmark.

Practice: The practice is that of Vajrapani, which is strength, and the clearing of obstacles. Become like the vajra—indestructible. Get a statue of Vajrapani or a stupa.

Mantra: OM VAJRA PANI HUM

He should avoid funerals. Cleanliness is very important, else the *nagas* (snakes) give a bad disease. He likes to travel. He has a deep mind, but is sometimes bad. Perhaps difficulty having children. If he has property, then farmland. The life is unstable, with a lot of ups and downs. There is sadness sometimes. People gossip about him. He does good things but others get the credit. He does not like to be lower than others, but finds little opportunity to rise. Whatever he has inside, stays with him. The *nagas* (snakes) are his protector. He is a vegetarian with four children. No wedding.

5 — Yellow

Length of Life: 50 years. There will be two difficult periods.
Birthmark: His birthmark is a certain nervousness.

Practice: The suggested practice is that of Shakyamuni Buddha, called the diamond vehicle (Dorje Chopa) (Prajnaparamita), cutting the vajra.

Mantra: TADYATA OM MUNE MUNE MAHAMUNI SHAKYA-MUNAYE SWAHA

This is a dharma person. This is also the astrologer's mewa. A monk's monk. He was a monk in the last life, reborn into a noble family in this life. Here is a very devoted person, with a stable mind. Very intelligent and religious. Obedient to his parents, he follows their customs or carries on their traditions. He does not travel much, or go far from his birthplace. He has a protector coming from his ancestors, whom he has ignored, and who is thus a little bit angry. He has strong dreams because his protector is angry. He is hard to please. Before becoming a monk, he was a saint, also a normal dharma teacher. He talks a lot, but often misses the point. He is very smart, a quick thinker. Should be a religious person in this life. He is restless, moving here and there. He has very high expectations of others. He always helps others, but they become his enemies. They gossip about him. He has five children. He has wealth in the form of property, houses, land. He will live long if he is religious. He is virtuous and educated. His possessions can be somewhat unstable. If female, he gets more gossip from others. If he is angry, it is difficult to please him. He has a good and stable mind. Tends to diseases of the gall-bladder, heart attack.

6 — White

Length of life: 70 years. There will be five difficult periods.
Birthmark: Calf of the left leg.

Practice: The practice suggested is that of the long-life (and purification) deity Vijaya Vsnisa (Tsuk Tor Nam Gyal Ma).

Mantra: OM AMRITA A YUR DADE SWAHA

He is intelligent. His mood and appearance are always changing. He travels a lot. If female, then will have nice speech, but the mind is not good. Receives protection from his own local deities. Possibly, he could be very poor. He will not be living near his birthplace, but instead, elsewhere. He will be able to build himself up greater than his parents. He is seldom sick, but if sick, he will be hard to cure. He has many relatives, none of whom offer him much help. There will be many enemies. He does good for others, but is still blamed. He will have three to five children. Children possibly handicapped. There is not much power in the family, but wife is powerful. He is quite bad-tempered.

7 — Red

Length of Life: 80 years and there will be four difficult periods.
Birthmark: On the backside or chest.

Practice: The practice is that of tara (green Tara), and thus healing, protection, wealth and a good birth.

Mantra: OM TARE TUTTARE TURE SWAHA

If female, then she likes to sleep. If married, it will not last long. He likes to fight, has a strong body and a ruddy complexion. Possibly may succumb from a sudden disease. Could die from his love of meat and similar things. His generation always shows suicide and murder. Seven children. The life very unstable.

8 — White

Length of Life: 50 years and there are three difficult periods.
Birthmark: On right cheek.

Practice: The suggested practice is that of Shakyamuni Buddha called the diamond vehicle (Dorje Chopa) (Prajnaparamita), cutting the vajra.

Mantra: TADYATA OM MUNE MUNE MAHAMUNI SHAKYA-MUNAYE SWAHA

He should avoid dirty things, stay clean. There is protection by local deities. He could go to another place from where born. Pleasant but proud. Good hands for arts and crafts. Older life will be better than younger life. He is religious and virtuous. Could have four to six children. Elegant people like him. The bad people don't like him. Could have a tendency to gossip, causing bad relations.

9 — Maroon

Length of Life: 73 years with five difficult periods.
Birthmark: On face, neck, or left leg.

Practice: Suggested practice is that of Manjushri, the development of the mind and intellect.

Mantra: OM ARA PATSA NA DHI

An image of one holding seven glorious flowers in hands. If he keeps flowers well, then will be a very rich man. Could be proud or greedy. His older life will be better than young life. Very brave. He may well live other than where born. Wealth includes cows, animals, livestock in general. Has to keep his wealth with care, or obstacles could destroy it. This is a good mewa for females, but not for monks or Bon.

LOG-MEN (NOT TURNING BACK)

A term meaning not-turning-back or not-coming-back. Here again, this is calculated differently for males and females. For males, always start with the sign of the Tiger and for the element, take the son of the birth power element. For me, the son of Iron (my power element) is Water, so start with Tiger Water and count up from there in the ascending order to the current agesign. Remember each element is counted twice. So we have Tiger Water, Tiger Hare, and so on. The sign and element combination that corresponds to your agesign is the LOG-MEN.

Females start with the Monkey sign and use the mother of their birth power element and count in reverse direction to the current agesign. That sign and element is their LOG-MEN.

For males, if LOG-MEN is the sign Dog, then it is called NAM-GO (Door of the Sky), while if the sign is Pig then it is called SA-GO (Door of the Earth). If NAM-GO, then it is important to avoid climbing, high places, etc. for that year. If SA-GO, then avoid digging, foundation work, anything underground for that year.

For females, the sign of the Dragon marks NAM-GO and the sign of the Snake marks a SA-GO year.

DEU

DEU is an integral part of the Tibetan astrology system, a means of awarding O's (good marks) or X's (bad marks) for the current year to your major elements: Life force, power, bodily health, luck and soul. This is also part of KEG-TSI which is the yearly calculation of the life obstacles.

It is somewhat complex, but well worth working out. To begin, compare your major birth elements and those of the current year elements as follows. For example, using the power element as example:

If the current year's power element is:

> Mother of my birth power: mark 000 (best rating).
> Friend of my birth power: mark 00 (2nd best).
> Son of my birth power: mark 0X (4th best).
> Enemy of my birth power: mark XX (6th best/least good).

If it is the same as my birth power then:

> Water or Earth: mark 0 (3rd best).
> Fire, Iron, or Wood: mark X (5th best)

It is important to calculate these for all of the major elements for each year.

WEEK DAYS

The day after the New Moon is the 1st day of the month, and whatever day of the week it is *colors* the whole month with the tone or quality of the planet of that day (Sun for Sunday, etc.). Also, the son of the 1st day's element is equally powerful for that whole month. The mother of that element is medium powerful, and the friend or enemy is bad for that entire month. See Table 22.

Example: if Sunday is the first day of the month (as in Table 23) then every Sunday in that month is very powerful, but if Sunday is friend or enemy (or otherwise not very good), then it dampens the best day of the month.

Table 22. Week Days.

PLANET	DAY	ELEMENT	DIRECTION
Sun	Sunday	Fire	South
Moon	Monday	Water	North
Mars	Tuesday	Fire	South
Mercury	Wednesday	Water	North
Jupiter	Thursday	Wood	East
Venus	Friday	Iron	West
Saturn	Saturday	Earth	SE, NW, SW, NE
Rahu	All Days	All Elements	All Directions

Further, if the first day of the month falls on a Sunday, then the planet is Sun, and the element Fire. Therefore, the son of Fire is *Earth*. Earth is powerful for the month. The mother of Fire is Wood, so Wood is medium powerful that month. The friend of Fire is Iron, and the enemy of Fire is Water. Fire and Water are bad for that month.

WEEK DAY CYCLES

Depending upon the animal sign for the year of your birth, three days of the week will have a special significance for you. According to John Reynolds in his *1978 Tibetan Astrological Calendar*, "Days which are best and good are considered to be auspicious for undertaking projects, for doing business and similar activities; while days which are bad are considered inauspicious for any activity at all. In addition, birth on a good or best day indicates long life, while birth on a bad day portends an early death." Using the animal sign for the year of your birth, enter the information, as in Table 23, page 188, which is an example.

Table 23. Days of the Week Cycles.

SIGN	BEST	GOOD	BAD
Snake	Tuesday	Friday	Monday
Horse	Tuesday	Friday	Wednesday
Sheep	Friday	Monday	Thursday
Monkey	Friday	Monday	Thursday
Bird	Friday	Thursday	Tuesday
Dog	Monday	Wednesday	Thursday
Pig	Wednesday	Tuesday	Saturday
Mouse	Wednesday	Tuesday	Saturday
Ox	Saturday	Wednesday	Thursday
Tiger	Thursday	Saturday	Friday
Hare	Thursday	Saturday	Friday
Dragon	Sunday	Wednesday	Thursday

LUNAR DAYS OF THE MONTH

Certain days of the month are auspicious and inauspicious for a given person. There are three favorable days each month, called foundation days, power days, and success days. There are also three unfavorable days, called obstacle days, disturbance days, and enemy days. In general, it is advised to begin things and take care of important business on the favorable days, and avoid such enterprise on the unfavorable days. The numbers in this table refer to the lunar days of the month for each sign. See Table 24. F = Foundation, P = Power, S = Success, O = Obstacles, D = Disturbance, E = Enemy

According to John Reynolds in his *1978 Tibetan Astrological Calendar,* "When the monthly and weekly cycles oppose each other on

Table 24. Auspicious Days.

Animal	F	P	S	O	D	E
Snake	13	12	6	8	9	9
Horse	17	12	6	20	5	27
Sheep	8	1	2	20	5	27
Monkey	8	1	2	9	10	17
Bird	14	7	25	3	11	24
Dog	9	27	5	11	3	12
Pig	2	8	11	26	3	12
Mouse	20	6	3	26	10	23
Ox	17	14	12	12	18	5
Tiger	5	27	9	14	12	3
Hare	7	27	12	26	25	18
Dragon	3	12	17	8	9	11

the same day, the former is the more powerful due to the planetary energies, but nonetheless, they act together. If, during the monthly cycle, opposing forces manifest on the same lunar day, these two complement each other."

Lunar Days 1, 2, 26—Good for making offerings, requests of high personages, taking vows, religious practices, and in general, the obtaining of something desired.

Lunar Days 3, 11, 20, 23—Excellent days for strong, firm actions; good for beginning construction or obtaining high offices.

Lunar Days 4, 13, 16, 25—Days of quickness, clarity, skill and cleverness; indicative of success in competitions.

Lunar Days 5, 8, 17, 18—Very bad reaction days; unethical activities will succeed, moral action will not.

Lunar Days 1, 9, 10, 19, 24—Generally good for activities such as marriages, large purchases, collections, teaching, initiation, blessings, building and ceremonies in general.

Lunar Days 2, 15—Barren. Many events will not occur. Neither good or bad for building, meditation practice and certain ceremonies. Nothing should be undertaken between midnight and 3 A.M.

LUNAR DAYS FOR TRAVEL

According to John Reynolds in his *1978 Tibetan Astrological Calendar*, certain lunar days are good (or not) for travel. Table 25 shows the days that John Reynolds offers:

Table 25. Travel Days.

1, 2, 3, 16, 17, 18	Generally good.
4, 19	Unsuccessful.
5, 20	Good for business.
6, 21	One should not travel.
7, 22	Fine for travel.
8, 23	Disturbing for emotions.
9, 24	Success in covering long distances.
10, 25	Fruitful travel.
11, 26	Spiritual.
12, 27	Wisdom.
13, 29	Activity benefits one.
15, 30	One should not travel.

TIBETAN NEW YEAR: LO-SAR

LO-SAR (Tibetan New Year) is the nearest New Moon to February 1st. If there are two New Moons, then take the second one. LO-SAR is the first sunrise after the New Moon—the next day.

DAR-GHE: TRADITIONAL ASSIGNMENT

In Table 26, numbers 3–8 are good ones and 9–12 and 1–2 are the bad ones. Numbers 3 and 4 are the worst of the good ones, 5 and 6 are medium good, and 7 and 8 are the best of the good. Likewise, numbers

Table 26. DAR-GHE (going up, increasing).

X	Worst (Best of)	1) Ug-len (First breath)
X	Worst (Best of)	2) Gnal-ney (Conception)
0	Good (Worst of)	3) Lue-Dzog (Body Complete, full term)
0	Good (Worst of)	4) Tse-Pa (Birth)
00	Good (Medium)	5) True-Jay (Bathing the baby)
00	Good (Medium)	6) Goe-Gon (Putting on clothes)
000	Good (Best of)	7) Ley-Jey (Working)
000	Good (Best of)	8) Gar-wa (Prime, full-filled)
XX	Bad (Medium)	9) Gue-Pa (Decaying)
XX	Bad (Medium)	10) Na-wa (Sick)
XXX	Worst (Worst of)	11) Shi-wa (Death)
XXX	Worst (Worst of 12)	Dur-shug (Burial)

1 and 2 are the best of the worst, 9 and 10 are medium bad and 11 and 12 are the worst of the worst.

Note: Father's death year sign, if same as current year, then not so good. If descending parkha is the same for both husband and wife, not so good. This is true of family members in general.

LO-KHAK

You might expect that a year which has the same sign as your birth year would be luck or auspicious. Not in the Tibetan system. If your birth sign and the current year sign are the same (every 12 years) then this is an example of LO-KHAK, which is very inauspicious. For men, the year before a LO-KHAK (termed NANG-KHAK) is a little more diffi-cult than the LO-KHAK itself, for women, it is the year after LO-KHAK (termed CHI-KHAK) that is difficult.

Birth and one year
12 to 13 years of age
24 to 25 years of age
36 to 37 years of age
48 to 49 years of age
60 to 61 years of age
72 to 73 years of age
84 to 85 years of age
96 to 97 years of age

During a LO-KHAK year, there are reputedly six months of particular danger when you are most vulnerable[2]:

Bird Month . . . . 2nd half very bad;
Dog Month . . . . 1st half very bad;
Pig Month. . . . . Passable;
Mouse Month . . . . . 2nd half very bad;
Ox Month . . . . 1st half very bad;
Tiger Month . . . . . . Passable;

---

[2] John Reynolds, *Astrological Calendar & Almanac 1978*, page 10.

Hare Month . . . . . . 2nd half very bad;
Dragon Month. . . . . Entire month very bad;
Snake Month. . . . . . 1st half very bad;
Horse Month. . . . . . Passable;
Sheep Month. . . . . . 2nd half very bad;
Monkey Month . . . . Entire month very bad;
Bird Month . . . . 1st half very bad.

If the current year sign is the 7th or opposite of the birth sign, this is called DON-ZUR and is also bad. If the current year is the 5th sign (i.e., Dragon-Monkey), then this is also not good. If the current year is the same element as the birth element, then this, too, is not so good.

SHI-SHEY

SHI-SHEY refers to the signs that are four up and back from the birth-year sign. For example, my birth in 1941 in the year of the Snake makes the Tiger and the Monkey signs fit this description (always counting from the birth sign as 1). If the current year is either of these signs, then it is called SHI-SHEY—which is not so good.

Also, for the current year sign, count four up and four back and the months of that year with the same sign are called "black months." If these months are Tiger, Monkey, Pig, or Snake, then the whole month is black, but the first ten days are the worst, the second ten days a little better, and the last ten days better still.

If the month signs are the Mouse, Horse, Bird, and Hare, then the days of the month from 10th–20th are the bad ones. If the month signs are Ox, Sheep, Dog, or Dragon, then the last 10 days of the month are bad. All days being calculated from the New Moon.

If the current year is Tiger, Monkey, Pig, or Snake and if the year's mewa is 2-Black, then the whole year is a black year.

THE SEVEN OBSTACLES

Quite a bit is made of the so-called seven obstacles. Each of these eventualities affects the entire current year, from LO-SAR to LO-SAR. In the following list, the term Current Year Sign refers to the Animal Zodiac Sign for the current year. The seven obstacles occur when:

1. If the Current Year Sign is your Birth Year Sign;

2. If the Current Year Sign is opposite your Birth Year Sign;

3. If the Current Year Sign is the animal sign adjacent (either side) your Birth Year Animal Sign *PLUS* the same element as your birth year element. For example, Snake has Dragon and Horse on either side;

4. If the Current Year Sign is one of three Destroyers (Friends). (See Table 3, page 162);

5. If Wife and Husband have the same descending parkha for the current year;

6. If the Current Year Animal Sign is the sign for the year Father or Grandfather died;

7. If descending parkha is the birth parkha.

FOUR MEWA OBSTACLES

1. Descending Mewa = Current Year Mewa;

2. Descending Mewa = Birth Mewa;

3. Descending Mewa = Two Black;

4. The Element of the Descending Mewa = Element of the Enemy of the Birth Mewa.

APPENDIX
TIBETAN ASTROLOGICAL TABLES

Here are some of the main calculations for each year in the current century and then some. You can use that as a guide to get you started.

Year	1900	1901	1902	1903	1904
Element	Iron	Iron	Water	Water	Wood
Zodiac	Mouse	Ox	Tiger	Hare	Dragon
Parkha	Li South	Khon SW	Dha West	Khen NW	Kham North
Mewa	1 White	9 Maroon	8 White	7 Red	6 White
Life Force	Water	Earth	Wood	Wood	Earth
Health	Earth	Earth	Iron	Iron	Fire
Power	Iron	Iron	Water	Water	Wood
Luck	Wood	Water	Iron	Fire	Wood
Soul	Iron	Fire	Water	Water	Fire

Year	1905	1906	1907	1908	1909
Element	Wood	Fire	Fire	Earth	Earth
Zodiac	Snake	Horse	Sheep	Monkey	Bird
Parkha	Gin NE	Zin East	Zon SE	Li South	Khon SW
Mewa	5 Yellow	4 Green	3 Indigo	2 Black	1 White
Life Force	Fire	Fire	Earth	Iron	Iron
Health	Fire	Water	Water	Earth	Earth
Power	Wood	Fire	Fire	Earth	Earth
Luck	Water	Iron	Fire	Wood	Water
Soul	Wood	Wood	Fire	Earth	Earth

Year	1910	1911	1912	1913	1914
Element	Iron	Iron	Water	Water	Wood
Zodiac	Dog	Pig	Mouse	Ox	Tiger
Parkha	Dha West	Khen NW	Kham North	Gin NE	Zin East
Mewa	9 Maroon	8 White	7 Red	6 White	5 Yellow
Life Force	Earth	Water	Water	Earth	Wood
Health	Iron	Iron	Wood	Wood	Water
Power	Iron	Iron	Water	Water	Wood
Luck	Iron	Fire	Wood	Water	Iron
Soul	Fire	Iron	Iron	Fire	Water

Year	1915	1916	1917	1918	1919
Element	Wood	Fire	Fire	Earth	Earth
Zodiac	Hare	Dragon	Snake	Horse	Sheep
Parkha	Zon SE	Li South	Khon SW	Dha West	Khen NW
Mewa	4 Green	3 Indigo	2 Black	1 White	9 Maroon
Life Force	Wood	Earth	Fire	Fire	Earth
Health	Water	Earth	Earth	Fire	Fire
Power	Wood	Fire	Fire	Earth	Earth
Luck	Fire	Wood	Water	Iron	Fire
Soul	Water	Fire	Wood	Wood	Fire

Year	1920	1921	1922	1923	1924
Element	Iron	Iron	Water	Water	Wood
Zodiac	Monkey	Bird	Dog	Pig	Mouse
Parkha	Kham North	Gin NE	Zin East	Zon SE	Li South
Mewa	8 White	7 Red	6 White	5 Yellow	4 Green
Life Force	Iron	Iron	Earth	Water	Water
Health	Wood	Wood	Water	Water	Iron
Power	Iron	Iron	Water	Water	Wood
Luck	Wood	Water	Iron	Fire	Wood
Soul	Earth	Earth	Fire	Iron	Iron

Year	1925	1926	1927	1928	1929
Element	Wood	Fire	Fire-	Earth	Earth
Zodiac	Ox	Tiger	Hare	Dragon	Snake
Parkha	Khon SW	Dha West	Khen NW	Kham North	Gin NE
Mewa	3 Indigo	2 Black	1 White	9 Maroon	8 White
Life Force	Earth	Wood	Wood	Earth	Fire
Health	Iron	Fire	Fire	Wood	Wood
Power	Wood	Fire	Fire	Earth	Earth
Luck	Water	Iron	Fire	Wood	Water
Soul	Fire	Water	Water	Fire	Wood

Year	1930	1931	1932	1933	1934
Element	Iron	Iron	Water	Water	Wood
Zodiac	Horse	Sheep	Monkey	Bird	Dog
Parkha	Zin East	Zon SE	Li South	Khon SW	Dha West
Mewa	7 Red	6 White	5 Yellow	4 Green	3 Indigo
Life Force	Fire	Earth	Iron	Iron	Earth
Health	Earth	Earth	Iron	Iron	Fire
Power	Iron	Iron	Water	Water	Wood
Luck	Iron	Fire	Wood	Water	Iron
Soul	Wood	Fire	Earth	Earth	Fire

Year	1935	1936	1937	1938	1939
Element	Wood	Fire	Fire	Earth	Earth
Zodiac	Pig	Mouse	Ox	Tiger	Hare
Parkha	Khen NW	Kham North	Gin NE	Zin East	Zon SE
Mewa	2 Black	1 White	9 Maroon	8 White	7 Red
Life Force	Water	Water	Earth	Wood	Wood
Health	Fire	Water	Water	Earth	Earth
Power	Wood	Fire	Fire	Earth	Earth
Luck	Fire	Wood	Water	Iron	Fire
Soul	Iron	Iron	Fire	Water	Water

Year	1940	1941	1942	1943	1944
Element	Iron	Iron	Water	Water	Wood
Zodiac	Dragon	Snake	Horse	Sheep	Monkey
Parkha	Li South	Khon SW	Dha West	Khen NW	Kham North
Mewa	6 White	5 Yellow	4 Green	3 Indigo	2 Black
Life Force	Earth	Fire	Fire	Earth	Iron
Health	Iron	Iron	Wood	Wood	Water
Power	Iron	Iron	Water	Water	Wood
Luck	Wood	Water	Iron	Fire	Wood
Soul	Fire	Wood	Wood	Fire	Earth

Year	1945	1946	1947	1948	1949
Element	Wood	Fire	Fire	Earth	Earth
Zodiac	Bird	Dog	Pig	Mouse	Ox
Parkha	Gin NE	Zin East	Zon SE	Li South	Khon SW
Mewa	1 White	9 Maroon	8 White	7 Red	6 White
Life Force	Iron	Earth	Water	Water	Earth
Health	Water	Earth	Earth	Fire	Fire
Power	Wood	Fire	Fire	Earth	Earth
Luck	Water	Iron	Fire	Wood	Water
Soul	Earth	Fire	Iron	Iron	Fire

Year	1950	1951	1952	1953	1954
Element	Iron	Iron	Water	Water	Wood
Zodiac	Tiger	Hare	Dragon	Snake	Horse
Parkha	Dha West	Khen NW	Kham North	Gin NE	Zin East
Mewa	5 Yellow	4 Green	3 Indigo	2 Black	1 White
Life Force	Wood	Wood	Earth	Fire	Fire
Health	Wood	Wood	Water	Water	Iron
Power	Iron	Iron	Water	Water	Wood
Luck	Iron	Fire	Wood	Water	Iron
Soul	Water	Water	Fire	Wood	Wood

Year	1955	1956	1957	1958	1959
Element	Wood	Fire	Fire	Earth	Earth
Zodiac	Sheep	Monkey	Bird	Dog	Pig
Parkha	Zon SE	Li South	Khon SW	Dha West	Khen NW
Mewa	9 Maroon	8 White	7 Red	6 White	5 Yellow
Life Force	Earth	Iron	Iron	Earth	Water
Health	Iron	Fire	Fire	Wood	Wood
Power	Wood	Fire	Fire	Earth	Earth
Luck	Fire	Wood	Water	Iron	Fire
Soul	Fire	Earth	Earth	Fire	Iron

Year	1960	1961	1962	1963	1964
Element	Iron	Iron	Water	Water	Wood
Zodiac	Mouse	Ox	Tiger	Hare	Dragon
Parkha	Kham North	Gin NE	Zin East	Zon SE	Li South
Mewa	4 Green	3 Indigo	2 Black	1 White	9 Maroon
Life Force	Water	Earth	Wood	Wood	Earth
Health	Earth	Earth	Iron	Iron	Fire
Power	Iron	Iron	Water	Water	Wood
Luck	Wood	Water	Iron	Fire	Wood
Soul	Iron	Fire	Water	Water	Fire

Year	1965	1966	1967	1968	1969
Element	Wood	Fire	Fire	Earth	Earth
Zodiac	Snake	Horse	Sheep	Monkey	Bird
Parkha	Khon SW	Dha West	Khen NW	Kham North	Gin NE
Mewa	8 White	7 Red	6 White	5 Yellow	4 Green
Life Force	Fire	Fire	Earth	Iron	Iron
Health	Fire	Water	Water	Earth	Earth
Power	Wood	Fire	Fire	Earth	Earth
Luck	Water	Iron	Fire	Wood	Water
Soul	Wood	Wood	Fire	Earth	Earth

Year	1970	1971	1972	1973	1974
Element	Iron	Iron	Water	Water	Wood
Zodiac	Dog	Pig	Mouse	Ox	Tiger
Parkha	Zin East	Zon SE	Li South	Khon SW	Dha West
Mewa	3 Indigo	2 Black	1 White	9 Maroon	8 White
Life Force	Earth	Water	Water	Earth	Wood
Health	Iron	Iron	Wood	Wood	Water
Power	Iron	Iron	Water	Water	Wood
Luck	Iron	Fire	Wood	Water	Iron
Soul	Fire	Iron	Iron	Fire	Water

Year	1975	1976	1977	1978	1979
Element	Wood	Fire	Fire	Earth	Earth
Zodiac	Hare	Dragon	Snake	Horse	Sheep
Parkha	Khen NW	Kham North	Gin NE	Zin East	Zon SE
Mewa	7 Red	6 White	5 Yellow	4 Green	3 Indigo
Life Force	Wood	Earth	Fire	Fire	Earth
Health	Water	Earth	Earth	Fire	Fire
Power	Wood	Fire	Fire	Earth	Earth
Luck	Fire	Wood	Water	Iron	Fire
Soul	Water	Fire	Wood	Wood	Fire

Year	1980	1981	1982	1983	1984
Element	Iron	Iron	Water	Water	Wood
Zodiac	Monkey	Bird	Dog	Pig	Mouse
Parkha	Li South	Khon SW	Dha West	Khen NW	Kham North
Mewa	2 Black	1 White	9 Maroon	8 White	7 Red
Life Force	Iron	Iron	Earth	Water	Water
Health	Wood	Wood	Water	Water	Iron
Power	Iron	Iron	Water	Water	Wood
Luck	Wood	Water	Iron	Fire	Wood
Soul	Earth	Earth	Fire	Iron	Iron

Year	1985	1986	1987	1988	1989
Element	Wood	Fire	Fire	Earth	Earth
Zodiac	Ox	Tiger	Hare	Dragon	Snake
Parkha	Gin NE	Zin East	Zon SE	Li South	Khon SW
Mewa	6 White	5 Yellow	4 Green	3 Indigo	2 Black
Life Force	Earth	Wood	Wood	Earth	Fire
Health	Iron	Fire	Fire	Wood	Wood
Power	Wood	Fire	Fire	Earth	Earth
Luck	Water	Iron	Fire	Wood	Water
Soul	Fire	Water	Water	Fire	Wood

Year	1990	1991	1992	1993	1994
Element	Iron	Iron	Water	Water	Wood
Zodiac	Horse	Sheep	Monkey	Bird	Dog
Parkha	Dha West	Khen NW	Kham North	Gin NE	Zin East
Mewa	1 White	9 Maroon	8 White	7 Red	6 White
Life Force	Fire	Earth	Iron	Iron	Earth
Health	Earth	Earth	Iron	Iron	Fire
Power	Iron	Iron	Water	Water	Wood
Luck	Iron	Fire	Wood	Water	Iron
Soul	Wood	Fire	Earth	Earth	Fire

Year	1995	1996	1997	1998	1999
Element	Wood	Fire	Fire	Earth	Earth
Zodiac	Pig	Mouse	Ox	Tiger	Hare
Parkha	Zon SE	Li South	Khon SW	Dha West	Khen NW
Mewa	5 Yellow	4 Green	3 Indigo	2 Black	1 White
Life Force	Water	Water	Earth	Wood	Wood
Health	Fire	Water	Water	Earth	Earth
Power	Wood	Fire	Fire	Earth	Earth
Luck	Fire	Wood	Water	Iron	Fire
Soul	Iron	Iron	Fire	Water	Water

Year	2000	2001	2002	2003	2004
Element	Iron	Iron	Water	Water	Wood
Zodiac	Dragon	Snake	Horse	Sheep	Monkey
Parkha	Kham North	Gin NE	Zin East	Zon SE	Li South
Mewa	9 Maroon	8 White	7 Red	6 White	5 Yellow
Life Force	Earth	Fire	Fire	Earth	Iron
Health	Iron	Iron	Wood	Wood	Water
Power	Iron	Iron	Water	Water	Wood
Luck	Wood	Water	Iron	Fire	Wood
Soul	Fire	Wood	Wood	Fire	Earth

Year	2005	2006	2007	2008	2009
Element	Wood	Fire	Fire	Earth	Earth
Zodiac	Bird	Dog	Pig	Mouse	Ox
Parkha	Khon SW	Dha West	Khen NW	Kham North	Gin NE
Mewa	4 Green	3 Indigo	2 Black	1 White	9 Maroon
Life Force	Iron	Earth	Water	Water	Earth
Health	Water	Earth	Earth	Fire	Fire
Power	Wood	Fire	Fire	Earth	Earth
Luck	Water	Iron	Fire	Wood	Water
Soul	Earth	Fire	Iron	Iron	Fire

Year	2010	2011	2012	2013	2014
Element	Iron	Iron	Water	Water	Wood
Zodiac	Tiger	Hare	Dragon	Snake	Horse
Parkha	Zin East	Zon SE	Li South	Khon SW	Dha West
Mewa	8 White	7 Red	6 White	5 Yellow	4 Green
Life Force	Wood	Wood	Earth	Fire	Fire
Health	Wood	Wood	Water	Water	Iron
Power	Iron	Iron	Water	Water	Wood
Luck	Iron	Fire	Fire	Water	Iron
Soul	Water	Water	Fire	Wood	Wood

Year	2015	2016	2017	2018	2019
Element	Wood	Fire	Fire	Earth	Earth
Zodiac	Sheep	Monkey	Bird	Dog	Pig
Parkha	Khen NW	Kham North	Gin NE	Zin East	Zon SE
Mewa	3 Indigo	2 Black	1 White	9 Maroon	8 White
Life Force	Earth	Iron	Iron	Earth	Water
Health	Iron	Fire	Fire	Wood	Wood
Power	Wood	Fire	Fire	Earth	Earth
Luck	Fire	Wood	Water	Iron	Fire
Soul	Fire	Earth	Earth	Fire	Iron

Year	2020	2021	2022	2023	2024
Element	Iron	Iron	Water	Water	Wood
Zodiac	Mouse	Ox	Tiger	Hare	Dragon
Parkha	Li South	Khon SW	Dha West	Khen NW	Kham North
Mewa	7 Red	6 White	5 Yellow	4 Green	3 Indigo
Life Force	Water	Earth	Wood	Wood	Earth
Health	Earth	Earth	Iron	Iron	Fire
Power	Iron	Iron	Water	Water	Wood
Luck	Wood	Water	Iron	Fire	Wood
Soul	Iron	Fire	Water	Water	Fire

Year	2025	2026	2027	2028	2029
Element	Wood	Fire	Fire	Earth	Earth
Zodiac	Snake	Horse	Sheep	Monkey	Bird
Parkha	Gin NE	Zin East	Zon SE	Li South	Khon SW
Mewa	2 Black	1 White	9 Maroon	8 White	7 Red
Life Force	Fire	Fire	Earth	Iron	Iron
Health	Fire	Water	Water	Earth	Earth
Power	Wood	Fire	Fire	Earth	Earth
Luck	Water	Iron	Fire	Wood	Water
Soul	Wood	Wood	Fire	Earth	Earth

Year	2030	2031	2032	2033	2034
Element	Iron	Iron	Water	Water	Wood
Zodiac	Dog	Pig	Mouse	Ox	Tiger
Parkha	Dha West	Khen NW	Kham North	Gin NE	Zin East
Mewa	6 White	5 Yellow	4 Green	3 Indigo	2 Black
Life Force	Earth	Water	Water	Earth	Wood
Health	Iron	Iron	Wood	Wood	Water
Power	Iron	Iron	Water	Water	Wood
Luck	Iron	Fire	Wood	Water	Iron
Soul	Fire	Iron	Iron	Fire	Water

Year	2035	2036	2037	2038	2039
Element	Wood	Fire	Fire	Earth	Earth
Zodiac	Hare	Dragon	Snake	Horse	Sheep
Parkha	Zon SE	Li South	Khon SW	Dha West	Khen NW
Mewa	1 White	9 Maroon	8 White	7 Red	6 White
Life Force	Wood	Earth	Fire	Fire	Earth
Health	Water	Earth	Earth	Fire	Fire
Power	Wood	Fire	Fire	Earth	Earth
Luck	Fire	Wood	Water	Iron	Fire
Soul	Water	Fire	Wood	Wood	Fire

Year	2040	2041	2042	2043	2044
Element	Iron	Iron	Water	Water	Wood
Zodiac	Monkey	Bird	Dog	Pig	Mouse
Parakha	Kham North	Gin NE	Zin East	Zon SE	Li South
Mewa	5 Yellow	4 Green	3 Indigo	2 Black	1 White
Life Force	Iron	Iron	Earth	Water	Water
Health	Wood	Wood	Water	Water	Iron
Power	Iron	Iron	Water	Water	Wood
Luck	Wood	Water	Iron	Fire	Wood
Soul	Earth	Earth	Fire	Iron	Iron

Note to Appendix: Tables for 1900–2025 of the main Tibetan astrological factors. Please note the following gives main factors for everyone, except where the calculation requires the use of an individual. In that case, Michael Erlewine (July 18, 1941) has been used, so that you have some example:

Year:	Year
Element:	Year Element for Everyone
Zodiac:	Zodiac for Everyone
Parkha:	Descending Parkha for M. Erlewine
Mewa:	Mewa for Everyone
Life Force:	Life Force for Everyone
Health:	Health for Everyone
Power:	Power for Everyone
Luck:	Luck for Everyone
Soul:	Soul for Everyone

REFERENCES

Some material in this article is the result of personal discussions with a number of high lamas in the Karma Kagyu Lineage, including H. E. Tai Situ, Rinpoche, H. E. Shamar, Rinpoche, Ven. Thrangu, Rinpoche, Ven. Khenpo Tsultrim Gyatso, Rinpoche, Ven. Bardor Tulku, Rinpoche and, in particular, Ven. Khenpo Karthar, Rinpoche.

Erlewine, Michael. *The Vision of the Eclipse*, AFA/Circle Books Calendar, 1980s.

———. *Lunar Gaps*, Matrix Journal, 1990.

———. *Science and the Lunation Cycle*, Matrix Journal, 1990.

———. *Yearly Lunar Practice Calendar*, from KTD Dharma Goods, 315 Marion Avenue, Big Rapids, MI 49307.

Iyer, N. P. Subramania. *Kalaprakasika*, Ranjan Publications, 1982.

Karthar, Ven. Khenpo, Rinpoche. From a teaching on Buddhist Festivals, given Big Rapids, MI in mid-1980s.

Pillai, D. Bahadur L. D. Swamikannuu. *Indian Chronology*, Asian Educational Services, 1982.

———. *Panchang and Horoscope*, Asian Educational Services, 1985.

Prakashananda, Swami. Personal communication.

Reynolds, John (aka Acharya Vajranatha). *Tibetan Astrology*, article.

――――. *Tibetan Astrology*, NCGR Newsletter.

――――. *1978 Tibetan Astrological Calendar & Almanac*, Kalachakra Publications, Katmandu, Nepal.

――――. Personal discussions, seminars, calendar, papers. n.d.

Sundar Das, Shyam. Personal communication.

Wangchug, Sange. Personal communication, teaching, and translation of Tibetan texts.

ABOUT THE AUTHOR

Michael Erlewine, director of Matrix Software, is active in a variety of areas, including: astrology, Tibetan Buddhism, music and film reviews, new age subjects, and online networking.

Erlewine is a systems programmer and the CEO of Matrix Software, the largest center for astrological programming and research in the Western hemisphere. The center includes the prestigious Heart Center Library, the largest non-profit astrological library that is open to the public on a year-round basis. Michael has been a practicing astrologer for over 30 years, with an international reputation in the field. He has made many original contributions to astrology including: Local Space (astro-locality technique), Interface Nodes, deep-space astrology, and pioneering contributions in heliocentric astrology. Erlewine was the first astrologer to offer astrological computer programs to the general public (1977). His astrological books include *The Sun is Shining, Astrophysical Directions, Manual of Computer Programming for Astrologers,* and *Interface Nodes.* He also serves as the editor of the *Astro★Talk Bulletin, Matrix Journal* (a technical research journal for astrologers), and the ongoing *Astro Index Encyclopedia* project. He has won a number of awards from the astrological community including: PAI (Professional Astrologers, Inc.), the American Federation of Astrologers, and the U.A.C. Regulus Award.

Michael Erlewine is also very active in Tibetan Buddhism (serving on a number of boards) and as the director of Heart Center Karma Thegsum Choling, a main center in North America for the translation, transcription, and publication of texts and teachings of the Karma Kagyu lineage of Tibetan Buddhism.

A former musician, he is the managing editor of AMG (All-Music Guide and All-Movie Guide)—perhaps the largest database of music and film ratings and reviews on the planet. AMG has a number of books and CD-ROMs published and also licenses data on a wide variety of online networks and other electronic formats (CompuServe, E-World, MSN, and the World Wide Web).

Erlewine is now engaged in producing The New Age Forum (the largest collection of new age experts and information) for The Microsoft Network (MSN) and as a World Wide Web Internet site (TheNewAge.com). Erlewine, married for some 25 years, lives with his family (four children) in Big Rapids, Michigan.

Michael Erlewine can be reached at Matrix Software, 315 Marion Avenue, Big Rapids, MI 49307. Phone 616 796-6398, Fax 616 796-3060, E-mail Michael@THENEWAGE.com.

HART deFouw

CHAPTER 5

THE HUMANISM
OF VEDIC ASTROLOGY

HUMANISM SELF-EVIDENTLY concerns itself with the essence of human existence. Even though cultural concepts about the significance and purpose of our existence have changed over the centuries, at its core, humanism remains an outlook that centers on people and their values, their capacities, and their worth, without compromising their interests, needs, and welfare. A humane astrology—be it ancient or modern, Western or Eastern—endeavors to illuminate the human condition.

Astrology that fails to dignify and improve the condition of our lives becomes essentially inhuman. In recognition of this, the tradition of Vedic astrology that developed in India over the last 3,000 years embeds its techniques and understandings in a matrix of humanistic thought. Yet the wealth of humanism in Vedic astrology is often not obvious to the casual modern observer who typically sees in Vedic astrology a predictive event-oriented system that resembles a strain of medieval astrology that is avoided by most contemporary Western astrologers.

Westerners who encounter the many poorly translated texts of Vedic astrology understandably believe it to be a mechanistic and fate-oriented system. Such texts typically and ominously declare in their aphorisms on individual horoscope interpretation that Mars and the North Node of the Moon in the 2nd house will indicate a spouse who dies of snake-bite on the second day after marriage; that Mars in the 4th house and Saturn in the 10th house will cause death through a lion; and that the ruler of the Ascendant and the Sun in the 6th, 8th, or 12th houses indicates afflictions through fire.

These texts also announce somewhat more benignly that the ruler of the 8th house in the 8th house bestows long life; that Jupiter in the 7th house will create attachment to the spouse; and that the lord of the

Ascendant in the 2nd or 9th house indicates the acquisition of a treasure. These and thousands (perhaps even millions) of similar authoritative statements violate the cultural paradigm of many a modern Westerner, who is typically oriented toward choice and free will, and who at the very least ultimately agrees with Polish-born American writer Isaac Beshivus Singer's statement:"We have to believe in free will. We have no choice."

The ancient classical texts of Vedic astrology are written in uncompromised language that leaves little room for interpretation. Coupled with the conspicuous absence of philosophical context to soften the authoritarian aphorisms in the majority of the classical Vedic astrology texts, it is little wonder that many a modern astrologer bristles at their dictatorial style. After all, there are no death inflicting lions or poisonous snakes in most modern cities. Horoscopes abound with Mars and Saturn in the 4th and 10th house respectively, without the ascribed effect of death through a lion! But you still may not be safe, as the following famous Indian astrological story illustrates.

A great astrologer told an opulent and wise king that his son, the only heir to the kingdom, would never become king because the youthful prince was destined to be killed in his childhood by a rampaging boar. The horrified king, knowing the astrologer's venerable record of accurate predictions, took all possible precautions to prevent the killing of his son by a boar. On the morning of the predicted day of death, the young prince was locked in the upper room of the highest and most inaccessible tower of the palace. Guards were posted. All were prepared should a rabid death-dealing boar charge the tower at the destined time, but the fatal hour passed without the appearance of a boar. The astrologer, who was with the king throughout this critical time, assured the king that his prediction was accurate and that the prince was now sure to be dead by a boar, even though none had appeared. The king sent his attendants to fetch his son in order to solve the riddle. Within minutes, shrieks of grief came from the tower that cloistered the prince. The king rushed up the steps of the tower to find his dead son, his skull crushed by a boar-shaped stone sculpture that had dislodged from its decorative perch high on the wall of the room.

Lions, snakes, and boars aside, the story epitomizes the tenuous nature of life, and the convoluted relationship between free will and fate. Any free-will-oriented astrology that attempts to dignify human life through an accurate portrayal of human experience must honestly acknowledge that often things don't go our way, despite our best efforts,

THE HUMANISM OF VEDIC ASTROLOGY / 207

and any honest predictive astrology must acknowledge that predictions go wrong as often as they are right, especially when the predictions attain progressively greater specificity. On the one hand, the efforts to save the prince were ineffective, despite the king's motivated will to change the situation; on the other hand, the astrologer who accurately predicted the death of the prince failed to foresee that the boar would be a stone sculpture.

Some anti-predictionists might argue that if the astrologer had not made the prediction, the prince would not have been locked in the room with the death inflicting boar, but this is an unsound argument because we will never know what would have happened precisely because it didn't happen. It appears that astrologers see our psyche and our past, present, and future through a glass darkly. One consequence of this is that our choices in life remain acts of faith. We can only hallucinate the possible ramifications of choices other than the ones made because in the end, what is, is what is. As Winston Churchill once wrote, "Which brings me to my conclusion upon Free Will and Predestination, namely—let the reader mark it—that they are identical."

The story also obliquely demonstrates that a Vedic astrology stripped of its substantial oral tradition of instructive tales is akin to a peacock plucked of its dignified plumage or a nightingale without a voice. A good one fourth of my training with my Indian Vedic astrology teacher involved my listening to the infinitely varied and inspired stories that he could effortlessly and pointedly recount to enrich my understanding of specific astrological and life situations that I or my clients could encounter. Through such frequently repeated traditional stories, and through the personal anecdotes of seasoned, practicing, native Vedic astrologers, the dictatorial language of the classical ancient texts is humanized. After all, the venerable astrologer of the story ends up being both right and wrong—an all too human dilemma!

The difficulty inherent in Vedic astrological analysis is emphasized in the *Sapta Rishi Nadi*, a little known work that is a compilation of the conclusions of a council of ancient Vedic astrological seers who discuss a number of horoscopes in the presence of the Hindu goddess Parvati. These seers, among whom are some of the most revered names in the pantheon of Vedic astrology, sometimes are at odds with each other in their inferences about specific horoscopes described in the manuscript. On the occasion of such variant opinions, each sage argues eloquently in favor of his predictions, citing classical astrological rules in support of his conclusion.

In one instance, several venerable sages insist that the wife of a person whose particular horoscope is under analysis will die young due to the astrological combinations found, while other equally eminent seers interpret the same combinations as indicating long life. In other horoscopes, the debate concerns the prospect of having children, the type of career, and numerous other matters. The goddess Parvati is required to intervene and offer the final opinion when the great astrological sages fail to agree. The sages unquestioningly accept Parvati's decisions.

At the very least, the method encoded in the *Sapta Rishi Nadi* serves the purpose of pointing out that Vedic astrological analysis is complex at times, even for the masters. Aside from being an astrological document that encourages students to evaluate horoscopes from different angles, the *Sapta Rishi Nadi* also is an allegory which demonstrates that reasoning on the basis of astrological principles must sometimes be enhanced or supplanted by divine intuition, represented by the goddess Parvati. The august and predictive language of the classical texts is humanized. Even for the seers, to err is human, and to accept the verdict of the divine in the midst of ambiguity becomes the ideal.

The preceding stories emphasize the compelling need for a comprehension of the matrix within which classical Vedic astrology thrives. To fathom the effulgent soul of Vedic astrology, it is perhaps more important for a student to develop a coherent understanding of the spiritual, philosophical, psychological, and secular context within which Vedic astrology is practiced, than to grasp exclusively the skeleton of its astrological techniques. Whereas the techniques of Vedic astrology may be partly obtained with some effort from its classical texts and their commentaries, *the silent language of its humanism is not to be found overtly and extensively in its own literature.* Yet it is this very silent language that infuses Vedic astrology with its humanism, and with its profound counseling potential. It is the very glue that holds Vedic astrology together, separating it from mere fortune telling, devoid of humanistic counseling content.

The traditional branches of classical Indian knowledge, of which Vedic astrology is one, to this day are seen in India as complementary parts of a larger system of knowledge, a precurser of holistic thought, in which the part contributes to the whole, and the whole enhances the part. The traditional branches of classical Indian knowledge collectively form a greater totality aimed at illuminating the human condition. Lack of knowledge of the various parts of this greater whole diminishes the understanding of a situation. For example, little or no knowledge of philosophy, psychology, or medicine, reduces a Vedic astrologer's theoretical and practical knowledge of human behavior and disease. The tacit consensus of the need for a holistic understanding among practitioners of traditional forms of Indian knowledge encourages them to aquire some comprehension of the various Indian classical traditions, according to his or her ability and opportunity. At one point in my studies, my teacher went through the spiritual classic known as The Bhagavad Gita (The Song of God) with me, explaining to me in detail its sublime insights into the human condition so that I would be a better counseling astrologer!

This implicit acknowledgment of the interrelation of the various classical disciplines in Indian traditions in turn does not require the classical astrology texts to restate in detail the principles of philosophy, medicine, spirituality, ritual, and the like. In this grand classical Indian tradition, it is incumbent on Vedic astrologers to get their noses out of technique-bound astrology texts, and to put their noses into the fragrance of life, a fragrance whose meaning is enhanced through an understanding of the organized principles of philosophy, medicine, and other traditional disciplines. This interwoven study of the various classical Indian subjects that address the vital concerns of humans is similar to the Western concept of a well-rounded education in the humanities. The Vedic astrologer learns how to think, and not only makes objective measurements, but interprets and applies them humanistically in different situations for unique individuals.

Just as a person is better known when one understands his or her background, so is Vedic astrology rendered humanistic once one assimilates the backdrop of ideas against which it is ideally practiced. Many of these ideas have entered the Western stream of awareness through the interest in Eastern thought. Other ideas used by Vedic astrologers also have parallels in Western thought: concepts like the law of cause and effect, transmigration of the soul, free will and fate, spiritual evolution, auto-behavioral conditioning, and other highly developed ideas.

TOWARD A NEO-VEDIC HUMANISTIC ASTROLOGY

With its emphasis on Indian religious, philosophical, and cultural concepts, is Vedic astrology too ethnocentric to be useful in the West? In its antiquated cultural milieux, it is undoubtedly too narrow for the West—perhaps even too narrow for modern India. For Vedic astrology to be useful and humanistic in modern times, its hallowed classical texts must be investigated, reinterpreted, and more overtly reintegrated with the rich philosophical heritage of India and with the traditions of the rest of the world. Undoubtedly, seen through the modern eye, Vedic astrology is ripe with antiquated notions, authoritarianism, chauvanism, and hyperbole. Yet to dismiss it as superstition, or as an idea whose time has come and gone, is surely a colossal modern conceit. It assumes that the cultures that gave us the brilliant religions and philosophies of Hinduism, Buddhism, Jainism, Vedanta, and Yoga; who produced the lofty thoughts of the Vedas, the Upanishads, the Puranas, and the great epics of the Ramayana and the Mahabharata; who dazzled the world with their precocious insight into mathematics, mysticism, and medicine, were capable of producing only meaningless superstitious drivel when it came to astrology.

Perhaps it is more reasonable to postulate that the meaningful essence of Vedic astrology needs to be winnowed from some of its restrictive trappings. From its substance must be woven a new style that is aligned with modern conditions, a style which does not sacrifice the original substance of Vedic astrology on the modern alter of fickle fashion. A balance must develop which honors the roots of Vedic astrology without allowing its past to choke the life from its unfolding present. Literal interpretation of classical Vedic astrological principles must give way to liberal renditions which translate its ancient principles into the language of modern circumstances. Freely understood and applied, the techniques and the outlook of a neo-Vedic astrology can help to illuminate the Westerner's and the modern Indian's path through life.

Daily, more and more people in our age of information are embracing the eclecticism born of a one planet/one people perspective. The Orient becomes more integrated with the Occident, and vice versa. And while the world moves toward the reality of a global village in diverse areas, the current of Vedic astrology gains momentum in the stream of modern Western astrological thought, just as the latter, itself, is starting to influence Vedic astrological thought. It seems inevitable that a neo-classical Vedic approach will be born as Vedic astrology acclimatizes to the global village of the modern and future world.

The birth pangs of a neo-Vedic astrology already are evident in the West and in India. In harmonizing Vedic astrology with a changing world, some Westerners (and some Indians) integrate Western astrological methods with Vedic ones. Others are fundamentalist proselytizers for the merits of Vedic astrology, often at the expense of other astrological systems. Still others in the Western and Eastern camps favor the strategy of the ostrich: if I ignore it, it will go away. A few aver that Vedic astrology is perfect, and that the world must change in order to fully appreciate it. Some take the "older it is the better it is" approach and lock in battle with the innovators, averring that if only the pure and original system were reconstructed, a glorious astrological renaissance would occur. All share in common a realization that in the global village, different astrological systems must adapt to the challenges presented by a global communal information environment.

In the evolving global village, the debate is no longer which system is superior, but how the concepts and methods of one system enhance the others. This eclectic and inclusive impulse in modern astrology is perhaps a theme of our times, having parallels in areas as diverse as religion (the adoption of components of Eastern religions by many Westerners), medicine (the greater acceptance of acupuncture, shiatsu and ayurveda), physics (as evidenced by popular books with titles like *The Tao of Physics* and *The Dancing Wu Li Masters*) and even popular music (as shown by the trend toward international musical themes by major popular recording artists). Even Western astrology, itself, is currently undergoing a renaissance, in the process reclaiming and re-evaluating its roots in classical Greek astrology, which, on several points, closely parallels Vedic astrology in substance and style, although there are many major differences as well.

THE CLASSICS OF VEDIC ASTROLOGY SPEAK

Whatever may be born of the cross-fertilization of these varied attitudes, a neo-Vedic astrology must not estrange itself from its basic mandate of illuminating the human condition. A great Vedic astrologer of antiquity wrote some fifteen centuries ago, "Just as the night without lamps and the day without the Sun are totally dark, so will a king grope in life like a blind man if not guided by a good astrologer.... Hence a king who desires victory, status, prosperity, pleasure and spiritual progress ought to employ a most knowledgeable astrologer" (*Brihat Samhita* 2.26–28). In our times of democracy and socialism, the common person is the "king" who becomes the beneficiary of skilled neo-Vedic astrology applied to modern conditions.

On the weight of its own authority, classical Vedic astrology supports its evolution and adaptation to different times and climes. Its most revered and authoritative work, the *Brihat Parashara Hora*, which is ascribed to Parashara, a great seer of Vedic times, says in this regard "[An astrologer] who likes astrology, who has self-mastery, who is intelligent, skilled, well-practiced, and logical in the calculations, grammar, and axioms [of astrology], and who has a knowledge of foreign places and time, will be true [in prediction]" (*Brihat Parashara Hora* 27.39–40). The inescapable reference to a knowledge of foreign lands and time, along with the emphasis on the qualities of the astrologer, suggests that Parashara encouraged adaptation of his aphorisms to different conditions, in the process perhaps anticipating the modern understanding of the conditioning effect of the triad of time, space, and observer on diverse phenomena, including human behavior.

The implications for a neo-Vedic astrology adjusting itself to modern conditions are immense. For example, it opens the door to modernizing some of the calculations of Vedic astrology, such as the use of the "true" instead of the "mean" nodes of the Moon. It also encourages the formulation of new interpretations for the many different planetary combinations. What may have been a combination for death at birth under ancient conditions may be a "routine" cesarean, a relatively common occurrence in modern society. Ancient attributions of death by lions and serpents may, in the modern context, be mishaps or traumas through pets or other animals. The finding of treasures may simply be an unexpected promotion involving a raise or an unanticipated refund from the taxman!

And yet, as I have demonstrated in public lectures and other writings, it remains uncanny how many of the ancient aphorisms will apply without modification, even in the modern context. For the combination of Saturn in the sidereal sign of Libra in the 4th house, a pertinent famous aphorism says in part "extolled by all ... wicked in disposition ... intrigues with [sexual] partners not her own ..." (*Phaladipika* 6.4). Marilyn Monroe had this combination, well supported by other indications.

She also had the lord of her 7th house exalted in a sidereal sign of Venus and aspected by Jupiter and Venus, the two great benefics of Vedic astrology. An aphorism of Parashara says: "If the lord of the 7th house is in a constellation of Venus or Saturn and be aspected by a benefic, there will be many spouses. The same will occur if the lord of the 7th house is exalted" (*Brihat Parashar Hora* 18.6). Both combinations applied to Monroe's horoscope. She had three husbands and many lovers. For Adolf Hitler, who had Mars in the sidereal sign of Aries in the 7th house, a renowned aphorism interpreting such a position of Mars says: "[W]ill have a long face, a forceful personality, great charisma, a love of fighting wars, much anger . . . is a protector of thieves . . . and dies by fire or weapons . . ." (*Brihat Parashara Hora* 75.3–7) all of which found expression in his life.

Parashara's statement, in support of the adaptation of his astrological principles to a different time and place, while opening the door to a neo-Vedic astrology adapted to our time that bears so little resemblance to ancient India, does not give license to whimsically concoct radically different foundational principles and practices for Vedic astrology. He specifically mentions that the astrologer should be "well-practiced" in the principles and axioms of the tradition. Before the known body of Vedic astrology is dramatically modified, it is imperative that the modifiers be familiar with its structure and its principles, so that the baby is not thrown out with the bath water—a phenomena that may have occured in Western astrology when it was progressively cut off from its roots in the attempt to modify it and to bring it into line with scientific materialism and other outlooks.

No matter what the subject, innovators are often able to innovate best after acquainting themselves with the knowledge that exists in their chosen discipline. Thus an Einstein masters the physics of his time and moves toward his theory of relativity as surely as a Martin Luther moves from his knowledge of traditional Catholicism to his historically innovative Lutheranism. Innovation and progression in a discipline are to be distinguished from iconoclastic chaos, anarchy, and confusion.

A simple example of the latter occurred during a recess in a seminar I once gave. A self-proclaimed advanced student of Vedic astrology approached me and asked me to comment on his Vedic horoscope. It was of concern to him (and to me) that I wasn't capable of correctly understanding the placements of the planets by house and by sign in the chart he had drawn and shown to me. It became apparent in the ensuing discussion that he had radically re-invented the traditional Vedic representation of a horoscope. Communication between us became confused because he did not know the standard method of chart representation that I was using in the seminar! Without a coherent understanding of the roots of Vedic astrology, such uncontained and random developments may pave the way to a Tower of Babel crisis for Vedic astrology in the West.

As a living tradition, Vedic astrology will continue to augment its traditional emphasis on the humanistic evolution of the individual, and a Vedic astrology reborn and fully integrated with its rich spiritual and philosophical heritage is ideally equipped to contribute to humanistic understandings of the human condition. Its spiritual, philosophical, psychological and mundane precepts encourage the individual to be a responsible participant in his or her evolution without fostering unbridled egotism. It manages this by encouraging an awareness of the matrix of forces within which human life evolves. The eternal questions raised by the human condition find answers in the classical and modern tradition of Vedic astrology, answers that were often formulated over centuries of inquiry and experience.

Most unfortunately, the presence of such answers in the classical Sanskrit works of Vedic astrology are often overlooked and under-valued by the modern reader. In a cultural milieu where manuscripts were painstakingly reproduced manually, a culturally defined economy of expression was important. The emphasis in the old astrological texts became that of a stylistic focus primarily on technique and method, not on philosophical enquiries integral to a humanistic astrology. The Indian astrological manuscripts of the past were not intended as self-explanatory expositions of *all* aspects of Vedic astrology. In the words of the Vedic astrology Sanskrit scholar, David Pingree: "The primary texts … are generally written in a very crabbed and obscure style designed to stimulate the student's memory of the procedure to be followed, but frequently not even pretending to provide the full algorithm for solving a particular problem; that was to be found, if not in the repetitiousness of the science, in the guru's oral tradition. …" (Pingree, p. 1).

For example, in the rules of Sanskrit composition, an idea or concept can be emphasized by placing it at the end of a chapter. With this in mind, what the casual reader may miss because an important notion is expressed but once to be lost in a sea of method and technique, the experienced reader will note as a point of emphasis. The occurrence of interesting philosophical asides in the last verse of some chapters of classical Vedic astrology texts is worthy of notice because they humanize Vedic astrology for a modern reader by building a bridge of continuity between the ancient and modern world.

To wit, almost like a modern author excusing himself from gender-biased writing, one classical authority states in the last verse of a chapter on astrology for women: "Whatever has been stated in this chapter should be wisely applied to females relating to their births, selection of grooms, marriage and query. These effects are applicable to their husbands also" (*Saravali* 46:32). In a significant aside in the last verse of another chapter describing astrological combinations for longevity, the same work states: "Only those who consume wholesome diet, those who are virtuous, those who have good conduct and who control their senses, will enjoy the longevity as laid down by the sages" (*Saravali* 41:25). Is this intended to emphasize the fact that astrology will operate within the context of a person's lifestyle? Most modern astrologers would agree that the principles of astrology find expression within the context provided by a person's milieu; astrological principles do not supercede the importance of an individual's environment.

Another work states, in the last verse of a chapter that describes the good and bad effects of transiting planets on a natal horoscope: "Planets are always favorable to one who is peaceful, who possesses self-control, who has earned wealth through virtuous means, and who is always observing ethical and moral conduct" (*Phaladipika* 26:50). An interesting emphasis by a classical author in a subject that is frequently associated exclusively with fate and destiny. Phaladipika's emphasized statement spans several centuries to align itself with a viewpoint valued by most astrologers today.

FREE WILL AND FATE

One of the eternal questions raised by the human condition is the issue of free will versus fate, which is not only pertinent to theologians and philosophers, but is of central importance to astrologers. If there is only free will, then presumably very little about a person's life is predictable because every well motivated human being will create the life of his or her choice. Judged by the historical and current human level of dissatisfaction, few have the life of their choice in all respects. If there is only predestination, then everything in life is theoretically predictable, and humans become automatons, a fact which is again contrary to experience because unforeseen surprises occur even in the most scripted of lives.

A genuine humanistic astrology must take up this question, for free will and fate are at the very center of human potential. Because of its centrality, whole societies, not to mention brilliant individuals, have polarized on the free will and fate debate. The post-industrial West is currently culturally in the grips of a "you can have it all if you only try" frenzy. (Just watch late night infomercial TV!) Most Indians are more comfortable aligning themselves predominantly with fate.

To emphasize the fatalist cultural tendency in India, an Indian yogi once told me the story of a man drowning in an Indian river. As the man's head went under the water for the third and final time, he wildly thrashed his hands above the water in a last attempt to attract a rescue. An Indian palmist who noticed the drowning man approached him. From the river's bank, he peered intently at the drowning man's hands. Suddenly, the palmist's look of concern melted into a smile of relief. He cupped his hands together to amplify his voice and shouted at the drowning man: "Don't worry, you have a long life line!" Having fulfilled his duty, the palmist promptly departed!

Yes, sometimes the Orientals are impoverished when their belief in destiny is carried to extremes. But before you proudly dust off your Free Will Club member card, may I remind you of Canute the Great, the 11th century English king, who, according to legend, failed to make the tide recede through an act of his kingly will. Or more disconcerting yet, sit down and count all of the legion times your own will was thwarted. East to West and back again—irrespective of culture, race and creed—people are consumed by this conundrum of free will and fate. The previous examples indicate that there are obviously times when an excessive commitment to the one or the other position has us play the fool.

Popular new age values suggest that we create our own reality; if we don't have what we consciously want, we just need to change our unconscious beliefs to attain the desired goal. How then can there be any basis for prediction? There is undoubtedly some truth in this viewpoint, but for this to become a viable strategy for fulfillment in life, one question that begs to be answered is: how can the conscious mind become aware of what is unconscious? Without an answer to this dilemma, self-empowerment philosophies remain castles in the air. Another important consideration in this cult of the will and choice is the extent to which beliefs operate within the parameters of natural and social laws. It often minimizes the fact that human possibility is ecologically embedded in the environment in its largest sense, which includes one's neurology, physiology, society, and so on. Does a mere non-belief in gravity enable a person to fly? Does one month of willful healthy living resolve many years of neglect? A humanistic Vedic astrology attempts to illuminate these areas by using the horoscope as a tool for insight by helping to define the nature and magnitude of a difficulty, its development and resolution over time.

The fate-oriented worldview of most Indian astrologers suggests that knowledge of even an unalterable future—which they believe can be acquired through Vedic astrology—empowers a person to be prepared for all circumstances in life. But the question that begs an answer here is: if all circumstances in life are predestined, what is the point in knowing the future? Is knowledge of the future intended to help a person simply to endure future circumstances or to change them? If it is exclusively the former, then the universal experience of the human will is disowned; if it is the latter, then life cannot be predestined. Although the methods of Vedic astrology undoubtedly render some prediction possible, no Vedic astrologer has a perfect record in prediction. Practically speaking, Vedic astrology is incapable of always predicting the future accurately and, to accommodate their idealism, some would have it that Vedic astrology is perfect, but Vedic astrologers are not.

In the one corner we have free will-oriented astrologers who sometimes lay exclusive claim to being true humanists. They imply that prediction is often detrimental and without foundation, an attitude that currently dominates Western astrologers, but one which may be shifting. In the other corner, we have fate-inclined astrologers, which includes the many native Vedic astrologers who make a tacit assumption about the prevalence of fate. They measure astrology's usefulness by its capacity to predict the future accurately. Interestingly, they also lay claim to humanism.

As a cultural cross-dresser who has enjoyed slipping in and out of occidental and oriental garb for the last twenty-seven years, I have watched Westerners astonished and dismayed by the Oriental's willingness to zealously predict events just as often as I have witnessed Easterners wonder at the reluctance of many Occidentals to forecast events. Some Western clients of mine have returned from visits to India complaining of the arrogance of some Hindu astrologer for emphatically predicting a divorce in a certain year, casually throwing in an unsolicited prediction of the exact year of the client's death to boot. My Indian clients often grumble that only a detailed psychological portrait was created by some Western astrologer whom they consulted, and that there was too little concrete information about their business prospects, the birth or marriage of their children, the outcome of their pending litigation, and the time for the approval for their immigration!

Since the free will or fate issue has been an unresolved topic for debate worldwide for many centuries, it is tempting to assume that it may be unresolvable. An unresolvable question is sometimes indicative of a question *that is formulated inappropriately*. It may be the case that free will *and* fate are dynamics that affect the human condition. It may even be that, paradoxically, one is the result of the other.

The apparent impasse between Western and Eastern notions of free will and fate can be addressed by a humanistic neo-Vedic astrology through the ancient Indian concept of karma—the law of cause and effect—according to which every action produces a result. Experience suggests that repetition of similar actions leads to an aggregate result that becomes a behavioral or circumstantial destination, or destiny. The aggregate result may be unstable, firm, or somewhere in between, depending on the two primary factors of conditioning: repetition and intensity. Within the parameters of natural and social law, intense single and/or repetitive actions usually lead to a fixed and well-defined outcome or destiny, while feeble single or repetitive actions tend to create less certain results. Viewed in this way, applications of free will eternally produce results which are later described as fate.

One of my Vedic astrology teacher's favorite analogies for the relationship between fate and free will was that of a car driver driving at 100 mph. At some point, the driver had *chosen* to make the effort necessary to accelerate to 100 mph and to maintain that speed. Suppose that something suddenly obstructs the vehicle's path. Free will is available to the driver to choose to pull on the wheel, honk the horn, forcefully apply the brake, and so on. Yet the vehicle also has a compelling forward momentum, a predictable fate that has arisen as a result of the driver's previous choices. If the previous choice would have been to drive at perhaps 50 mph, the act of will involved in swerving or braking to avoid the obstruction may have been less dangerous and more meaningful in producing the desired outcome because of the reduced momentum of the car.

The car analogy involves controlled variables, which is usually not the case in the complex web of life. Yet it contains the nucleus of a viable explanation of why people sometimes appear to be fated and swept along by a current of destiny, seemingly having their will thwarted. At other times their will is duly rewarded when the focused application of their will is supported by the established momentum in their life, or when their use of will is intense enough to overcome any momentum contrary to their goal. Vedic astrologers who attempt prediction are, in fact, trying *to gauge the momentum of a person's karma* toward different outcomes, even if they can only do this in broad terms.

REINCARNATION

Why are there such inequities among people? Practically speaking, few people seem to get their just desserts. To explain why one person is born in the lap of luxury while another is deprived of even subsistence food; why one experiences a sudden rise to dizzying heights of power only to experience a humiliating fall, while another rises steadily and preserves his or her gains; why one person expends his or her genius by age 30, and another only discovers his or her genius at age of 50—these and many other variables in life are explained typically by Indian astrologers through a belief in reincarnation. In Western literature, this is also known as the theory of the transmigration of the soul.

In the spiritual literature of the Upanishads, the oldest of which predate Buddhism, it is suggested that a being has more than one life, and that the doer of constructive deeds enjoys life, while the doer of destructive deeds suffers in life. A being will reap what it sows through its actions because of natural law, what the Hindus and Buddhists refer to as *dharma*. A well-defined destination may be forged as a result of actions that produce a firm destiny over the course of many lifetimes. A person may have pursued spiritual practices over several lifetimes and be born with a natural talent for spiritual understanding that is precocious in relation to the logic of their current life.

This expansive perspective of an incarnating being over many lifetimes leads most Indian Vedic astrologers to believe that the birth chart indicates the karmic propensities developed by the incarnating being during previous lives. The horoscope becomes a map of the karma of a person in the various areas of the current life. Depending on the past activities, the being may have a forceful momentum in areas such as marriage, children, education, and the like, that is ripe to be experienced.

Such karma will develop of its own accord, like a ripe fruit falling from a tree spontaneously. Having forgotten its past life activities, the incarnated soul believes itself to be swept along by its good or bad destiny in these areas of ripe karma. It feels its will to be unduly thwarted or rewarded depending on the notably desirable or undesirable results it experiences. In other areas of life, the soul may experience life operating within the predictable parameters of typical logical assumptions. In yet some other life activities, there may exist a formative momentum toward a goal that will yet require additional effort to mature.

From this viewpoint, even what seems to be fated in a life is actually the result of an entity's activities in previous lives. What may temporarily seem like unrewarded activities will ultimately cumulate and penetrate an achievement threshold beyond which it will be experienced as the desired result. This achievement threshold may be crossed later in a lifetime, or perhaps in a future incarnation. It may be tomorrow, next year, a decade from now, or in the second future incarnation! Paradoxically, reincarnation sugggests that even when dealing with situations that seem predestined, the application of will results in an inevitable outcome according to natural law, although the outcome may simply be separated from the willful activity by time.

There is a story about Swami Prabhupada Bhaktivedanta, the founder of the Hare Krishna movement. When he first arrived in the West, he was an unknown itinerant and poor monk. One day, an American who saw the Swami sitting by himself in a desolate park in New York, asked him who he was. Prabhupada replied that he was a famous Swami, the head of 108 temples around the world. The American was dubious of this dour monk's assertion and asked the Swami to show him one of the temples as proof. "Oh, I cannot do that because of a small problem," Prabhupada is said to have replied. "You see, I and my temples are separated by the small matter of time." By the time of his death, Prabhupada was a famous Swami and was the head of 108 temples world wide.

This anecdote illustrates the spirit that lies behind constructive use of the karmic theory. Prabhupada had an unshakable conviction that his activities would lead him to their inevitable result sooner or later in this lifetime or in the next. It is not the intention of Vedic astrology to squelch a person's conviction and commitment to his or her goals by a reference to destiny; rather, the intention is to inspire an individual to evaluate realistically what he or she wants to accomplish by assessing how assiduously and how long the person may be required to work toward a goal to enjoy its achievement. Viewed in this way, Vedic astrology becomes the means for pragmatically assessing one's potential and applying oneself to living up to one's destiny in those arenas where an intense momentum in one's destiny is implied by the horoscope, while adjusting to areas that may be difficult to enliven. Ultimately, nothing becomes impossible because the results of one's actions are forever creating a new destiny, even while one paradoxically experiences one's current fate in the form of circumstances to be modified. Of course, goals may take time and effort to achieve.

Humanistic Vedic astrology thus draws a clear line between its view of destiny and the concept of determinism, the theory that all human action is caused entirely by preceding events, and not by the exertion of the human will. If it had been the intention of the ancient masters of Vedic astrology to create a system of knowledge founded exclusively on the doctrine of determinism, their classical works would not have included exhortations to resolve, by the implemention of a variety of suggested solutions, the dynamic karmic tensions diagnosed by means of a Vedic horoscope. The great Parashara, himself, points to a concept of destiny that is distinct from determinism by devoting the last fourteen chapters of his ninety-seven chapter *Brihat Parashara Hora* to remedies that can be resorted to in the face of karmic afflictions shown by a horoscope.

HUMANISM AND KARMA

Given the fact that Vedic astrologers believe that the whole horoscope is a map of the person's karma, a Vedic astrologer often uses the horoscope to classify the karma of a person as good, bad, or somewhere in between. While the terms "good" and "bad" ultimately invite the problem of values, these same generalizations invite Vedic astrologers to categorize horoscopes as relatively good or bad. This does not mean that the owner of the horoscope is exclusively good or bad, but that the life experiences of a person may be generally and relatively of a desirable or undesirable type. True, often unpleasant experiences are character builders and harbingers of lessons to be learned, but despite such opportunities for enrichment, few people line up willingly for entrance into the school of hard knocks. Perhaps the language of Vedic astrology merely reflects the human propensity for seeking pleasure and avoiding pain.

Although a horoscope is often characterized by Vedic astrologers as relatively good or bad based on its planetary combinations, more explicit analysis of a person's karma involves assessment of the individual astrological houses, which have meanings similar to the Western astrological houses. Thus the 1st house of both systems represents the body and the personality of the person, the 2nd house indicates wealth or resources, the 9th house becomes the house of travels, and so on. There is some dissonance between the Vedic and Western astrological house attributions, a notable example being the 9th-house rulership of the father in Vedic astrology. An analysis of each of the houses gives a portrait of the horoscope owner's karmic patterns in important areas, like relationships, education, finance, spiritual practices, or any of the many other human endeavors.

Such detailed astrological house analysis may lead to the conclusion that the karma in marriage, for example, may be unstable, firm, or somewhere in between for either relative good or bad, keeping in mind that good and bad are defined by individual and cultural preferences. I have had some Western couples come to me confused as to why a Hindu astrologer—who believed that children are the crowning achievement of a marriage—deemed it to be a tragedy that their horoscopes indicated little likelihood of ever having children, when in fact the couple did not want any!

I have also had Eastern clients who are puzzled by Western astrologers who want to belabor the psychological implications of the client's relationship with his or her parents. As one such client, who had been separated from his parents early in life in order to go and live with a relative and further his education, said to me, "What's the point in such self-indulgence? The success my wife, children, and I enjoy today is the result of the benefit of my early education!"

The truth may lie somewhere in between a total event-oriented fatalistic astrology and one that is exclusively psychological, and spiritual. A spiritual, psychological, physiological, and event pattern analysis of the planetary combinations affecting each of the twelve astrological houses of a Vedic horoscope creates a comprehensive mosaic of a person's likely patterns over the course of a lifetime. Thus, for example, a horoscope may indicate mostly desirable experiences and events in the area of marriage, children, and parents, while concurrently implying difficult situations over the course of a lifetime in matters of education, health, and finance. One with difficult event patterns may nevertheless have great spiritual potentials; another with good event patterns may be inclined towards pessemism. Many other permutations become possible, and through an accurate assessment of such patterns, astrology becomes a diagnostic tool that sheds light on a person's overall patterns and their interaction.

This procedure humanizes the overall good or bad snapshot evaluation of a horoscope because it will be seen practically that, through the lens of Vedic astrological analysis, almost every astrological chart has combinations indicating difficulties in some areas of life, while also having astrological indicators of success in other aspects of life. Analysis of some less defined areas inevitably leads the Vedic astrologer to the middle ground between failure and success as well. In terms of the earlier car analogy, the vehicle of marriage or career may have compelling momentum toward effortlessness, strenuousness, or neutrality, depending on the nature of the astrological combinations.

The compelling nature of some of the adverse and beneficial combinations in a horoscope may indicate a type of karma that is so firm that it seems almost impossible to change by one's willful actions over a limited but extended period of time, be it a month, or a decade, or this life. It is in such realms of karma that prediction becomes possible. Some horoscopes abound with well-defined astrological combinations indicating well-defined karmic propensities. In such astrological charts, predictions are most likely to succeed. Other charts have only one or two houses with compelling combinations indicative of unyielding karma. These charts make dramatic prediction feasible in those areas, but less possible in the other areas of the person's life. Finally, a few charts have little in the way of compelling astrological evidence for firm karmas in any areas, and predictions become more and more uncertain.

For example, if by the rules of Vedic astrology, a person has in the Vedic chart Saturn, Rahu (North Node of the Moon) and Mars influencing the 7th house of marriage, without the intervention of any of the many modifications possible in a Vedic horoscope, the likelihood of a person not being able to sustain a long term partnership like marriage are high indeed. Under such circumstances, a Vedic astrologer may predict obstructions to marriage, such as its absence, or separation, divorce, infidelities, or perhaps ill health to the marital partner. (Should you have such a combination, remember that many modifications are possible.)

This exact combination exists in the horoscopes of the French writer Anais Nin[1] and the Indian yogi Swami Shivananda.[2] Nin became famous for her convoluted writings on sexuality, her affairs with notable people of her day—including the American writer Henry Miller, her incest with her father, and her unusual marriage, which involved multiple separations and infidelities. Swami Shivananda became famous as an unmarried celibate practitioner of yoga, his reputation remaining unsullied throughout his spiritual life.

The Vedic astrological reasons for the different development in the arenas of marriage and intimate sexual relations in the lives of these two famous people lies in the fact that Shivananda had in his horoscope astrological combinations known as *pravrajya yogas* (ascetic combinations) that are delineated in classical texts in a chapter exclusively dedicated to these combinations. Such a specialized chapter reccurs in most major classical works of Vedic astrology, perhaps as an acknowledgment of the importance of spiritual questing in ancient India.

Although these works praise combinations like the *pravrajya yogas* for success in spiritual endeavors, the fact remains that Shivananda's married life was obstructed, as indicated by the influence of Mars, Rahu and Saturn on his 7th house of marriage. Among his several ascetic combinations cited in classical texts are 1) if Saturn aspects the lord of the sign occupied by the Moon, and 2) if the lord of the Ascendant is aspected by Saturn (all according to the astrological aspects of Vedic astrology, which differ from those of Western astrology both in method and interpretation). Similar ascetic combinations are conspicuously absent in Nin's chart, which abounds in configurations for sensuality.

Because Vedic astrology can at times provide a karmic x-ray of a life, it is incumbent on a Vedic astrologer who presents the diagnoses to become a counselor who animates the x-ray, taking into consideration a client's values and potential to whatever extent these are known. The way in which the plot of the client's life story, and its possible resolution, is offered to the client will depend partly on the expectations and personal beliefs of the client, partly on the societal context within which the person exists, and partly on the attitude and skill of the astrologer.

When making a prediction concerning marriage, as in the cases of Shivananda and Nin, the astrologer must remain a soothsayer: he or she

---

[1] Anais Nin, born February 21, 1903 at 8:35 P.M. LMT, 2°E16′ 48°N53′.
[2] Swami Shivananda, born September 8, 1887 at 4:16 A.M. LMT 77°E40′ 8°N48′.

must be one who first and foremost soothes through the process of fore-telling the future to the extent that it can be foretold. On occasion this may mean short-term discomfort to a client in the interest of the client's long-term satisfaction in life. In support of the wise and humanistic use of Vedic astrological analysis, one of the greatest of Vedic astrologers wrote in the fifth century:"[An astrologer] must be eloquent, kind and sincere, a knower of time and place ... well versed in the art of curative and preventive behaviors ... and in the suggestion of preventive mea-sures ..." (*Varahamihira* 2.3).

Following the leads of classical Vedic astrology in the Indian con-text, it becomes necessary for the astrologer to recommend appropriate prayers, or other culturally sanctioned behaviors, whenever the client's interests are best served by such measures. In the Western context it is incumbent on the Vedic astrologer to adapt and to recommend remedial measures that are within the client's value system—perhaps psychologi-cal or financial counseling—to help him or her modify behavior and circumstances.

In the case of Swami Shivananda, noticing the ascetic spiritual combinations may enable a Vedic astrologer to contextualize the prob-lematic 7th house within the promise of spirituality, something highly valued and respected in Hindu culture. A feasible interpretation be-comes:"Although it may be inadvisable for you to marry, this will ben-efit you because your life will likely take you in the direction of a successful monastic life. By following this inclination toward renuncia-tion, you will be enhancing themes that are already strong in your na-ture and promise successful outcomes."

With Nin, the solution may be therapy, with a caution that the undertaking will likely be demanding and lengthy. Because her horo-scope contains promising Vedic astrological combinations for fame in writing, she could perhaps also be encouraged to write for catharsis, which she, of course, did through her famous voluminous diary and her semi-autobiographical books. No matter what a Vedic astrological diag-noses involves, it is incumbent on a Vedic astrologer to contribute to its humanistic use by the client.

Perhaps one of the major contrasts between the attitudes of a hu-manistic Vedic astrologer and a humanistic Western astrologer is that the Vedic astrologer more overtly tends to build a system of psychology that emphasizes the profound impact on the formation of one's life made by the events one experiences. This is not done to the exclusion of the innate force of character, but as a complement to it. The Vedic astrologer is curious to know in hindsight what the impact was of that accident or of that career success early in life. In foresight, he or she may caution of the difficulty arising from the posssibility of ill health in a coming year, or suggest the most supportive time for pursuing a promotion. In the event of the ill health, an ounce of prevention may constitute a pound of cure. In the career promotion scenario, a simple word to the wise may optimize the best use of a promising time.

Western astrology currently seems to approach its analysis predominantly from the inside out, to a large extent minimizing astrological focus on mundane events and maximizing the impact on one's life of psychological states. The modern Western astrologer tends to wonder what occurred in the world of career as a result of the intense focus on power or regeneration suggested by the transit of Pluto over the 10th house of career in a client's horoscope. Ultimately, both systems view the same situation through different lenses. Vedic astrology, despite its current focus on mundane events, is able to address psychological, spiritual, and mundane considerations—a fact often demonstrated by my teacher. Western astrology is also capable of addressing life's several dimensions, although its current emphasis is mostly psychological.

Counseling is enriched when the spiritual, psychological, *and* the mundane scripts that may occur in various areas of life are known. A person with the unmitigated 7th house combination involving Mars, Rahu and Saturn, is less likely to resolve marriage themes—even with the help of prayer and/or psychological counseling—than one who has less virulent horoscopic indications concerning partnerships like marriage. In fact, it may sometimes be more useful to counsel such a person to become equipped mentally *to accept* the themes in his or her relationships, while encouraging the person to put energies into other more promising areas of life. The very acceptance of a situation may sometimes bring about a revolutionary or magical change in a person's dynamics. As my Vedic astrologer teacher used to say: "You Westerners spend so much time trying to change your destiny, when it is hard enough to live up to it!"

Knowledge of the mundane experiences in a person's past is likely to shed light on the present and future, and an outline of likely future occurrences may empower a person to constructively interact with circumstantial developments. To anticipate circumstances in a person's life at different times, Vedic astrologers make a great deal of use of *dashas,* which are their equivalent of Western progression systems. The dashas are diverse ways to allocate rulership of segments of a person's life to either the sidereal signs of the zodiac, or to the planets of Vedic astrology. Such allocated segments will vary from person to person depending on variations in his or her horoscope. Thus, for one person a cycle of variable duration allocated to Taurus or to the Sun—depending on the system used—may start at age 30, for another at age 2, and yet another person may not experience such a cycle at all during the course of life. The most widely used of these systems is known as the *Vimshottari Dasha*. Its method of calculation can be obtained from any standard modern text on Vedic astrology.

These dashas indicate, through their involvement as signs and planets in the astrological combinations in a horoscope, the type of karmic developments likely to occur during the different years of one's life. For example, the sequence of the *Vimshottari Dasha* of Swami Shivananda was such that during the marriageable years from 22 to 29 he experienced seven years which fell under the rulership of the planet Mars. Keeping in mind that Mars is one of the three planets (Rahu and Saturn being the other two) that combine to adversely influence his 7th house of marriage, his karmic momentum during this period of time was toward marital difficulty or obstructions, and from a psychological perspective marriage may have been ill-advised. The next period for him from the age of 29 to 47 was that of Rahu, another of the planets obstructing his 7th house. Consequently his karmic momentum around obstruction in marriage was formidable during a total of twenty-five consecutive of his most marriageable years.

It is important to note that the "fated" marital karma of both Shivananda and Nin were resolvable and inspirational to a host of others. Shivananda's marital karma was valued by the monks around him as an inspiration to their drive toward spiritual realization. Nin's relationship karma became the source for much of her world famous *Diary of Anais Nin*, which inspired a generation of feminists. At its best, Vedic astrology makes use of destiny patterns to weave a meaningful and inspired story from the client's life pattern. Like a meteorologist who forecasts anticipated weather conditions so we can plan activities and dress for the weather, a humanistic Vedic astrologer predicts life conditions while keeping in mind Ralph Waldo Emerson's suggestion that, "This time, like all times, is a very good one, if we know what to do with it." The recipient of a forecast should keep in mind that the meteorologist and the astrologer will sometimes be wrong due to unanticipated variables in their respective models.

Sometimes, in the convoluted world of human dynamics even wrong can become right, and vice versa! An emotionally distraught Indian woman came to see me several years ago. Married for fifteen years, but childless, she was indoctrinated by those around her to believe a childless marriage to be a great tragedy. Life became intolerably unhappy for her and her husband. Upon hearing that aside from a short window of time in the next year, her horoscope indicated little likelihood of a child, an emotional catharsis took place that was as painful for her to experience as it was for me to witness. Over the several months that we maintained frequent contact, she adjusted herself to the possibility of life without a child of her own.

One day she called me and with a smile in her voice informed me she was pregnant. I was both delighted and perturbed, thinking myself to have been careless as an astrologer by having given her the original disturbing analyisis. To my surprise, she countered by saying she ascribed her pregnancy to the analysis. She explained that prior to the horoscope interpretation, she was so anxious about conception that she could not relax about coitus, suffering from pervasive performance anxiety. All strategies attempted, including modern fertility clinics, had failed over the fifteen years of anxiously trying for the conception of a child. After the astrological analysis, she said she adjusted herself to life without a child. She felt comforted that it was simply her destiny up to that point in time not to have had a child. She became more relaxed, and in a motivated but unexpectant mood, utilized the imminent window of time for pregnancy that her horoscope presented. She now has a healthy boy, and she remembers the astrological episode gratefully.

This case has several far-reaching implications. Some psychological astrologers would perhaps suggest that had she looked after her anxieties the outcome would have been the same. Yet despite modern professional counseling and fertility help, prior to the encounter with her destiny, she remained at an impasse. Although one anecdote does not validate Vedic astrology's capacity to accurately pinpoint the flowering of karma, it does illustrate how at the very least, it occasionally becomes a useful tool for helping others to achieve a desired outcome through analysis of the future.

Another dramatic example of the utility of being aware of one's destiny or karma lies in the following story. One of my Indian teachers predicted the imminent death of my friend, who was in his mid-40s.

This man was married and had a relatively young child. He was a very bold, forthright and courageous man, not prone to anxiety induced by undue imagination. My teacher put his astrological findings to my friend in this way: "There is a crossroads in your life next summer involving your health and longevity. I suggest that you start doing Maha Mritunjaya (a mantra famous for spiritual evolution and its health-bestowing properties). Also take out an insurance policy for your wife and child. If the summer passes without incident, you will be out a few dollars for the insurance premiums, and the mantra will have benefitted your soul's evolution. You will be at greater peace." And so it turned out that upon my friend's death at the predicted time from serious health complications, his survivors were financially secure. As a Hindu, my friend also was consoled and inspired through the the repetitions of the mantra prior to his death.

What all this boils down to is the ability and need of every humanistic astrologer to gauge each situation on its own merits, much like a doctor with a good bedside manner makes decisions about the impact of telling a client about a terminal disease in a certain manner. Relayed inappropriately and with little consideration of the patient's value system and circumstance, such news may speed the death of the patient, just as a sensitive and compassionate relaying of the medical condition may postpone, or even prevent, the logical prognosis in the case of another patient.

HUMANIZING VEDIC ASTROLOGERS

One day, several years ago, my Vedic astrology teacher was explaining to me the reasons why classical Vedic astrology was conceptually complete, even though it excludes the use of Uranus, Neptune, and Pluto, preferring to confine itself to use of the Sun, Moon, Mercury, Venus, Mars, Jupiter, Saturn, Rahu (North Node of the Moon) and Ketu (the South Node of the Moon). Among the many sophisticated philosophical and cosmological points he advanced to support his position, he pointed out that by using only nine "planets," Vedic astrology paralleled the modern number system in which the integers one to nine can be combined to describe a complex sum. My teacher went on to indicate that the inclusion of the cipher "0" enabled the integers one to nine to become mathematically more eloquent in expressing numerical concepts.

Consequently, he argued, Vedic astrology needed the astrological equivalent of the concept of "zero" to infinitely enrich the meanings of the astrological combinations of the nine planets. He suggested that the astrological equivalent of the mathematical cipher "0" was the Vedic astrologer, because the astrologer always enlivened the nine planets, enabling the whole of the horoscope to become greater than the sum of its astrological parts. In his inimitable style, my teacher concluded by cautioning me to remember I was therefore a "big zero" as a Vedic astrologer. My ego was reduced while paradoxically the importance of the role of the Vedic astrologer to Vedic astrology was affirmed! Once again the anecdotal oral tradition of Vedic astrology became a humanizing influence. People enliven astrology.

Because of the onus of responsibility on the astrologer to make responsible decisions about horoscope analysis, which in a Vedic tradition may include predictions, the ideal classical training of a traditional astrologer in India is rigorous. The best trainees evolve through an apprenticeship system. The vast array of theoretical knowledge is learned and practiced under the watchful eye of an experienced teacher who is central to the making of a Vedic astrologer. The ideal teacher's responsibility to the student is not simply one of spewing astrological techniques, but involves the process of awakening in the student a mature understanding and practical use of the spiritual, philosophical, psychological, and mundane insights and methods that enrich and humanize the analytical predictive techniques of Vedic astrology.

Several Indian philosophies assert that the whole of creation is one inseparable whole comprised of spirit and matter, in which matter is animated by spirit. Only when the spirit enlivens a human body is it self-aware, otherwise it becomes a corpse. As an expression of this philosophical tradition, the Vedic astrologer's role in astrological interpretation is that of the spirit which animates the horoscope reading. Without the input of the astrologer, the symbols of the horoscope are dead. The astrologer is empowered with the function of enhancing the self-awareness of the owner of a horoscope, and is trained to this end to know a good deal about life. Awareness becomes the fundamental instrument by which the client can improve the quality of life.

This view of the importance of the astrologer in Vedic astrology has a broad parallel within the modern scientific community in the enunciation of the Uncertainty Principle by the physicist Werner Heisenberg. His work in quantum mechanics led Heisenberg to claim that the "neutral" experimenter is as much a participant as an observer who influences the very nature of the matter in question. His work challenges the possibility of ultimately determining an objective framework through which one can totally distinguish cause from effect, and whether one can know an objective effect if one is always a part of its cause.

One implication of the Principle of Uncertainty for a neo-Vedic astrology is that only variable rules of horoscope interpretation can be established, because an individual astrologer and client will influence the objectivity of those rules. Another important implication for astrologers who do not wish to influence their clients to any extent by remaining totally neutral is that they may in fact be incapable of maintaining such objectivity. Of course, it goes without saying that the client will also influence the astrologer, invoking a humanistic dialogue on some level.

To fulfill this noble and responsible role in a person's evolution, a Vedic astrologer is encouraged to augment his or her knowledge about as many aspects of life as is possible. Self-knowledge is emphasized, for, through knowledge of the self, say the ancient sages of India, all other things will become known. The Vedic astrologer is encouraged not only to learn the rules and the techniques of the art of chart interpretation but to aspire to self-knowledge in order ultimately to serve best those who seek the counsel of Vedic astrology. If this is not a humanistic astrology, what is?

BIBLIOGRAPHY

Bhasin, J. N. *Commentary on the Sapta Rishi Nadi*. Durban, Delhi: Ranjan Publications, 1976.

Kalyan Varma. *Saravali*. Trans. by R. Santhanam. New Delhi: Ranjan Publications, 1983.

Maharshi Parashara. *Brihat Parashara Hora: Volume I & II*. Trans. by R. Santhanam and G. S. Kapoor. New Delhi: Ranjan Publications, 1984.

Mantreshwara. *Phaladipika*. Trans. V. Subrahmanya Shastri. Bangalore: Yugantara Press, 1961.

Pingree, David. *Jyotihsastra: Astral and Mathematical Literature*. Wiesbaden: Otto Harrassowitz, 1981.

Varahamihira. *Brihat Samhita: Part I & II*. Trans. M. Ramakrishna Bhat. Delhi: Motilal Banarsidass, 1981.

ABOUT THE AUTHOR

Hart deFouw has been studying and practicing Vedic astrology since 1968. He trained for fifteen years with his Indian Vedic astrology teacher, who also introduced him to other components of Indian culture that are relevant to Jyotish. Since 1988, he has traveled worldwide by invitation to give lectures, seminars, and consultations. Hart is the co-author (with Dr. Robert E. Svoboda) of a series of books on Vedic astrology, the first of which, *Light on Life: An Introduction to the Astrology of India*, was published in 1996 by Penguin Books. He is a visiting faculty member of the Ayurvedic Institute of New Mexico.

Readers who want to contact Hart deFouw can write to him at the following address:

Hart deFouw
115 Maplewood Avenue
Toronto
Ontario M6C 1J4
Canada
Phone: 416-653-4005
Fax: 416-653-6856

CHAPTER 6

THE EASTERN MOON
THROUGH WESTERN EYES

AS A WESTERN TROPICAL astrologer, you have undoubtedly studied the Moon and her cycles and phases in great detail, perhaps assuming there is nothing new under the Sun, so to speak, about the Moon and her symbolic usage in the horoscope. "The Eastern Moon Through Western Eyes" will show you from the Eastern, i.e., the Vedic perspective, that the easily observable Moon can be viewed from several vantage points that can add greater dimension to your astrological interpretations.

THE MONTHS OF THE MOON

Next to the ascending sign, the Moon is the most personal factor in a birth chart, moving 12 to 15 degrees in a given day, and changing zodiacal signs faster than any of the other planets. The Moon waxes and wanes from New Moon to New Moon in 29 days, 12 hours, 44 minutes, and 2.7 seconds. This cycle of activity is called the synodic month of the moon, from the Greek *sunodos*, meaning "copulation," as the Sun and Moon conjoin every New Moon, beginning a new cycle of birth.

The synodic month of the Moon is distinguished from the sidereal month of the Moon, in that the sidereal cycle of the Moon, from the Greek, *sidus*, meaning "star," refers to how long it takes the Moon to move against the backdrop of the fixed stars and come back to the same position relative to those fixed stars. This sidereal month of the Moon takes 27 days, 7 hours, 43 minutes, and 11.5 seconds.

234 / EASTERN SYSTEMS FOR WESTERN ASTROLOGERS

Just when you thought having two "months" for the Moon was confusing enough, we will yet discover that two additional "months" are also associated with the Moon. These are the *anomalistic month* and the *draconic month*. The anomalistic month measures the Moon's movement from one perigee, when the Moon is closest to the Earth, to the next perigee. This cycle takes 27 days, 13 hours, 18 minutes, and 37.5 seconds. The draconic month refers to the interval of time between succeeding conjunctions of the Moon with its North Nodes. This cycle takes 27 days, 5 hours, 5 minutes, and 35.8 seconds. As you can see, astrologers have at least four "months" associated with the Moon. These months are measured with a high degree of accuracy, right down to the second.

It is not surprising that the etymological roots of the words Moon and month are the same. The Greek word for Moon is *mene* and the Greek word for month is *men*. Old English equivalents are *mona* for moon and *monath* for month. They once referred to a like phenomena connected with the Earth's only satellite, but the word month in our language has now come to mean a period of time; a duration of activity. We use this word, strictly speaking, to measure an allotment of time, within the natural year, referenced to the Gregorian calendar. This calendar was introduced in 1582 by Pope Gregory the XIII as a revision of the Julian Calendar. This allotment of time we call a "month" is anything but precise, and is only now loosely associated with the Moon. Months are respectively 28, 29, 30, and 31 days long. Hardly the precise measurements, down to seconds we noticed for the synodic, sidereal, anomalistic, and draconic months of the Moon.

Our Gregorian calendar measures the tropical year, which is 365 days, 5 hours, 48 minutes, and 46 seconds long. This year of measurement is also commonly called the astronomical year, the equinoctial year, the natural year, the seasonal year, and the solar year. As with the months, there are also many types of years! The Gregorian calendar is a solar-based calendar, concerning itself with measuring the tropical year of the Earth, that is, the time it takes the Sun to move between one vernal equinox and the next. So, even though the words "month" and "Moon" share the same etymology, in our Western solar calendar, they have come through popular usage to measure different things.

The word "Moon" still refers to the celestial body from which we derive systems of measurement of clocklike precision. But the word "month," in our Western calendar, now refers to a segment of the tropical year connected to the Sun, with hardly the same degree of precession. Even though the etymologies are the same, the word "month" no longer references a measurement to the Moon, but rather references a measurement between the Earth and the Sun! It has lost its original meaning in our solar-based calendar.

There are further anomalies in our usage of the Gregorian solar calendar. The months September, October, November, and December refer to the ninth, and to the twelfth month respectively in Latin. The Latin prefixes *sep, oct, nov and dec* refer to the numbers seven through ten respectively, not the numbers nine to twelve! Another shift in measurement and in meaning has again occurred. It seems Julius and Augustus Caesar demanded their names literally go down through history, and to ensure this, they replaced the original seventh and eighth month names with their own names! This realigned inaccurately the remaining Latin months in the calendar, and this numerical distortion remains to this day. Our popular calendar just doesn't measure what it used to measure. It no longer predicts regularity of cycle without constant small adjustments, and the months have become solar-based, losing their original connection to the Moon, ironically, from which the word month was derived in the first place!

In adopting a solar calendar, many Westerners, exempting astronomers and astrologers, have lost touch with the natural lunation cycle. Much of the Western public does not know that the word "month" is a derivative of the word "Moon." They have lost touch with a natural, recurring, observable calendar, replacing it with a modern conventional one, which has become confused, distorted, and less connected to the night sky with age. Our usage of the solar calendar aligns us more in reference to the Sun's seasonal equinox and solstice points, rather than the Moon's monthly sidereal cycle, or synodic cycle of New to Full Moon. Our months do not start on the New Moon, and culminate with the Full Moon. Our months start on any given day of the week, and due to a phenomenon called the "Blue Moon," we can have two New, or two Full Moons, in any given month.

Because we reckon our months from a solar-based calendar, not a lunar-based one, the New and Full Moons progressively take place earlier and earlier every month until the whole synodic month of the Moon is contained in one of our calendar months. In such a month there will need to be two New, or two Full Moons, so as to start the synodic cycle off on the right track of one New and one Full Moon per Gregorian calendar month. Like the leap year adjustment, the Gregorian calendar uses the "Blue Moon" adjustment to realign us with the natural lunation cycle. This realignment, however, is but a temporary adjust-ment, for the whole process must start over again because of the dis-crepancy between the months of our solar calendar and the months of the synodic cycle of the Moon.

It was not always this way on the North American continent. How many times have we seen the typical Western movie in which the prover-bial Native American says: "They passed this way two Moons ago." Such films exemplify that the Native American Indians used a lunar-based cal-endar to measure time. Some may find this Native American reckoning of "Moons" a folksy, generalized description of an allotment of time, but their "Moon" was a directly observable, cyclic phenomenon, with a high degree of accuracy; more accurate and more observable than our modern month of 28, 29, 30, or 31 days—give or take "Blue Moon," and an oc-casional leap year. The Native American Indians adopted this natural cal-endar because of its easily observable regularity of cycle. They were not the only Indians to embrace this natural observable calendar.

CHANGING CALENDARS FROM WEST TO EAST: FROM SUN TO MOON

Like the Native American Indians, the Indians of ancient India utilized a soli-lunar calendar. This Moon-based calendar was used to calculate the most auspicious times for the various religious rituals the ancient Vedic people observed. The times of these rituals were usually just after the New and Full Moons. The people who determined the times these Vedic rituals were to be observed were known as *Jyotisins*, which means astrologer in Sanskrit. But the word *Jyotisin* also meant a mathematician and astronomer as well, for these individuals calculated a calendar based upon the observed movements of the Moon which was relied upon for religious purposes. Unlike the Western synodic month, that is, the 29.5 day cycle from New, to New Moon again, the Vedic people observed the aforesaid sidereal month. A sidereal month is not measured from the New Moon, but is measured according to how long it takes the Moon to orbit the Earth and cycle back to its original alignment with a par-ticular fixed star. The sidereal month is 27 days, 7 hours, 43 minutes and 11.5 seconds long. Outside of the two-day time difference, there is a greater difference between the sidereal month Eastern astrologers use, and the synodic month that Western astrologers use.

In order to calculate the sidereal month Eastern *Jyotishins* are required to know exactly where among the fixed stars, or sidereal constellations, the Moon is located. The sidereal month requires a knowledge of the fixed stars, or the sidereal zodiac. The calculation of the sidereal month requires a **direct observation** of where the Moon is located relative to the sidereal zodiac. In using the synodic cycle of the Moon, Western astrologers have concentrated on the observations of New and Full Moons, and the Moon's synodic regularity of cycle. They have ignored where the Moon was located against the backdrop of the fixed stars in the sidereal zodiac. Along with the timing of New and Full Moons, *Jyotishins* have directed their observations more to the varying sections of the night sky where the New and Full Moons appear.

Along with the sidereal month, Eastern astrologers also use the sidereal year, instead of the tropical year. The sidereal year is calculated by how long it takes the Sun to return to the same place among the fixed stars. The sidereal year is about twenty minutes longer than the tropical year, or natural year we use for our solar calendar. This discrepancy between the sidereal year and the tropical, or natural year, is due to the precession of the equinoxes. Twenty minutes may not seem like much, but multiplied by hundreds, even thousands of years of history, it makes a world, or more appropriately a constellation of difference.

PRECESSION OF THE EQUINOXES

The precession of the equinoxes is the continuous shift of the equinoxes backward, or westward through the sidereal zodiac at a rate of about 50 seconds per year, resulting in an ever-increasing difference between the sidereal zodiac and the tropical zodiac. According to Western sources, the phenomena of precession is said to have been discovered by the Greek Hipparchus in about 130 B.C. However, the Vedas, the sacred literature of ancient India, reputed to be over 5000 years old, present a factual record of ancient astronomical observations, for religious purposes, that reflect a much earlier knowledge of precession.

The ancient Vedic astrologers, as well as the modern ones, use the precession of the equinoxes regularly in their calendar and astrological calculations. Western astrologers do not, unless they hail from the Western sidereal school. This difference between the two zodiacs determines how both Eastern and Western astrologers observe the night sky and the movement and placement of the Moon.

Because there is a record of astronomical observances in the Vedas for thousands of years, Vedic scholars and Vedic astrologers can readily see that the seasonal points of the equinoxes and solstices now fall in different fixed star groupings than they did in the past. Precession of the equinoxes is an on going calculation for Vedic priests and Vedic astrologers. *Jyotish*, the Sanskrit word for astrology, is considered one of the highest Vedic sciences. It is called the "eye" of the Vedas, for Vedic astrology, with its sidereal calculations, laid the framework for the timing of the sacred rituals of the Hindu religion, and the development of a soli-lunar calendar. Knowledge of *Jyotish* required both a clear view and a clear understanding of precession in examining the night sky. In this way, one would be able to record where in the heavens the Moon was now waxing, the planets were now moving, and the equinoxes and solstices were slowly changing relative to the fixed stars.

THE NIGHT SKY AND
THE LUNAR CONSTELLATIONS

Because Vedic astrology uses the sidereal month of 27 days and 43 minutes, it has correspondingly broken down the Moon's movement during that time into 27 lunar constellations called the *Nakshatras,* from the Sanskrit, meaning "that which never decays."This equates one lunar day of the sidereal month with one Nakshatra. The Vedic priests and astrologers for thousands of years have observed the Moon's regular passage through these 27 Nakshatras, which are 13 degrees 20 minutes in length. The 27 Nakshatras are calculated utilizing the backdrop of the fixed stars in the sidereal zodiac.

Each month in the Hindu calendar is named after one of these Nakshatras, or lunar constellations, in which the easily observable Full Moon occurs that month. The New Moon is not used because its observation is hidden by its closeness to the Sun. Noting the Nakshatras named after each month, one also finds they note the beginning of the zodiacal sign in which they fall. This means that the Hindus, in designing their monthly system, were aware of both the lunar sidereal month, resulting in the use of the 27 Nakshatras, and the solar month, resulting in the use of the 12 signs of the zodiac. Thus we find the use of both the 27 lunar constellations and the 12 solar constellations incorporated simultaneously into their astrology. So Vedic astrologers calculate and measure from both the lunar constellations and the solar constellations.

Chinese and Arabic astrology also utilize the lunar constellations. Modern Western tropical astrologers rarely use the lunar mansions, or the sidereal month of the Moon. Instead, Western tropical astrologers largely calculate from the 12 solar signs. We can ask how much information about the Moon has been lost because of this modern practice in Western astrology. What kind of information has been lost?

Before we attempt to answer this question, let's examine another important point of information regarding the lunar constellations. Vedic astrologers also observed, through the recorded astronomical record of the Vedas, that the equinox would move back one Nakshatra, or lunar constellation, roughly every thousand years due to precession. Thus, the placement of the observed equinoxes would shift backward, or westward through all 27 Nakshatras in a complete cycle of precession cycle, or Great Year, in about 25,800 years, to come around once again to the same position in the night sky. This meant that the night sky that presented itself to their ancestors thousands of years ago, was not the night sky presently being viewed.

When the equinox retreated to a previous Nakshatra in one thousand years, or a previous sign in two thousand years, this precipitated a major reform of the calendar. This calendar reform was not just a good idea, it was a necessary calculation, for the practice of Vedic rituals were required to be aligned with certain New and Full Moons in certain portions of the night sky that now had to take place at different times of the year due to precession. Vedic culture was constantly aware of the slowly changing night sky. Only a culture which survived after thousands of years could have such a recorded knowledge. So the Vedic priests and *Jyotishins*, who continually reformed the calendar, were constantly aware of the changing sky, and although familiar with the tropical zodiac, adopted the sidereal zodiac to keep their religious rites in accordance with the fixed stars of their ancestors who recorded these rites in the Vedas.

So what does this all mean? Simply put, it means using the sidereal zodiac and the Nakshatras, you can go out on any given night and find the Moon among the fixed stars of say, the constellation Leo. Further, you can pinpoint the Moon more specifically in the lunar constellation, or Nakshatra called *Magha*, in the sidereal sign of Leo, highlighted by one of those fixed stars, the first magnitude triple star, *Regulus*, visible to your naked, sky watching eye. Using a sidereal precessional calendar and sidereal ephemeris, and a belief in reincarnation, you could view the Moon in the constellation of Leo, in the Nakshatra of Magha, one thousand years earlier, or one thousand years later, and it would still be close to the fixed star Regulus, just like today! Due to precession, the Moon would align with Regulus, in the constellation of Leo, in the Nakshatra of Magha, in a different part of the night sky, but you would know where in the night sky, due to your ancestors telling you to keep a sky-watching eye out for that first magnitude star, Regulus, marking the heart of the Lion. You would see, as your ancestors would have seen, the beautiful sight of a dim New Moon, brightened by Regulus' bluish, white light. A contemporary Western tropical astrologer equipped with a tropical calendar and tropical ephemeris, and even a first-rate telescope would not be greeted by the sight of the Moon in Leo, close to the heart of the Lion. A contemporary Western tropical astrologer would not see most of the stars of the constellation Leo, never mind Regulus. Why?

Before I answer this question, I will repeat the previous question again: Why has so much information about the Moon been lost to Western astrologers? Frankly, because the tropical zodiac does not take into account the phenomenon of precession. When todays' tropical astrologer consults a tropical ephemeris and sees that the Moon is coming into the sign of Leo, he or she will rush outside and gaze toward the heavens only to find the Moon in the constellation of Cancer, not in the constellation of Leo. Confusing you say? If astrology is based upon the observable position of the Moon and stars, why is the Moon not in the sign of Leo? Are we betrayed by the night sky?

You see, the tropical sign of Leo, is not the constellation of Leo. Due to precession, the tropical sign of Leo is removed by some 23-24 degrees from the sidereal sign of Leo. These signs are no longer in the same place in the night sky. This confuses many Western astrologers to no end. The tropical ephemeris does not line up with the night sky, because the tropical zodiac is based on the seasonal movements of the Sun, relative to the Earth, not relative to the night sky and the fixed stars. Because of this discrepancy, Western tropical astrology has chosen to concentrate on the synodic cycle of the Moon, rather than the Moon's confusing, actual location in the night sky.

Western tropical astrology has thereby enriched our understanding of the *synodic* cycle of New and Full Moons, and the phases of the Moon which are rich in archetypal and personality symbolism. However, in the process we have sacrificed an understanding of the *sidereal* cycle of the Moon, replete with the symbolic richness of the fixed stars and the primordial lore of the sidereal constellations. These different vantage points are due to the Moon's confusing tropical position, no longer relative to these fixed stars and constellations. This discrepancy need not further confuse us. Rather, let's understand what each branch of astrology, West and East, has to reveal about the Moon and through this understanding, synthesize these two great systems into a greater, more complete coherent understanding of the Moon.

THE TROPICAL WESTERN MOON

Let's take a quick overview of how the Moon is observed and interpreted by most tropical Western astrologers. The study of the Moon in Western astrology has been an examination of the dynamics inherent within the synodic cycle. Since childhood, everyone has been exposed to the four phases of the Moon: these being the New Moon, First Quarter, Full and Last Quarter Moon. These phases are listed on most Western calendars. The waxing and waning of the Moon, within the synodic cycle, obviously carried great importance to Western astrologers of the past. New Moons were the beginning of the synodic cycle and the Moon grew in strength until the Full Moon was reached. For centuries, Western astrologers utilized the New Moon for planting crops, or starting some project that was to come to some point of culmination, or fruition during the Full Moon. The synodic month of the Moon is fully utilized by Western astrology. Beyond the activity of the synodic cycle, what other types of activities and energies was the Moon personally representative of in a typical Western horoscope?

MONDAY, MONDAY—CAN'T TRUST THAT DAY

As the old Mamas and Papas pop hit of the 60s exclaims, the Moon's day, Monday, is not to be trusted. This is because the Moon represents what is ephemeral and passing. What is here today, may be gone tomorrow.

The Moon represents feelings and moods, all types of fluctuations in Western astrology. Each day the Earth's rotation with the Moon creates the rising and falling of the tides. Oysters and clams open their shells to feed in accordance with the Moon's passage overhead. The Moon is observed as a planet of rhythm in Western tropical astrology. The feminine rhythm menses, is named after the Greek word for Moon and month. The rhythms of daily life fall under the rulership of the Moon.

The Moon has rulership over women in general, and ones relationship to women and mother. The Moon, and it's position in the horoscope, is associated with your childhood, your family, and the maternal relationship.

The Moon is further associated with all forms of habit. These are merely feelings and moods, which have become ingrained over time. Habits are types of unconscious feeling or thinking patterns which have an association with the past. Thus, the Moon is associated with things that have been brought over from the past, such as childhood behavioral patterns, all ingrained patterns of feeling, thinking and relating, and, of course, memory. The Moon is further associated with characteristics inherited from the family, and past generations. Something has been inherited from your race, ethnicity, and family. The Moon represents these collective experiences from the past.

The Moon is generally considered to be a passive, reactive force within the birth chart. In conscious expression, its associations are the reactive mind, the sympathetic nervous system, and the inherited disposition. In Western astrology, feelings, and their ability to change at any given moment generally sum up the meaning of the Moon.

THE MOON AND PERSONALITY

In addition to the general personality characteristics inherited from race, ethnicity and family, the Moon by sign is associated with more specific personality traits. By element and modality the Moon tells a great deal about us. Fixed Moons (Taurus, Leo, Scorpio, and Aquarius) are less likely to change than the mutable Moons (Gemini, Virgo, Sagittarius, and Pisces). By element, the air Moons (Gemini, Libra, and Aquarius), are said to be more social, and intellectually oriented than the earth Moons (Taurus, Virgo, and Capricorn), which are said to be more practical and business-oriented. This, of course, is a generalized, superficial description by sign only, not considering aspects and the Moon's position in the chart. Of course, if the Moon is in an angle, lunar traits will express themselves more strongly into the life. House position shows where the personality traits of the Moon are expressed in the person's life. In summation: the Moon sign of an individual is indicative of a certain lunar personality type. In addition, the phase of the Moon one was born under further reflects a deeper personality type.

DANE RUDHYAR: THE LUNATION CYCLE

Western astrology's understanding of the lunar personality type further evolved through the concepts Dane Rudhyar revealed in his work: *The Lunation Cycle*. His theories changed the way today's Western astrologer understands the Moon. He developed a prototype of cycles in examining the synodic lunar month that was latter to become the humanistic movement in Western astrology. Rudhyar's work viewed the synodic cycle of the Moon as a dynamic archetypal cycle, which could be applied to any two celestial bodies. In examining the synodic lunar month, from New to Full Moon, Rudhyar found a dynamic pattern of relationship between the Sun and the Moon, which he expanded into eight lunation types of personality. Gone forever were the four phases of the Moon for Western tropical astrologers. They were replaced by the eight phases of Rudhyar's lunation cycle, and a deeper understanding and emphasis on the holistic nature of the lunar cycle itself were revealed.

Dane Rudyar's lunation cycle first conceptualized the synodic cycle of the Moon as an archetypal symbolic cycle reflecting the life process. Like the ancient Greeks in their word for month, *sunodos*, meaning "copulation," Rudhyar viewed the waxing and waning of the Moon; the regular cycle of increasing and decreasing light, as a dynamic symbol for the life process itself. Rudhyar envisioned that from a darkened seed state, represented by the darkened New Moon, all things were born. During the New phase, the Moon was infused by the brilliant spirit of the Sun. This impulse of spirit grew in the womb of the waxing Moon and became revealed for all to see in the symbolic light of the Full Moon. The impulse started at the New Moon and fulfilled at the Full

Moon, was then disseminated symbolically as the Moon waned, until the light of the spirit of this Moon became exhausted in preparation for the next infusion of spirit at the next New Moon. The synodic lunation cycle became a symbolic representation of all cyclic activity. In practice, a Western astrologer could apply the principles in Rudhyar's lunation cycle to any two related dynamics in the birth chart. Thus, the astrologer could advise a client when to open a new business, start a new relationship, etc., and advise the timely unfolding of this new project based on Rudhyar's lunation principles.

More importantly, Rudhyar's examination of the synodic lunation cycle would change the way Western astrologers would view the various personality types associated with the Moon. No longer would astrologers note the Moon just by sign; they would come to examine the Moon by what Rudhyar called the Moon's "phase relationship."

Dane Rudhyar's lunation cycle was not just an archetypal representation of the way life cycles flowed, it became an astrological personality inventory. He divided the eight phases of the Moon into eight distinct personality types. These eight types followed the waxing and waning of the Moon. They are as follows: from the New Moon waxing to the Full Moon; the *Crescent Moon Type*, the *First Quarter Type*, the *Gibbous Type*, and the *Full Moon Type*. From the Full Moon waning to the New Moon; the *Disseminating Type*, the *Last Quarter Type*, the *Balsamic Type*, and the *New Moon Type*.

Rudhyar divided the four lunar types from New Moon to Full, as *instinctive types*, for the light of consciousness was yet full. He divided the four lunar types from Full Moon to New, as *conscious types*, as the light had now reached it fullness. He further characterized his eight lunar types by their organic process. In the instinctive half of the lunar cycle, New Moon personality types are *projecting* and the most instinctive, Crescent personality types are *action oriented*, First Quarter personality types are *struggling to build* a form that is represented by the coming Full Moon, and thus experienced what Rudhyar called "crises in action." Gibbous personality types are *analyzing*. In the conscious half of the lunar cycle, Full Moon personality types represent the culmination of consciousness in that they *think before they act*. Disseminating personality types are concerned with the *distribution of consciousness*. Last Quarter personality types are concerned with the *reorientation of consciousness* and are directed toward the next New Moon and thus experience what Rudhyar called "crises in consciousness," and Balsamic Moon types are introverted and *future oriented* toward the next New Moon impulse. Rudhyar himself was a future oriented Balsamic type.

With the personality inventory inherent within the lunation cycle, Dane Rudhyar gave added dimension and depth to the Moon's interpretation in Western astrology. Some astrologers have attempted to link his personality inventory with others in psychology, such as the Meyers-Briggs personality inventory. Other noted Western astrologers, Michael Meyer and Marc Robertson, further developed Dane Rudhyar's concepts and lunar personality types in their books, *A Handbook for the Humanistic Astrologer*, and *Not a Sign in the Sky, But A Living Person*. These works examine and further develop in great detail the humanistic movement in Western astrology. They flesh out the various lunar personality types Rudhyar briefly described in *The Lunation Cycle*, and combine these lunar personality types with astrological time-tested lunar principles.

Rudhyar's humanistic movement changed the face and practice of Western tropical astrology. His personality inventory, based on the Moon phase relationship at birth, personalized the generalized synodic cycle of the Moon in chart interpretation. In this way tropical Western astrologers delineated the lunar personality, not just a static analysis by the Moon's sign and house placement, but dynamically, referencing the individual lunar personality type to the larger organic cycle of the synodic month. Rudhyar's work once again linked astrologers back to the night sky, and something which could be easily observed—the waxing and waning of the synodic cycle of the Moon

Moving the Moon in Western Astrology

Western tropical astrology uses the transits, and more importantly the progressions, of the Moon as a tool for timing in the astrological chart.

Most Western practitioners use the transiting synodic cycle of the Moon to determine the current areas of activity in the chart. There will generally be thirteen New and Full Moons within the horoscope in a given year, give or take a "Blue Moon." As these Moons progressively fall from house to house, they activate the chart by the transiting synodic cycle. Each house is activated monthly, synodically speaking, until the year is complete. This is a powerful forecasting tool used by nearly every professional Western tropical astrologer. Further, when the transiting New or Full Moon happens to be an eclipse, the effects of its transit are intensified and prolonged. In practice, Western tropical astrologers will usually give a Solar Eclipse (New Moon), and Lunar Eclipse (Full Moon) a longer duration of activity, often up to six months, which is the time of the next eclipse. It is interesting to note that while the synodic lunation's progress through the houses is sequential numerically; that is the houses 1, 2, 3, etc., the eclipse patterns progress inversely; that is 3, 2, 1, etc.. This symbolically connects Western tropical astrologers with a cycle that is likened to the precession of the equinoxes.

Aside from transits, there is, perhaps, no greater popular timing indicator, in the Western chart, than the use of the Secondary Progressed Moon. In using the Secondary Progressed Moon, astrologers liken the motion of the Moon in one day to the movement of the Moon in the course of a year. As the Moon moves 12 to 15 degrees in any day, the Secondary Progressed Moon moves the same number of degrees over the months of a year. In this way, the synodic month of the Moon, which is 29 days, 12 hours, 44 minutes, and some seconds, becomes a major life cycle lasting some 29.5 years by Secondary Progression. In this way, the Secondary Progressed Moon can activate a house for two-and-a-half years, or longer, depending on the speed of the Moon and the size of the astrological house. One can see an area of personal emphasis that will be in prolonged focus due to the Secondary Progressed Moon.

Dane Rudhyar emphasized that one should observe the Secondary Progressed New and Full Moons that occur within a horoscope. They are indicative of the initiation and fruition of a much greater organic cycle within the life of the individual. He observed that Secondary Progressed New Moons, in practice, were often associated with new beginnings, such as moves, relationships, and employment. Secondary Progressed Full Moons were associated with the fruition and at times closure of things begun at the Secondary Progressed New Moons. He instructed, that the use of the secondary progressed synodic cycle could be used to forecast the unfolding of the major events in a person's life.

So, in conclusion, the archetypal synodic cycle is utilized by Western tropical astrologers to indicate personality, and by transit and progression is used to time events in the horoscope. Now, let's turn to the Eastern sidereal cycle of the Moon, and how Eastern sidereal astrologers, that is, Vedic astrologers, observe the Moon.

THE SIDEREAL EASTERN MOON

While Western tropical astrologers concentrate on the synodic cycle of the Moon, Eastern sidereal astrologers, hereafter called Vedic astrologers, concentrate on the sidereal cycle of the Moon.

The word used for the Moon in Sanskrit is *chandra*, which etymologically is derived from the Sanskrit work *chandramas*, which means, "the shinning Moon." The root of the word *chandramas* comes from the Sanskrit word *ma*, which means "to measure." Like the Greek root *men*, for month, the derivation of the word for Moon in Sanskrit is also associated with measuring the passage of time. To accomplish this, the Hindus of India adopted a soli-lunar calendar, as opposed to a solar calendar that most Western cultures observe.

The sidereal month of the Vedic calendar is measured in 27 days, 12 hours, 43 minutes, and a few seconds. As previously mentioned, this equates one day with one of the 27 lunar constellations, or Nakshatras. Remember also, that each month of the Vedic year is named after one of the lunar constellations, or Nakshatras, that the Full Moon of that Month falls in. This connects the Vedic calendar to the lunar principle. But the Vedic year, for sacrificial rites, begins at the winter solstice, and thus symbolically is associated with the rebirth of the Sun at the winter solstice. This also relates the Vedic calendar to the solar principle, as well. So the months are named after the Moon's Nakshatra, and the Vedic sacrifices follow a calendar marked by the Sun's seasons, equinoxes and the solstice points. Indeed, this elaborate soli-lunar calendar was used in ancient India, and still is used today.

MANY HAPPY RETURNS AND THE LUNAR MONTH

While Western tropical astrologers celebrate their birthday, or solar return, at the precise moment the Sun returns to the same tropical zodiacal degree, Vedic astrologers, and Hindus, celebrate their birthday on the day of the month of their birth in which the Moon returns to the Nakshatra in which it was posited at birth. This lunar return is also celebrated as the person's monthly star day. One immediately sees that the sidereal monthly calendar has taken a decidedly lunar turn. Unlike the Western birthday, this birthday is easily observable in the night sky.

The use of the Nakshatras, and the correspondence to the sidereal cycle of the Moon, references Vedic astrologers more directly to the night sky than their Western counterparts, who rely more on the synodic cycle of the Moon. Vedic astrologers also use the synodic cycle of the Moon, consisting of 29-½ days. This lunar month, from New to Full, to New Moon again, is broken into 30 lunar days called *Thithis*. These in turn are broken down into one half lunar days called *Karanas*, of which there are 60. A good sidereal astrological almanac, called a *Panchangam* (five divisions), lists the Thithis, Karanas, and Nakshatra days, as well as other information for Vedic astrological use.

Certain Nakshatra days, often called star days listed in a *Panchangam*, are auspicious for initiating specific activities or religious rites. For example, the lunar day of the *First Nakshatra Aswini* is auspicious for travel, beginning lessons, and buying or selling vehicles. The lunar day of the *Third Nakshatra Krittika* is good for quick actions, accepting fire in religious rites, and competition in general. The lunar day of the *Fifteenth Nakshatra Swati* is auspicious for construction of religious buildings, planting seeds, and the making of tools or weapons. The lunar day of the *Twenty-fourth Nakshatra Shatabhishak* is good for manufacturing transportation vehicles, entering new houses, and beginning land rites. The *Twenty-seventh Lunar Day, Nakshatra Revati*, is auspicious for building houses, constructing religious buildings, making jewelry and performing marriage.

In a like manner, certain of the lunar days, or Thithis are auspicious for specific activities. For example, the *First* and the *Sixteenth Thithis* are auspicious for marriage and festivals. The *Seventh* and *Twenty-second Thithis* are auspicious for affairs relating to vehicles and starting a trip. The *Fifteenth Thithi,* which is the Full Moon, is auspicious for all rightful actions, religious ceremonies, and household affairs. The *Thirtieth Thithi*, or New Moon, is auspicious for fire rituals, performing religious rites for the departed, and making offerings. All of this can be found in a good *Panchagam*, or sidereal almanac, such as the yearly *Sidereal Astrological Almanac* by Molly Seeligson and Sally Gorell of Personal Insight Data Services, or the *Vedic Astrology Ephemeris and Lunar Calendar* by Bill Levacy of the Educational Sciences Corporation of America.

As seen, the 27 lunar Nakshatras, and 30 lunar days are each auspicious in a different way. Further, each of the 30 lunar days, or Thithis, are not of equal importance. The synodic month has moments of increased activity and increased importance at various junctions. A full examination of the increased importance of particular Thithis is beyond the

scope of this article, but a revealing, in-depth examination of this phenomenon is presented in Michael Erlewine's article, "Lunar Gaps: Taking
Advantage of the Lunar Cycle" in Llewellyn's *Astrology's Special Measurements.* This article is well worth reading for anyone interested in how
Eastern culture views and utilizes the Thithis in everyday use, as well as
spiritual practice.

THE MOON: MYTH AND MEANING IN EASTERN ASTROLOGY

Where Western astrologers see the "the man in the Moon," Eastern astrologers see "a rabbit in the Moon." In India, where the ecliptic passes
more directly above, the Moon appears differently than it does in our
more northerly skies. Vedic mythology has long equated the Moon with
a rabbit, or with a hare, who hops along in the night sky from one
Nakshatra to another, quicker than any of the other planets. In Vedic
mythology, the god Shiva, representative of the planet Saturn, is often
linked with the Moon. Here a symbolic connection is seen between the
29.5-year return cycle of Saturn, and the 29.5-day synodic cycle of the
Moon. It becomes easy to understand the connection of the Moon with
Shiva, remembering the aforesaid 29.5-year cycle of the Secondary Progressed Moon. The Moon and Saturn also rule signs directly opposite
one another.

In Vedic mythology, the Moon is the God Shiva's brother-in-law. In
being lord of the Nakshatras, the Moon is married to the 27 goddesses
of the lunar constellations. No wonder the Moon hops about like a rabbit! Chandra, or the Moon, did not treat all of his wives with equal
favor. He made a favorite of *Rohini,* represented by the Nakshatra of the
same name, which falls in the sidereal constellation of Taurus, in which
the Moon is exalted. The Vedic God Daksa, who is father of the twenty-
seven daughters of the lunar constellations, cursed the Moon because
of this favoritism, and caused him to die of consumption. But all the
Moon's wives pleaded for his return, so Daksa removed the original
curse, and made it progressive over the course of a lunar month, which
accounts for the phenomena of the waxing and waning Moon.

The Moon is also associated with the God Soma in Vedic mythology. In Vedic sacrifices, Soma is also the intoxicating ritual drink associated with this God. This intoxicating drink, which comes from a plant,
was considered by Vedic priests as an *amrita,* or nectar of immortality.

Soma was consumed at many important Vedic rituals, and in time became increasingly associated with the Moon. From this myth, we see a profound association of the Moon with changes in consciousness. It is, therefore, not surprising to find that in Vedic Astrology, the Moon itself is a symbol of consciousness, or an indicator of the mind.

Many Western students of Vedic astrology are shocked to find that Eastern astrologers associate the Moon with the mind. Western astrologers often insist that this cannot be correct, for Mercury certainly has dominion over the mind. Let's open a discussion here as to the nature of consciousness, or mind that Vedic astrologers are talking about. The Moon in Vedic astrology is seen as the vehicle of awareness. Awareness includes the senses, and is called the mind. What you have become aware of is a Moon function. What you choose to do with your awareness is a Mercury function. So the Moon in Vedic astrology is associated with consciousness and the mind, and Mercury is associated with the evaluative intellect, which builds on the original awareness of the mind.

Let's illustrate this by a simple example. You come upon a grove of apples and you see that the apples have fallen to the ground. The smell of the ripe apples wafts through the air, and you taste a fallen apple. It tastes sweet. This is the vehicle of the mind, telling you the apples are ripe. Now, you may decide to gather all the apples for yourself. You may hire someone to pick the apples at a very inexpensive price, and later charge more for the apples than you paid to pick them. You may walk away and let someone else pick the ripe apples. You may have become bored reading this example! This is your choice, the choice of the evaluative, or discriminating intellect. It is a further development in the process of consciousness, called intellect. It is different from the innocent awareness of the mind, as represented by the Moon.

That is why Mercury, or the Greek God Hermes, is the God of commerce. Please notice that there is *merc* in the middle of the word commerce. Commerce, in ancient Greece, was carried out at stone pilings called *herma*, that stood at the crossroads between cities. Commerce is an evaluative conscious process reserved for the discriminating intellect, or mercantile mind. Many times the mercantile intellect takes advantage of the innocent mind!

There is another myth in Vedic lore where the Moon abducted the Goddess Tara, wife of Brihaspati, or Jupiter. From this abduction, a child was born, called Budha. This is the name given to Mercury in Vedic astrology. So Budha, or Mercury is born of the Moon in the

Vedic myths. His original Sanskrit name is *Saumaya*, which means "son of the Moon." It is further interesting to note that the Moon, as innocent, pure consciousness, has no planetary enemies in Vedic astrology, while Mercury's only planetary enemy is the Moon. Vedic astrology reveals an eternal truth: pure consciousness has many friends, and no enemies, while the evaluative, rational intellect often fears the pure conscious mind!

THE WAXING AND WANING EASTERN MOON

We have seen in the previous explanations that the Moon is powerfully associated with consciousness. In the various Vedic myths, the Moon has been depicted as male, but in practice, it represents the passive, responsive feminine principle.

In the practice of Vedic astrology, the Moon is of supreme importance. It is the most important and personal of all the planetary principles. Where Western astrology follows the Sun sign in a solar calendar year, Vedic astrology gives paramount importance to the Moon sign and Moon phase, in its soli-lunar calendar year. As said, the Moon relates to the mind and consciousness, and all that follows from it. When the Moon is waxing, bright, and moving toward the full, it is considered a first rate benefic influence in Vedic astrology. When the Moon is waning, loosing light, it is considered a malefic influence in Vedic astrology. The general principle of practice is that a bright Moon brings auspicious results, and the dark Moon brings decidedly less than auspicious results. The Moon is considered particularly weak the last few days before the New Moon. This corresponds to the balsamic phase in Western astrology. The Moon is not particularly strong at the New, but from the new phase on, it continues to wax, becoming bright after the first quarter phase, and highly benefic at the Full.

To be born on a Full Moon is considered very fortunate and auspicious in Vedic astrology, whereas, in Western astrology the conflicting aspect of the Moon opposite the Sun is often regarded as a focus of tension. The Moon continues to be bright in its waning cycle, although diminishing in strength, until about the third quarter phase is reached. From here on, the Moon is decidedly weak and malefic in influence.

In summation, a bright Moon is seen as very beneficial; this generally represents the Moon from the waxing first quarter phase until the waning third quarter phase. The dark Moon is generally conceded to be weak and negative in influence. This dark Moon is from the waning third quarter phase to the waxing first quarter phase. The strength, or weakness, described here relates to the indications of the Moon, as well as the area of life represented by the Moon's rulership within a given chart.

The Moon in Vedic astrology is a *karaka*, or indicator of many things. Like in Western astrology, it represents the mother and women in general. It not only relates to personal consciousness, but mass consciousness, as well. The stronger the waxing Moon by sign and house placement, the stronger the awareness of the mind of the individual. A strong, bright Moon, is often indicative of a strong desire to educate the mind by schooling and meditation. The Moon is seen as an indicator of happiness, or general peace of mind. In India, where poverty is generally greater than Western societies, a comfortable life brings peace of mind and freedom from worry. The tendency to worry, is associated with a weak, or afflicted Moon, in that the mental function is not stable. A well placed, strong Moon, is seen as one of the greatest assets in the Vedic chart. It generally indicates good family, good association with women and the mother, and the ability to come before the public and achieve fame and recognition. A weak, poorly placed Moon, is generally considered to bring poverty and a restless, worried mind, unable to commit things to memory.

A strong Moon is indicative of grace and beauty, sensitivity and deep insight. When the Moon is weak, the person is said to go unrecognized, and as in Western astrology, have some issues related to women or being cared for and nurtured by family. As in Western astrology, the Moon rules the sign Cancer, and is exalted in Taurus. It is fallen in the sign of Scorpio. The Moon rules the 4th house, as in Western astrology, and is associated with the family. But the Moon is only associated with the mother through the 4th house, while the father is only associated with the 9th and 10th houses.

The Moon's most powerful position is the *Kendras*, or angles, and the 4th house is the most powerful angle the Moon can be placed in. Here the Moon receives what is called *dik bala*, or directional strength, and unless afflicted, gives strong familial connections, and generally favors good education and overall happiness.

Another important consideration in Vedic astrology is the Moon's associations. As the Moon represents the mind, it becomes important that the Moon be associated with planets, either in the same sign, or the preceding or antecedent signs. A disconnected Moon, without any associations, brings listlessness and a sense of not being connected to the greater whole. The isolated, unaspected Moon goes under the name of a particular *yoga*, that is a planetary combination, known as *Kemedruma yoga*. The isolated and unaspected Moon of such a yoga is said to bring sorrow and mental restlessness, no recognition, resulting in a loss of peace of mind and happiness.

In contrast, when planets are on either side of the Moon, this planetary yoga is called *Dhurdhura yoga,* and is said to bring about mental well being and riches, as well as good family and good associations.

In conclusion, there is a qualitative difference in how a strong, bright connected Moon acts through the birth chart, and how a weak, disconnected, dark Moon acts through the birth chart. There is almost no similarity between the two Moons. The disconnected, dark Moon brings troubling results, particularly if the Moon is in its sign of Fall, the sidereal sign of Scorpio. The connected, full Moon brings bounty and all good things, particularly if the Moon is in its own sidereal sign Cancer, or the sidereal sign of its exaltation, Taurus. In Vedic astrology, all Moon's are not created equal. It further becomes of supreme importance to see what lunar constellation, or Nakshatra, the Moon was in on the day you were born. Many other finer interpretations will follow from this stellar placement.

THE NAKSHATRAS

Perhaps the most ancient and distinguishing characteristic of Vedic astrology is the use of the lunar constellations, or Nakshatras, from the Sanskrit (meaning "that which never decays"). The Nakshatras are the oldest astrological references recorded in the most ancient of the four Vedas, the Rig Veda, considered by many Vedic scholars to be over 5000 years old. The Nakshatras are not only richly symbolic, but are actually observable constellations in the sidereal zodiac, linking Vedic astrology with the fixed stars of the night sky. As discussed, it is still possible now, as it was thousands of years ago, to go out at night and observe the Moon in proximity to the fixed star Regulus, and know that the Moon has begun its sojourn well into the Nakshatra of Magha.

The calendar of the Hindus is soli-lunar, as it observes the motion of both the Sun and Moon. The months of the Indian calendar follow the sidereal cycle of the Moon, which is a little longer than 27 days, the Hindus, for the most part, have developed a system of 27 lunar constellations, corresponding to the Moon's movement with a given day of the sidereal month. In the ancient past, the actual length of the lunar constellations was more in accordance with the actual size of the sidereal constellations than today. With the latter addition of the zodiac, the Nakshatras each became 13 degrees 20 minutes in length, which easily divided the path of the ecliptic into 27 equal parts. Further, each Nakshatra was subdivided into 4 equal parts, called *padas,* each 3 degrees 20 minutes in length. This divides the path of the ecliptic into 108 sections. Each part, or *pada,* of the night sky symbolically belonged to one of the 108 gods of the Vedic tradition.

Each of the 27 Nakshatras is ruled over by one the nine planets, or *grahas,* used in Vedic astrology. Because Vedic astrology is thousands of years old, and the trans–Saturnian planets were first discovered in 1781 with the discovery of Uranus, they are not used in the ancient rulership system of the Nakshatras. The nine *grahas* used are the seven planets; Sun, Moon, Mercury, Venus, Mars, Jupiter, and Saturn, plus the North and South Nodes of the Moon.

These nine planets fit evenly into the rulership scheme of the 27 Nakshatras, with each planet ruling three of the lunar constellations. On a finer level of interpretation, the four subdivisions, or *padas,* of each Nakshatra, each have their own planetary ruler.

In addition, each of the 27 Nakshatras has a Vedic deity presiding over it. The ancient Atharva and Yajur Vedas give complete details on the Vedic deities presiding over the Nakshatras. Each asterism is divided by sexual polarity, being male or female in disposition, as well as being categorized by belonging to a particular social caste. The Nakshatras further fall into three temperament categories; god, human, and demon. These temperaments describe where, in the three worlds of the Vedas, the consciousness of the Nakshatra is directed, and are not necessarily meant to be pejoratively judgmental.

Perhaps the most exciting feature of the Nakshatras, for the purposes of this article, are the various fixed stars of the sidereal constellations that each of the Nakshatras are associated with. These fixed stars share a rich history of myth and lore that is thousands of years old. I want to share a brief snapshot of each of the 27 Nakshatras, showing planetary rulership, presiding deity, and most importantly, naming the prominent fixed stars associated with each of the Nakshatras.

The *First Nakshatra* is called *Ashwini* and it extends the first 13 degrees and 20 minutes of the sidereal sign of Aries. It's planetary ruler is Ketu, the South Node of the Moon. It's polarity is male and the temperament is that of a godly nature. Aswini is symbolized by a horse, or a horse's head. The preceding deities are the Ashwins, Dasara and Nasatya, the identical twins of the Sun. They are associated with horses, after whom the constellation was named. They bring help, truthfulness, and understanding to humanity. The prominent fixed star of Aswinis is known to Westerners by its Arabic name, *El Sharatan*, from the Arabic which means, "the two signs." It is a pearl white star located on the horn of the Ram, and, like the Ram, its nature is bold and outspoken, and at times violent.

The *Second Nakshatra* is called *Bharani*, and it falls between 13 degrees 20 minutes and 26 degrees 40 minutes of the sidereal constellation of Aries. The planetary ruler is Venus. The gender polarity is male and the temperament is that of human nature. The presiding deity is the Vedic god Yama, the god of death, and the King of Dharma, or purpose in life. This asterism gives one his or her duty in life. The Nakshatras symbol is the *Yoni*, or female reproductive organ. *Bharani* means "bearing," in the sense of carrying. One of the prominent stars of this asterism is known to Westerners by the Arabic name, *Almach*. Almach is a binary star situated on the left foot of Andromeda. It gives honor and artistic ability in accordance with the Venus rulership of this Nakshatra. Another star, *Menkar*, situated in the jaw of the Whale, is associated with disgrace, loss of fortune and trouble with legacies, indicative of the ruling Vedic deity Yama, god of death.

The *Third Nakshatra* is called *Krittika* and falls between 26 degrees 40 minutes of the sidereal constellation of Aries and 10 degrees Taurus. Krittika is ruled by the Sun. Its gender polarity is female, and its temperament is of a demon nature. The presiding deity is the Vedic god of fire, Agni. Agni connects the realm of the gods with the realm of humanity, for in the Vedic sacrifice, fire carried the offerings from our world to the world of the gods. Another important deity associated with this asterism is Karttikeya, which loosely means "son of Krittika." He is the Vedic god of war. The symbol for this Nakshatra is a razor. It is associated with the fire sacrifice and war. The fixed stars of Krittika are "the Cutters," implied in the razor symbol of the Nakshatra. The Cutters are the six brightest stars of the Pleiades: Alcyone, Celaeno, Electra, Taygete, Maia, and Asterope. The sisters are said to be the wives of the

Seven *Risis*, associated with the stars of the Great Bear. Alceyone is the brightest star of the Pleiades, situated on the shoulder of the Bull. One of the "Weeping Sisters," Alceyone, is said to be a star of sorrow, as well as a star of eminence, success and prominence. Krittika also contains the fixed star Algol, said in fixed star lore to be one of the most violent and evil of the stars, indicative of the war-like characteristics of this Nakshatra.

The *Fourth Nakshatra* is known as *Rohini*, and it falls between 10 degrees and 23 degrees 20 minutes of the sidereal constellation Taurus. Rohini is ruled by the Moon. Its' gender polarity is female, and the temperament is of a human nature. The presiding deity is Brahma, the Vedic god of creation. The name *Rohini* is associated with the growing process. The Moon not only rules this asterism, but it is the Moon's favorite placement. This comes from the aforesaid myth in which Rohini was the favorite wife of all the Moon's wives. The symbol for this asterism is a chariot, a royal vehicle worthy of carrying the creative force. The symbol of the royal chariot links Rohini with the first royal fixed star, Aldebaren, situated in the Bull's left eye. This star is associated with honor, intelligence, eloquence and public honors. Lore has it, that Aldeberan gives extraordinary energy and enthusiasm. Lore suggests there is also danger from violence and sickness.

The *Fifth Nakshatra* is called *Mrigashira*, and it falls between 23 degrees 20 minutes of the sidereal constellation of Taurus and 6 degrees 40 minutes of Gemini. Mrigashira is ruled by Mars. This asterism is of a female polarity, and the temperament is of a godly nature. The presiding Vedic deity is *Soma*, who is associated with the Moon. More modern Vedic astrologers associate this asterism with Chandra, another deity for the Moon. The symbol for this Nakshatra is the head of a deer, which relates to the face of the Moon. The root word *mrga* means " to hunt," and so it is not surprising that the stars of this asterism are the group of three stars in the West that represent the head of Orion, the hunter. This asterism contains the star Bellatrix, a pale-yellow star situated on the left shoulder of Orion. The name means the "Female Warrior." Lore suggests this star gives great civil, or military honor.

The *Sixth Nakshatra* is called *Ardra*, and it falls between 6 degrees 40 minutes and 20 degrees of the sidereal constellation of Gemini. It is ruled by Rahu, the North Node of the Moon. The asterism is female in polarity and the temperament is of a human nature. The presiding Vedic deity is Rudra, the Vedic storm god, known as "the Howler," and "the One who Weeps."The symbols for this Nakshatra are a precious stone, or a tear drop, in keeping with the attributes of Rudra, and the prominent fixed star of this asterism.The star is Betelgeuse, the bright star situated on the right shoulder of Orion.The lore surrounding this star declares it gives marital honor and wealth.When the Moon is in Ardra with Betelgeuse, it gives a very active mind. Ups and downs in the career are indicated, but eventually is said to give power and preferment.

The *Seventh Nakshatra* is called *Punarvasu*, and it falls between 20 degrees of the sidereal constellation of Gemini and 3 degrees 20 minutes of Cancer.The planetary ruler of this asterism is Jupiter. Punarvasu is of the female polarity and the temperament is that of a godly nature.The presiding deity is the Vedic goddess Aditi.Aditi is the "unbounded one," and she is depicted in the Vedas as having her legs widely spread, so as to give birth to the gods.A Bow, or a quiver of arrows, is the symbol of this asterism, and this relates it to the martial fixed stars contained in this Nakshatra, Castor and Pollux—the twins. Castor is a bright-white star situated in the head of the Northern Twin. He was the mortal of the twins known for his skill in horsemanship. Lore suggests this star gives a keen intellect, sudden fame and honor, sometimes followed by loss of fortune. Pollux is an orange-colored star situated in the head of the Southern Twin. Pollux was the immortal twin known for his skill in boxing. Lore suggests this star gives a spirited, courageous nature, at times cruel and heartless.

The *Eighth Nakshatra* is called *Pushya*, and it falls between 3 degrees 20 minutes and 16 degrees 40 minutes of the sidereal constellation of Cancer.The planetary ruler is Saturn. Pushya is of the male polarity, and has the temperament which is godly in nature.The reigning Vedic deity is Brihaspati, the Guru to the gods. He represents wisdom, nourishment, and good fortune in general. Pushya means "nourishment," and this Nakshatra is often symbolized as a cow's udder.The asterism is noted by three stars in the constellation of Cancer. In Western mythology, the North and the South Asellis refer to the asses ridden by Bacchus and Vulcan during the war between the gods and the Titans. Eastern lore has it that these fixed stars relate to giving care reflecting the nourishing nature of this asterism.

The *Ninth Nakshatra* is called *Ashlesha* and it falls between 16 degrees 40 minutes of the sidereal constellation of Cancer and 0 degrees of Leo. The planetary ruler of this asterism is Mercury. The polarity is male, and the temperament is of a demon nature. The presiding deities are the *Nagas*, the semi-divine serpent beings of Vedic lore. *Ashlesha* means "The Embracer," and the symbol for this asterism is a serpent, representing great wisdom and the mystery of the sexual embrace and the flow of Kundalini energy. The stars of this Nakshatra are the ring of stars that form the head of the Hydra, a serpent-like creature of Greek myth. The fixed star known to Westerners as Acubens falls within the night sky of this asterism. Acubens is a white star, situated on the southern claw of the Crab. Lore has it that this star is a "sheltering place." It is noted as being persevering and idealistic. Lore further suggests this star is good for the study of astrology, writing, and affairs related to the public.

The *Tenth Nakshatra* is known as *Magha* and it falls between 0 degrees and 13 degrees 20 minutes of the sidereal constellation of Leo. Now that the cycle of nine planetary rulerships is complete, it starts all over again with Magha's planetary ruler being Ketu, the South Node of the Moon. Magha is of the male polarity and the temperament is of a demon nature. The reigning Vedic deities are the Pitras, the Fathers, the deified ancestors who are ruled over by the god of death, Yama. Magha means "the Mighty One," and the symbol for this Nakshatra is a royal chamber containing a throne. Magha is one of the brightest Nakshatras and the royal aspects are represented by the royal fixed star, Regulus. Magha also contains Al Jabhah, Algieba, Adhafera and Algenubi. Regulus is a white star situated in the heart of the Lion. Lore suggests it brings great fame, gives high and lofty ideals with magnanimity as well as a thirst for power. Algenubi is situated in the mouth of the Lion, and lore suggests it gives artistic ability, along with an egocentric, bombastic nature.

The *Eleventh Nakshatra* is called *Purva Phaguni* and it falls between 13 degrees 20 minutes to 26 degrees 40 minutes of the sidereal constellation of Leo. The planetary ruler is Venus. This asterism is of the female polarity and the temperament is that of a human nature. The reigning Vedic deity is Bhaga, the god of fortune who brings marital happiness and pleasure. The name of this asterism means, "the Former Reddish One," and the symbol for this Nakshatra is a swinging hammock, representing well being, ease, and enjoyment, as well as the pleasures of the bed. One of the stars of this asterism with which Westerners are familiar is called Zosma, located on the back of the Lion. In a typical Leo fashion, the lore surrounding this star is one of egotism and selfish indulgence corresponding to the ease of that swinging hammock, which is the symbol of this asterism.

The *Twelfth Nakshatra* is called *Uttara Phalguni* and it falls between 26 degrees 40 minutes of the sidereal constellation of Leo and 10 degrees of Virgo. The planetary ruler is the Sun. The Nakshatra is of the male polarity and the temperament is of a human nature. The presiding Vedic deity is Aryaman, the god of hospitality. He is concerned with patronage, favor, kindness and fortune, and often invoked with Bhaga. The name of this asterism means, "the Latter Reddish One," and it is symbolized by a small bed. Located in this asterism is the fixed star Denebola, situated in the Lion's tail. Lore suggests this star gives a fast mind and a noble disposition, with much generosity and high honors, but also association with people of low reputation.

The *Thirteenth Nakshatra* is called *Hasta* and it falls between 10 degrees and 23 degrees 20 minutes of the sidereal constellation of Virgo. Hasta's planetary ruler is the Moon. This asterism is of the female polarity and has a godly temperament. The ruling Vedic deity is Savitr, a Sun god who gives life and assists in childbirth. *Hasta* means "the Hand," and is symbolized by one. It is associated with life and creativity, as well as what can be held in the hands. This asterism is associated with five stars, representing the five digits of the hand. Two of its stars with which Westerners are familiar are Alchiba and Algorab. Algorab is a double, pale-yellow star situated on the right wing of the Crow. Lore has it that this star brings charm and success in business, but eventual falls from favor.

The *Fourteenth Nakshatra* is called *Chitra* and falls between 23 degrees 20 minutes of the sidereal constellation of Virgo and 6 degrees 40 minutes of Libra. The planetary ruler is Mars. The polarity is female and the temperament is of a demon nature. The presiding Vedic deity is Tvastra, the celestial carpenter and architect. He possesses the power to shape how humanity will see the world. The symbol for this asterism is a bright jewel, or a pearl. The name for this Nakshatra can also mean a painting, or a work of art, reflecting the nature of its deity, the heavenly carpenter, Tvastra. The bright star of this asterism is Spica, a brilliant white star in the Wheat Ear of Virgo. Lore suggests it gives success and riches and a love of the sciences and arts.

The *Fifteenth Nakshatra* is called *Swati* and falls between 6 degrees 40 minutes and 20 degrees of the sidereal constellation of Libra. Its planetary ruler is Rahu, the North Node of the Moon. Swati is of the male polarity, and the temperament is of a godly nature. The presiding Vedic deity is Vayu, the Wind god, who rules over all forms of air, including the breath of life. The symbol for this asterism is coral. The prominent star of this Nakshatra, with which Westerners are familiar, is Arcturus, a golden-yellow star situated on the left knee of Bootes. Lore suggests it gives riches, renown, prosperity, success in the fine arts and self determination like Swatis' deity Vayu, whose Sanskrit name translates to "self going."

The *Sixteenth Nakshatra* is called *Vashaka* and it falls between 23 degrees of the sidereal constellation of Libra and 3 degrees 20 minutes of Scorpio. The planetary ruler of this asterism is Jupiter. The polarity is female and the temperament is that of a demon nature. Vashaka is reigned over by two Vedic gods, Indra, King of the Gods, and Agni, the Fire God. The name *Vashaka* means, "Forked," or "Two-branched," reflecting the two Vedic deities ruling this asterism. The stars of this Nakshatra are known to us by their Arabic names and are Zuben el Genubi and Zuben el Hakhrabi. The lore surrounding Zuben el Genubi suggests the ability to concentrate on objectives and overcome obstacles in life. This star is said to be very social, clever, yet unforgiving, and revengeful in nature.

The *Seventeenth Nakshatra* is called *Anuradha* and falls between 3 degrees 20 minutes and 16 degrees 40 minutes of the sidereal constellation of Scorpio. The planetary ruler is Saturn. This asterism is female in polarity and has the temperament which is godly in nature. The presiding Vedic deity is Mitra, the god of friendship. This Nakshatra symbolizes friendship with the implied meaning of a helper, or co-worker. The symbol for this asterism is a Lotus Flower. The name refers to Radha, who was Lord Krishna's female consort. The Nakshatra contains three stars, two with which Western astrologers are familiar. These are Isidis and Graffias. Isidus is situated near the right claw of the Scorpion. Lore has it that it inspires religiosity and interest in astrology, as well as immorality and shamelessness. Graffias, a pale white star situated on the head of the Scorpion, is said to cause wealth and fame, but not of lasting nature. Lore has it that this star causes extreme malevolence and violence.

The *Eighteenth Nakshatra* is called *Jyestha* and falls between 16 degrees 40 minutes of the sidereal constellation of Scorpio and 0 degrees of Sagittarius. The planetary ruler is Mercury. Jyestha is of the male polarity, and the temperament is of a demon nature. The presiding Vedic deity is Indra, King of the Gods. *Jyestha* means; "the Eldest," and symbolizes that which is eldest, particularly the oldest and most powerful.

The symbol for this asterism is an earring. The prominent star of this Nakshatra is Antares, the bright red star situated in the body, at the heart of the Scorpion. This is the third of the royal stars, and fixed star lore suggests it prefers high intelligence, honors, and power, but with sudden loss. Lore has it that it is a military, as well as a political star.

The *Nineteenth Nakshatra* is called *Mula* and it spans the first 13 degrees and 20 minutes of the sidereal constellation of Sagittarius. Once again we have completed nine Nakshatras and so the planetary rulers start again with Ketu, the South Node of the Moon. The polarity of Mula is male, and the temperament is of a demon nature. The presiding Vedic deity is Nritta, the Goddess of Destruction, a demon exemplifying evil and decay. Surprisingly, her Nakshatra symbolizes non-violence. *Mula* means, "the Root," and the symbol is an elephant goad, or a tied bunch of roots, and this asterism symbolizes all things that are rooted and bound. Its stars form the tail of the Scorpion. Fixed star lore has it that the star Lesath, situated on the tail of the Scorpion brings good judgment, keen mind and good fortune. Lore also suggests that this star brings people before the public, and produces an interest in things of a spiritual and religious nature, such as astrology.

The *Twentieth Nakshatra* is called *Purvashada*, and falls between 13 degrees 20 minutes and 26 degrees 40 minutes of the sidereal sign of Sagittarius. The planetary ruler is Venus. The polarity is male and the temperament is of a human nature. The reigning Vedic deity is Apah, the Waters personified as goddesses. The deity is a symbol of all pervasiveness and patience. The name means, "the Former Unconquered," for like water the power of resistance and patience of this asterism is immense. The symbol is the tusk of an elephant, a universal symbol of patience. The prominent star of this Nakshatra is Kaus Borealis, on the bow of the Archer. Lore has it that this star is associated with idealistic, altruistic qualities, and that it indicates a strong sense of justice with leadership ability.

The *Twenty-first Nakshatra* is called *Uttarashada* and falls between 26 degrees 40 minutes of the sidereal sign of Sagittarius and 10 degrees of Capricorn. The planetary ruler is the Sun. The polarity is male and the temperament is that of a human nature. The ruling Vedic deities are the Viswa Devas, or All-Gods, a group of divine brothers. The name of the Nakshatra means "the Latter Unconquered." Like the former, it is patient, enduring, and invincible in adversity. A small cot is the symbol of this asterism. It consists of three stars. One famous star of this

Nakshatra, with which Western astrologers are familiar, is Wega, sometimes called Vega. Wega is a pale sapphire star situated on the lower part of the Lyre. Lore has it that this star gives great artistic ability in music, dance, as well as leadership ability. A good star for wealth and dealing with the government.

The *Twenty-second Nakshatra* is called *Shravana* and falls between 10 degrees and 23 degrees 20 minutes of the sidereal constellation of Capricorn. The planetary ruler is the Moon. Shravana is of the male polarity, and has a temperament which is human in nature. The presiding Vedic deity is Vishnu, the Preserver. Vishnu is responsible for preserving the universe, as he dreams the world's existence while he reclines on the Naga Ananta. The symbol for this asterism is an Ear. The name means "to hear." This asterism symbolizes hearing, listening, and learning. These three traits are corner stones of the great verbal Vedic tradition. Shravana consists of three bright stars, Altair, Ashain and Tarazed. Altair is a pale-yellow star situated in the neck of the Eagle. Lore has it that this star confers a bold, valiant and ambitious nature that leads to positions of leadership and command. Altair is said to create sudden wealth, but trouble with the law.

The *Twenty-third Nakshatra* is called *Dhanishta* and falls between 23 degrees 20 minutes of the sidereal constellation of Capricorn and 6 degrees 40 minutes of Aquarius. The planetary ruler is Mars. The polarity of this asterism is female, and the temperament is of a demon nature. The ruling Vedic deity are the Vasus, the gods of light. *Dhanista* means "the Wealthiest." This asterism is also called by the name *Shravistha*, which means "the Most Famous." This Nakshatra is symbolized by a drum, suggesting sound and musical ability. A prominent star associated here is Sadalsuud, a pale-yellow star situated on the left shoulder of Aquarius. Lore suggests this star gives visionary and intuitive ability. Good for astrology, writing, and public affairs.

The *Twenty-fourth Nakshatra* is called *Shatabhishak*, which falls between 6 degrees 40 minutes and 20 degrees of the sidereal constellation of Aquarius. The planetary ruler is Rahu, the North Node of the Moon. The polarity of this asterism is female, and the temperament is of the demon nature. The Vedic deity associated with Shatabhishak is Varuna, god of the Sky and Waters. The name means "possessing a hundred physicians," or "possessing a hundred stars." You may be in need of one of the physicians at this point, having absorbed so much information. The symbol for Shatabhishak is a hundred-petaled flower, representing

the hundred stars of this Nakshatra. One of the prominent stars Westerners are familiar with is Sadalmelik, situated on the right shoulder of
Aquarius. Lore indicates it gives high ideals and a philosophical nature.
Honors and gains follow, but are said not to last. The fourth, and final of
the royal stars, Fomulhaut, is also found in this part of the heavens. Lore
has it that this star is either very fortunate or very unfortunate. It is a
noted star of mystical ability and spiritual mastery.

The *Twenty-fifth Nakshatra* is called *Purva Bhadra* and falls between
20 degrees of Aquarius and 3 degrees 20 minutes of Pisces. The planetary ruler is Jupiter. The polarity is male, and the asterism has a temperament which is of human nature. The Vedic deity presiding is *Aja Ekapad*,
the One-Footed Goat. The symbol for this asterism is the two posts of
a bed. The name means "One who Possesses Lucky Feet." The prominent stars of this Nakshatra known to Westerners are Markab and Scheat.
Markab is a white star situated on the wing of Pegasus. Lore suggests it
gives honors and success, as well as a headstrong nature. It is said to also
be a fated star of great sorrow. *Scheat* is a yellow star situated on the left
leg of Pegasus. Lore has it that it gives literary and poetic ability, but also
extreme misfortune and suffering.

The *Twenty-sixth Nakshatra* is called *Uttara Bhadra*, and falls between
3 degrees 20 minutes and 16 degrees 40 minutes of the sidereal constellation of Pisces. It is ruled by Saturn. It is of a female polarity, and the
temperament is of human nature. The presiding Vedic deity is Ahir-
budhanya, the Serpent of the Deep. The name of this asterism means
"the Latter One who Possesses Lucky Feet." The symbol of this
Nakshatra is the number two, and also the feet of a bench. The two
Bhadra asterisms together form the rectangle of stars we know in the
West as *Pegasus*. This is the bed, or bench these two asterisms refer to.
One of its prominent stars known to Westerners is Algenib. Algenib is a
white star situated at the tip of the wing of Pegasus. Lore suggests it
gives great courage and fighting spirit, as well as the ability to shoulder
great responsibility. It also is said to confer a sharp mind and good ora-
tory abilities.

The *Twenty-seventh*, and last Nakshatra is called *Revati*, and extends
the balance of the sidereal constellation of Pisces, from 16 degrees 40
minutes to 0 degrees of Aries. Completing the cycle of planetary rulerships, this asterism is ruled by Mercury. The polarity is female and the
temperament is that of a godly nature. The reigning Vedic deity of
Revati is Pushan, the Nourisher. He is also the patron god of travelers,

and is invoked for safe passage and prosperity. The name *Revati* means "wealthy" indicative of the aforesaid prosperity and completed journey, symbolized by this last of the Nakshatras. The symbol for this asterism is the fish, suggesting abundance and fertility. The Nakshatra is made up of a large group of faint stars, which includes Piscium. A prominent star in this portion of the heavens known to Westerners by its Arabic name is, Al Pherg. Al Pherg is located in the cord near the tail of the Northern Fish. Lore has it that this star confers an authoritarian and daring nature, as well as great organizational ability and a promise of final success.

With these thumbnail descriptions of the 27 Nakshatras, Western astrologers can begin to add greater depth to the Moon position in any given horoscope. Proceed as usual, examining the sign the Moon is in at birth, as well as its phase relationship in the Western tropical chart. Then add the Nakshatra that the Moon is placed within at birth. One can bring a wealth of additional information to bear on the Moon's astrological interpretation. One can incorporate the planetary Nakshatra rulers, in addition to the sidereal zodiacal sign rulers, creating a finer level of interpretation. One can add the long-standing tradition of Vedic myths, in addition to the Greek myths, that Western astrologers bring to their interpretation. This is based on the presiding Vedic deities of each Nakshatra. But, for Western astrologers, perhaps the most important revelation, in addition to the concurrent use of the synodic and sidereal cycle of the Moon, is the moving Moon's alignment with the various fixed stars of the night sky. As said, each Nakshatra has an observable group of prominent fixed stars associated with it, many of these familiar to Westerner astrologers by their Arabic names. Here is found a rich symbolic lore from the Arabs, Babylonians, Greeks, Persians, and finally now the Hindus.

To exemplify this, we will use the horoscope of the great Eastern and Western Guru and preceptor, and founder of the Self Realization Fellowship movement, Paramahansa Yoga, who has his Moon in the tropical sign of Leo. See figure 1. His Moon is in the 12th house, within eight degrees of the Ascendant. Its phase relationship, in the synodic lunation cycle, is the Disseminating phase, after the Full Moon. It is true that Yogananda was a founder of ashrams, spiritual churches, and organizations, all associated with the 12th house. Disseminating Moon types are said to disseminate and spread the ideas, which come into illumination at the Full phase of the Moon. It is also true that Yogananda was a preacher, lecturer, and disseminator of spiritual ideas on meditation and self-realization. From the Western perspective, all of this is undeniably true. Now, from the Eastern perspective, we can add greater depth to the Moon interpretation in his chart. In the sidereal, Vedic chart, Yogananda's Moon is also in the sign of Leo, but in the sidereal constellation of Leo. Yogananda's Moon falls in the Nakshatra of Magha, who is ruled over by the planet *Ketu*, the South Node of the Moon. In Vedic astrology, the Moon's South Node is known as a mystical and spiritual planet, which gives spiritual insight and renunciate tendencies (see "Mythic Measurements of the Moon's Nodes," by Dennis Flaherty, in Llewellyn's

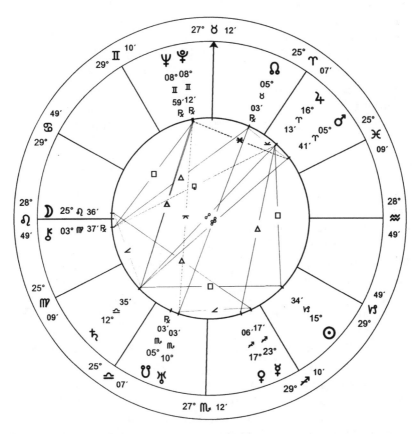

Figure 1. Paramahansa Yogananda. Born January 5, 1983, 8:39 P.M. LMT, Gorakhpur, India. Placidus houses. Data from Lois Rodden's Astrodata II, as "A" data, *Mercury Hour*, July 1976, as according to the Sri.

266 / EASTERN SYSTEMS FOR WESTERN ASTROLOGERS

anthology, *Astrology's Special Measurements*). No argument here, Yogananda was a celibate, spiritual priest. The presiding Vedic deities of Magha are the Pitras, the deified ancestors. With Magha there is a need to carry on the lineage of the past, that is why it is so important for Hindu families to have a son, for daughters are expected to join the husbands family at marriage. It is true that Yogananda carried on the lineage, or the tradition of his Guru Sri Yukteswar, who in turn had carried it forth from his Guru, etc.

Further, Yogananda's Moon is in close proximity to the fixed star Regulus, in the Nakshatra of Magha. Remember, Regulus is the "Little King," the "Mighty One," which is said to bring great recognition. Yogananda achieved widespread public acceptance, as well as brilliant fame in his lifetime and thereafter. His fame is still growing today, close to one hundred years after his birth! All this is true. One can easily see, by this brief example, that the inclusion of the Nakshatras, their planetary rulers, presiding deities and myths, and the fixed stars with-in these Nakshatas will flesh out in dramatic detail any interpretation of the Moon beyond its position by sign, house and phase! Try this technique using Vedic principles, your chart interpretation will be enriched.

MOVING THE EASTERN MOON

Vedic astrologers consider the transits of the Moon, not only through the sidereal signs and Nakshatras, but through the houses as well. In addition to examining the transiting Moon through the houses of the natal chart, or *Rasi*, as the Hindus call it, Vedic astrology also examines the Moon's transits from the natal Moon position as well. There is a further development of this method by examining the transiting Moon from the Nakshatra the Moon occupies at birth, giving a total of 27 placements of the transiting Moon! The placement of the Moon in this practice is divided into three parts, or *pariyayas* in Sanskrit. Each of the three pariyayas reflects nine of the 27 Nakshatras. There is much history and lore surrounding the Moon's transit within a paripaya. In the first paripaya, the first, fourth, sixth, eighth, and ninth Nakshatra positions from the birth Moon are said to be auspicious. In the second pariyaya, the transiting Moon only has half the strength that it does in the first. Hindu lore has it that the Nakshatras of the third pariyaya from the birth Moon have no adverse effect. Tradition further states that the 22nd and the 27th Nakshatra from the Moon's birth position should be avoided for starting certain activities. For the starting of important projects the transit of the Moon through the second, third, sixth, ninth, tenth, eleventh, eighteenth, twenty-second, twenty-fifth, and twenty-sixth positions from the birth Moon should be avoided.

New and Full Moons aside, Eastern astrology does not treat all transits of the Moon through the houses and Nakshatras equally. As can be seen, the birth Nakshatra of the Moon is the foundation for these calculations. In addition, the birth position of the Moon is of even greater importance for determining life events, for this position is the foundation for the directional system of the Hindus, called the Dasas.

Where Western tropical astrology uses the movements of the Secondary Progressed Moon to time events of the horoscope, Eastern Vedic astrology uses the Dasa system of directions based on the Moons Nakshatra position at birth to time events in the life. Each of the Nakshatras previously mentioned has a planetary ruler beyond the planetary ruler of the sign the Nakshatra falls in. The planetary ruler of the Nakshatra that the Moon is posited in at birth starts the Dasa system for the course of the person's life. Remember that Hindus celebrate their birthday in the month of their birth when the Moon returns to where it was in the night sky on the day of their birth. The Moon is of paramount importance in Vedic astrology, as it forms the basis for all predictions concerning the unfolding of the pattern inherent within the natal chart.

The most popular Dasa system used in Vedic astrology is the Vimsottari system. In this system, each of the nine planets is allotted a particular length of time. The length of each planet's cycle is fixed and the period of duration of all nine planets totals 120 years. This is said by the ancient Vedic seers of India to be the total life span available to humanity.

The Vimsottari Dasa system has a total of nine planetary periods that occur in a specific fixed order. The beginning of this planetary directional system is solely determined by the planet that rules the Nakshatra the Moon was in at birth. Like Yoganada, if the Moon was in the Nakshatra of Magha when you were born, its planetary ruler Ketu, the South Node of the Moon, would start the Dasa periods for you. From there, the life progresses through the various planetary cycles, all determined by the natal Moon position in your chart. It is beyond the scope of this article to give a full accounting of the Vimsottari Dasa system. There are many fine books discussing the planetary periods in complete detail. From this brief analysis one can see how all-important the natal position of the Eastern Moon is. Its natal position is the most important factor in determining the unfolding of the promised heavenly gifts of the natal chart.

CONCLUSION

Following our examination of both the Western and Eastern Moon, it is readily apparent how much interpretative depth and profundity can be gained by the use of both the synodic and the sidereal cycles of the Moon. Each has something of special importance to add to your understanding of the Moon. The observable sidereal zodiac of Vedic astrology returns the Western astrologer to the source of our cosmic science; the fixed stars of the ever-changing night sky. The use of the Nakshatras, once again, returns the Western astrologers lunar gaze to those ancient visible stars. These stars of the night sky are rich in ancient stellar lore and myths.

The East is known for its great Gurus and great Yogis, but I'll finish this chapter here quoting a famous Western Yogi. In the time honored words of one of the West's great Yogis, Yogi Berra, former coach of the New York Yankees baseball team: "You can observe a lot by watching!" Take the knowledge of the West with the wisdom of the East and watch the Moon's passage through the night sky, and I guarantee you'll observe a lot!

BIBLIOGRAPHY

Behari, Bepin. *Myths and Symbols of Vedic Astrology*. Salt Lake City, UT: Passage Press, 1990.

De Luce, Robert. *Constellational Astrology*. Los Angeles, CA: Deluce Publishing Company, 1963

Flaherty, Dennis. "The Blue Moon Blues," in *The Mountain Astrologer*. Boulder, CO, July 1993.

Frawley, David. *Gods, Sages and Kings*. Salt Lake City, UT: Passage Press, 1991.

Gorrell, Sally, and Molly Seeligson, *The Sidereal Almanac.* Eureka Springs, AK: Personal Insight Data Services, 1994.

Jordon, Michael. *Encyclopedia of Gods.* New York: Facts on File, 1993.

Roebuck, Valarie, J. *The Circle of Stars.* Rockport, MA: Element, 1992.

Robson, Vivian, E. *The Fixed Stars and Constellations in Astrology.* New York: Samuel Weiser, 1969.

Rosenberg, Diana, K. *Fixed Star Workbook.* New York: Privately published, 1992.

Rudhyar, Dane. *The Lunation Cycle.* Santa Fe, NM: Aurora Press, 1967.

ABOUT THE AUTHOR

Dennis Flaherty is a certified, professional east/west astrologer, with over twenty years of experience. He holds degrees in English and Sociology from the University of Massachusetts. He is past president of the Washington State Astrological Association, and currently serves on the Steering Committees of the Association For Astrological Networking (AFAN), and the American Council on Vedic Astrology (ACVA).

Flaherty was nominated for a Regulus Award at the United Astrology Congress (UAC) of 1992, and was conferred the title *Jyotish Kovid* in 1994, and *Jyotish Vachaspati* in 1996, by the Indian Council of Astrological Sciences (ICAS), in Madras, India.

He frequently writes for *The Mountain Astrologer, Astraea Magazine,* and the *Ascendant.* He is the author of "Mythic Measurements of the Moon's Nodes," in the Llewellyn Anthology, *Astrology's Special Measurement,* (1994). He is the founder and director of the east/west astrology curriculum at Greenlake Metaphysics, in Seattle, Washington, where he teaches classes in both Western, tropical astrology, and Vedic, sidereal astrology. One of his visions has been the development of Eastern astrology for the Western mind; to that end he co-sponsors the International Symposiums on Vedic Astrology and the Sacred Astrology Symposium.

Dennis Flaherty conducts a private consulting practice in Seattle at Greenlake Metaphysics at 7212 Woodlawn Ave NE, Seattle, WA 98115. Phone (206) 525-2229.

JAMES T. BRAHA

CHAPTER 7

PREDICTION EAST

IN THIS CHAPTER, I WILL present some fundamental techniques of Hindu astrology. Hindu astrology is different from the Western system, and readers must be on guard not to mix Western astrological knowledge and attitudes with what is taught here. It cannot be emphasized enough that *none* of what is mentioned here should be applied to one's Western horoscope. Having taught Hindu astrology to Westerners for some ten years now, I am quite aware that many astrologers will, unfortunately, try to mix Hindu techniques with their Western charts. Doing so will produce inaccurate information at best and detrimental effects at worst. Regarding the wearing of planetary gemstones (see pages 287–288), applying Hindu astrological prescriptions to one's Western horoscope can be decidedly harmful.

Transposing a Western horoscope to a Hindu one is simple, and readers should either calculate their Hindu horoscope by following the instructions given in this chapter or else write to one of the horoscope services I mention later. Because Western astrologers habitually apply Hindu techniques to their Western birthcharts, cautionary reminders are given several times throughout this chapter.

Hindu astrology is much more intricate and detailed than recent Western astrology (I say "recent Western astrology" because the system is currently undergoing a profound renaissance with the advent of "Project Hindsight," an endeavor pioneered by Robert Hand and others to translate all Greek and Latin ancient astrological scriptures; Project Hindsight demonstrates that traditional Western astrology is far more rich and complex than has been practiced in the past few centuries).

Due to space constrictions, the material presented here is by no means a thorough introduction to Hindu astrology. My purpose is simply to give readers a sense of the predictive nature of the Eastern approach. Please realize that the information on planets in houses, which forms the bulk of this chapter, must not be applied too literally to one's horoscope. Full accuracy of planets in houses can only be obtained by taking into account a multitude of factors: the zodiac signs, house rulerships, friendly signs versus enemy signs, and planetary aspects (which are calculated quite differently than Western planetary aspects).

For example, the explanation of Jupiter in the 5th house states that a person gets wonderful children, speculates successfully, and has strong artistic talent. This, however, will be completely inaccurate if Jupiter occupies the 5th degree of Sidereal Capricorn—the highest degree of debilitation for Jupiter! Jupiter in the 5th house is also harmed if the Ascendant of the chart happens to be the sign of Taurus, in which case Jupiter rules the *dusthana* or "grief producing" 8th house.

Further, benefic planets in houses do not function very well if they are aspected by malefic planets. Malefic planets in Hindu astrology are the Sun (which is so hot it burns its associations), Mars, Saturn, Rahu (North Node), and Ketu (South Node). On the other hand, malefic planets in houses may give excellent results if they occupy their own or exaltation signs, or if they are aspected by benefic planets, such as Moon, Venus, Jupiter, or Mercury.

Astrologers who are fascinated by the following material should obtain my Hindu astrology textbook or any other fundamental text on the subject *written by a Westerner.* Hindu astrology books written by Indians, although filled with valuable knowledge, are, for a number of reasons, extremely difficult for Westerners until the basics of the system are clearly understood.

One final note: Indian astrology is known by three names. Hindu astrology, Vedic astrology, or *Jyotish. Jyotish* is the Sanskrit name, and it means "science of light." The term Vedic astrology refers to the astrology taught through the Vedas, the Indian body of knowledge which predates religion and is said to have been cognized by sages or enlightened beings. Hindu astrology simply means Indian astrology as practiced by the majority of Indians, the Hindus. I prefer the term Hindu over Vedic because I believe that too much of original Vedic astrology has been both lost (especially information about *nakshatras*, or lunar mansions) or mixed with Western concepts.

Several of the most fundamental terms used in Indian astrology are of Greek origin *(kendra, trikona, apoklima, hora)* and have no meaning whatever in Sanskrit, the ancient language of the Vedas. It strains the imagination to think that Vedic astrologers thousands of years ago would simply combine Greek terms with their system of astrology. The more logical scenario is that the Vedic system was influenced by invading cultures over the centuries, or that, in time, Vedic astrologers did borrow workable techniques from the Greeks.

Interestingly, many apparently Hindu astrological methods are being uncovered in the Greek and Latin astrological translations within the work of Project Hindsight mentioned earlier. One could easily surmise that the Greeks borrowed *their* knowledge from Vedic astrology, but if so, why would they not have taken advantage of the Vedic nakshatras (lunar mansions), one of the most valuable features of Hindu astrology? The fact that scriptural information on nakshatras in India is almost non-existent implies to me that most of the truly Vedic astrological knowledge is either lost or held by some few Indian astrologers who have not yet seen fit to bring it out in written form.

In any case, for those who do not like the term Vedic astrology because of its potential inaccuracy, nor the term Hindu astrology because of its religious overtones, the word *Jyotish* is perfect if one is comfortable with a foreign term.

THE SIDEREAL ZODIAC

Hindu astrology employs exclusively the Sidereal, or constellation-based, zodiac. This is different from the Western system where most, though not all, astrologers use the Tropical or season-based zodiac. Because Hindu astrology is currently gaining great popularity in the West, and because there has been considerable confusion about the different zodiacs, it is important to address the issue thoroughly. The matter is also critical because many New Agers and disciples of spiritual movements these days consider anything Eastern to be deep, pure and profound, and anything Western to be shallow, superficial, and tainted. Where astrology is concerned, this is a very sad mistake.

A zodiac is an imaginary circle in the heavens, inside which the Sun, Moon, and planets travel in their orbits. In order to plot the positions of the heavenly bodies, it is necessary to determine a starting point within the circle. To construct a starting point, it is necessary to establish a reference point, some kind of fixed element to be used as a backdrop to the ever-orbiting planets, the Sun and the Moon. Here is where the difference between the two zodiacs lies. The Sidereal zodiac uses as its reference point the positions of "fixed stars." In other words, the Sidereal zodiac is calculated by determining the positions of the planets and the Sun and Moon in relation to a stationary point in the sky, a particular "fixed star" cluster, which is delegated as the first degree of Aries. Aries then becomes the first of twelve 30° zodiac "signs" (portions of space) making up the 360° zodiac.

The Tropical zodiac uses an entirely different, but equally fixed, reference point. For measuring purposes, it uses the equinoxes (the relationship between the Sun and the Earth which creates the four seasons: the Spring Equinox, the Summer Solstice, the Autumnal Equinox and the Winter Solstice). The starting point of the Tropical zodiac, also called the first degree of Aries, is determined by the Spring Equinox, the 1st day of Spring. Each year when Spring arrives, the position of the Sun within the imaginary circle establishes the first degree of Aries. All other planets are then calculated in relation to the Sun. This works well because the Sun moves approximately 360 degrees in one year, the same number of degrees in the zodiac, and because the first day of Spring occurs at the exact same time each year (even though our yearly calendar makes it seem to vary by a day or two).

Tropical astrology is not based upon a fixed position in the heavens, as is the Sidereal zodiac. It is based upon an undeviating, similarly fixed, atmospherical condition called the four seasons—specifically, Spring.

For thousands of years, there has been confusion and disagreement as to whether both zodiacs are legitimate, and if so, which one is preferable, producing the most accurate results. Astrologers who have studied and practiced both systems, using the Tropical zodiac for Western astrology and the Sidereal for Hindu astrology, almost always conclude that both work because they have experienced accurate results from both. (It is possible that the information gained from Tropical or seasonally-based, astrology, may relate somewhat more to a person's psychology and behavior than events and circumstances.) Unfortunately, most astrologers are not expert in both Hindu and Western astrology, and have therefore confronted the question of the two zodiacs only from a theoretical perspective.

Unfortunately most people, astrologers and astronomers often included, overlook the fact that the zodiacs are based on different principles and have different reference points for determining the first degree of Aries. Therefore, when the first degree of Aries in the Tropical zodiac differs from the first degree of Aries in the Sidereal system, it is assumed that one zodiac is incorrect. *This is not the case.*

The problem is exacerbated by the fact that there is a consistent mathematical relationship between the two zodiacs, so that the first degree of Aries in the Sidereal zodiac is always a perfect mathematical formula away from the first degree of Aries in the Tropical zodiac. This can also make it appear that the two zodiacs are based upon the same reference point, but that one zodiac has somehow been miscalculated.

The mathematical difference between the two zodiacs—specifically the difference between the first degree of Aries in the Tropical zodiac and the first degree of Aries in the Sidereal zodiac—is known by Hindu astrologers as the *ayanamsa* (pronounced aya-nam-sha). The *ayanamsa*, though able to be precisely calculated for any single moment, is a moving figure. For example, in 1900 the difference between the first degree of Aries in the Tropical zodiac and the first degree of Aries in the Sidereal zodiac was 22°27'. In 1970, the *ayanamsa* was 23°26', a difference of approximately one degree. This motion of approximately one degree every seventy-two years between zodiac starting points describes the "precession of the equinoxes." The precession of the equinoxes reflects the perpetual, though extremely slight, tilt of the Earth.

In our present day, the way astronomers arrive at the starting point of the Sidereal zodiac is by using the calculated positions of the Tropical zodiac and then taking into account the movement of the precession of the equinoxes. Because the starting points of the zodiacs are always moving apart from each other (within a circle), there are times when the starting points do coincide. Therefore, astronomers try to determine exactly what year the first degree of Aries was the same in both zodiacs. From there, they simply begin to subtract approximately one zodiac degree for every seventy-two years and thus arrive at the current Sidereal first degree of Aries. There are slight disagreements among astronomers as to the exact year in which the zodiacs coincided. But the Indian government has sanctioned the work of N. C. Lahiri, and it is therefore his *ayanamsa* which is most widely used for astrological purposes.

My experience in trying different *ayanamsas* is that Lahiri's ayanamsa is the accurate one. (There are about three or four popular ones. They produce differences of only two or three zodiac degrees from Lahiri's.) Hindu astrology texts generally offer a few different ones so astrologers are free to choose for themselves.

In trying to come to terms with the two zodiacs, please consider that different techniques often produce the same results. Different spiritual paths lead to the same enlightenment. There is good reason that Tropically-based Western astrology has endured for thousands of years in the West and Sidereally-based Hindu astrology has endured in the East.

THE CHAKRA: THE BIRTHCHART

There are two prevalent Hindu horoscope formats, one that comes from South India and one from North India. The designs have no effect on the results and are simply a matter of tradition. The South Indian method is somewhat more popular in India, and that is the one taught here.

Contrary to the Western birthchart, wherein the houses are fixed (if the chart were a clock, twelve o'clock is the 10th house and nine o'clock is the 1st house) and the signs rotate, the South Indian chart has the signs fixed and the houses rotating. In other words, *zodiac signs always*

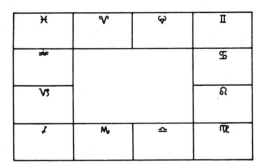

Figure 1. South Indian Chart.

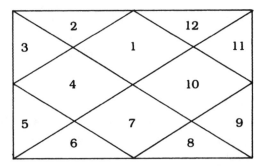

Figure 2. North Indian Chart

fit the same squares (the top left square is always Pisces and the bottom right square is always Virgo) and the house numbers rotate. The 1st house, whichever square it might be, is denoted by a diagonal line within the square. Another difference from Western astrology is that the chart flows in a *clockwise* direction rather than counterclockwise.

As for the "house systems," there are two that are generally used in India. One is older and more traditional, and the other is somewhat more contemporary. The older method is the one used in this chapter. This is the "equal house" system, meaning that if the 1st house begins at 10° Capricorn, then all other houses begin also at 10° (i.e., 2nd house starts at 10° Aquarius, 3rd house at 10° Pisces, and so on).

In the traditional Hindu chart system, the degree of the house cusp is completely irrelevant. This means that although the 1st house may begin at 25° of Scorpio, even a planet in 2° Scorpio occupies the 1st

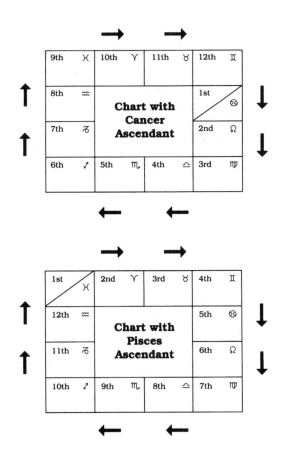

Figure 3. Two charts with different Ascendants.

house. This differs from Western astrology in that all planets in degrees less than the Ascendant will occupy the 12th house.

In typical Western house systems, the 1st house may start at the middle of one sign and continue until the middle of the next sign (e.g., from 3° Leo to 3° Virgo, or from 20° Gemini to 20° Cancer). This does not happen in the traditional Hindu equal house system. (It does occur in the contemporary Hindu chart method, but that is not the method we are using.)

To put it simply, planets in the second SIGN from the Ascendant occupy the 2nd house. Planets in the 5th sign from the Ascendant, occupy the 5th house. The Ascendant degree is irrelevant in positioning the planets (the Ascendant degree is not insignificant in other ways, only in terms of determining the other houses).

DRAWING THE CHART

In order to transform a Western birthchart (calculated with the Tropical zodiac) to a Hindu one (that employs the Sidereal zodiac), all that is necessary is to subtract the *ayanamsa*, the figure that accounts for the precession of the equinox, or tilting of the Earth, from the positions of the Ascendant, the planets, and the North and South Nodes. (Uranus, Neptune, and Pluto may be disregarded, since they are not utilized in ancient Hindu astrology.)

The precession of the equinox moves approximately $50\frac{1}{4}$ seconds per year. Table 1 shows some *ayanamsas* during the 20th century.

Table 1. Lahiri Ayanamsas During this Century.

January 1, 1900	22°27'59"	January 1, 1960	23°17'54"
January 1, 1910	22°35'51"	January 1, 1970	23°26'21"
January 1, 1920	22°44'43"	January 1, 1980	23°34'31"
January 1, 1930	22°52'40"	January 1, 1990	23°43'14"
January 1, 1940	23°01'21"	January 1, 2000	23°51'11"
January 1, 1950	23°09'34"	January 1, 2010	24°00'04"

In order to determine approximate ayanamsas for years in between the ones listed in Table 1, use 50.25 seconds per year. (But remember that the precession moves *approximately* 50.25 seconds of arc per year. Therefore, your final calculation for the ayanamsa will be close but not exact.) As an example birthchart, let us use the chart of Richard Nixon. His birth data is JANUARY 9, 1913, 9:35 P.M., PST, longitude 117W49, latitude 33N59.

Tropical Zodiac Positions:

Ascendant	Virgo	17°34′
Sun	Capricorn	19°24′
Moon	Aquarius	20°08′
Mars	Sagittarius	29°45′
Mercury	Capricorn	00°01′
Jupiter	Capricorn	01°40′
Venus	Pisces	03°29′
Saturn	Taurus	27°29′
Rahu (N. Node)	Aries	07°15′
Ketu (S. Node)	Libra	07°15′

The easiest way to proceed is to first reduce the sign degree of each item to its proper degree within the 360° zodiac. Therefore Table 2 (page 280) will be helpful.

Nixon was born in 1913, three years after the 1910 *ayanamsa* of 22° 35′ 51″. Therefore, add $50\frac{1}{4}$ seconds for each of these three years:

50.25″	22° 35′ 51″
x 3	+ 2′ 51″
150′ 75″ divided by 60 = 2° 51′	22° 38′ 42″

The final figure, 22° 38′ 42″ is a close approximation of the *ayanamsa* (because, as already mentioned, the precession moves *approximately* 50.25″). The exact *ayanamsa* was 22° 38′ 31″. For our purposes, we will simply use 22° 38″.

Examples

The Sun at 19° ♑ 24′ = 289° 24′ minus 22° 38′ = 266° 46′ = 26° ♐ 46′.
The Moon at 20° ♒ 08′ = 320° 08′ minus 22° 38′ = 297° 30′ = 27° ♑ 30′.
Rahu (N. Node) at 7° ♈ 15′ (add 360° since 22° 38′ cannot be subtracted from 7° 15′) = 367° 15′ minus 22° 38′ = 344° 37′ = 14′ ♓ 37′

Table 2. Degrees in the Zodiac.

Aries	0°– 29°59'	Libra	180°–209°59'
Taurus	30°– 59°59'	Scorpio	210°–239°59'
Gemini	60°– 89°59'	Sagittarius	240°–269°59'
Cancer	90°–119°59'	Capricorn	270°–299°59'
Leo	120°–149°59'	Aquarius	300°–329°59'
Virgo	150°–179°59'	Pisces	330°–360°

For those who wish to quickly transpose Western charts into their Hindu Sidereal counterparts, there is an easy way to do this that produces approximately accurate Hindu birthcharts. The technique is a simplified way to make zodiac subtractions and works easily for all planets and Ascendants, except those that occupy 22 or 23 degrees of a sign. During the entire 20th century, the *ayanamsa* is approximately 23 degrees, so that is the figure to subtract from the Ascendant, planets and the nodes. Subtracting 23 degrees from planets located between 24 degrees and 30 degrees is simple. Subtracting 23 degrees from, say, 10 degrees (or any figure below 23 degrees) becomes confusing. To make the calculation easy, just add 7 degrees to the figure (in this case, add 7 to 10) and then subtract a sign. This works because 7 and 23 equals 30, the number of degrees in each sign. You can also order your chart from a chart service.[1]

For example, the Moon in Richard Nixon's Western chart is approximately 20°≈. Therefore, to find the Sidereal position of the Moon, add 7 degrees to 20 and subtract a zodiac sign. The result is 27° ♉. Remember that this is only a quick way to gain an approximate Hindu chart and cannot work for planets occupying a degree near the *ayanamsa* (22 or 23 degrees during 20th-century births). The exact figures of such

---

[1]Computer chart services to order Hindu charts (with *dasa bhuktis*):

Astro Communications Services Inc.
P.O. Box 34487
San Diego, CA 92163-4487
Phone 1-800-888-9983

Astrogram
3600 N. Lake Shore Dr. #1817
Chicago, IL 60613
Phone (312) 589-6314

planets as well as the exact *ayanamsa* are necessary in order to determine whether such planets fall in the final degree of one sign or the earliest degree of the next sign.

THE YEARS EACH PLANET "MATURES"

In Hindu astrology there is an important phenomenon known as the great years of the planets. (See Table 3.) During the great year of a particular planet, that planet "matures," or comes of age, and manifests its full effects. This is a once in a lifetime episode. For example, it is typical for people to begin exhibiting leadership qualities around their 36th year (age 35) because that is when Saturn matures. Many people begin to write, or do some of their best writing or finest self-expression, during their 32nd year (age 31), the great year of Mercury. It is common for people to become more aggressive or sexual during their 28th year (age 27) the great year of Mars and so on.

During the great year of a planet, the person experiences an integrating effect relating to the nature of the planet as well as to the houses that planet rules in the person's birthchart. For instance, if Saturn rules the 1st house (Capricorn or Aquarius Ascendant), then during the 36th year the person experiences his or her personal power in a way never before fully realized. From that point on, the person is finally aware of his or her full potential in that realm.

Table 3. Great Years of the Planets.

Jupiter	−16th year (from age 15 to 16)
The Sun	−22nd year (from age 21 to 22)
The Moon	−24th year (from age 23 to 24)
Venus	−25th year (from age 24 to 25)
Mars	−28th year (from age 27 to 28)
Mercury	−32nd year (from age 31 to 32)
Saturn	−36th year (from age 35 to 36)
Rahu (North Node)	−42nd year (from age 41 to 42)
Ketu (South Node)	−48th year (from age 47 to 48)

If the person has a Cancer Ascendant, then the person does not fully realize his or her career potential until the 28th year, the year that Mars matures, because Mars is the ruler of the Aries 10th house (career). Until the 28th year, the person with the Cancer Ascendant has simply been investigating and experimenting with Mars energy. Even if the person was successful in professional life before Mars matured, there is still a significant increase in professional power and a greater grasp of one's purpose or life calling when Mars, as ruler of the 10th house, matures.

As another example, a person with a Leo Ascendant begins to know his or her full potential with financial earnings after the 32nd year because, for a Leo Ascendant, Mercury rules the 2nd house (Virgo) and Mercury matures in the 32nd year. Until the 32nd year, the Leo-Ascendant person is still investigating and learning about his or her money matters.

If the planet that is maturing happens to be extremely afflicted, the great year of the planet may be terrible. For example, if Venus, the planet of love, is fallen (in Virgo) and is aspected by malefic planets like Saturn and Ketu, the person may suffer terribly in love matters during his or her 25th year of life (age 24). The person also experiences difficulties in the areas of life that Venus rules and occupies in the birthchart.

To summarize, then, there are two significant effects from the maturation of planets in the sidereal Hindu horoscope. First, each planet gives its full effects and displays its full potential, for good or bad, in its great year. Second, until a planet has matured, it cannot produce the full capacity of its significations, as a planet symbol and in connection with its house rulerships.

Regarding the great years of the planets, there are two planets in each Hindu horoscope of which an astrologer must take careful note. The first one is the planet ruling the Ascendant (known in Hindu astrology as the Ascendant "lord" or Ascendant "ruler"). The year of maturity for the Ascendant-ruler is especially important because that is the year when a person is finally capable of taking responsibility for his or her power, destiny, and purpose. Individuals often experience great evolutionary and life-supporting changes during the year their Ascendant lord matures (astrologers must not apply this, or any Hindu astrology techniques, to their Western horoscope Ascendant).

For example, it is typical for women who have been enduring terrible marriages to choose divorce during the great year of their Ascendant-ruler because they are now integrated in their power and self-esteem. Both men and women often make crucial commitments to their life path or other important issues at this time. In my astrological practice with thousands of clients over the years, I have found the great year of the Ascendant-ruler to be one of the most consistently accurate features of birthchart interpretation.

The second most important planetary great year to consider is the planet known as the *yogakaraka*, or union indicator (*yoga* means "union," *karaka* means "indicator"). The *yogakaraka* is the most special or benefi- cial planet for an Ascendant *by virtue of the houses that it rules*. As such, the year that a person's *yogakaraka* planet matures is generally a period of ad- vancement and promotion. The *yogakaraka* for each Ascendant is listed in the left column of Table 4, page 284. (See the "best" column in the "good and bad planet" section.)

In Hindu astrology, planets carry with them a benefic or malefic influence not only by their intrinsic nature, but also due to the quality of the houses that they rule. There are a vast array of rules governing the benefic or malefic nature of the houses, but some of the simplest ones to remember concern the *dusthanas* and *trikonas*. The 6th, 8th and 12th houses are *dusthanas* or "grief-producing" houses, and therefore any planet ruling one of the these houses carries a certain degree of negative energy regardless of its fundamental nature. On the other hand, the 5th and 9th houses—the *trikonas* or trinal houses—are the best houses of a Hindu horoscope, and therefore the planetary rulers of the 5th and 9th houses carry a significant amount of positive energy regardless of their benefic or malefic intrinsic nature.

There are, however, many more rules than these and the matter quickly becomes complicated when, for example, one planet simultane- ously rules a *trikona* and a *dusthana* house. How does one judge the benefic or malefic nature of Mars' rulership energy in the case of a Sagittarius Ascendant where Mars rules the 12th house *(dusthana)* and the 5th house *(trikona)*? (In Hindu astrology, there are no intercepted houses and therefore every planet except the Sun and Moon rules two houses.) The same problem occurs for the Libra and Aries Ascendant horoscopes where Mercury rules the 9th and 12th houses for the Libra Ascendant and Jupiter rules the 9th and 12th for the Aries Ascendant.

Without going into all of the detailed rationale of rulership judg- ments given by the ancient Hindu astrological seers, Table 4 (page 284), shows the *yogakaraka*, the best planet for an Ascendant, as well as the good and bad planets (planets that receive beneficial or malefic energy by virtue of rulership) for each Ascendant. Please bear in mind, however,

Table 4. Benefics or Malefics by Virtue of House Rulerships.*

GOOD AND BAD PLANETS FOR EACH ASCENDANT BY VIRTUE OF RULERSHIP				PLANETARY COMBINATIONS FORMING RAJAYOGAS	
Asc.	Best	Good	Bad		
♈	♃	♂☉	♀☿☽♄	♈	☉♃
♉	♄	☿♂☉	♃☽	♉	♄
♊	♀		♂☉♃♄	♊	♀☿
♋	♂	♃	☿♀♄	♋	♂
♌	♂	☉	☿♀	♌	♃♂
♍	♀		☽♂♃	♍	♀☿
♎	♄	☿♂♀	☽☉♃	♎	♄
♏	☽	☉♂♃	☿♀	♏	☉☽
♐	☉	♂	☿♀♄	♐	♂♃
♑	♀	☿♄	♂♃☽	♑	♀☿
♒	♀	♄♂☉	☽♃	♒	♂♀
♓	♂	☽	♄☉☿♀	♓	☽♂ OR ♃♂

*Planets not listed as good or bad for each ascendant are considered neutral by virtue of their rulership.

that the energy a planet contains by virtue of rulership is only half of the picture. The other half is the benefic or malefic fundamental nature of the planet itself (Jupiter, Venus, Moon, and Mercury[2] are natural bene-

[2]Technically, Mercury is a neutral planet that takes on benefic or malefic quality depending on its aspects. In practice, however, Mercury is, by nature, a completely benefic influence unless it is strongly aspected by one or more malefic planets.

fics while Mars, Saturn, Rahu, Ketu, and the Sun are natural malefics.) Please bear in mind that planets not listed in either the good or bad column are considered neutral by virtue of rulership and that neutral truly means neutral (for some unknown reason, beginning astrologers are typically discouraged about neutral planets).

EXAMPLES OF MATURITY OF PLANETS

Two good examples of the significance of the great years of planets (Table 5) can be seen in the charts of Jimmy Carter and Robert De Niro. Jimmy Carter's horoscope (figure 4, page 286) indicates leadership ability due to exalted Saturn in the 1st house. Although a strong Mars is typical in the horoscopes of presidents, Hindu astrological scriptures declare that an angular, well-placed and well aspected Saturn makes a person "leader of his/her village." Saturn is well-placed, not merely because it is in its exaltation sign (Libra), but also because it is the *yogakaraka*, the best planet for a Libra Ascendant as shown in Table 4.

Saturn matures in the 36th year of life and it was shortly after that (age 37) that Jimmy Carter decided to run for public office. While he may have considered a political life in earlier years, it was only after Saturn matured that he felt fully ready for leadership.

Table 5. The Most Important Planetary Years.

ASCENDANT	ASCENDANT RULER	YOGAKARAKA PLANET
Aries	Mars (28th year)	Jupiter (16th year)
Taurus	Venus (25th year)	Saturn (36th year)
Gemini	Mercury (32nd year)	Venus (25th year)
Cancer	Moon (24th year)	Mars (28th year)
Leo	Sun (22nd year)	Mars (28th year)
Virgo	Mercury (32nd year)	Venus (25th year)
Libra	Venus (25th year)	Saturn (36th year)
Scorpio	Mars (28th year)	Moon (24th year)
Sagittarius	Jupiter (16th year)	Sun (22nd year)
Capricorn	Saturn (36th year)	Venus (25th year)
Aquarius	Saturn (36th year	Venus (25th year)
Pisces	Jupiter (16th year)	Mars (28th year)

In Robert De Niro's horoscope (figure 5) Mercury is the ruler of the Ascendant or 1st house, and the great year for Mercury is the 32nd (age 31 to 32). Mercury in De Niro's chart is very well disposed because it is forming what is called a *rajayoga*, a royal union, with Venus. When Mercury matured, De Niro burst onto the scene in 1972 with his Oscar-winning performance in "The Godfather." De Niro had made several movies and been well received before "The Godfather," but once the Ascendant-ruler of his horoscope matured, he began to manifest his *full* potential. Everything up to that point was, ultimately, experimentation.

I first discovered the power and significance of the great years of the planets in 1984, during my second visit to India. I was greatly perplexed about a client of mine who had attempted suicide during a relatively harmless *dasa-bhukti* period. Further, there were no obvious indications of difficulties indicated from transits occurring at the time. My mentor, P. M. Padia, looked at the horoscope and quickly noted that the suicide attempt happened during the 32nd year of the person's life—the great year of Mercury.

♓	♈	♈	♊
♒ ♂ 03°05′			♋ ☊ 27°40′
♑ ☋ 27°40′		**RASI**	♌ ♀ 00°33′ ☿ 28°24′
♐	♏ ♃ 21°38′	♐ 21°01′ ♄ 09°08′ ☌ 03°18′	♍ ☉ 15°16′

Figure 4. Jimmy Carter's Rasi Chart. Born October 1, 1924, 7:00 A.M. CST, Plains, GA (32N02, 84W24). Source: According to Lois Rodden, Marion March from birth certificate.

10th ♓	11th ♈	12th ♉ ♂ 3°	1st ♊ ♄ 1° Asc. 22°21
9th ♒ ☽ 21°			2nd ♋ ♃ 17° ☊ 22°
8th ♑ ☋ 22°			3rd ♌ ☉ 0°27′ ☿ 25° ♀ ℞ 27°
7th ♐	6th ♏	5th ♎	4th ♍

Figure 5. Robert de Niro's Rasi Chart. Born August 17, 1943, 3:00 A.M. EWT, Brooklyn, NY (40N38, 73N56). Source: Neil Marbell quotes a colleague, "from him." Lois Rodden data base.

Mercury ruled the 1st house of the chart and was "hemmed in by malefics"in the 8th house, the house ruling death. In this particular case, Mercury was placed in between Mars and the Sun, being no more than 3° away from either of the planets (Sun is a harmful planet in Hindu astrology, burning its associations by combustion). When Mercury matured, it manifested its full results and the person experienced the full extent of his mental functioning. His usual nervousness and tendency toward depression increased significantly. As ruler of the 1st house (personality and confidence), this heavily afflicted Mercury manifested severe feelings of insecurity and inadequacy. Thoughts about death were, of course, due to Mercury's occupation of the 8th house.

Regarding my own chart, the great year of Saturn has been very important to me. At age 33, during my studies in India, I remember wondering whether I would ever have the successful career I envisioned for myself. After P. M. Padia had, night after night, demonstrated his astrological excellence, I put my serious (and quite private) question to him: "Will I ever get fame in my life?" I asked. "Yes," he answered, "but not until your 36th year—the year that Saturn matures." Saturn is the ruler of my 10th house (career) and is extremely powerful and well-aspected in my chart. In mid-1986, my first book was published. By October (the beginning of my 36th year of life), I was rapidly becoming known in astrological communities around the globe.

GEMSTONES, MANTRAS, AND YAGYAS

Much of the beauty of Hindu predictive astrology lies in its powerful methods to alleviate karmic difficulties appearing in one's birthchart. Astrological *upayes* (antidotes to obstacles and difficulties) are, necessarily, an essential feature of Hindu astrology. After all, what is the point of a completely predictive system—a system that makes it easy to foresee difficult and sometimes life-threatening periods—if one does not have the means to alter the problem? Who would want to know the future if nothing can be done about it? In Hindu astrology, much *can* be done. Therefore, Hindu astrologers are famous for prescribing gemstones, mantras, and *yagyas*, which are now briefly described. Prescribing *upayes*, particularly gemstones, requires some mastery of Hindu astrology and therefore only simple material is presented here.

THE SUN: The gem is red ruby (chrome pyrope and red garnets are secondary stones).

THE MOON: The gem is pearl (moonstone is a secondary stone).

MARS: The gem is red coral.

RAHU: The gem is hessonite.

JUPITER: The gem is yellow sapphire (yellow topaz is a secondary stone).

SATURN: The gem is blue sapphire (tanzanite is a secondary stone).

MERCURY: The gem is emerald (tourmaline is a secondary stone).

KETU: The gem is chrysoberyl (turquoise is a secondary stone).

VENUS: The gem is diamond (white sapphire is a secondary stone).

Astrologers differ in their methods of prescribing gemstones, but there are some fundamental, generally agreed upon procedures. The two most traditional recommendations are that a person should permanently wear the gemstone corresponding to his or her birth planet (the planet that rules the Ascendant or 1st house) as well as temporarily wearing the gemstone corresponding to the current planetary *dasa* (planetary period lasting anywhere between six and twenty years, depending on the planet involved). Because determining a person's *dasa* periods is too detailed to address in this small chapter, readers who are interested can mail away to one of the horoscope services (see footnote on page 280) or purchase one of the many Hindu astrological software programs that now exist for personal computers. For now, let us concern ourselves with the gemstone of the birth planet.

The gemstone for a person with a Scorpio Ascendant is red coral—the stone for Mars—because Mars rules Scorpio. A person with a Sagittarius Ascendant must wear yellow sapphire because that is the stone of Jupiter, which rules Sagittarius. (Westerners beware that these recommendations are ONLY TO BE PRESCRIBED FOR ONE'S HINDU BIRTHCHART CALCULATED BY THE SIDEREAL ZODIAC. Wearing improper astrological gemstones is harmful.) By wearing the gemstone that corresponds to the 1st house, the most important house of a horoscope, the person strengthens confidence, self-esteem, general well-being, support of nature and the ability to gain recognition. Everyone should wear his or her birthstone.

Gemstones of natural malefic planets (Sun, Mars, Saturn, Rahu, and Ketu) should not be worn unless the Ascendant is ruled by a malefic (i.e., Saturn's gem is the birthstone for a person with Capricorn or

Aquarius Ascendant, Mars' gem is the birthstone for Aries, and so on) or unless the person is in the midst of a *dasa* of a malefic planet. The effects of gemstones are subtle, but they are profound enough for relatively sensitive individuals to notice a positive difference in their lives. A few examples may be helpful.

In my horoscope, Venus is the birth planet because Venus rules my Ascendant (Taurus). Venus was heavily afflicted on the day of my birth, being posited one degree away from malefic Ketu (South Node) and two degrees away from malefic Mars. This has significantly harmed my confidence, recognition, general well-being, and all the other 1st-house significations mentioned above. On top of this, Mars and Ketu being next to the Ascendant-Ruler have brought about a powerfully introspective and mystical nature, since Ketu represents metaphysical and astral phenomenon and Mars rules the 12th house of my horoscope, the house of spiritual and other-worldly experiences.

Aside from my intense mystical and spiritual tendencies, during most of my adult life, I experienced a disturbing sense of alienation from the rest of the world, particularly in the evenings. In my early 30s, when began wearing my Hindu astrological birthstone (diamond for Venus) the disturbing moods disappeared entirely in a matter of months! Confidence was strengthened, and I experienced greater equanimity in love matters (strengthening Venus naturally improves the realm of love). But the best effect was the elimination of my alienating moods.

In the same way that gems can produce desireable effects, wearing the wrong stones can be harmful. Some years ago, a client who had been out of work for over one year sought out my services. The Ascendant of her horoscope was Virgo, and therefore Mercury was her birth planet, making emerald the stone she should have been wearing for confidence, general well-being, and so on. In her case, having a Virgo Ascendant meant that Mercury was also ruling her 10th house, the realm of career success—of which she was having none. As it happened, this woman's need for a Mercury stone (green emerald) was far greater than the average Virgo Ascendant because Mercury in her horoscope was heavily afflicted by being only two degrees away from malefic Saturn. As I was advising her to purchase an emerald (or green tourmaline if she could not afford emerald), I noticed on her finger a very large, three or four carat, blue sapphire, the stone for Saturn. Because Saturn was the planet harming Mercury, the planet of confidence and career in her chart, strengthening Saturn was the worst thing she could be doing.

I quickly advised her to remove the sapphire and obtain an emerald or tourmaline. About two or three weeks later, this client called to say that after removing the large blue sapphire she began to feel tremendously lighter and more at ease, and was surprised at the harmful effect her blue sapphire had been causing. And then she excitedly exclaimed "Oh, guess what? I found the perfect job."

While not all experiences are as dramatic as these, gemstones are quite powerful. Indeed, the way many people in India choose their gems is by taping a particular stone to their body for a few hours and noticing how their mood is affected, as well as paying close attention to what kind of news comes to them.

I am reminded of a close friend who some years ago called me from out of town just to say hello. Knowing his chart by heart, I remembered that he was just about to enter a planetary *dasa* that would be phenomenally fortunate for wealth, and I told him so. He was thrilled and took my prediction seriously because, over the years, my astrological advice to him had been quite accurate. He then said that he was in the process of deciding whether or not to buy a very expensive 26-carat yellow sapphire (the Jupiter gemstone) that he had taped to his chest that morning. When I told him to monitor the news coming his way that day, he declared that he would buy the gemstone immediately because he was overjoyed at the news I had just given him! Jupiter is the planet of luck and money and while wearing this giant, extremely high-quality yellow sapphire, he learned that he was about to make more money than ever before. (My friend was already a millionaire, so the ramifications of my statement were profound.)

Gemstones can also be worn to strengthen afflicted planets unrelated to one's birth planet or one's *dasas*. And they can be worn to strengthen already beneficial planetary influences, thereby creating even more good fortune for a person. Determining which planets can be strengthened without harming other birthchart features, however, requires expertise in Hindu astrology, and beginners should consult an expert.

Gemstones should be natural, of very high quality, and should not be heated, dyed, or chemically altered. The stones should touch the skin, if possible. As a general rule, most astrologers advise wearing stones that are two carats or larger. If this is not possible, one should consider purchasing a slightly smaller gem or a "secondary" stone, a stone which is similar in color and chemical properties to the traditional gem (since the effect of secondary stones are weaker, the size should be increased). It cannot be overemphasized that gem size and quality are crucial. Do not expect an extremely flawed stone to have a positive effect. Do not expect that wearing several tiny stones adding up to two or three carats will have a positive effect. It is far better to wear a large, high quality *upa-ratna* (secondary stone) than a tiny or flawed gem.

Perhaps the most powerful *upaye* of all is called a *yagya* (also spelled *yajna*). A *yagya* is a religious or spiritual ceremony performed by a Hindu priest in order to alleviate karmic difficulties. It is a kind of offering or sacrifice, in which a priest appeals to the planetary beings or the forces of nature (or the gods) for grace and intervention on behalf of the person requesting the *yagya*. During the *yagya*, the priest lights a fire, burns incense, and throws rice and ghee (clarified butter) into the flames. This symbolizes the burning of negative karma from the past so the person may be relieved of the most intense influences of past destructive actions. During the *yagya*, the priest continuously chants astrological mantras. Astrological mantras are Sanskrit prayers which entreat higher evolutionary beings to remove obstacles in the person's life.

Yagyas are extremely powerful and should be prescribed during a *dasa* or *bhukti* (*dasa* periods are broken down into shorter time frames, or sub-periods, within the *dasa* called *bhuktis*) that is difficult or life-threatening. *Yagyas* can also be done during good periods to help fulfill heartfelt desires or to remove unrelenting impediments in life. I have had several *yagyas* performed during rough periods and can attest to their force and efficacy. I will give a few examples.

A few years ago, a friend of mine was involved in a bitter divorce and was having big troubles in court, including problems gaining equal custody (weekend visitations) of his daughter. At the time, he was in a Jupiter *bhukti* within a Venus *dasa* and Jupiter in his horoscope occupies its *neecha* or "fallen" sign, Capricorn. Because Jupiter is the *karaka* (indicator) of law and children (among other things) and because Jupiter is in its worst sign in his chart, my friend was having trouble in both areas. Based on this information, I recommended that he obtain a *yagya* as soon as possible. Since there were no Hindu priests in South Florida, I gave him the phone number of a priest in Pittsburgh named Pandu, who did the *yagya* long distance. Within one week after the ceremony, the judge in the court case, who was quite old and conservative, was called out of town and replaced by a 35-year-old woman who saw matters quite differently than the elderly judge. Suddenly, the court decided that my friend deserved to have equal custody rights of his daughter.

Furthermore, a statement was put into the divorce decree that my friend's soon to be ex-wife had been intentionally manipulating their daughter to have negative feelings about her father. The purpose of stating the matter for the record was to make it more difficult for the wife to continue harassing her husband in court, which the judge felt she was doing to get revenge.

I was so impressed with the results of my friend's *yagya* that I decided to call the same priest for help with some debilitating health problems I was experiencing. About a year earlier, I had entered one of the most troublesome *dasa-bhuktis* of my life (Rahu-Venus). Because Venus rules my 1st and 6th houses, it is the planet directly connected to my health. As already explained, Venus is severely afflicted because it is conjunct Mars and Ketu (South Node). Venus periods and sub-periods are always delicate for me, but the Venus sub-period within the Rahu *dasa* was extremely harsh because Venus is exactly opposite Rahu natally. In any case, during the Rahu-Venus period, my health was so sensitive and my immune system so weak that I was habitually catching colds and the flu whenever I was under even the *slightest* stress. Medical doctors could find nothing wrong with my health and had no idea why I was continually getting sick.

I told Pandu of my health problems and requested him to perform my *yagya* on a Friday, because that is the day ruling Venus, the planet causing problems. As it happened, the *yagya* was performed the day before a weekend bookselling convention where I would be selling my astrology books. When I awoke on Saturday, I saw that it was raining heavily outside and realized I would very likely be getting sick. The previous book conventions I had attended were extremely demanding, and in this instance, I would be carrying numerous heavy boxes of books from the outside rain into an artificially controlled and heavily air conditioned environment. There was no doubt I would end the weekend with a cold.

As it turned out, I carried the heavy boxes of books I needed, walked endlessly around the convention center for two days meeting publishers, booksellers, and bookbuyers, and even walked outside in the rain to get lunch! On Monday evening I was surprised on two counts. First, I had escaped getting sick. Second, a friend and his wife remarked that I looked healthier than ever and that, in their words, my face was glowing. Within weeks of the *yagya* my strength and vitality improved dramatically and my health, though far from perfect, was on the upswing.

The yagya had proved more effective than months of vitamins, acupuncture, special diets and visits to traditional doctors.

Yagyas can be obtained by calling any Hindu temple in the U.S. or India that employs a Hindu priest.[3]

There are many kinds of *yagyas* available. There are *yagyas* for wealth, childbirth, removal of obstacles, family happiness, acquisition of a spouse, and so on. For the purposes of ameliorating a difficult period or subperiod, the *nava graha* or nine-planet *yagya* is usually recommended because it is both effective and easily affordable. The usual donation for the two-hour ceremony is around $150 as of this writing.

It is preferable to be present with the priest during the *yagya*, but if this is impossible, the ceremony can be performed in absentia with fine results. Another way to heal afflicted planets and difficult dasas and bhuktis is to chant astrological mantras. These are the same mantras that the Hindu priest performing a *yagya* chants, although *yagyas* include additional ceremonial material. Some Westerners will find chanting astrological mantras comfortable while others may not. Those with strong interest should consult any of my three texts on Hindu astrology mentioned at the start of this chapter.

KUJADOSHA—MARS AFFLICTION HARMING MARRIED LIFE

There is an important astrological condition in Hindu astrology called *Kujadosha* (pronounced koo-ja-doe-sha) or "Mars affliction" which harms married life and portends divorce. *Kujadosha* (sometimes called *mangaldosha*, since *Kuja* and *Mangal* are both names for Mars), occurs when Mars

---

[3] To find a Hindu priest in the United States, consult your local phone directory under the heading: Churches and Temples. If no Hindu temple exists, consult one of the temples below:

Hindu Temple of Greater Chicago
P.O. Box 99
12 South 701 Lemont Road
Lemont, IL 60439
Phone (708) 972-0300

Sri Shirdi Sai Baba Temple
3744 Old William Penn Highway
Pittsburgh, PA 15235
Contact Pandu Malyala
Phone (412) 374-9244,
or (412) 823-1296

occupies the 1st house (unless it occupies Aries), the 4th house (unless occupying Scorpio), the 7th house (unless in Capricorn or Pisces), the 8th house (unless in Cancer), and the 12th house (unless in Sagittarius). (Western astrologers are cautioned to apply this information only to Hindu horoscopes using the Sidereal zodiac.) The reason these Mars placements harm married life is because, in all these cases, Mars throws a *drishti* (a "glance" or aspect) onto either the 7th house (marriage) or the 2nd house (family life).

A person with *kujadosha* is attracted to partners who eventually cause major problems and, in most cases, divorce. The antidote for a person who has *kujadosha* is to marry another person who also has *kujadosha*! In this way, the person marries someone who is also paying karmic love debts and is unconsciously waiting to be victimized. Thus, *neither* person gets victimized, and the difficult love karma for both individuals is postponed until a future lifetime. In India, where marriages are prearranged, astrologers always match *kujadosha* individuals with other "Mars-afflicted" individuals.

Kujadosha is a fairly common phenomenon as will be realized when reading the Mars descriptions of planets through the houses. Those with the condition should marry slightly later in life (late 20s or early 30s) and try to approach relationships with as much logic and common sense as possible. Persons with *kujadosha* must not simply follow their impulses and passions in choosing mates. Doing so almost ensures trouble in the realm of love because the person is easily charmed by individuals who are, ultimately, cold, callous or unfeeling. Before committing oneself to a partner, the person must determine that his or her mate is sensitive, caring, and compassionate in love matters. Otherwise, disaster is very likely.

RAHU AND KETU

Rahu and Ketu are not heavenly bodies, but calculated points in the sky, which, in Western astrology, are known as the Moon's nodes. Rahu (North Node) and Ketu (South Node) are called "shadowy planets" and there is a distinctive story about them.

During the beginning of creation, Lord Vishnu was conferring immortality on all the planetary beings by feeding them a special potion called *amrita*. Somehow a *rakshasa*, a serpent demon, entered the room and drank the potion. The Sun and Moon saw the demon and alerted Lord Vishnu who quickly grabbed a sword and cut it in two. Unfortunately, however, the giant serpent had already gained immortality. Thus, it became two halves of a demon that forever live in our lives.

Rahu is the head of the demon and it represents insatiable cravings and desires for worldly success. Rahu's house placement reveals the specific direction the cravings will take both natally and in Rahu's *dasas* and *bhuktis* (periods and subperiods). Rahu periods often bring abundant material success and worldly power but very little happiness or contentment because Rahu is the planet of *insatiable* desires.

Ketu, the body of the serpent, is the exact opposite of Rahu in that it represents everything spiritual, astral and otherworldly. Because it is an otherworldly influence, it causes serious disturbances to earthly and practical matters unless it is well placed by sign or the aspects it receives. Planets conjunct Ketu become strange, weird, unconscious, or uncontrollable forces in a person's life. For example, if Venus is conjunct Ketu the person is likely to be attracted to lovers who are strange, weird, married, emotionally unavailable, or addicted to drugs or alcohol. If Mercury is conjunct Ketu, the person's mind is constantly wavering, as if the mind is functioning partially on the earth plane and partly on the astral or spiritual plane.

A person undergoing a Ketu period or subperiod, is likely to experience increased introspection, psychic ability, and a desire for seclusion and spiritual evolution.

PLANETS IN THE HOUSES

The 1st House
The 1st house, or Ascendant, is in many ways the most important house of all because it reveals how a person is received by the world. It denotes whether or not one can gain fame and recognition, as well as signifying a person's innate confidence and self-esteem. Also seen from the 1st house is one's appearance, happiness, well-being, health, and the person's general experience of early childhood. The 1st house is a *kendra* or angular house. *Kendras* are the most powerful houses and they confer power and strength to any occupying planets.

The 1st house corresponds to a fire sign (Aries) and is therefore a *dharma* house, a house relating to one's purpose and mission in life.

Surya—The Sun in the 1st House: The Sun, considered a malefic planet in *Jyotish*, harms the 1st house causing irritability, hot temper, and lack of confidence. Despite these feelings, the person APPEARS proud and very confident. There are leadership ability, powerful ego, good recognition achieved in life and a close relationship to father.

Chandra—The Moon in the 1st House: Emotional and moody nature, sensitive and vulnerable, very attractive and magnetic, large beautiful eyes, sociable, good in professions dealing with the public. Gains good fame and recognition. Self-indulgent; life is overly personal and there is too much attention on oneself. Because the Moon rules the mind (specifically the common sense portion of the mind), the person has a strong mental and intellectual nature.

Kuja—Mars in the 1st House: Assertive and aggressive personality, hot temper, physical body overheats easily. Brave, courageous, excels in sports. Leadership ability—but the person must beware of dominating others. Excellent mechanical ability, able to fulfill desires easily. Ambitious, independent, competitive. Accident-prone, scars on face. Mars in the 1st causes Kujadosha; a karmic condition harming married life (see page 293 for full explanation).

Buddha—Mercury in the 1st House: An intellectual and communicative nature, youthful appearance throughout life, strong intelligence, good at writing and teaching, able to charm others, friendly. If Mercury is afflicted or badly aspected, the person will be nervous, easily excitable, or mentally unstable. The closer Mercury is to the Ascendant, the more likelihood the person is a twin. Gains evolution through Lord Vishnu, the God of the intellect, and gains evolution through Zen, astrology, intellectual seminars, and other truth-oriented religions.

Guru—Jupiter in the 1st House: Tremendous luck, a religious or spiritual nature, gains fame and recognition with ease, protected from harm, divinely blessed, strong morals, wonderful childhood, good longevity. Happiness throughout life is assured. Married life is enhanced due

PREDICTION EAST / 297

to Jupiter's "glance" upon the 7th house. Worships Lord Krishna and gains evolution through devotion and prayer.

Sukra—Venus in the 1st House: Happy, healthy, charming personality, beautiful appearance, well-loved, wonderful childhood, artistic nature, kind-hearted and can forgive anyone. Strong passions, attractive to opposite sex, marries early in life. Many comforts throughout life. Tendency to overindulge in sweets and other pleasures. Married life is enhanced due to the aspect Venus throws onto the 7th house.

Sani—Saturn in the 1st House: Thin or ascetic appearance, serious and humble personality, lacking in confidence, self-critical, censors his or her talents and abilities. Unhappy youth, difficult childbirth. Responsible, disciplined, patient, unattached to worldly pleasures. Worships Lord Shiva, the god of austerity, and gains evolution through meditation, fasting, avoidance of senses and other austerities.

Rahu—The North Node in the 1st House: Handsome or beautiful appearance, peculiar or egocentric personality, big ego but little true confidence, continual ups and downs in married life, interest in spiritual and occult subjects. The person craves worldly power and material benefits. Power greatly increases in the 42nd year (the Great Year of Rahu).

Ketu—The South Node in the 1st House: Introverted and introspective personality, shy, tends toward invisibility. Strong spiritual nature, interested in *moksha* (enlightenment or final liberation). Intuitive and psychic, good powers of discrimination, enjoys yoga. Health is sensitive, must beware of poisons or contaminated foods. Married life is filled with ups and downs.

The 2nd House
The 2nd house represents money, education, family life, writing, speaking, imagination, truthfulness or the tendency to lie, the face and the food one eats.

Unlike Western astrology, where the 3rd house governs writings, communications, and all intellectual functions, these significations are attributed to the 2nd house in Hindu astrology. Poets, writers, lecturers, and counselors, etc., are seen through the 2nd house. The mind, however, is ruled by neither the 2nd nor the 3rd house in the Hindu system. It is represented by the 5th house. Lyndon Johnson had five planets in the 2nd house, and was one of the only U.S. presidents who was a school teacher. Appropriate to his horoscope, he taught public speaking and debate.

Another 2nd house distinction is family life, which is governed by the 4th house in Western astrology. If malefic planets occupy the 2nd house of a Hindu horoscope, the person will experience friction with his family. For this reason, the 2nd house must be analyzed in order to obtain an accurate picture of a person's marital happiness.

The 2nd house signifies a person's speech (whether sweet or foul) and the tendency to lie. Richard Nixon's 2nd house was extremely afflicted. His speech, in private, was often vulgar and his tendency to lie is well known.

Although the 1st house represents one's general appearance and the head, it is the 2nd house that rules the face. If benefic planets like Venus or Jupiter occupy the 2nd house (and are unafflicted by sign or aspect), the person is likely to be extremely goodlooking.

The 2nd house corresponds to an earth sign and is therefore an *artha* house, a house relating to wealth.

Surya—The Sun in the 2nd House: Loves money, interest in education and knowledge, good teaching ability, has to work hard for money, person eats bad foods, speaks harshly, family life is mildly disturbed.

Chandra—The Moon in the 2nd House: Wealthy, soft-spoken, beautiful face, loves knowledge and education, happy family life, well-educated, may become a teacher, wealth fluctuates, earns money through the public or females, eats good foods, excellent memory, becomes an authority figure in his or her field because of ability to retain knowledge.

Kuja—Mars in the 2nd House: Earns good wealth through tedious jobs or very hard work, may earn money through immoral or illegal means, speaks harshly, tends to lie, eats bad foods, scars on face, family life is harmed and married life strained, argumentative, difficulties in schooling, makes a poor teacher due to impatience and narrow attitude toward knowledge.

Buddha—Mercury in the 2nd House: The consummate teacher and writer, witty, clever, speaks well, excellent with words and knowledge, good in school, happy family life, wonderful imagination, youthful face. Speech problems if Mercury is afflicted or badly aspected. Writes beautiful poetry and music.

Guru—Jupiter in the 2nd House: Wealthy, pretty face, happy family life, great imagination, earns money through moral or charitable acts, fine education, happy schooling, eats good foods, truthful, may be an excellent astrologer because of the ability to memorize information and because of Jupiter's "glance" onto the 8th house.

Sukra—Venus in the 2nd House: Beautiful face, gains wealth easily, happy family life, great ability to write poetry and music, speaks sweetly and beautifully, eats good foods, speaks only truth.

Sani—Saturn in the 2nd House: Difficulties making money, poverty, unhappy family life, eats bad foods, education suffers, unattractive or rapidly aging face, has to work hard for money. Earns money through businesses of carpentry, coal, metal, or construction. Imagination is limited.

Rahu—The North Node in the 2nd House: Very bad for family life and happiness in general, argues with spouse and loved ones. Eats bad foods, may use alcohol or drugs. Difficulties in schooling, problems with teachers, uses foul language. Diseases of the face and mouth. Craves tremendous wealth and will get it if the rest of the horoscope is strong.

Ketu—The South Node in the 2nd House: Very bad for family life and happiness in general, argues with spouse and loved ones, tendency to lie, problems in education, speaking disorders, diseases of the face and mouth. Earns money through mystical or spiritual work. Eats bad foods, may use drugs and alcohol.

The 3rd House

The 3rd house represents the fine arts of music, dance and drama (painting and crafts are ruled by the 5th house). It has to do with one's voice and singing ability. Actors and performers are seen from the 3rd house (as opposed to the 5th house in Western astrology). The 3rd house also governs *all* brothers and sisters except the eldest (the eldest sibling is ruled by the 11th house).

The 3rd house signifies desires, one's own efforts, ambition and energy level. If the 3rd house is strong, a person fulfills desires easily, with little resistance from the world. A weak 3rd house makes a person lazy, lethargic, and frustrated from an inability to fulfill daily desires (11th house rules *major* desires).

The 3rd house governs courage, firmness of personality and willpower. If the 3rd house is strong, the person can succeed at any endeavor because of his or her ability to focus powerfully and persist until victory. Even if the rest of the birthchart is afflicted, the person can get what he or she wants through sheer will.

The 3rd house is an *upachaya* or "growing" house. This means that planets in the 3rd house grow stronger and more prominent as the years go by. It also means that malefic planets (Sun, Mars, Saturn, Rahu, and Ketu) are well placed in the 3rd house and give primarily good results.

The 3rd house corresponds to an air sign (Gemini) and is therefore a *kama* house, a house relating to desires.

Surya—The Sun in the 3rd House: Deep interest in music, dance, or drama. Extremely strong willed, fulfills desires easily, brave, adventurous. Powerful ambitions, Strong connection to brothers and sisters even though mild discord with them. Next born sibling is male.

Chandra—The Moon in the 3rd House: Many brothers and sisters, happiness from brothers and sisters, loves the fine arts, extremely active and energetic. May choose a career in music, dance or drama. Very strong desire nature, fulfills desires easily. The Moon suffers in the 3rd house, causing troubles with mother and females in general, as well as a general lack of happiness throughout life.

Kuja—Mars in the 3rd House: Stubborn and strong willed, adventurous, brave, and courageous, intense desire nature, fulfills desires easily, argues and competes with brothers and sisters, suffering on account of brothers and sisters, great manual dexterity and mechanical ability, can succeed at anything due to ability to concentrate and focus his or her energies.

Buddha—Mercury in the 3rd House: Talent in publishing, nice voice, good singing ability, changeable desires, fulfills desires easily, many brothers and sisters and good relations with them, next-born sibling is intelligent and intellectual, good in business.

Guru—Jupiter in the 3rd House: Artistically talented, good singing voice, fulfills desires effortlessly, can succeed in any endeavor due to strong will and focused energy, many brothers and sisters, happiness from siblings, next-born sibling may be famous or special. Tremendous energy level, excellent in public relations career, takes care of errands without loss of energy. Highly motivated.

Sukra—Venus in the 3rd House: The consummate artist. Talented in music, dance, or drama. Beautiful singing voice. Highly energetic, thrilled to be alive, runs errands without loss of energy, good in public relations career, fulfills desires easily, happiness from brothers and sisters, next-born sibling is female. Very strong desire nature.

Sani—Saturn in the 3rd House: Difficulty in fulfilling daily desires, stubborn-minded and strong willed, works extremely hard with little help from others, engages in physical labor for career, efficient at executing tasks. Few siblings, no happiness from siblings, next-born sibling suffers a lot. Lazy and lethargic, lacks motivation. Problems or defects with hands if Saturn is afflicted or badly aspected.

Rahu—The North Node in the 3rd House: Extremely strong willed, fulfills desires easily due to strong focus and concentration, adventurous, excited, motivated. Courageous and adventurous. Powerful desires to communicate. Talent in music, dance or drama, fine arts. Next-born sibling is worldly and materialistic. Ambitious and determined, overcomes enemies.

Ketu—The South Node in the 3rd House: Strong willed, stubborn, peculiar or eccentric personality, fulfills desires easily. Brave, courageous and adventurous. Irritation and suffering on account of siblings. Next-born sibling is shy, spiritual, introverted or introspective.

The 4th House

The 4th house governs home, land, real estate, fixed assets, and the person's mother. It also represents happiness as well as the heart, both physical and emotional (in Western astrology, the heart is ruled by the 5th house).

Benefic planets occupying the 4th house make a person happy and blissful, no matter how objectively good or bad his or her experiences of life may be. Malefics in the 4th house can make a person powerful and successful, since the planets are strengthened by the angularity of the 4th house. However, they ruin a person's happiness in a major way. The only astrological influence that can balance an afflicted 4th house is a benefic 5th house, which gives the person an optimistic mind to counteract the disturbances of the heart.

The 4th house relates to academic degrees (but not schooling, which is a 2nd house matter). A person may get great education and knowledge but if the 4th house is weak, he or she may fail to obtain a degree.

The 4th house also governs endings of all matters.

The 4th house is a *kendra* or angular house, and it therefore confers power and strength to occupying planets. It corresponds to a water sign (Cancer) and is therefore a *moksha* house—a house of spiritual enlightenment or final liberation.

Surya—The Sun in the 4th House: Difficulties with land or real estate, impaired happiness, problems with mother, powerful mother, strong confidence, leadership ability, wields power, difficulties to get educational degrees, heart problems.

Chandra—The Moon in the 4th House: Benefits from mother, close ties to mother, happiness throughout life, blessed with abundant comforts, lives in beautiful surroundings, gets wonderful homes and cars, plentiful jewelry, many female friends, may own boats.

Kuja—Mars in the 4th House: Suffers on account of mother, argues with mother, hot-tempered mother, anger and unhappiness throughout life. Person is assertive and aggressive. Problems with cars and houses. Intense and passionate nature. Endings of matters are fraught with friction and tension, Mars in the 4th house causes Kujadosha, a condition spoiling married life (see page 293 for full explanation).

Buddha—Mercury in the 4th House: Intelligent and communicative, gets fine educational degrees, owns nice homes and cars, plentiful jewelry, gets many comforts in life, enjoys music and fine arts, has many friends, fortunate endings.

Sukra—Venus in the 4th House: Happiness throughout life, kind-hearted and can forgive anyone, wonderful relationship with mother, endings of matters are smooth and peaceful, loves arts, possible artistic career, owns nice homes and cars, may own boats, gets plenty of jewelry, lives in beautiful surroundings, very well-liked, fortunate in love.

Guru—Jupiter in the 4th House: Happy and content, loves religion and philosophy, gets beautiful homes, nice cars and boats, enjoys many comforts and luxuries, happy relationship with mother, mother is religious or spiritual, many fine educational degrees, inherits ancestral wealth, successful, strong luck, generous and warm-hearted, good morals, blessed, lucky endings, end of life is spiritual.

Sani—Saturn in the 4th House: Unhappy or depressed, suffering on account of mother, mother's life is tedious or miserable. Major ups and downs in life—can reach pinnacle of success and depths of despair, unhappy endings, end of life is lonely or austere, Problems with cars, difficulty gaining educational degrees, overly serious, detached or ascetic nature. Gets evolution from Lord Shiva (evolution via austerity, meditation, and avoidance of the senses).

Rahu—The North Node in the 4th House: Big cravings for power and material success, problems with mother. Mother is materialistic, worldly, domineering and manipulative. Many dramatic changes throughout life, owns large homes, intense endings, moves away from parents.

Ketu—The South Node in the 4th House: Innately spiritual, loves yoga, discriminating nature, problems with mother. Mother is weird, strange, or mentally imbalanced. Mother is introspective or spiritual. Problems with homes and cars, owns homes with termites or insects, leaves home early in life, difficulties gaining academic degrees, heart problems.

The 5th House

The 5th house rules children, sports, and kingship (politics). It also governs mantras and spiritual techniques, but not religion or higher knowledge, which are 9th house affairs.

The 5th house represents morals and good deeds, and has much to do with a person's character. If the 5th house is strong and well-aspected, the person will exhibit the finer qualities of life. He or she is likely to be honest, humble and dignified rather than arrogant or pompous.

The 5th house rules the mind, unlike in Western astrology, in which the 3rd house takes that honor. Intelligence, peace of mind, mental balance, depression or optimism are all seen through the 5th house.

Also, the highly important signification of *poorvapunya*, or past-life credit, is seen through this house. While the entire horoscope results to some extent from past-life activities, the 5th house specifically shows effects that must occur in this life because of karma that has been building lifetime after lifetime. For example, Richard Nixon came to a Mercury *dasa* (17-year Mercury period) right before his presidential downfall. Mercury was dreadfully afflicted in the 5th house of his birthchart. His downfall was caused by Mercurial problems: lying, tape recorders, the press, college students, and the intelligencia. As another example, if the ruler of the 10th house (career) occupies the 5th house, without affliction, then the person gets career success because of diligent professional work performed in a past life.

Even though the 3rd house is the most important house of art, the 5th house rules painting and crafts. The 5th is also gambling, speculations, and the stomach, which is ruled by the 4th house in Western astrology.

The 5th house is a *trikona*, or trinal house, thereby conferring fortune and benefits to any occupying planets. The 5th and 9th houses are the best houses in a Hindu horoscope. Planets that are associated with the 5th house in any way (by rulership, or aspects, etc.) flourish.

The 5th house corresponds to a fire sign (Leo) and is therefore a *dharma* house, a house relating to one's purpose and mission in life.

Surya—The Sun in the 5th House: Leadership ability, career in politics due to past-life credit, talent in sports, intelligent, sharp mind, irritable or hot-tempered, male children, benefits from father and government, enjoys art (painting and crafts) deep interest in mantras and spiritual practices, likes to speculate, strong confidence.

Chandra—The Moon in the 5th House: Brilliant mind, passionate beliefs, learns very quickly, has special or famous children, talent and deep interest in the arts, benefits from mother and females due to past-life credit, marries for love, profitable speculations, enjoys spiritual techniques, good morals, strong sense of devotion.

Kuja—Mars in the 5th House: Hot-tempered, practical-minded, disturbed mind. Talented in technical fields, such as law, architecture, engineering, or drafting. Excellent in sports and politics due to past-life credit, little or no desire for children, uninterested in spiritual techniques or performing good deeds, stomach ailments.

Buddha—Mercury in the 5th House: The consummate thinker, extremely objective mind, may give birth to twins, happiness from children, literary ability due to past-life efforts, talent in chanting mantras, good in astrology and other mental subjects, virtuous and refined, talent in drawing and painting, loves music.

Guru—Jupiter in the 5th House: Extremely lucky due to past-life credit, pious and virtuous, strong morals, gains from gambling and speculations, excellent intelligence, superiority complex, happiness from children, male children, religious or spiritual children, enjoys sports, practices spiritual techniques, happy mind, enjoys prayer and chanting mantras, strong life purpose, gains great wealth.

Sukra—Venus in the 5th House: Talent in arts due to past-life credit, happiness in love, optimistic mind, successful investments, knowledge of mantras, romantic and passionate. Lives a wealthy and comfortable life.

Sani—Saturn in the 5th House: Slow or depressed mind, overly serious, extremely logical and deep mind, few children, difficulties on account of children, danger of abortions or unwanted pregnancies, difficulties in love affairs. Powerful sense of responsibility, discipline, patience and humility due to past-life credit. Losses from speculations. Career involving intellectual or mental activities, may give out mantras in career. Feels misunderstood, becomes frustrated with shallow or non-thinking persons.

Rahu—The North Node in the 5th House: Mental unrest due to powerful cravings in the mind, practical-minded, ability to manipulate life to fulfill desires, success after 42nd year of life (when Rahu matures), powerful children, difficulties with children, stomach problems, problems in love affairs.

Ketu—The South Node in the 5th House: Minor mental irritations, few children. Begets children that are spiritual, shy or introspective. Strong intuition and psychic ability due to past-life credit, good discriminative ability, interest in spiritual subjects.

The 6th House

The 6th house is a *dusthana* or "grief-producing" house that causes destruction to its occupants and associations. The 8th and 12th houses are also *dusthanas*, but the 6th house is slightly better than the 8th and 12th because it is an *upachaya* or "growing house." This means that planets in the 6th house, though certainly harmed, may improve in time if the person is diligent in working with the energies involved.

As an *upachaya*, the 6th house is able to accommodate the influence of malefic planets (Sun, Mars, Saturn, Rahu, and Ketu) and actually benefits by their presence. Benefic planets are harmed by 6th house, destructiveness, even though the 6th house, itself, benefits by the presence of benefic planets.

The 6th house represents the ability to defeat enemies, competitors, jealous people, and anyone who stands in the person's way of success and fulfillment. It also signifies daily work, health, self-improvement, illnesses, diseases, healing ability, nursing or medical work, the restaurant and catering field, service-oriented work, co-workers, bosses, maids and servants, tendency to be charged in court cases, detail work, and the person's appetite.

The 6th house corresponds to an earth sign and is therefore an *artha* house—a house of wealth.

Surya—The Sun in the 6th House: Defeats enemies and competitors with ease, wins in court cases, enjoys service jobs, interest in healing profession, gains good fame or recognition, political or leadership ability, very strong health, good appetite and vitality. Difficulties with father in early years. Sensitivity in the heart if the Sun is afflicted or in an unfriendly sign.

Chandra—Moon in the 6th House: Sickly during early childhood. Suffering on account of mother, mother's life is problematic. Weakness or sensitivity with breast, brain, stomach, and (for a woman) menstrual cycle. Emotional difficulties or lack of mental peace throughout life. Attracts jealous people. Excellent at detail work, healing ability, good in nursing or medical field, good in restaurant or catering business.

Kuja—Mars in the 6th House: Swiftly defeats enemies and rises above competitors. Excels in technical fields, such as architecture, drafting, law, and engineering. Strong sex drive, courageous and adventurous. Problems with weak blood if Mars is afflicted, or in an unfriendly sign.

Buddha—Mercury in the 6th House: Obstacles in schooling, difficulties with speech. Weakness of lungs, intestines, and nervous system. Excels in debating, quarrelsome, likes to brag, prideful, good at self-expression after having difficulties in this realm during childhood, works in literary field, writes articles or books, knowledge of health matters, defeats enemies through his or her intellect. Nervous disorders, easily excitable.

Guru—Jupiter in the 6th House: Impaired luck, disappointments with religion, problems with spiritual teachers, good health, sensitive liver and possible allergies, good at detail work, enjoys service and daily job, few children, able to overcome enemies and jealous people. Good worker, gets along well with bosses and co-workers. Very well-liked.

Sukra—Venus in the 6th House: Problems in love matters, weak or sensitive reproductive system, venereal diseases, good health. Works with arts, jewelry, crafts, or sweets. Excellent in detail work, career in accounting, success in daily job, enjoys service, gets along well with co-workers. Few enemies, very well-liked.

Sani—Saturn in the 6th House: Big appetite, tremendous ability to defeat enemies and competitors, rises to the top of chosen field, excellent health. May work with carpentry, mining, coal, or real estate, difficulties or tediousness in daily job, problems with bosses and co-workers. If Saturn is afflicted or in an unfriendly sign, the person may have problems with arthritis or paralysis.

Rahu—The North Node in the 6th House: Excellent health, strong vitality, powerful appetite, great ability to defeat enemies and competitors, hard-working, good at detail work, enjoys service, troubles with co-workers.

Ketu—The South Node in the 6th House: Strong appetite, may work in the health field doing spiritual or metaphysical healing, difficulties with co-workers, problems with maids and servants. Because malefics are good influences in the 6th house, Ketu also gives robust health, strong vitality, and the ability to defeat enemies and competitors with ease.

The 7th House
The 7th house represents married life, the spouse, sexual passions and love partners. The 7th house is a *kendra*, or angular, house conferring strength and power and planets to any occupying planets.

The 7th house is expansive in nature and therefore it has some connection to success in business.

Also, if the 7th house is severely afflicted, the person will leave his or her birthplace and live in a foreign country, something that is considered a terrible fate from the Indian perspective.

The 7th house corresponds to an air sign (Libra), and is therefore a *kama* house—a house of desires. If the 7th house is strong, the person fulfills his or her daily desires easily.

Surya—The Sun in the 7th House: The Sun, which is known as the *atma-karaka* or indicator of the soul, in the 7th house gives a preoccupation with relationships and married life. But as a natural malefic in Hindu astrology, it causes big problems in marriage. Marries later in life, delays or obstacles in marriage, insufficient dowry or marries outside his or her religion, dominating or bossy spouse, spouse of low character. Possibility of divorce is high but it is the spouse who decides to end the marriage. Feels an overwhelming need to be in relationship. Attractive to the opposite sex, easily obtains his or her desired partner.

Chandra—The Moon in the 7th House: Extreme happiness in marriage, head over heels in love throughout life, spouse is emotionally nurturing. Gets a spouse who is brilliant, special, or famous. Strong bond in marriage, big passions, able to obtain the partner he or she desires. The Moon as a changeable planet (constantly waxing and waning) indicates a tendency to get numerous partners. In a polygamous society, this person would have more partners than anyone.

Kuja—Mars in the 7th House: Marries too early due to physical attraction, friction in married life, divorce is a near certainty, person loves to fight with his or her partner (consciously or unconsciously), powerful sexual passion, sexually experimental, very attractive to the opposite sex, skilled in the art of sexual pleasure, possibility of becoming widowed. Succeeds in business. Mars in the 7th house causes *Kujadosha*, or Mars affliction, a condition harming married life (for a full explanation see page 293).

Buddha—Mercury in the 7th House: Gets an intelligent and youthful looking spouse, numerous partners, minimal sexual passions, weak marriage bond caused by an emotionally detached spouse, exceptionally skilled in business and commerce, success in writing and communicative endeavors.

Guru—Jupiter in the 7th House: Surpasses his parents in prosperity and achievement. Lucky, goodlooking, honored and extremely respected. Gets a beautiful, special, or wealthy spouse. Happy married life, religious or spiritual spouse, strong sexual passions, able to obtain his or her desired partners, succeeds in business.

Sukra—Venus in the 7th House: Strong sexual passions, happy and romantic married life. Gets a beautiful, artistic, and youthful looking spouse. Possibility of numerous marriages due to intensely sensual nature, skilled in the art of sexual pleasures. Venus in any angular house indicates a kind, compassionate and forgiving nature.

Sani—Saturn in the 7th House: Bad luck in married life, approaches marriage from a position of scarcity, mistreated by spouse, possibility of becoming widowed. Saturn in any angular house creates major ups and downs in life, may reach pinnacle of success or depths of despair. Person is overly responsible in love matters. Attracts a partner who is older, authoritative, thin, or ascetic. Extremes of sexual passions (either frigid or powerfully indulging). Tendency to live in foreign countries.

Rahu—The North Node in the 7th House: Disturbed married life, constant ups and downs with spouse, insatiable desires to be in relationship. Person attracts a spouse who is powerful, worldly, materialistic. Spouse may also be bossy, domineering, and manipulative.

Ketu—The South Node in the 7th House: Constant ups and downs in married life, many minor disagreements in marriage. Attracts a partner who is shy, introverted, introspective, weird, metaphysical, or spiritual. Spouse may be weak, sickly, or of low character. Must beware of illusion or deception in the marital sphere. Attracts partners who are involved in drugs or alcohol.

The 8th House

The 8th house is a *dusthana*, or "grief-producing" house, that causes destruction to its occupants and associations. Planets in the 8th house are harmed in a serious way, and do not improve much in time. However, the 8th house is also the house of astrology, metaphysics, psychic ability, and intuition, and planets in the 8th create talent in these important fields.

The 8th house also represents longevity, means of death, joint finances, money from partners, wills and inheritances, money from unearned means (insurance companies, lotteries, and so on) and alimony.

Sexual attractiveness, but not sexual enjoyment or sexual passion, is seen from the 8th house. Sex symbols, such as Marilyn Monroe and Paul Newman have strong 8th houses. Also ruled by the 8th house are: virility, chronic illnesses, the reproductive system, and secretive matters, such as activities with the CIA, KGB, or any other "underground" organization.

The 8th house corresponds to a water sign (Scorpio) and is therefore a *moksha* house, a house of spiritual enlightenment and final liberation.

Surya—The Sun in the 8th House: Confidence is impaired, shy, there is a weak sense of dignity and authority, a tendency to be embarrassed or humiliated, problems with father. Father may suffer much or die early. Great interest in metaphysical subjects, strong intuition, talent in occult arts, sensitivity with reproductive system, weak eyesight, career ups and downs. Difficulties with government officials, bosses, and authoritarians. Few children.

Chandra—The Moon in the 8th House: Emotional suffering, disturbed peace of mind, many psychological complexes, oversensitive, lack of luck and fortune, many childhood illnesses, mother suffers or dies early, poor eyesight. Talent in metaphysical and occult subjects, very psychic, strong intuition, long life, gains money from spouse, money from wills and legacies, strong reproductive system, sexually attractive. Chronic illnesses. Difficulties with breast, brain, and menstrual cycle. Problems with women. Good spiritual and mystical experiences throughout life.

Kuja—Mars in the 8th House: Arguments due to joint finances, death by accident, illnesses or diseases of the reproductive system, accidents, weak blood, problems with brothers and sisters, difficulties with landed property, problems with wills and legacies, has to work hard for money. Strong gusto for life. Mars in the 8th house causes Kujadosha, a condition harming married life (for a full explanation see page 293).

Buddha—Mercury in the 8th House: Mental suffering, worrying, little peace of mind, interruption of schooling. Good longevity. Gains money from unearned means such as wills, legacies, insurance companies, and lotteries. Because Mercury (the planet of intellectual functions) aspects the 2nd house (writing and speaking) when it occupies the 8th house, the person writes and speaks well. Good imagination, earns well. Weak virility, impaired nervous system, lacks confidence. The person is very refined in character.

Guru—Jupiter in the 8th House: Very long life, gains great wealth from marriage partner. Benefits from wills, legacies, insurance companies, and other financial sources of unearned means. Strong reproductive system, sexually attractive, loves astrology and metaphysics, strong intuition, and psychic ability, good spiritual experiences throughout life. Problems in religion, disappointments on the spiritual path, arguments or dissension with gurus and mentors, upsets with religious figures. Dies a peaceful and painless death.

Sukra—Venus in the 8th House: Troubles in love life, general happiness is impaired. Sexually attractive, vibrant, energetic, strong vitality and gusto for life, money through wills and legacies. Dies a peaceful and painless death. Talent in occult arts, interest in astrology and metaphysics, psychic, intuitive. Sexual diseases if Venus is afflicted or in an unfriendly sign.

Sani—Saturn in the 8th House: Saturn as *ayushkaraka* (indicator of longevity) in the house of longevity gives the longest of lives. Much hardship, tensions in family life, difficulties earning wealth, problems in joint finances or with alimony, difficulties collecting wills, no money from "unearned" means (insurance companies, lotteries, and so on).

Rahu—The North Node in the 8th House: This is a very bad placement for family life and happiness in general. Separations from friends and family, problems in joint finances, lack of domestic harmony, constant ups and downs, many expenses throughout life. Cravings for mystical or spiritual knowledge, talent in the occult arts. Sexual attractiveness, long life.

Ketu—The South Node in the 8th House: Very bad for domestic harmony and happiness in general. Many separations from friends and family. Troubles with joint finances, inability to collect from wills and legacies, chronic illnesses, reproductive ailments. Talent in spiritual and metaphysical subjects, loves astrology.

The 9th House

The 9th house is the best, most auspicious, house of a Hindu horoscope. Planets occupying the 9th house are strengthened and their energies function gracefully and beneficially.

The 9th house represents luck, fortune, travel, religion (not spirituality or evolutionary growth, which are 12th house significations), spiritual mentors and gurus, higher knowledge and faith in God.

As the house of luck, the 9th influences the person's ability to attain solutions throughout life. These solutions often occur due to the person's strong sense of faith.

In Southern India, the 9th house is considered to represent the father, because there a person's father functions somewhat as a guru to his children. In Northern India, the 10th house represents the father. In my experience, I have noticed that both houses have a distinct bearing on the father.

The 9th house corresponds to a fire sign (Sagittarius) and is therefore a *dharma* house, a house relating to one's purpose and mission in life.

Surya—The Sun in the 9th House: Tremendous interest in religion and philosophy, loves higher knowledge, likely to follow a different religion than the one given at birth, enjoys spiritual practices, loves to travel. Has a powerful and long-lived father, father may be wealthy and successful. Strong morals, good character, performs good deeds. There may be mild disturbances or disagreements with one's father as well as one's religious mentors and spiritual gurus, particularly if the Sun is poorly aspected or occupying an unfriendly sign.

Chandra—The Moon in the 9th House: Great luck and fortune, many blessings throughout life, much happiness, tremendous faith in God, loves religion and philosophy, gets good spiritual mentors and gurus, gets abundant higher knowledge, benefits from mother, mother is special or long-lived. Many visits to foreign countries, solutions to problems come easily and swiftly.

Kuja—Mars in the 9th House: Suffers on account of father, great interest in religion, disagreements with religious teachers or spiritual gurus, too dogmatic or fervent in religious beliefs, good at promoting philosophy or religion, strong drive and ambitions, owns land or real estate, long distance travel occasionally meets with discord.

Buddha—Mercury in the 9th House: Tremendous understanding of religion and philosophy, scholarly, well-educated, may translate scriptural knowledge, good at teaching higher knowledge, gets good religious teachers and spiritual gurus, good relationship with his or her father. Cultured, refined, well-mannered.

Guru—Jupiter in the 9th House: Divinely blessed, the consummate spiritual disciple, unshakable faith in God, very lucky with religious teachers and spiritual gurus, lives for spiritual knowledge, travels for religious pilgrimages or spiritual purposes, instant solutions to problems, charitable, good morals, loves meditation, has many fine children, plenty of wisdom, talent in law, may promote religion or help raise people's consciousness.

Sukra—Venus in the 9th House: Lucky, strong faith in God, gets good mentors and gurus, religion and philosophy bring only happiness, gets a bubbly or good-natured guru. Love matters are favored, strong artistic talent, gets a religious or spiritual spouse, marries a foreigner. Happiness from father, father is wealthy or fortunate. Gets abundant wealth and comforts throughout life.

Sani—Saturn in the 9th House: Luck is spoiled, difficulties with father, father may suffer or live a very hard life, troubles with religious teachers or spiritual gurus, problems with foreigners, difficulty to get higher knowledge, obstacles or delays during long distance travels. Saturn in the 9th can mean no interest at all in religion and philosophy or intense commitment in that realm, depending on the rest of the horoscope and Saturn's sign placement and house rulerships.

Rahu—The North Node in the 9th House: Cravings for religious and spiritual knowledge, many long distance travels, enhanced ability to gain worldly power and wealth, difficulties with father, father suffers a lot. Worldly power increases during 42nd year (when Rahu matures).

Ketu—The South Node in the 9th House: Minor disturbances with religious teachers and spiritual gurus, disturbed relationship with father, father suffers a lot or has problems with alcohol, gets a mystical or spiritual father. Faith is weak, little interest in religious or spiritual knowledge. Strong tendencies toward occultism or metaphysics. Troubles during long-distance travels. Gets a guru who is particularly reclusive.

The 10th House

The 10th house is a *kendra*, or angular, house, bestowing power to any occupying planets. It represents career success, profession, *dharma* (life purpose), honor, fame and deeds that benefit society.

The 10th house relates to holy pilgrimages. If spiritual planets (Jupiter, Ketu, etc.) occupy the 10th house, the person makes plenty of spiritual journeys. Also seen from the 10th house are: government officials, authority figures, and notable persons.

The 10th house is an *upachaya*, or "growing," house. This means that planets in the 10th house grow stronger and more prominent as the years go by. It also means that malefic planets (Sun, Mars, Saturn, Rahu, and Ketu) in the 10th house give primarily good results.

The 10th house corresponds to an earth sign and is therefore an *artha* house, a house relating to wealth.

Surya—The Sun in the 10th House: Powerful career success, leadership ability, tendency to be a boss, rises to a high position, gains fame easily, strong confidence, benefits from government or takes a government job. Performs good deeds for society. Has a powerful or successful father.

Chandra—The Moon in the 10th House: Fine reputation, much fame, high public achievements early in life, loves to perform for the public, tends toward artistic or high profile careers, numerous careers throughout life (Moon is a changeable influence—always waxing and waning), able to incite the masses, benefits from mother and females. Has a powerful or successful mother. General success and happiness throughout life, many accomplishments.

Kuja—Mars in the 10th House: Great success and achievement in career, mechanical ability, enjoys technical professions (architecture, engineering, law, drafting), military career, enjoys bossing other people, extremely ambitious, may create enemies because of ruthlessness in professional life, respected and powerful, potential friction and disturbances with both parents.

Buddha—Mercury in the 10th House: Fine reputation, successful career in communications or literary field, strong intellectual abilities, good speaker, great talent in business and commerce, performs good deeds for society, musical talent, smart in professional life.

Guru—Jupiter in the 10th House: Successful career, honor and fame, performs good deeds for society, attracted to careers that raise consciousness, desires to educate the public, lucky, gains wealth easily, gets plenty of comforts in life, benefits from government and authority figures, enjoys holy pilgrimages, good relationship with father (and with mother due to the aspect Jupiter in the 10th throws onto the 4th).

Sukra—Venus in the 10th House: Successful career, honored or famous, career in performing arts, lucky with the public, happy, gets plenty of jewelry and other comforts, good relationship with father (and with mother, due to the aspect Venus in the 10th throws onto the 4th), gets nice cars and homes.

Sani—Saturn in the 10th House: Leadership ability, excels at organizing for the public, strong desires to affect the masses. This placement can make or break a person's life, depending on whether or not the person pursues the powerful career he or she desires, or censors talents due to confidence problems. Major ups and downs in life (person can reach pinnacle of success as well as depths of despair). Career may involve construction, real estate, carpentry, or tedious jobs.

Rahu—The North Node in the 10th House: Powerful and renowned career, honored or famous, excels in professions dealing with the public, leaves home early to pursue a career, supports his or her parents early in life, performs important deeds for society, many spiritual pilgrimages throughout life. May be attracted to a spouse outside his or her religion.

Ketu—The South Node in the 10th House: Successful career, easily fulfills professional ambitions, desires to educate the masses or raise peoples' consciousness, excels in spiritual or mystical careers, talented in ancient or metaphysical healing arts.

The 11th House

The 11th house is the house of financial gains and profits through side ventures. Side ventures means interests that are distinctly separate from one's daily work. However, real estate and speculations (gambling or stock market involvement) do not come under 11th house significations as they are specifically ruled by the 4th and 5th houses respectively.

The 11th house also rules the eldest sibling (not older siblings—just the eldest), friends and groups.

A person's major goals and desires in life are seen through the 11th house (daily desires are ruled by the 3rd house). Although the 3rd house rules the fine arts of music, dance, and drama in Hindu astrology, the 11th house is also strongly connected to dancing.

The 11th house is an *upachaya* or "growing" house. This means that planets occupying the 11th house become stronger influences as time goes by. It also means that malefic planets in the 11th house give primarily beneficial results.

The 11th house corresponds to an air sign (Aquarius) and is therefore a *kama* house—a house relating to desires.

Surya—The Sun in the 11th House: Able to earn wealth from side ventures, strong bond with friends, many male friends, gets powerful friends, loves group activity, earns good money, strong connection to eldest sibling, eldest sibling is male. Confidence and leadership ability grow stronger as life goes on. Able to fulfill major goals and desires in life.

Chandra—The Moon in the 11th House: Prosperous, earns great wealth through side ventures, quickly becomes wealthy, loves to be with friends and groups, gets famous or special friends, especially female friends, fulfills major goals easily, happy relationship with eldest sibling, eldest sibling is special or renowned, opportunities continually arise throughout life, person lives life in accordance with his or her dreams and visions. Loves to dance.

Kuja—Mars in the 11th House: Ambitious, fulfills major goals and desires easily, plentiful opportunities, earns wealth from side ventures, prosperous, courageous. Little happiness from eldest sibling, friction or fighting with eldest sibling, friction or fighting with friends, agitation and disruption in group activity.

Buddha—Mercury in the 11th House: Wealthy, successful, talented in business and commerce, plenty of opportunities, earns money from side ventures, intelligent and brilliant, good relationship with eldest sibling, eldest sibling is communicative, enjoys friends and groups, has intelligent friends, able to fulfill major desires.

Guru—Jupiter in the 11th House: Person has the "midas touch." Neverending opportunities to earn wealth, earns money from side ventures, easily fulfills major goals and desires, has excellent luck with friends and in group activities, gets wealthy or famous friends, benefits greatly from eldest sibling, eldest sibling is fortunate and lucky, major goals and desires may be religious or spiritual. Loves to dance.

Sukra—Venus in the 11th House: Fulfills major goals and desires easily, wealthy and prosperous, earns money from side ventures, lucky with opportunity, has many fine friends, friends are artistic and female, loves to dance, major goals in life may be artistic, enjoys abundant luxuries and comforts, happiness from eldest sibling. Eldest sibling may be artistic, special, or lucky.

Sani—Saturn in the 11th House: Becomes wealthy slowly during later years, succeeds in side ventures involving construction or buildings, few friends, older or ascetic friends, suffers in group activity, no happiness from eldest sibling (either has no elder sibling or suffers in his or her relationship to eldest sibling). Fulfills major goals in life but only through hard work and great effort.

Rahu—The North Node in the 11th House: Wealthy, prosperous, can make millions through side ventures, very intense goals and desires in life which are likely to be fulfilled, abundant opportunities, gets friends that are powerful and materialistic, troubled relationship with eldest sibling, eldest sibling may be domineering or manipulative.

Ketu—The South Node in the 11th House: Gains wealth through side ventures, major goals may be spiritual or otherworldly, strange disturbances with friends and groups. Gets friends that are weird, strange, or spiritual. Unhappy relationship with eldest sibling. Eldest sibling is odd or spiritual.

The 12th House

The 12th house is a *dusthana*, or "grief-producing," house that causes destruction to its occupants and associations. Planets occupying the 12th house are harmed in a serious way and do not much improve in time. On the positive side, however, the 12th house represents *moksha* (enlightenment or final liberation). Planets in the 12th house give an interest in meditation and other evolutionary paths. They also create a great deal of spiritual growth throughout life despite the suffering the person undergoes due to the harm that the 12th house causes to the occupying planets.

The 12th house rules debts and expenses, as well as *remote* foreign countries (specifically, exotic or spiritual lands such as India, Nepal, Tibet, Israel, and Africa).

Also governed by the 12th house are: beds and everything that occurs in the bedroom, sexual pleasure (but not sexual passions or sexual appearance), problems from thieves and robbers, prisons, and hospitals.

The 12th house corresponds to a water sign (Pisces) and is therefore a *moksha* house, a house of spiritual enlightenment or final liberation.

Surya—The Sun in the 12th House: Shy, lacks confidence, introspective, periodic need for seclusion, difficulties attaining worldly success. Loves meditation, interest in enlightenment or final liberation, may choose monastic life. No leadership ability, difficulties asserting oneself. Suffering on account of father, father may be sickly or short-lived, poor eyesight, danger of imprisonment, many dealings with remote foreign countries. Weak heart if the Sun is badly aspected.

Chandra—The Moon in the 12th House: Much emotional suffering throughout life, many fears or psychological complexes, disturbed peace of mind, unhappy childhood, continual illnesses during childhood, poor memory, few comforts, feels undeserving, difficulties attaining abundance, hard to gain fame or recognition. Suffering on account of mother, mother is sick or dies early. Loves meditation and other evolutionary techniques, travels often to remote foreign countries for spiritual purposes, makes tremendous spiritual advancement over the course of life, has good spiritual experiences. Sleeps on nice beds, enjoys great sexual pleasure.

Kuja—Mars in the 12th House: Strong sex drive, much sexual pleasure, spends a lot of money, many debts and expenses, difficulty asserting oneself, weak blood, troubles with brothers and sisters, problems in remote foreign countries, strong desire for spiritual growth. Mars in the 8th house causes *Kujadosha*, a condition harming married life (for a full explanation see page 293).

Buddha—Mercury in the 12th House: Troubles in education, mental disturbances, weak confidence, weak nervous system, thrifty, able to hold onto wealth, good experiences in remote foreign countries for spiritual purposes, interest in *moksha* (enlightenment or final liberation).

Guru—Jupiter in the 12th House: Interrupted religious or spiritual life, obstacles or troubles with gurus, problems with universities and other institutions of higher learning. Gains tremendous spiritual evolution throughout life, loves meditation and other spiritual techniques, able to hold onto wealth, rarely disturbed by unforseen debts and expenses, spends money for spiritual or charitable purposes. Gets abundant sexual pleasure, sleeps in fine beds, goes to highest heavenly plane after death.

Sukra—Venus in the 12th House: Troubles in love life, difficulties with females, thrifty, few debts and expenses, gets bargains, great sexual pleasure, happiness in remote foreign countries for spiritual purposes, plenty of spiritual evolution, loves meditation, spends money entertaining others and throwing parties, goes to a heavenly plane after death.

Sani—Saturn in the 12th House: Career ups and downs, sleeps on hard beds, no happiness in bedroom, trouble with discipline and patience, curtailed longevity, gets extreme sexual pleasure or none at all (depending on Saturn's sign placement and aspects to Saturn).

Rahu—The North Node in the 12th House: Craves spiritual evolution, enjoys meditation and other evolutionary techniques, spends much money, meets with large debts and expenses, strong sex drive, plenty of sexual pleasure.

Ketu—The South Node in the 12th House: Gains tremendous spiritual evolution throughout life, loves meditation, good discriminative ability, very psychic and intuitive, troubles in the bedroom, little sexual pleasure, bothered by thieves and robbers, trouble in the left ear, cannot save money.

CLOSING

Having gained some sense of the nature of Hindu predictive astrology, you are now, hopefully, in a better position to determine whether further study is appropriate. For those who wish to continue, the rewards are great. As a practicing astrologer who uses both Hindu and traditional Western astrology for each horoscope interpretation, I must say that the two systems complement each other extraordinarily well. Nothing so marvelously reveals a person's psychology, personality, and behavioral traits as the planetary aspects and tropical zodiac sign positions in a Western horoscope. On the other hand, determining a person's *dharma* (life purpose) and the actual events and circumstances of one's life is so perfectly facilitated from the Hindu birthchart.

The marvelous *dasa-bhukti* system of planetary periods, which could not be presented here due to space constrictions, is an unparalleled gift to astrologers wishing to predict the futures of their clients. It is to the largest extent the *dasa-bhukti* system that is responsible for so many stories throughout the world regarding remarkably accurate predictions made by Hindu astrologers.

It has always been my belief that drawing accurate astrological conclusions and making reliable predictions, whether about a person's behavior or their events and circumstances, depends more on essential and fundamental astrological techniques than complicated, tedious, highly obscure and/or new-fangled methods. Astrologers who have knowledge of a person's Hindu as well as Western horoscope, have two sets of powerful fundamentals with which to compare and judge. Knowing that the Western chart is free-will oriented and more revealing of the person's psychology, the astrologer processes the Western data appropriately while simultaneously considering how the Hindu, fate-oriented data applies. In many cases the Hindu and Western birthcharts will be similar in their indications of positive or negative implications thereby giving the astrologer greater confidence in his or her conclusions.

However, in other cases, the charts are extremely different and this is perhaps when the greatest advantage is gained. If a person's Western horoscope is highly afflicted, but the Hindu chart is strong and beneficial, it means that the person's karma—the material success and benefits they deserve to experience—is strong but that their psychology and internal makeup can easily hold them back if they give too much credence to their thoughts and feelings. Contrarily, if a person's Hindu horoscope is weak but their Western one is strong, it means that the person deserves weak or inferior material success and benefits, but can profoundly influence the situation through thoughts, feelings, and new ways of being; in other words through free will.

I could go on and on promoting the case that astrologers should learn *both* Hindu and Western astrology, but since I have devoted an entire book to that subject *(Astro-Logos: Revelations of a Hindu Astrologer)*, interested readers can obtain that text. It is worth repeating that the information in this chapter is but a "taste" of Hindu predictive astrology. No details have been given regarding Hindu astrological *yogas* (planetary unions), nor the peculiar Eastern method of astrological aspects, nor *chandra lagna* (the house placements of the planets in relation to the Moon—i.e., a planet opposite the Moon is seen as a 7th house planet), nor the nearly endless maze of astrological techniques that has been developed over so many thousands of years. Those who want to learn the system more fully should consult my textbook *Ancient Hindu Astrology for the Modern Western Astrologer* or one of the four other Hindu astrology books written by Westerners. Students who are particularly interested learning about *dasa bhukti* periods may also look into my fourth book, *How To Predict Your Future: Secrets of Eastern and Western Astrology.*

Finally, those who still have doubts about Hindu astrology, please consider the following conversation that took place in Benares, India some twelve years ago. It is an excerpt from the first Hindu astrology reading of my life. I was then 31 years old.

Astrologer Shastri: You are going to write some books.
Braha: What!!!
Shastri: You are going to write some books.
Braha: Are you sure?
Shastri: Yes.
Braha: How many?
Shastri: A few. Five or six.
Braha: Are you sure?
Shastri: Yes.
Braha: But are you sure? I mean, are you positive?
Shastri: My dear friend, astrology is not an absolute science.
Braha: Ahhhhh ...
Shastri: But you will write books!

ABOUT THE AUTHOR

James Braha is internationally recognized as the astrologer who first brought Hindu, or Vedic, astrology to the West in understandable form through his groundbreaking book *Ancient Hindu Astrology for the Modern Western Astrologer.* He is also the author of *How to Predict Your Future: Secrets of Eastern and Western Astrology, How to be a Great Astrologer: The Planetary Aspects Explained* and *Astro-Logos: Revelations of a Hindu Astrologer.* Braha is the recipient of the *Jyotish Kovida* award from the Indian Council of Astrological Sciences. He lectures throughout the U.S. and Europe.

Braha graduated as an actor from the fine arts department of Carnegie-Mellon University in 1973. He then became interested in spiritual subjects and spent seven years teaching meditation throughout the United States. Braha began his astrological studies in 1979 and eventually came to believe that, while Western astrology is profound in its descriptions of character and personality assessment, the system leaves something to be desired regarding predictions of events and circumstances. In search of missing links, he made two journeys to New Delhi and Bombay in 1983 and 1984 where he studied privately with astrologer/author R. Santhanam and with P. M. Padia.

Although Braha acknowledges that both Hindu and Western astrology are complete in themselves, he has gained the most accuracy by using the two systems side by side. Therefore, his main commitment during the last ten years has been to train astrologers to practice Hindu and Western astrology, using the Hindu system more for prediction purposes and Western astrology primarily for its spiritual and psychological advantages.

Braha maintains a busy astrological practice in Sarasota, Florida and most of his work occurs on the telephone with clients who have read his books. He self-publishes all his books under the name Hermetician Press.

Readers may write to him at the following address:

James T. Braha
P.O. Box 552
Longboat Key, FL 34228-1020
Phone: 941-387-9101

Richard Houck

CHAPTER 8

Life & Death—
East & West

O NE OF THE KEY QUESTS to fascinate mankind concerns the possibility of knowing one's own date of death. Because this information is generally considered unknowable, even as it is critical at the unconscious level, psychoanalytic theory asserts that the latent fears and anxieties associated with this "occult" dilemma can often manifest in poor adaptation to life through a broad variety of involuted pathways.

As I slowly shifted my personal orientation from Western to Eastern (i.e., Indian or Vedic) astrology, I became fascinated by the much more open attitude of Indian books and periodicals to this topic vis à vis the West. Of course, this reflects key elements of the East's religious culture, but it also reflects what I was finding to be a vastly more competent, and sophisticated, astrological foundation.

I had also become convinced beyond all personal doubt that, as Edgar Cayce, Alice Bailey, and most other powerful psychics assert, the Tropical (or seasonal) zodiac is an error. But, since this is a long and arduous argument with many complex threads, it will not be addressed in this brief chapter.

However, even though we will start out just assuming that certain Eastern fundamentals are true, it nevertheless remains the case that the Western astrological tradition has some wonderful techniques that confirm the message, and strengthen the timing, of Eastern methods. A key objective of my book, *The Astrology of Death*, was to illustrate how an integrated methodology can be demonstrated to yield even better results, both theoretically and through the accumulated weight of anecdote.

As a follow-on to that effort, the main purpose of this chapter is to highlight a subset of summary-level technical considerations that anchor Hindu thinking about death timing, and then to demonstrate how these considerations can be blended with some key Western techniques. For ease of "digestion," the Eastern methods will be simplified and adapted to make them more accessible to what is expected to be the likely mindset of the Western reader.

Ultimately, however, in order to really understand what will be presented here, any stimulated reader should feel the need to undertake a more extended study. Finally, since many readers of this chapter may have already read my book on this topic, I will also introduce several new, or extended, ideas for further consideration.

MY OWN DATE OF DEATH
GIVEN VIA NADI GRANTHA

After *The Astrology of Death* was released, I found myself promoting it in a variety of public fora such as lectures, bookstores, and so forth. One of the questions I was repeatedly asked was if I knew when I, myself, was going to die. Although I did not discuss this in my book, the answer is: I think so. Specifically, my estimation is September 13, 2031.

And this alleged fact, based upon a certain amount of "cheating" as described below, provides the opportunity to begin this review with some insight into the range of Hindu astrology. Ultimately, this exotic beginning will provide a springboard back to some key fundamentals.

Several years ago, through quite a shadowy procedure, I had put myself on a waiting list to receive something called a Nadi Grantha reading (*nadi grantha* actually refers to books of degree-related information that were trance-channeled by ancient masters). These readings are generally only given in India by a subset of specially-trained astrologers who also have access to certain 5,000-year-old palm leaves. On these preserved leaves are Sanskrit texts. When you show up for your consultation, the reader will ask for your birth data. Using this information, he will then index through these leaves in order to pull a subset of them, and he will often ask you a question or two in order to complete determination of his selection.

The reader will then proceed to *read your life story, including all key life events and their implications, from these leaves.* But he doesn't stop with where you are right now. His reading will also explain what will happen to you over the remaining term of your life. It will also extend to a review of the past eight lives that led up to, and therefore contributed to the creation of, your current life. My reader felt the spontaneous need to apologize for this limitation of eight (!), but it suggested to me the possibility that lives may be lived in blocks of eight (eight bits in a byte, after all!). In any case, as a matter of course, the date of death is also provided. These leaves therefore correspond to what Western astrologers probably have heard referred to as the "akashic records."

Some reviewers of my book, with their intellectual Western need to personally believe in a certain type of "free will," expressed concern about the enhanced level of "fatalism" that they thought my book implied. All I can say is, I'm sure glad they didn't hear about the Nadi Grantha experience! However, let me briefly say that even experiencing the reality of a Nadi Grantha reading does not dissuade me from the reality of free will. It just makes a statement about "soul time."

A question that typically comes to mind is: why aren't there billions of these leaves? One answer often given is that the leaves were only written for those who were destined to ultimately consult them (some even say that the consultation is itself written on the leaves). While this seems efficient enough, it may actually be untrue. The volume of leaves is manageable because what the reader is really pulling is a *symbolic pattern* of life events and experiences that corresponds to the life of tens of thousands of individuals who have been born at various points in Earth's space and time. In other words, the exact template of my personal life experiences exactly overlays the lives of many others. And this "template" information is then blended, to a certain extent, with the person's unique natal chart.

As a word to the wise, I should mention that, due to the great interest in this knowledge among people who are perhaps *not* destined to have such a reading, a minor fraudulent "industry" has developed in India to address the market demand. Due to the greater power of just normal Hindu astrology, a standard astrologer can often simulate a reading that will trick the unwary Westerner into concluding, at least for a while, that they have had a real Nadi Grantha reading. My guess is that legitimate Indian astrologers probably don't worry about this very much on the grounds that it is perhaps your destiny to be tricked. It is my contention that it may be possible to validate the reading, including the past life remarks. That is the subject of yet another discourse, but I shall nevertheless pick up the thread of this issue at the close of this article.

In Hindu astrology, the Sun rules the soul along with the planet at the highest sidereal degree. My Sun is a double soul ruler since it is also the "planet" at the highest sidereal degree, being in the last half of the last degree of Pisces. Therefore it may be of interest to note that I suddenly received this enlightenment about my year of death ("in the Fall, at age 84") on September 30, 1994—only two weeks after my book was released. And this was when transiting Uranus was within two days of being completely stationary square to my Sun, with an applying orb of only 9 minutes!

Only two days later, which was the exact date of the Uranus station, and using the techniques in my book, I was able to validate further the assertion of the Nadi Grantha reader, and then identify the *exact* date of death. This was important to me since I had been given estimated dates of death by otherwise good Western psychics, but since their information would not validate astrologically, I would not accept it. This one validated perfectly.

So, in the absence of other living volunteers, I will therefore kill *myself* off by using my own chart as an anchoring theme chart to highlight a number of the key points that were made in *The Astrology of Death*. The key points to be made with regard to this chart will then be reinforced with supporting data from a variety of other people who have already died.

THE EASTERN VERSUS WESTERN CHART

Before getting into some technical death theory, it's important to anchor your understanding of a fundamental conversion that must first occur. Your Western chart must first be converted to an Eastern chart. This is best demonstrated by an example. See figures 1 and 2 (pages 329–330). The former is my standard Western chart (04/13/47 @ 00:51 CST in Des Moines, Iowa). The second chart is what the former should look like after you have converted it. There are three steps:

Step #1: Subtract the *ayanamsha* value off of every planet and angle in your chart. The ayanamsha is the amount of arc that the Western, tropical, or seasonal zodiac has precessed forward from the Eastern sidereal, or star-based, zodiac since the year they began to diverge. While the exact

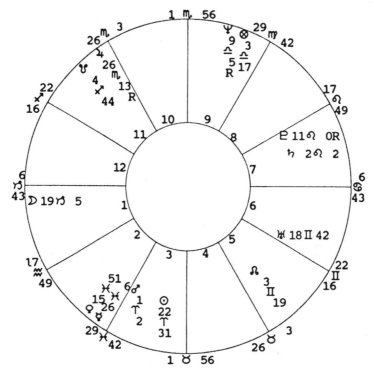

Figure 1. Richard Houck. April 13, 1947, 00:51 A.M., CST, Des Moines, Iowa. Tropical. Placidus Houses.

amount is disputed, the values I strongly suggest you use (in degrees/minutes/seconds) are: 22/22/45 (for 01/01/1900) or 23/04/17 (for 01/01/1950).

I picked these two dates since Western software can often convert to sidereal if you supply information in this format. Alternatively, if an *ayanamsha* value for *Lahiri* is automatically supplied by your software, use the Lahiri value minus (in degrees/minutes/seconds) 00/05/10, and you will get the same result.

Step #2: Convert your chart to a full-sign house system as per the example. When my Capricorn ASC was backed up, it became Sagittarius. So the entire 1st house is SA (from 00–29 degrees), the entire 2nd house is Capricorn (from 00–29 degrees), and so on. The ASC ("A") is just put into the 1st house as a sensitive point.

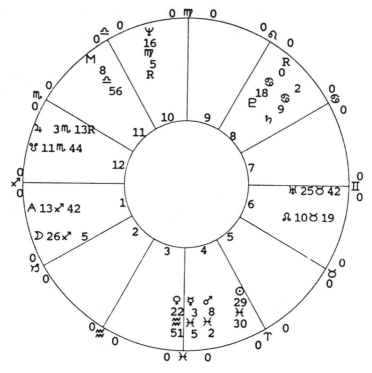

Figure 2. Richard Houck. April 13, 1947, 00:51 A.M., CST, Des Moines, Iowa. Eastern Sidereal.

Step #3: Put your Midheaven (MC) into whatever house it ends up in, but note that the cusp of the 10th is no longer defined by the MC; the 10th is just the 10th sign/house from the 1st sign/house. Hindu astrology does not make as much use of the MC as the West does, but do insert it anyway ("M") since we will be using it in our hybrid system. For the same reason, put in the three outer planets, even though Hindu astrology does not use them, but do not use them as rulers of houses. So, using the more classical rulerships, every inner planet rules two houses except the Sun and the Moon.

The chart that a classical Hindu astrologer uses looks exactly like the second example. The only difference is that he converts it to a rectangular or triangular chart format. These alternate formats are only matters of style and not of content. They allow the astrologer's eye to make more rapid visual associations of a certain type.

Western astrologers have long been puzzled about what planets have the power to signal death. Hindu astrologers refer to such planets as *marakas*, and they have some specific ideas about how to derive them. Superficially, from the point of view of a form-oriented observer, death would seem to be signaled by a hard Saturn or Pluto transit or progressed event. But experienced observation proves that such is often not the case. In fact, Venus or Jupiter often seem to be clearly involved—but not consistently.

Alternatively, the ruler of the 8th, or the degree on its cusp, is said to have something to do with death. But experience makes it obvious that this house in a Western chart has no consistent usefulness or applicability. If it were that easy, astrologers could consistently predict death. But the reality is that their skill set in this matter is, in fact, quite limited. Now that we have anchored ourselves in the classical Indian zodiac and house system, perhaps we can proceed forward more productively.

THE TRUE HOUSES OF LIFE AND DEATH

Western astrologers have it quite backwards in a number of ways, and this sub-section will begin to unravel the problem. First, there are actually three *life* houses in the Hindu chart. About the first of these, there is no contention with the West. The *1st* house is a life house. Among other things, it symbolizes the general body we have taken on, as a cloak, in this particular lifetime. When it is strong, it contributes tone values of strength, force and vitality. However, I should note here "for the record" that the factors which make a house strong in the East are often not the same as in the West. But again I will have to pass on this issue to stay with the larger issues.

But here some new wrinkles begin. The *8th* house is the second *life* house. The reason is because it rules those aspects of the life force that function at a deeper level of pulsation. This is the level of occult energy that contributes to regeneration. This is the fundamentally anabolic house of sex. And, of all the houses, what other house but the 8th could possibly symbolize, in general, the key occult concepts of both kundalini and the chakras?

So there is only one way the 8th can function as a morbid or terminal house in the chart of any particular individual. And that is if it, or its ruler, is *weak*, and thus the underlying vitality becomes exposed. But, in that case, the 8th house becomes the *object*, and not the "cause," of a death-related transaction.

I do want to respond to the valid concern that there must be *some* house in astrology theory that signifies every single concept that can be conceived. So what house signifies the *concept* of death? Yes, the 8th, but this is because of its occult support of life. Thus, for example, if a question is asked about death under a circumstance that would generate a horary (or *prashna*) chart, the 8th could be analyzed with regard to the question. Along this line, it could also contribute information to queries about the cause or nature of a death, or about death-related issues in general. But that is about the extent of it.

By the way, just as there must be a house that symbolically correlates to the concept of death, so must there also be a correlated planet. As we might suspect in a system that does not use Pluto, Saturn fills this role. In Hindu terminology, Saturn becomes the general *karaka*, or indicator, of the concept of death. But this leads us into a type of minor paradox.

Because of the frequent misplacement, by Western astrologers, of planets into the wrong signs and houses, Indian astrologers have been able to notice something important that Western astrologers have not: when Saturn is located in the natal 8th house, it frequently results in a *long* life. This is a "gross level" statement, and is subject to a lot of further qualification (the condition of Saturn, aspects upon the 8th house and other life houses, the status of the ruler of the 8th, and so forth). But it is basically true for two reasons.

The first reason is because Saturn slows everything down, and it essentially becomes a type of "modulator" of whatever comes under its sphere of influence. As we have already noted, the 8th house is a life house at the level of occult pulsation. Certain schools of biological thought argue that any particular body may be genetically pre-programmed to have only a fixed number of cell divisions allocated to it at birth. With Saturn in the 8th, the basal metabolism thus becomes much more regulated and is treated more prudently. Thus Saturn, as the ruler of time, essentially forces the metabolic clock to run slower.

Before getting to the second reason linking Saturn to longevity, let's briefly shift attention to two related questions that more immediately come to mind. These two points will, in fact, lay the groundwork that allows us to sneak up on the second longevity point. This, in turn, will provide a key clue that will unlock the secret of the true indicators of death.

Question #1: Why *does* Saturn link to death? There are many reasons, but part of the clue is found in all ancient medical texts that comment upon what is fundamentally required to support life. The key words you see over and over are: *deficiency* and *toxemia*. Thus death is more likely to occur when our bodies fail to adequately assimilate enough good things, or when our bodies fail to adequately dispose of enough bad things.

The Sanskrit word for Saturn is *Sani*. What famous plumbing product is still found on store shelves worldwide? Sani-Flush. What is the name of the Hindu god that rules death? Yama. In what part of the symbolic human body is Yama said to reside? The rectum. So, while the marketing hype of the Western world is always promoting the eating of this or that to support anabolism, Hinduism wisely reminds us that the catabolic disposal of blockages is equally important. At whatever symbolic level, he who is consistently blocked in the free flow of energy, soon dies.

Question #2: What about the issue of wills and legacies? Hasn't it always struck you as odd that the 8th house would allegedly rule both death and, at the same time, the resources of the dead? How can a house rule its own concept *and* the 2nd-house idea from its own concept? Yet is seems quite clear that the 8th is the resources of others (the 7th). Might this say something about the 7th? With this important question, we are at the edge of understanding the second main reason that Saturn rules longevity. And when we understand this, then it will become clear what factors must necessarily rule death.

Let's presume that the "natural" house distribution is the one that supports life. This is the one that symbolically associates "Mars with Aries with the 1st house." If this is the fundamental layout for the concept of life, then what might be the fundamental layout to support death? Did you know that Manilus, Alan Leo, and others referred to the cusp of the 7th as the "Portal of Death?" Reason: this is where the source of all life, the Sun, "dies" every evening. So let's begin by wondering if the layout for death might logically be found by flipping the standard "life zodiac" upside down.

When we do this, Libra is rising. What does Libra-rising do for Saturn, the natural karaka of death? It gives it incredible status because

Saturn becomes a *rajayoga* all by itself when Libra is rising. (Here we need to digress for a moment. What is a "rajayoga?" *Raj* means "king" and *yoga* means "union." So a rajayoga is a "kingly union." Rajayogas are usually the combination of two special planets in the same house. For each rising sign, these two planets are selected because they rule a certain combination of good houses. So wherever this joint combination occurs, great value and performance strength is brought to that receiving house. In rough terms, and eliminating much qualification, a rajayoga in the Eastern system tends to occur when the ruler of either the 5th or the 9th ends up in the same house as the ruler of one of the angles, or *kendras*.)

When Libra rises, it works out to be the case that Saturn, all by itself, rules both the angular Capricorn 4th and the Aquarius 5th. Thus, by looking at the zodiac upside down, the karaka of death manages to achieve a lot of status all by itself. This would make sense when life is inverted. But there is still another occult link back to longevity.

Notice further that when Libra is rising, Venus rules both of the life houses (the 1st and the Taurus 8th). And Saturn is exalted in Venus' sign (Libra) which, by the way, helps explain why so many extremely wealthy individuals have a certain kind of very hard aspect between Venus and Saturn. Thus Hindu astrologers have made another key observation that Western astrologers have been unable to notice: when Venus is natally in the 8th house in the Eastern chart, these people tend to have an exceptional amount of life vitality, particularly if Venus is well reinforced (some perceive this as exceptional "sex appeal," and so forth).

Clearly this should not be the case if the 8th were a death house instead of a life house. But since we now see that Venus actually thrives in its own ruling house (which is now Taurus, instead of Scorpio where it would be detrimentally placed) this makes sense and therefore tends to fend off death.

You may recall my earlier assertion that there were *three* life houses. We have discussed the 1st and the 8th, so this leads us to the final one. Often, when a Hindu astrologer is engaged in a deduction about an issue, he will look at the symbolically appropriate house *and* the house that is the same number of houses from that house.

So, in thinking about life, he will look at the 1st from the 1st (which remains the 1st) and the 8th from the 8th which you know is the *3rd*. Hindu astrology asserts that the 3rd house has a lot to do with the release of local activity energy as seen in an elevated level of courage, enthusiasm, motivation, adventure, and desire, especially when the 3rd is well reinforced.

Now, if the 1st, 8th and 3rd are the life houses, what houses, and their rulers, might hold sway over death? Let's logically start out by simply considering the houses that oppose them. For the 1st, this would be the 7th. The 7th itself symbolically implies a 180-degree aspect with reference to the 1st—an opposition. And notice that using our upside-down "death zodiac," this is an Aries house ruled by Mars, the simple and straightforward killer of ancient astrology. Notice also how this disposes of the "wills and legacies" problem. If, as I am arguing, the 7th rules death, then it would make simple sense for the 8th, as 2nd from the 7th, to rule the products of a death-dealing house, i.e., wills and legacies.

The 8th house is opposed by the 2nd. Notice once again that, using our upside-down death zodiac, the Scorpio 2nd is also ruled by Mars. So we get a confirming message here. And this whole message is reinforced from yet another perspective: what house "secretly undermines" the 1st? The 12th. What is the 12th from the life-giving 3rd? Here we are back at the Mars-ruled 2nd. What is the 12th from the life giving 8th? Well here we are back at the Mars-ruled 7th.

What about the 7th from the 3rd which is the 9th? Here an exception is made because this house is one of the two best houses in the Hindu horoscope presentation. And using our upside-down death zodiac, it is ruled by Mercury which, as a general rule, has almost no status to kill. And, to reinforce the point further, any involvement with the 9th house is almost always considered protective.

So where does this leave us? The initial key conclusion is this: The 1st, 3rd and 8th houses sustain life. Therefore the rulers of these houses cannot bring about death even if they are natural malefics. However, an important point to note is that if these houses, or their rulers, are very debilitated natally, then they can be a factor in death. But this is only true in the same sense that a deer, by virtue of being wounded, can be designated as the cause of its own death as a result of ultimately being attacked by a lion. Therefore, debilitated rulers of these houses become the object, and not the subject, of a similar planetary transaction.

Further, the true active "agents" of death are the rulers of the 2nd and the 7th, with the 12th also on the watch list. And this is true even if they are natural benefics. But it is symmetrically true, relative to the last paragraph, that if these houses or their rulers are weak, then their ability to "induce" death is reduced, and other factors and combinations become more relevant.

At this point I should introduce a key rule: the Sun and the Moon absolutely cannot become active agents of death (and this is also true of Mercury under many circumstances). If either one happens to rule the 2nd or the 7th they cannot function as marakas, and other patterns must do the job. But again, if they rule the life houses and are natally weak, they can be agents in death, but only via invocation as a result of becoming involved with more powerful factors during certain debilitated cycles.

All this has been a rather lengthy buildup to establish a simple general rule. But before you go off with your analytical gun half-cocked, it is now *very* important for you to realize that these simple rules are subject to massive refinement and qualification, and such qualification, via rules and a large base of examples, constituted a significant core of *The Astrology of Death*.

There are also quite a number of detailed methods for the calculation of longevity *(ayurdaya)* that are distinctive to Hindu astrology. These generally involve variations on the assignment of unique weighted values to each planet in the person's basic natal *(rasi)* chart. These numerical values are then further modified depending upon a host of considerations that affect the strength or status of each planet.

In my book, I made the assertion that some of the more effective methods with which to predict death are actually outside the "mainstream" of Hindu astrology, but I didn't go into these secondary methods. One of the lesser used, but still respected, methods is that of Jaimini. The calculation of my *ayurdaya* by the Jaimini method yields 83 years, 10 months and 6 days. This compares most favorably with the number of years given by the Nadi Grantha reader which was 84 years and about 5 months.

Note that these detailed calculations are generally only performed by a Hindu astrologer within the context of a prior determination, which is commonly done, as to whether the person will lead a short, medium, or long life. There is a fundamental set of calculations that underlies this, and it is supplemented by an enormous base of "yogas" (distinctive, and often complex, planetary combinations) that further confirm the validity of the main short/medium/long calculation.

EASTERN AND WESTERN SYNTHESIS

In the above commentary, I made occasional reference to the importance of being able to assess the *status* of planets at various points in their cycles. Other than transits (common to both systems), this article will highlight two methods that are relatively unknown and unused by the typical Western astrologer. One of these is Eastern and the other is Western. But what pulls them together is that they are both fundamentally *lunar* in their foundation, *and* they give off highly synergistic messages. This is true even though I haven't found any person or reference that can identify a conceptual link between the two.

Method #1 (Eastern)—The Vimsottari Dasa/Bhukti system: This method is initially grounded in the placement of the natal Moon in one of the 27 *nakshatras* (also known as "constellations" or "lunar mansions"), each of which covers about 13+ degrees of the sidereal zodiac. By rulership, there are actually three "sets" of nine nakshatras, since there are only nine planetary factors (seven planets and the two lunar nodes) that must rule all 27 nakshatras.

Imagine that there is a continuous loop of tape, and on that tape are marked 120 years. These years are broken down into main planetary segments (called the *Dasa* or *Dasha* periods) in a fixed sequence, but the lengths vary depending upon each planet. The fixed sequence (and length in years) is as follows: Sun (6), Moon (10), Mars (7), lunar North Node, or *Rahu* (18), Jupiter (16), Saturn (19), Mercury (17), lunar South Node, or *Ketu* (7) and Venus (20).

"Inside" each of these planetary periods is another set of time periods in identical planetary sequence that are in the same relative time proportion to each other, but they are compressed or expanded to reflect the varying length of each Dasa. These sub-periods are referred to as the *Bhukti* periods. There are even further levels of refinement (down to about the duration of a heartbeat!), but we will hold the discussion at these two levels.

As an example of all this, see Table 1 (pages 338–339). This is a portion of my personal Dasa/Bhukti listing which we will be using to illustrate and confirm my estimated date of death. I entered onto this 120-year "tape loop" at the very end of the Venus Dasa. The reason I started in Venus is because when I was born, my Moon was located at the very end of the nakshatra called *Poorva Ashada*, and this lunar mansion is

Table 1. A Portion of Richard Houck's Dasa/Bhukti List.

JUPITER	Jupiter	beginning on 02/30/1989	at age	41y	10m	17d	for	25m	18d
JUPITER	Saturn	beginning on 04/18/1991	at age	44y	0m	5d	for	30m	12d
JUPITER	Mercury	beginning on 10/30/1993	at age	46y	6m	17d	for	27m	6d
JUPITER	Ketu	beginning on 02/06/1996	at age	48y	9m	23d	for	11m	6d
JUPITER	Venus	beginning on 01/12/1997	at age	49y	8m	29d	for	32m	0d
JUPITER	Sun	beginning on 09/12/1999	at age	52y	4m	29d	for	9m	18d
JUPITER	Moon	beginning on 06/30/2000	at age	53y	2m	17d	for	16m	0d
JUPITER	Mars	beginning on 10/30/2001	at age	54y	6m	17d	for	11m	6d
JUPITER	Rahu	beginning on 10/06/2002	at age	55y	5m	23d	for	28m	24d
SATURN	Saturn	beginning on 02/30/2005	at age	57y	10m	17d	for	36m	3d
SATURN	Mercury	beginning on 03/03/2008	at age	60y	10m	20d	for	32m	9d
SATURN	Ketu	beginning on 11/12/2010	at age	63y	6m	29d	for	13m	9d
SATURN	Venus	beginning on 12/21/2011	at age	64y	8m	8d	for	38m	0d
SATURN	Sun	beginning on 02/21/2015	at age	67y	10m	8d	for	11m	12d
SATURN	Moon	beginning on 02/03/2016	at age	68y	9m	20d	for	19m	0d
SATURN	Mars	beginning on 09/03/2017	at age	70y	4m	20d	for	13m	9d
SATURN	Rahu	beginning on 10/12/2018	at age	71y	5m	29d	for	34m	6d
SATURN	Jupiter	beginning on 08/18/2021	at age	74y	4m	5d	for	30m	12d

Table 1. A Portion of Richard Houck's Dasa/Bhukti List (cont.).

MERCURY	Mercury	beginning on	02/30/2024	at age	76Y	10m	17d	for	28m	27d
MERCURY	Ketu	beginning on	07/27/2026	at age	79Y	3m	14d	for	11m	27d
MERCURY	Venus	beginning on	07/24/2027	at age	80Y	3m	11d	for	34m	0d
MERCURY	Sun	beginning on	05/24/2030	at age	83Y	1m	11d	for	10m	6d
MERCURY	Moon	beginning on	03/30/2031	at age	83Y	11m	17d	for	17m	0d
MERCURY	Mars	beginning on	08/30/2032	at age	85Y	4m	17d	for	11m	27d
MERCURY	Rahu	beginning on	08/27/2033	at age	86Y	4m	14d	for	30m	18d
MERCURY	Jupiter	beginning on	03/15/2036	at age	88Y	11m	2d	for	27m	6d
MERCURY	Saturn	beginning on	06/21/2038	at age	91Y	2m	8d	for	32m	9d
KETU	Ketu	beginning on	02/30/2041	at age	93Y	10m	17d	for	4m	27d
KETU	Venus	beginning on	07/27/2041	at age	94Y	3m	14d	for	14m	0d
KETU	Sun	beginning on	09/27/2042	at age	95Y	5m	14d	for	4m	6d
KETU	Moon	beginning on	02/03/2043	at age	95Y	9m	20d	for	7m	0d
KETU	Mars	beginning on	09/03/2043	at age	96Y	4m	20d	for	4m	27d
KETU	Rahu	beginning on	01/30/2044	at age	96Y	9m	17d	for	12m	18d
KETU	Jupiter	beginning on	02/18/2045	at age	97Y	10m	5d	for	11m	6d
KETU	Saturn	beginning on	01/24/2046	at age	98Y	9m	11d	for	13m	9d
KETU	Mercury	beginning on	03/03/2047	at age	99Y	10m	20d	for	11m	27d

one of the three ruled by Venus. So, in a nutshell, that is basically how it works. To learn more about this calculation, I suggest the very clear modern classic, written by James Braha, titled *Ancient Hindu Astrology for the Modern Western Astrologer* (Hermetician Press).

The Dasa/Bhukti listing is used by nearly all Hindu astrologers to make excellent forecasts about the twists and turns of life's karma. The Dasa period generally functions as the backdrop, while the Bhukti factor is in the foreground providing more immediate modification and coloration to the Dasa factor. So there are fundamentally two planets "on stage" during various periods of time, and note that these are being activated at their (previously latent) *natal* positions. This confirms the ancient idea that before anything can happen in the life, it must first be "promised" in the natal chart itself.

As already mentioned, this procedure has a fundamentally *lunar* foundation, and it therefore stands in counterpoint to the popular techniques of Solar Arc, Secondary Progression, and other solar thinking that tends to be more dominant in the West. Indeed, in the West, when one person asks another, "What's your sign?" they are asking about the Sun sign. But in the East, they are asking about the Moon sign or the rising sign (sidereal, of course).

Remember when I introduced the idea of certain planets *(marakas)* formally achieving the power to signal death? Typically, this will be said to occur during the Dasa and/or Bhukti of such a planet. But my research experience seemed to indicate that it was quite a bit more complex than initially expected. So I began to seek a technique that would confirm a possible death message from the Dasa/Bhukti system. And I found such a confirming technique in tertiary progressions.

Method #2 (Western)—Tertiary Progressions: Tertiary progressions are also a lunar-based technique. In various metaphysical sources it has often been suggested that 1,000 months of life may be one of the best standards of a good lifespan. In calendar months, this corresponds to about 84 years which Western astrologers recognize as about one full Uranus cycle (and roughly three Saturn cycles). Further, this number is a compound of the two key occult numbers of 7 and 12.

1,008 calendar months of life (84 years) will give you about 1,111 *lunar* months. By this I am referring to the tropical equinoctal Moon (zero Aries to zero Aries), and its value is 27.321582 (note: this is very close to the non-precessed sidereal value of 27.321661, so for all practical progression purposes you may use either). This method of progression equates each day in your life to each calendar month of this length. Therefore, for example, if you live to the age of 84, then you will have worked your way through about three years in the ephemeris from the date you were born.

Thus, in the course of such a life, you will experience roughly 50 progressed planetary stations, 10 progressed eclipses and many progressed sign ingresses (sidereal, of course). Progressed Mercury will circle your chart about twice, and will itself have about 20 progressed stations. This has tremendous implications if you have sidereal Gemini or Virgo rising, and/or if you are in a Mercury Dasa or Bhukti at the time. The same is true for all the other planetary stations relative to their sign rulers.

It's clear how fast the planets move under such a scheme—about ever 27.3 calendar days they transit the distance of one line in the ephemeris. So the tertiary Moon moves about ½ a degree per day (therefore it resides in each sign about two months), and the tertiary Sun will move about one degree per month (about equal to the secondary Moon with which the Western astrologer is probably more familiar).

Under this scheme, we will choose to progress your MC by the amount of this tertiary solar arc, i.e., roughly a degree per month, and the tertiary ASC will just be a slight variation on this, since it is derived normally per the Table of Houses. Consequently you may estimate that, in the course of using tertiary angles for rectification, every week of event error, as demonstrated by the progressed angles, will correlate to about one minute of birth time error. Finally, note that the tertiary angles will pass about 2-½ years in each sign/house, and you will immediately recognize how this correlates to transiting Saturn and the secondary Moon.

Having reviewed Dasa/Bhukti planets and tertiary progressed planets, let me state three preliminary rules that apply to their usefulness and interaction as they relate to the subject of death. To my knowledge, the last two rules and relationships have never before been documented, so in my book I took the bemused liberty of modestly labeling them "Houck's Laws."

1. Progressed planetary stations contribute the value of intensified amplitude to any symbolic message that is otherwise being formed in the chart. The quality of this amplitude will relate directly to the fundamental nature of the planet.

2. Almost invariably, there will be an *appropriate* correlation between the current Dasa (or Bhukti planet) and a progressed planetary station. This will often signal death if subsidiary factors confirm (although these confirming factors will receive little development in this conceptual synopsis).

3. You may *routinely* expect appropriate progressed angle and planet hits in an exact 4th harmonic relationship to a current maraka. Exact eclipse hits may also be routinely expected within the context of such a pattern.

Let's take a moment here to define the word "exact," and also to comment briefly upon eclipses. Whenever astrologers talk about a transiting or progressed conjunction, square, or opposition from or to an angle or planet, I believe they should hold to a maximum orb of one degree. All my work conforms to this standard (and the vast majority of it is just applying aspects). Also I should mention that, in conformity with Indian thinking on this matter, I do not attribute to any planet, except Jupiter, the power to cast a trine.

With regard to eclipses, my book highlighted the complex issues of chart sensitization via prenatal and progressed eclipses. And any particular point in a chart (planet or angle) becomes extremely sensitized if it is hit directly by one of these eclipses. Remember that ancient astrologers almost invariably considered eclipses to be "evil" due to their interrupt quality as it applies to "The Lights" of life, i.e., the Sun and the Moon.

The last transiting solar and lunar eclipses before death are almost invariably very important signals, and they should also conform to the standard of a maximum orb of one degree. I say "almost" because the strong presentation of such transiting eclipses is most apparent when a person dies during the Dasa or Bhukti of one of the nodes, or when the nodes are tightly linked to critical points within the natal or progressed chart.

EXAMPLE: THE AUTHOR'S CHART

Let's now take a break from all this abstract theory, and review its application against the assertion of the Nadi Grantha reader that my date of death will be in the Fall of 2031. Looking back at figure 2 (page 330), and Table 1 (page 338), we will first do a brief review of the relevant natal elements, and then the transitory considerations. Then I will reinforce the assertions with related examples. Some of this reasoning may sound peculiar to the Western ear, but it will sensitize you to some of the Eastern thinking about this matter.

Q: What are the marakas in this chart?

A: The ruler of the 2nd is Saturn, and the ruler of the 7th is Mercury.

Q: Do we have reason to conclude that these really can function as marakas?

A: Yes. Let's review the natal status of both, starting with Mercury.

Although Mercury is in Jupiter's sign and also receives a perfect 120-degree trine from Jupiter itself, Mercury is nevertheless fallen and with Mars. The support from Jupiter may be expected to provide quite a bit of protection throughout the life. Also, although two natural malefics (yes, the Sun is a malefic in the East) are in the same house with Mercury, each rules one of the two best houses in the Hindu system (5th and 9th). But, since we all must die of something, this is nevertheless an ultimately weak point. It suggests a stroke, or some similar brain-related pathology, and the family relative I most take after (my paternal grandfather) died at age 84 of a stroke. (The exact octile between Mercury and my slow 8th house Pluto adds supporting emphasis.)

For Saturn, let's first note a few "positives." It also rules one of the life houses (the 3rd), and is further located in a life house (the 8th). It gains some strength by being quite slow at birth (it was stationary ten days before birth, just as Pluto, also in the 8th, was stationary ten days after birth). And, as already noted, Saturn in the 8th (a life house) promotes longevity. Finally, Saturn is in Jupiter's exaltation sign, and Jupiter itself aspects the 8th house thus strengthening the 8th (note: in Hindu astrology, planets aspect not only other planets but also other *houses*, with various predictable effects).

On the negative side: Saturn also does rule the 2nd, it is the natural karaka of death, and it is not strong by sign (note: Hindu astrology does not have the concept of "detriment," only "fall"). But for me, based upon my review of many death charts, a key negative factor is that it is

344 / EASTERN SYSTEMS FOR WESTERN ASTROLOGERS

exactly linked, by tight square, to the IC. So Saturn will be a significant factor at death for almost that reason alone.

There is a third planet I should comment upon: the Moon. It is considered generally good to have the Moon in the 1st house, and in the case of this Moon, ancient texts specifically state that there is no harm in its rulership of the 8th. And we already know that the Moon absolutely cannot be an agent of death. But, since it contributes to the ebb and flow of energy management, it can be a victim within a technical death complex.

Something also to note here is that the Moon is perfectly quincunx to Uranus. Uranus also has no "power to kill." But keep in mind that, even as noted in ancient Hindu texts, the quincunx aspect inherently implies 6th and 8th house concepts relative to the 1st. The fact that this Moon is actually in the 1st, and Uranus in the 6th, implies a "lightning strike" quality relative to the Moon. And in the Hindu system, the Moon rules the true core of the mind. Mercury, in contrast, only rules communication and the more overt computational aspects of the mind. So I would expect a strike against the Moon to play into any final death pattern, again, as victim and not as agent.

Q: So, do these factors play out on the suggested death date?

A: Yes. Here is a pattern of six key considerations.

However, be advised that the various degrees I will cite for transiting, progressed and eclipsed positions will be *expressed* tropically. This is purely as a courtesy, so that the likely Western astrologer can run a simulation with his or her own software, and/or can verify my statements by following along in a standard Western ephemeris. But keep in mind two points:

• I consider the natal houses, rulers, and planetary placements to be as shown in figure 2 (page 330).

• By age 84, slightly over one degree of precession will have occurred. This will modestly affect transits (but not progressions), i.e., transiting aspects that are exact tropically will be applying by one degree sidereally.

The following six points will show where relevant factors will stand on September 13, 2031:

1. As noted on Table 1 (page 338), I will be in a *Mercury* Dasa and *Moon* Bhukti. We've already seen that Mercury is a confirmed maraka, and that the 1st house Moon can be at risk.

2. The equivalent tertiary progression date is 15 May 1950. On this date, the tertiary Moon is at 11 Taurus 38. This tertiary Moon position is perfectly square to the slow natal Pluto in the 8th which is at 11 Leo 00 (side note: some contemporary Indian astrologers think that Yama, the Hindu god of death, may actually be Pluto).

3. We find that both of these points (at 11 degrees of the Tropical fixed signs) are doubly reinforced from two further points of view. First, the equivalent secondary progression date is 6 July 1947. On the projected date of death, my secondary progressed ASC will be at 11 Taurus 31, perfectly conjunct the tertiary Moon and square natal Pluto (as per point #2 made above). Second, on this date, transiting Pluto will be at 11 Aquarius 38, square the tertiary Moon *to the minute.*

It is amazing (but common) to see that the Hindu system, seemingly unaware of Pluto, highlighted (via the Dasa/Bhukti system) the "benefic" Moon at death (with, of course, no mention of a "tertiary" Moon), just as the Western system highlighted the tertiary Moon via its conjunction with the secondary progressed ASC, as each will be jointly hammered by "both" Plutos.

4. With regard to Saturn, I said its natal configuration indicated that it would absolutely be a strong factor at my death. If you look up in your ephemeris for the tertiary progressed date of 15 May 1950, you will see that it is also the *exact date* that tertiary Saturn goes fully stationary. This is a life grinding to a complete stop (as similarly illustrated in a variety of cases in *The Astrology of Death*).

Following are some additional supporting considerations:

5. Tertiary Saturn will be stopped at 12 Virgo 35. Transiting maraka Mercury will be exactly conjunct it at 12 Virgo, and transiting Mars will be exactly square it at 12 Sagittarius. Recall that I will be in a Mercury Dasa, and fallen Mercury is with Mars in my natal Eastern chart. By the way, secondary progressed Mars will have come up to 3 Gemini 56; this is the midpoint of the natal true South Node (Ketu) at

3 Gemini 19 and the Mean Node at 4 Gemini 44. This secondary Mars is also exactly conjunct the tertiary IC of 3-GE-51 (remember: natal Saturn is exactly square the natal IC). So both common methods of progression tie directly into the karmic nodes (which sidereally are in the 6th and 12th). This will be going on while tertiary Jupiter, ruler of the natal 1st, is at 4 Pisces 44, thus square the natal Mean Lunar Nodes *to the minute* of arc.

6. Speaking of the nodes, what about eclipses? Since the true ruler (Jupiter) of the true 1st house (see figure 2, page 330) is actually in the 12th with the nodal axis, we can therefore always expect some eclipse action, in addition to mere nodal indicators, at death. You recall, at point #5 just above, that tertiary Saturn had stopped at 12 Virgo, and was being squared by transiting Mars at 12 Sagittarius.

Now note further that when I am 51 years of age, there will be a secondary progressed eclipse in my 12th house at 12 Sagittarius 22 (see 6/3/47), and this is perfectly square to my tertiary progressed Saturn at death which will be totally stopped at 12 Virgo 35 (and conjoined by transiting Mars). If any secondary progressed eclipses occur in a person's life, then that point is permanently and significantly sensitized for the remainder of the life. And if it happens to hit a natal planet or angle (which here it does not), that puts that natal factor in almost a "special" dimension. As a final personal eclipse comment, the last solar eclipse before I was born was at 0 Sagittarius 50 (on 11/23/46). At death, the secondary mean nodes will be at 0 Sagittarius 16.

HINTS OF CONFIRMATION

Does all this build a valid death pattern? Yes. But based upon a quick review of the upcoming Dasa and Bhukti periods, it would seem that there could be one or two other potential death periods (such as Saturn/Mercury). But these periods would have to be reviewed individually with an informed knowledge of what the pattern should look like (and to exclude other kinds of deaths). In any case, all we are trying to do now is introduce some of the basic astrological ideas surrounding death simply by validating the shortcut provided by the Nadi Grantha reader.

Support Discussion

There are numerous charts in *The Astrology of Death* that validate many of the points made in my personal example. Let me expend a few more pages doing a high-level review of some of these cases that support concepts introduced to this point.

It was stated that the Sun and Moon can never be marakas except by invoking a stronger malefic already in a hard natal 4th harmonic aspect, and sample cases have validated that death can occur during the Dasa or Bhukti of such normally life-sustaining factors. In one example, a male died during a Sun Bhukti. But what you would have to notice is that natally his Sun was exactly square to Saturn. There was another case of a middle-aged male whose mother died during his Moon Bhukti. But his natal Moon, unseen by Hindu methods, was conjunct natal Pluto.

And, as a third example, former TV anchor, Jessica Savitch, died during a (1st house) Moon Bhukti although, from a Hindu viewpoint, her natal Moon was in very good condition. But, unseen by the Hindu system, was the fact that her natal Moon was exactly conjunct natal Uranus which contributed a huge unseen instability. Of course, many other cycle patterns have to confirm the animation of such latent natal aspects.

We also learned that Mercury, although not much predisposed toward death-related activities, can be a maraka, depending upon related stressful circumstances. In my personal chart, you saw how Mercury will always invoke Mars (and Pluto) during Mercury's period. Time and again, you will see how a neutral, weak or even benefic factor can *invoke* a stronger, more aggressive factor during the period of the invoking planet.

Another example of this is the death of former President Richard Nixon. He had natal Mercury exactly conjunct Mars. Thus he also died of a stroke when he went into a Mercury Bhukti, and this was at the exact same month that his tertiary Mars went stationary ("Houck's Law"). As usual, there were numerous other confirming factors in the chart, including the fact that transiting Pluto was in his 4th and opposing his natal Saturn *to the minute* of orb. (Karmically, we could speculate that this might still have been more trivial for Mr. Nixon than his expulsion from office, since the expulsion occurred the exact year of a secondary Pluto station.)

We noticed that, at death, relevant planets will often go stationary by progression, and this will typically have an appropriate connection to the Dasa/Bhukti planets. Among the many cases cited to support this is Conor Clapton who fell over fifty stories to his death on a progressed Uranus station. And his mother, Lory del Santo, was having a progressed Pluto station.

A father, born on a natal Pluto station, was killed by his son, when the father was having a progressed Saturn station. H. R. Haldeman, President Nixon's former Chief of Staff, who was born with an exact Mercury/Saturn conjunction, died the exact month of a tertiary Saturn station. And the case was given of a former head of the Republican National Committee who also died the exact month of a tertiary Saturn station.

Anyone born with one or more natal stationary planets (especially, it seems, Mars or Uranus) should monitor those planets to see whether they will play into a death configuration. Examples are politicians (such as Abraham Lincoln or John Kennedy), and performers (such as Elvis Presley), and include the case of a famous statistical researcher who was born with a natal stationary Mars in the 12th who committed suicide very shortly after moving into his Mars Dasa. Luis Donaldo Colosio, the assassinated Mexican presidential candidate, was also born with a natal stationary Mars in his 12th. In his case, it ruled the 2nd and 7th, thus making it a classic maraka. He was assassinated when this natal stationary Mars (hiding in his 12th and ruling his 7th) progressed exactly to his MC.

Actually, charts of countries may also demonstrate relevant progressed stations at the death of a national leader. For example, in the case of Colosio, both tertiary and secondary Neptune were essentially stationary in the chart of Mexico (using the standard timed constitutional chart of 01/31/1917). Along this same line, in an article I wrote that was postmarked 12/1/93, I pointed out that North Korea (born 9/12/1948) would be having a tertiary progressed Saturn station exactly seven months in the future. Thus it was that seven months later Kim Il Sung dropped dead, and this produced the spectacle of over two million people weeping in the streets on 7/19/1994. And Kuwait had a "near death experience" when it was attacked during its own secondary Neptune station (this was by Saddam Hussein during the exact month of his own tertiary Pluto station). And this list can go on and on.

Not only the rulers of the 2nd and 7th are marakas. It can also be the case that planets actually in these houses, depending on the pattern and configuration, can also be marakas. And this can be the case even when these planets are natural benefics. For example, 5-year-old Conor Clapton, mentioned earlier, natally had Venus in his 2nd and Jupiter in his 7th. He died during a Jupiter Dasa and Venus Bhukti. But one would have to notice the secondary progressed Uranus station, the exact Neptune problems, the eclipses and so forth, to suggest that this would manifest as death.

Here are two little subtleties (among dozens) about benefics: if a benefic has maraka status and also rules an angle, then it has more power of release and is therefore more dangerous. Also, even if the ruler of the 12th is a benefic, if it is conjunct a hard-core maraka, then the benefic itself becomes dangerous. Can you see why these rules are so?

Speaking of benefics, one of the great things about the sidereal zodiac is that mutual receptions actually begin to work consistently, and are always very informative (by the way, if one of the planets rules the 1st, this will suggest a kind of dual personality). Thus, due to the ability of mutual receptions to shift death clues, this will often permit subtle insights into why death occurred during the period of a planet that would itself not seem to support the death.

But more commonly, it is malefics, and not benefics, in the Eastern 2nd or 7th house that are a problem, and these aren't even necessarily Hindu planets. For example, one case cited among many was that of a 15-year-old female with Pluto in the sidereal 2nd with the natal ASC 15 degrees from this Pluto. As the ASC arced down to touch Pluto, she committed suicide. But, as usual, other factors supported the analysis.

Let's close out this section of supportive examples by reviewing two final points: the first is eclipses, and the second is Dasa/Bhukti shifts. Eclipses are a huge topic, and case studies in *The Astrology of Death* saturated the issue from a variety of perspectives. For me, it was interesting to discover ultimately, and quite by accident, that four of the cases I had randomly selected had all died just after the same last total solar eclipse of 8 Cancer 57 that occurred on 6/30/1992. Tennis star Arthur Ashe died on 2/6/1993, German Chancellor Willy Brandt died on 10/8/1992, German Green Party politician Petra Kelly died on 10/19/1992, and a non-public person was killed in an argument over a pack of cigarettes on 7/4/1992.

In the case of Ashe, this eclipse exactly conjoined his natal Mercury (ruler of his 1st) at 8 Cancer 46, and transiting Mars would ultimately station on this point at 8 Cancer 41 (he died when Mars was slow and retrograde at 9 Cancer 10). For Willy Brandt, his natal ASC was 9 Aries 1; thus the eclipse perfectly squared it. Petra Kelly's natal ASC was 8 Cancer 38, thus the eclipse perfectly conjoined it. Finally, the fellow who was killed in the argument, only four days after the eclipse, had his tertiary Sun at 8 Cancer 57. As you can see, this was conjunct the prior eclipse *to the minute* of arc. Almost without exception then, there is just no escaping eclipses before death. They are excellent timers and indicators.

Now to the second point: If my ayanamsha is truly precise, do any deaths occur on the exact date of a Dasa or Bhukti shift? The answer is yes, since this ayanamsha was originally refined using three clients all of whom were entering into a Mars Bhukti. One had been stung by eleven bees, the second had been involved in a plane hijacking, and the third had been hit in the face with a board and then beaten unconscious. Once their birth times were validated beyond doubt (via other methods), it coincidentally became the case that they were *all* entering into a Mars Bhukti on the *exact* date of their respective events.

This was confirmed by other cases. For example, a young man, who had the natal ruler of the 1st exactly conjunct the natal North Node *(Rahu)* in his 12th, disappeared, and was ultimately found to have been killed, on the exact day he entered into a South Node *(Ketu)* Bhukti. In another case, a homeless person died the last day of a Saturn Bhukti (and per "Houck's Law" this was also the exact month of a tertiary Saturn station). Finally, the famous singer, Karen Carpenter, died the very last day of a 20-year Venus Dasa. So, yes, deaths can, and do, occur on the exact date of Dasa and Bhukti shifts.

NEW ISSUES AND DIRECTIONS

Certainly it is fascinating to discover that the timing of death can be forecast. While this has many useful and interesting implications, it ultimately leads to a new level of dissatisfaction. For it seems to be in human nature that, as soon as we know when, we want to know why.

Now let's go full circle. Returning to the beginning of this article, in reviewing the Nadi Grantha reading that set up this entire discussion, I made the passing remark that it may very well be possible to validate such a reading, and the past-life context that it provided, and I promised to at least pick up some threads of this issue at the close of this article.

So I will close out with a loopy story that, as of the moment at least, goes nowhere, and indeed, it seems to dissipate into the ether. But I think this is a temporary condition. I suspect that, as per the famous observation, "the opera ain't over until the fat lady sings." Watch the following swirl of "coincidence," and be advised that, in the future, we will attempt to develop a methodology to validate the past-life statements of the Nadi Grantha reader. The "we" is me and one of the players introduced in the vignette which immediately follows.

In September of 1994, my company was the sole sponsor of the largest Hindu astrology conference ever held on the east coast of the United States. This event drew interested attendees and speakers from around the world. As the program evolved, I was approached by a person based in Europe who wanted to speak. He supplied a complete copy of a lecture on Hindu medical astrology that he claimed to have written, along with an excellent resume.

His claims were difficult to verify since they all occurred outside of the United States. So I assigned him only a single simple lecture topic until I could learn more about him. The topic I selected for him was "Shad Bala" a pointing system which has to do with planetary strengths. Remember this topic selection; it is one of the "threads" we will be picking up later.

About a week after the conference brochure was printed, I happened to read a long, and very interesting, article by the female lawyer for Ted Bundy. Readers may remember that Ted Bundy was executed for murdering numerous females. This incited me to want to review Ted Bundy's chart. I knew I had a copy somewhere, but the first place I went to look was in a book sub-titled *Profiles In Crime* assembled by Lois Rodden. It shows the charts of hundreds of psychopaths and sociopaths along with some pithy commentary.

It turned out that Ted Bundy's chart was not in the main part of the book, nor in the "extra data" section. But, on the page right next to where Ted Bundy's chart data might have been, was the birth data for a professional international con man, he who had maneuvered himself onto my tentative conference speaker slate! How we eventually exposed him, with solid verification of his lies, is an interesting story in its own right, but it is peripheral to our task here.

Historically, until Pluto recently entered sidereal Scorpio (12/1992 and 10/1993), there have been very few people, other than myself, who have written or lectured on the topic of death. One of these people is

Lois Rodden who edited the book noted above. She then put me in touch with Marcello Borges, whom she thinks highly of (and vice versa). A resident of Sao Paulo, Brazil, Mr. Borges is the person who originally submitted the con man's validated birth data, and partial criminal record, for Ms. Rodden's book.

[Readers may be amused by two parenthetical side notes. I learned that the con man actually owns this particular book, but he did not know that he was in it. Via fax, I pointed this out to him on 8/5/1994, a day that Pluto went stationary and perfectly square to his MC! Also, included with my fax to him was a copy of a letter I had received from Dr. B. V. Raman, one of India's most famous astrologers. This letter specifically refuted hand-written assertions from the con man that he had studied, over extended periods, directly under Dr. Raman. Dr. Raman had never heard of him.]

I then began to correspond with Mr. Borges. But before I comment upon that, and keeping his location in mind (Sao Paulo, Brazil), let's bring in another player. After my book came out (9/1994), I received a letter from Dr. Margaret Millard, a retired M.D. now living in England. She asked to review my book on behalf of *Considerations* magazine. It turned out that she herself had written a fairly recent article for *Considerations*. The article was titled "The Death Chart," and it described what she considered to be eighteen indicators of impending death.

So now I found another person writing on death. But the "coincidences" hardly end there. She sent back a wonderful review, and among many interesting comments, her accompanying letter included the remark that when she was 19 years old, she rescued a *Dr. Houck* in September, 1936, from being washed out to sea. As she wrote, "It was in Brazil, at a coffee port at the end of the railway from *Sao Paulo* to the coast." This particularly struck me because I was already aware of the fact that Uranus in my current natal chart is *exactly* conjunct the IC when you relocate my chart to the coastal area just slightly east of Sao Paulo. I knew this because I had been wanting to visit it, but wondered what this aspect was all about. I immediately began to amuse myself by wondering if I had been "Dr. Houck," and whether Dr. Millard had rescued me ten years before my next birth! And thus I had come back with my current chart reflecting Sao Paulo as an "exciting" place.

But I quickly set aside this amusing speculation because of the past-life information given by the Nadi Grantha reader, which I had already had "confirmed" at earlier points in my life, by other powerful psychics.

Plus, of course, past-life names don't work like that. But now let's return momentarily for some additional comments from the Nadi Grantha reader. Each remark will be mentioned for a subsequent purpose.

He stated that in the past life immediately preceding this one I was in the military (clarity note: the chronologically most recent past life only carries a *piece* of the karmic elements that drive this life). In that life, he stated that I was a *map maker,* and had an excellent talent at targeting sites for the successful delivery of military ordinance. This resulted in a lot of damage and loss, and he proceeded to explain how this created the formation of certain yogas in my current chart, and the subsequent effect of these yogas at various Dasa/Bhukti cycles. Without going into the detail, suffice it to say that this validated my current life experience.

[Parenthetically, let me donate one paragraph of this "coincidence" to yet another player. On September 17, 1994 I met a woman who immediately demonstrated a very positive attraction to me (her data: 01 February 1964 at 11:56 A.M. EST, 40N39 & 78W56). This was undoubtedly due to the fact that my Jupiter, ruler of my 1st, is conjunct her Descendant within minutes of orb. And she had moved into a Venus Dasa only days before. All I knew about her occupation was that she was in the field of graphic arts. In October, after I told her about the remarks of the Nadi Grantha reader, she gasped and said, "Do you know what I do for a living?" It turns out that she has a very classified position with a defense contractor. She is a *map maker* who uniquely articulates geography, via computer software, for nuclear targeting. And my 8th house Saturn is only one degree from her IC.]

Next fact up: I had tried, for a number of years, to locate a book titled *Toward a New Astrology* by Ry Redd. I had the impression that this was a very original work that pulled together many unique concepts, and articulated new theories regarding reincarnation and astrology. This book was said to synthesize the implications of Edgar Cayce's channeled remarks, combined with Persian and Hindu astrology, the Hebrew Kabbala, Jungian archetypes, and the ideas of Rudolph Steiner. This latter philosopher, scientist, and mystic has always interested me in an odd way (perhaps because his Mercury is within a degree of mine?).

Mr. Redd's book was published in the mid-1980s in Virginia Beach, VA, but when I called the A.R.E. bookstore, located in Virginia Beach, they acted like they had never heard of either him or his book. It seemed that both Mr. Redd and his book had disappeared. I was about to engage a book search service, but I kept hesitating.

On September 8, 1994 I received my first letter from Mr. Borges in Sao Paulo. At this point, he knew nothing about me except my unfortunate involvement with the person he had exposed via Lois Rodden's book. His extensive letter made a number of shocking points (that went beyond the "mere" fact that we have many of the exact same interests, read the same books, admire many of the same unusual authors, belong to the same organizations, and so forth). Here are three of the most salient:

1. He had written an article, that had been published, titled "The Astrology of Death." This was the exact title of my book. He enclosed this article, and I was impressed by the spectrum of cross-cultural spiritual considerations he brought to this topic. The focus was upon death charts, and quite precise related speculations about reincarnation, i.e., astrological degree themes from life to life.

2. He has written a book (in Portuguese) whose translated title is *Holistic Balancing Techniques.* In his words, "It shows how one may balance a chart, from the Shad Bala value of each planet, using metals, gems, music, colors, etc., as well as the possible past lives profile the strong and weak planets may show." Remember now that this concept of "Shad Bala" is the one I originally assigned to the con man to speak on without any suggestion on his part. It turns out that Mr. Borges had taught this concept to this fellow, before Mr. Borges realized whom he was dealing with—a "double blind coincidence."

But the "coincidence" again extends further. One of the things the Nadi Grantha reader had told me is that, from 1995–1996, I would begin writing on two more topics. He said I would be joined in this effort by someone I already know. He said this subject would give people unique therapeutic knowledge of the physical body and its regulation via "the spectral elements associated with astrology." This would seem to be the exact subject that Mr. Borges had already written his book on.

3. But here it gets even more strange. Now I will again quote directly from the letter of Mr. Borges introducing himself to me (keep in mind that Mr. Borges knew nothing about my frustration regarding Ry Redd's book): "In 1988, I read a book called *Towards A New Astrology* by Ry Redd, and started to correspond with him. I then invited him to visit Brazil and give a lecture at a conference in Rio in 1989. Then he actu-

ally moved to Brazil and was a guest at my house for a month. His work was the key to my present astrological concept, based as it was on Edgar Cayce readings and on Vedic Astrology. In case you knew him, unfortunately Ry drowned in February, 1994, while swimming off the coast of Sao Paulo."

So now both Dr. Houck and Ry Redd had nearly, or actually, drowned off the coast of Sao Paulo, and this somehow linked me together with Lois Rodden, Dr. Margaret Millard, and Marcello Borges (who lives in Sao Paulo), and all of whom have either written, or lectured, on the rather unique subject of death. Further note this: in his letter, Mr. Borges gave his birth data as 1 March 1955 at 3:10 P.M., BZT in Sao Paulo. For zone 3 standard time, this gives him a Descendant of 12 Capricorn 59. If you look at the last eclipse the month before Dr. Houck almost drowned in September, 1936, it was at 12 Capricorn 51, only eight minutes of orb from Mr. Borges' Descendant. Now might there be a link between Dr. Houck and Mr. Borges, or someone he knew?

And remember when I mentioned that my Uranus is exactly upon my IC when it is relocated to this coastal city? That Uranus turns out to be the exact 12th house (Placidus) cusp of Mr. Borges, and some occult traditions associate the 12th house with the immediately prior life. And Mr. Borges also has his Mars exactly upon my (non-relocated) IC. A final point to note: while my Saturn is slow and square the IC, his Saturn is stopped.

I wrote to Mr. Borges advising him of much of this. In his reply of October 26, 1994 (which included sending me his own copy of Ry Redd's book, plus his own) he stated, in part, the following:

"Ever since I was in my teens, I have been obsessed with maps: reproductions of ancient world maps, South and North American maps, European maps, artists' renditions of Atlantis, etc. My home office is covered with them! More, I have long become convinced that, in my immediately prior life, I was an American officer or marine in WW II, killed by a German soldier who shot me in the head. The American way of life has always been my own; I learned English since I was 5 or 6, reading *MAD Magazine*. In another lifetime, I was a navigator. We should work together to refine a method to prove the basis of our obvious connection."

His remarks incite more counterpoint. First, in my home office, I *also* have many reproductions of ancient world maps. Second, a friend of mine who works at the Pentagon (in nuclear targeting!) told me that the specific detail supplied by the Nadi Grantha reader could only have applied to WW II, and to no other war (my own father fought in this war, and I was born shortly after it ended).

Third, I have actually written on the subject of *MAD Magazine* as one of the major cultural influences of the 20th century. It began publishing in 11/1952, and this was the exact month that Neptune and Pluto were both changing sidereal signs—including a Pluto station at exact zero—thus causing instant massive popularity among many of those children who are now assuming positions of authority across the United States.

Finally, I have been intrigued by my ongoing vague reluctance to visit Germany. It turns out that in Germany, Uranus is exactly upon my relocated ascendant while Pluto is also exactly upon my relocated IC (this spot is located in what was formerly called East Germany, southwest of Berlin). It had already been one of my evolving theories, yet to be "tested" or "proven" by whatever occult means, that these points of double angularity upon the Earth are actually places where we have had intense past lives that exhibited the quality of the planetary symbolism (note: in India, I have the Sun on the MC and Saturn on the ASC—an ascetic authority?). So this may have something to do with Marcello Borges' comment about being shot by a German soldier in a prior life combined with the Nadi Grantha reader's comments on my military "map karma."

If you can stand one final "coincidence" about all this, shortly after my book came out I was contacted by an enthusiastic reader in Berlin, Germany who is a book translator by occupation. She was considering translating it, but wanted to know more about its sales performance, etc. But she also wrote: "Do you know a technique named 'Combin?' It is not a composite, but kind of a meeting point in space and time (dates, times, and places). I found something very interesting. When you do a combin between your horoscope and mine, and then relocate it to my birthplace (Berlin), we get Pluto exactly upon the ASC. If we relocate it to your birthplace (Des Moines) we have Uranus conjunct the IC." She also added (with reference to our individual charts): "The ruler of your 1st is almost exactly conjunct the ruler of my 1st, your Mars is exactly conjunct my South Node, your Jupiter is exactly conjunct my Sun...." Perhaps another fellow soldier? I was afraid to ask about how many maps she owns!

I'll close here, after littering these final pages with these vague and inconclusive threads, but also with a final jog to your memory. Those readers who have reached a reasonable age may very well recall that, just in the course of reading their daily newspaper, a strange story surfaces every now and then where a search team of one or more Tibetan Buddhist monks eventually shows up on someone's doorstep and declare it likely that the person living there is the reincarnation of someone who was very important in the past within their tradition. You may at least recall the story with regard to the discovery of the most recent Dalai Lama himself.

This identical thing actually occurred within ten miles of my current home in Gaithersburg, MD, and the event eventually received extensive publicity around the world. In 1987, a housewife with two children was approached by an authority from the Palyul monastery in Bylakuppe, India. The woman was so apparently clueless that she even offered him some hot dogs for lunch. He declared her the reincarnation of a woman who had overseen over 100,000 monks and nuns plus hundreds of monasteries throughout Tibet (I will spare you dates, titles, etc.). Enthroned in 1988 as Jetsunma Ahkon Lhamo, she has set up a major center in Poolsville, MD, and has already accomplished amazing things. It couldn't be more obvious that she actually *is* the reincarnation of the person they claimed, since very sophisticated Buddhist teachings have been pouring out of her ever since, and a whole host of amazing stories—including what might be called "miracles"—already surround her new reality. For those who are attuned to this topic, this is Vajrayana Buddhism according to the Nyingma tradition of Tibet.

How do these search teams *do* that? It is Mr. Borges contention, via interesting extracts taken from various obscure research texts, that the information is contained in the chart of the person's prior death. Parenthetically and if so, it seems quite certain that the Buddhist archivists were unlikely to lose track of Jetsunma's chart because at the same Poolesville monastary they have on display the preserved cremated remains of her 17th century body. (But here I should also note that Tibetan Buddhism does not actually emphasize astrology, and the search confirmation process typically involves a variety of occult interrogations.)

Indeed, as the three wise astrologers followed "stars" looking for the birth of Jesus Christ, some occult texts suggest that they were working from the death chart of Zend, the father of Zoroaster. As you may know,

Edgar Cayce repeatedly emphasized the concept that, between Earth lives, a soul sojourns near, or under the influence of, a specific planet. And this may very well correlate to the Eastern concept of the *loka,* where the soul resides between Earth-based reincarnations.

Since most of Tibetan spiritual science originated in India, this idea of a planetary sojourn, in turn, leads us back once again to the Hindu concept of *Shad Bala* where various methodologies define the relative strength of each planet in a person's chart. Combine the concept of the strongest (i.e., most influential) chart planets with a compass-based Local Space Chart, particularly those related ideas popularized by Western astrologer Steve Cozzi, and there would seem to exist ample components for further investigation.

As time permits, Mr. Borges and I will set to work to clarify this mystery to the extent we can. To move the matter beyond mere speculation, the most key problem is to find sets of two reliably-timed charts about which an assertion can be made that the Earth-based incarnation of one chart preceded the Earth-based incarnation of the second. The works of Edgar Cayce provide a lot of helpful material in this regard because he often gives specific information about the reincarnation of various individuals. One of India's most respected astrologers, K. N. Rao, also has about ten sets of these. And there are other sources, but securing good data remains the biggest initial barrier. Complicating matters is my knowledge that there is also an occult concept of partial souls. Might we all just be experiencing bits and pieces of each other? The reader is encouraged to forward any related theories, comparable experiences, or useful data to the author by way of the publisher. And meanwhile, if I prove to be wrong about my estimated date of death, in my next life I plan to exit the astrology business and secure a nice 6th house occupation instead!

ABOUT THE AUTHOR

Richard Houck, President of ARC Associates, Inc., in metro Washington, DC, provides research and consulting services for the time cycle management requirements of corporate, political, and professional clients. His highly-acclaimed book, *The Astrology of Death,* broke through many barriers of thought and technique in astrology.

Rick has lectured to many diverse groups about astrology—from psychotherapy students, to country clubs, and monasteries. He has a special interest and recognized reputation in documented forecasting. Interviewed at length on cable and network television, he is also the author of over 100 postmarked articles distributed primarily to other astrologers. Quoted in non-astrological newspapers, and in publications such as *Today's Investor*, his astrological work was featured twice on the cover of *Leaders* magazine, a closed-circulation periodical distributed only to the world's top leaders.

In September 1994, ARC Associates, Inc. also sponsored the largest Hindu astrology conference ever held on the east coast of the United States. In early 1997, it also published the anthology *Hindu Astrology Lessons*.

Prior to incorporating ARC Associates, Rick worked primarily as an investigative assurance specialist in the security, integrity, and control of very large computerized systems. He has held significant management positions in organizations such as Arthur Andersen & Co. and Intelsat, the international governmental consortium that runs the world satellite network.

Readers who want to contact Richard Houck may write to the following address:

Richard Houck
P.O. Box 8925
Gaithersburg, MD 20898
Phone/Fax: 301-353-0212
E-Mail: RichardHouck@worldnet.att.net

INDEX

J
Jagger, Mick, 45
je tsai, 123, 131, 132
jung-tsi, 149, 172
Jones, Marc Edmund, 1, 43
Jupiter, 4, 250, 257, 260,
263, 272
Jyestha, 260
jyotish, 238, 272
jyotisin, 236, 237

K
Kalachakra System, 149
karaka, 332
karanas, 248
karma, 218, 321
karmic
difficulties, alleviat-
ing, 291
relationships, 180
Karma Kagyu tradition,
149
Kar-Tsi, 149
Karttikeya, 255
Kaus Borealis, 261
Kelly, Petra, 349, 350
Kemedruma yoga, 253
kendra, 272
Kennedy, John, 139, 348
Ketu, see houses
kham, 174
King of Dharma, 255
King Wen, 39, 40
Krittika, 255
Kriya Yoga, 7, 29, 34
Kriyananda, Goswami, 1
Kuei, Dr. Chen Yi, 97
kujadosha, 293, 294
kundalini, 8
kundalini energy, 258
Kuwait, 348
Kwei, 118
kwei gong, 132

L
Lahiri, N. C., 275, 329
law of cause and effect, 218

Leadbeater, C.W., 145
Lesath, 261
Levacy, Bill, 248
Life and Death—East and
West, 325
Lincoln, Abraham, 348
Lin, Michael, 110, 114
Lo, Ana, 97
log-men, 185
loka, 358
lo-kak, 192
long life, 332
Lo-Sar, 191
lotus flower, 260
lucky feet, 263
lunar
cycle, 150
days, 154, 187, 188
days for travel, 190
dharma protector,
days, 154
eclipses, 155
feast days, 155
full and new moon,
154
gaps, 151–153, 249
healing days, 156
mansions, 337
month, 247
more protector days,
156
purification days,
154
lunation cycle, 243
Luther, Martin, 19, 20

M
magha, 240, 253, 258, 266
magic square, 177
nine, 178
Maha Mritunjava, 229
Manipura chakra, 3
Mandate of Heaven, 112
mantras, 287
marakas, 331
Markab, 263
Mars, 4, 259, 262

affliction, 293
Master Lo, 107, 120
meditation, 145, 153
Menkar, 255
Mercury, 4, 250, 251, 257,
260
Metal, 115–117
mewas, 156, 176, 177
1 white, 180
2 black, 181
3 blue, 181
4 green, 182
5 yellow, 182
6 white, 183
7 red, 184
8 white, 184
9 maroon, 185
descending, 179
Mexico, 348
Meyers-Briggs personality
inventory, 245
Millard, Dr. Margaret, 352
mind practice, 146, 147
ming, 109
Mitra, 260
Monday, 241
monkey, 108, 165
Monroe, Marilyn, 212
Moon, 4, 5, 151, 234, 247,
249, 259
action oriented type,
244
analyzing type, 244
and mind, 250
and personality, 242
archetypal synodic
cycle, 246
balsamic phase, 251
balsamic type, 244
blue, 236, 245
conscious type, 244
crescent type, 244
dik bala, 252
directional strength,
252
disseminating type,
244

distribution of con-
sciousness type,
244
Eastern, waxing and
waning, 251
eclipse pattern, 246
first quarter type, 244
full, 244, 251
future-oriented type,
245
gibbous type, 244
instinctive type, 244
karaka, 252
kendras, 252
last quarter type, 244
lunar eclipse, 246
months of, 233
moving Eastern
moon, 266
moving the Western
moon, 245
new type, 244
nodes, 294
north node, 262
orientation of con-
sciousness type,
244
pariyayas, 266
phase, 251
projecting type, 244
secondary progressed,
246
sidereal cycle, 254
sign, 251
solar eclipse, 246
struggling to build a
form type, 244
synodic month, 233
think before they act
type, 244
tropical Western, 240
wives, 256
Moore, Thomas, vii
month
anomalistic, 234
direction, 172
draconic, 234
mouse, 163

Mrigashira, 256
Mula, 261
muladhara chakra, 2
Myer, Michael, 245
myth and meaning in
Eastern astrology,
249

N
Naga, 258
Naga Ananta, 262
nadi, 8
three channels, 7
Nadi Grantha, 326, 350
Nakshatras, 238, 247, 249,
253, 254
first, 255
first Aswini, 248
second, 255
third, 255
third Krithka, 248
fourth, 256
fifth, 256
sixth, 256
seventh, 257
eighth, 257
ninth, 257
tenth, 258
eleventh, 258
twelfth, 259
thirteenth, 259
fourteenth, 259
fifteenth, 259
fifteenth Swati, 248
sixteenth, 260
seventeenth, 260
eighteenth, 260
nineteenth, 261
twentieth, 261
twenty-first, 261
twenty-second, 248
twenty-third, 262
twenty-fourth, 262
twenty-fourth
Shatabhishak,
248
twenty-fifth, 263
twenty-sixth, 263

twenty-seventh, 263,
266
twenty-seventh
Revati, 248
of magha, 253
Nasatya, 255
Neo-Vedic Humanistic as-
trology, 209
night sky and lunar con-
stellations, 238
Nin, Anais, 224, 227
Nixon, Richard, 280, 347
North Korea, 348
not turning back, 185
Nritta, 261

O
obstacles
four mewa, 194
seven, 193
opposites, 161
Orion, 256
ox, 108

P
padas, 254
Panchangam, 248
parkha
descending, 174
eight, 173
I Ching, 172
Paramahansa Yoga, 264,
265
Parashara, 212, 213
Parvati, 207, 208
Pegasus, 263
Pentans, 40
Phaladipika, 212, 215
pun, 121
pien tsai, 125, 132
pig, 108, 165
pingala, 8, 35
Pingree, David, 214
Piscium, 264
Pitras, 258, 266
planets, 9
and the chakras, 4
in houses, 271, 295